MICHIGAN LEGAL STUDIES

Diplomats, Scientists, and Politicians

Diplomats, Scientists, and Politicians

The United States and the Nuclear Test Ban Negotiations

by
Harold Karan Jacobson
and
Eric Stein

The University of Michigan Press
Ann Arbor

PUBLISHED UNDER THE AUSPICES OF
THE UNIVERSITY OF MICHIGAN LAW SCHOOL
(WHICH, HOWEVER, ASSUMES NO RESPONSIBILITY FOR THE VIEWS EXPRESSED)
WITH THE AID OF FUNDS DERIVED FROM
GIFTS TO THE UNIVERSITY OF MICHIGAN
BY WILLIAM W. COOK.

Preface

This study began in 1961 as a limited attempt to assess the impact of science and modern technology on the negotiating process and concepts of international organization, using the test ban negotiations then in progress as a case study. When the Moscow Treaty was signed, however, it seemed wise to broaden the focus and to capture as many of the details as we could that might help to explain this first formal arms control agreement between East and West in the nuclear age. Our analysis is clearly not definitive, but hopefully, it will be a useful source, even after all relevant documents have been published. We hope also that the study will fulfill something of its original purpose.

The principal written sources have been the records of the negotiations and the memoirs thus far published. In addition, a large number of the participants have been interviewed. These include President Eisenhower, all three of the Special Assistants to the President for Science and Technology who were involved, Ambassador Arthur H. Dean, Adrian S. Fisher, John J. McNaughton, various other officials of the Arms Control and Disarmament Agency, the Atomic Energy Commission, the Department of Defense, the Department of State, and most of the American scientists who took part, including Robert F. Bacher, Hans A. Bethe, James B. Fisk, Wolfgang K. H. Panofsky, and Edward Teller. Several United Nations and United Kingdom officials were also interviewed. For obvious reasons, there are no citations for any of the material gained through interviews.

The study was undertaken as part of The University of Michigan Law School's Atomic Energy Research Project. We are indebted to the director of that project, Professor Samuel D. Estep, for his assistance. We appreciate the financial support of the Ford Foundation and The University of Michigan Phoenix Project which made the study possible. We are especially grateful to the many individuals who kindly submitted to our interviews.

Agnes Cacamindin, Judith Lane, Lynne Edelstein, Helen Jussila, and Judith Rote all helped in the preparation of the book by serving as research assistants, and the last named did the onerous task of checking the notes. Alice J. Russell's invaluable contribution was in editing the manuscript. Eleanor Herp unflinchingly bore the brunt of the typing. This book would not exist without their help. Abraham Bargman, Bernhard G. Bechhoefer, Elisabeth Case, Inis L. Claude, Jr., Philip J. Farley, Lawrence S. Finkelstein, Warren E. Hewitt, Fred C. Iklé, George M. Kavanagh, John H. Morse, Mrs. Alva Myrdal, Wolfgang K. H. Panofsky, E. Raymond Platig, Marshall D. Shulman, Rudolph K. Skeete, J. David Singer, Ronald I. Spiers, Jerome B. Wiesner, Christopher Wright, and Ciro Elliott Zoppo all read part or all of the manuscript, and we and the book have benefited greatly from their wisdom.

Of course, we alone are responsible for whatever errors of commission and omission the study may contain.

HAROLD KARAN JACOBSON
ERIC STEIN

Ann Arbor, Michigan

Contents

PART III

The Path to the Moscow Treaty

PART IV

Some Concluding Observations

PART I

BY WAY OF INTRODUCTION

Chapter I

The Nuclear Age, the United States, and the Test Ban Negotiations

I

The Moscow Treaty: A Turning Point?

In Moscow, on July 25, 1963, representatives of the Soviet Union, the United Kingdom, and the United States initialed the Treaty Banning Nuclear Weapon Tests in the Atmosphere, in Outer Space, and Under Water. Eleven days later, again in Moscow, the foreign ministers of the three states signed the Treaty, which became the first major formal arms control agreement between the two sides in the Cold War. Moreover, the Treaty dealt—although in a very limited fashion only—with the most awesome aspect of the competition between East and West, the nuclear-missile arms race.

Eighteen years earlier, almost to the day, on July 26, 1945, the first test detonation of a nuclear device occurred at Alamogordo, New Mexico, and the first detonation of a nuclear weapon in war devastated Hiroshima on August 6, 1945. These events had introduced a new phase into mankind's existence. The two events in Moscow in 1963, falling as they did, seemed to suggest, at the least, a punctuation of this phase. More generally, they offered hope that mankind had begun to take steps to control the destructive potential of modern technology, of which the development of nuclear weapons has been but one aspect. For the United States, which had first developed nuclear weapons and had created the largest stockpile, and probably for most of the world, the Moscow Treaty represented the first concrete step toward a goal that had been sought since the very outset of the nuclear age.

II

The United States and the Nuclear Age

The Changed International System

To begin to assess the significance of the Moscow Treaty, it is necessary to recall that the advent of nuclear weapons in 1945 fundamentally altered the international political system. Although the full dimensions of this revolution were then and still remain obscure, certain salient features were immediately apparent. Nuclear weapons increased the potential human and physical costs of war to such an extent that its traditional role as the *ultima ratio* in international politics was brought sharply into question and a search for new means for the peaceful adjustment of conflicts appeared particularly urgent. Again, because of the enormous destructive capacity of nuclear weapons and the cost and complexity of building a nuclear arsenal and appropriate delivery systems, the distinction between those states which possessed such weapons and those which did not seemed greater than any difference in the power position of states that had previously existed. As a consequence of these developments, many of the traditional modes and patterns of international politics appeared to be fundamentally altered. Alliances seemed not to mean the same thing that they had prior to the summer of 1945. The tasks and techniques of diplomacy seemed to acquire new dimensions. Concepts of international organization assumed new meanings. Some analysts even questioned whether or not the territorial state continued to have relevance.[1]

The changes in the international system bore especially heavily on the United States as the state which had introduced nuclear weapons and which, at first at any rate, would have the greatest capacity to develop them. To compound the complexity, these changes occurred at precisely the same time that the United States was forced to abandon finally its isolationist stance and to accept seemingly permanent and deep involvement in international affairs. The balance of power in Europe which had helped to guarantee America's security in the nineteenth century probably ceased to exist during the First World War and certainly was no longer operative after the Second World War.[2] Instead of being able to rely on the exertion of others to protect its security, the United States now had to undertake that task itself. Moreover, it became increasingly apparent that the security of a large number of other

[1]John H. Herz, for one. See his *International Politics in the Atomic Age* (1959), p. 22.
[2]For an excellent analysis of these developments and their implications for the United States see Hajo Holborn, *The Political Collapse of Europe* (1951).

states was dependent upon American efforts. Thus, in 1945, the problems of adjustment for the United States were piled one on top of the other. The United States faced a changed world and faced it from a new perspective.

Weapons Development versus Weapons Control: Two Conflicting Strains in American Policy

From the outset, American attitudes and policies toward nuclear weapons have been characterized by a deep ambivalence. On the one hand, the United States has felt that for reasons of its security it could not forego the development of nuclear weapons; yet at the same time, it has found the development of these weapons and dependence on them distasteful and has continually sought some means of controlling them. Prominent among the sources of this ambivalence has been the fact that nuclear weapons and other aspects of modern military technology have enormously increased the vulnerability of the United States. The relative predominance of one or the other of the two conflicting strains—and the resulting policy mixture—have, of course, varied with time, but both of these strains have been constant components of American thought and actions, causing important stresses and uncertainties in the policy-making process and in American negotiating postures.

The policy strain which caused the United States to develop nuclear weapons—and which motivated the development of its nuclear arsenal—was based upon the consideration that in the mid-twentieth-century world of sovereign and often sharply clashing states, American security depended first and foremost upon American power, particularly the national military establishment based broadly upon the immense American industrial capacity and steadily evolving technology. The initial decisions to develop nuclear weapons were made with the knowledge that Nazi Germany was also pursuing this goal and at least partly because of the fear that it might succeed.[3] In addition, nuclear weapons were viewed as a possible means of shortening the Second World War, and the President's decision to employ them in Japan was basically motivated by this

[3]See Louis Morton, "The Decision to Use the Atomic Bomb," in U.S. Department of the Army, Office of the Chief of Military History, *Command Decisions* (Washington, D.C.: Government Printing Office, 1960), pp. 493-518, at 494.

purpose. These decisions were made in wartime secrecy, and despite the wartime emergency, not without soul searching on the part of those who made them. It is thus not surprising that American plans for the control of nuclear weapons—reflecting the second policy strain—began to evolve almost simultaneously with the initial use of these weapons. But for a variety of reasons, negotiations to establish international control foundered.[4] As the failure of these negotiations emerged, so did the deep Soviet-American clash about the nature of the post-war world. The United States came to perceive the Soviet Union as an expansionist power with virtually unlimited objectives, the achievement of most of which would seriously jeopardize fundamental American interests. In this situation, the build-up of the nuclear arsenal again seemed to offer an important means of gaining security, particularly in view of Soviet superiority in manpower and conventional weapons. Beyond that, there was always the fear that the Soviet Union might make a technological breakthrough which it would then exploit for its purposes, a fear which became particularly acute after the USSR's first detonation of a nuclear device in 1949, several years ahead of American expectations.[5] As during the Nazi period, therefore, it was not even necessary to face the issue of the value of nuclear weapons on its merits in order to advocate their development; one could simply argue the inexorable necessity of keeping ahead of the other side.

Although the tempo of the nuclear arms race quickened as the years went by, the United States never completely abandoned the quest for the control of these weapons. Moreover, several new factors emerged bearing upon this issue. First and foremost was the increase in Soviet nuclear power. As the USSR's nuclear stockpile grew, and it became apparent that the Soviet Union could devastate the United States just about as easily as the United States could wreck the Soviet Union, the role that nuclear weapons could and should play in American strategies was increasingly called into

[4]For accounts of the negotiations see Bernhard G. Bechhoefer, *Postwar Negotiations for Arms Control* (1961), and Joseph L. Nogee, *Soviet Policy Towards International Control of Atomic Energy* (1961).

[5]How the Soviet detonation spurred the United States to develop its nuclear capacity still further is shown in Warner R. Schilling, "The H-Bomb Decision: How to Decide Without Actually Choosing," *Political Science Quarterly*, Vol. LXXVI, No. 1. (March 1961), pp. 24-46.

question. And if a world in which two states had large numbers of nuclear weapons and ample means to deliver them seemed frightening, the prospect of a world in which this capacity was dispersed among additional states was even more horrendous. Even if the majority of Americans active in foreign policy did not see increased prospects for the control of nuclear weapons, they certainly saw increased need for such control.

Linking the Control of Nuclear Weapons with Improved World Order: Another Source of Ambivalence

Another complicating element in the evolution of American policy arose from the fact that the search for means of controlling nuclear weapons inevitably became linked with one of the themes which had characterized American foreign policy since the beginning of the twentieth century, the search for institutional means of regulating the conduct of world politics.[6] One reason was that in the American view, it was precisely the absence of effective international institutions that compelled the United States to rely primarily on national military power for its security and to develop nuclear weapons as an essential component of that power. Another reason was that it seemed to be difficult to seek control arrangements for one of the most crucial elements in the relations among states without considering other relevant elements and the problem of world order in general. The existence of the United Nations and the tasks that it assumed in the field of regulation of armaments was a further reason for the linkage.

Like the American attitude toward nuclear weapons, that toward the problem of creating a more effective world order was also characterized by a fundamental ambiguity. On the one hand the United States envisaged the image of a future world in which international institutions would have significant powers with a corresponding reduction in the powers of states; on the other, it was very reluctant to see any derogation of its own sovereignty. From the early days of the twentieth century, American policies concerning

[6]For a critical analysis of this strain see Roland N. Stromberg, *Collective Security and American Foreign Policy: From the League of Nations to NATO* (1963). How it affects contemporary American policy can be seen in former Deputy Assistant Secretary of State Richard N. Gardner's *In Pursuit of World Order: U.S. Foreign Policy and International Organizations* (1964).

these matters were characterized by a series of compromises and followed a zig-zag path. This was dramatized by the American pressure for and subsequent rejection of the League of Nations. Although the scale of oscillation appears to have narrowed after the Second World War, the ambiguity has remained clearly discernible, for instance in the American posture toward the United Nations. Thus the linking of this strain of American foreign policy with developing American attitudes and policies toward the control of nuclear weapons tied the latter to a fairly well developed, yet complicated and sometimes conflicting, set of concepts.

The linkage had consequences for both components. On the one hand, American thinking on the framework for the control of nuclear weapons tended to be cast into predetermined molds. Universal international organizations, such as the United Nations and the specialized agencies, were used as models, without much thought being given to the relationship between the specific weapons control functions to be performed and the nature of the organization required. On the other hand, as the United States began to grapple with the problem of controlling nuclear weapons, it was forced to reappraise certain of its views concerning international organization. For example, the question immediately arose as to whether or not it would be possible to control nuclear weapons completely without at the same time controlling all uses of nuclear energy. If the answer was negative, what would be the impact on the traditional doctrine of domestic jurisdiction?

In the years after 1945 both the changes in the international system wrought by the advent of nuclear weapons and the new status of the United States within that system compelled a broader reevaluation of American concepts of world order. Old concepts generally were questioned and reformulated. What did security mean in the new age? Under the circumstances, what would an organized and orderly system for the conduct of international politics be like? What was the relationship between the reconciliation of the conflicting aims and ambitions of states and the control of violence?

Since these concepts originated within the international political system, their development was inevitably and profoundly affected by the conduct of other actors within this system and especially of the state that the United States perceived as the principal threat, the USSR. This interaction was characterized by a process of bargaining which went on formally and informally, explicitly and implicitly, all of the time.[7] In the American view, the need for nuclear weapons, the need for their control, and the requirements for that control were all intimately related to Soviet behavior.

New Actors in the Security Policy Process, the Scientists

Just as the new age required a new conceptual understanding of the changed world on the part of American policy-makers, opinion leaders, and the informed segments of the public, it also required adjustments in the processes for formulating and implementing security policy. One crucial new requirement was to bring scientists into the policy process.[8] In the first place, they alone could provide the knowledge which would be essential for rational policy formulation with respect to many key issues. Again, many of those scientists who had participated in unlocking the secret of the atom, felt that they had a special responsibility concerning the use to which their discoveries were put, and demanded a voice in policy-making. In an open society, and with a base of new-found prestige, they were in a good position to realize their demands. Finally, scientists became involved in yet another role: the implementation of certain policies, once formulated, also required the services of scientists, including their participation in international negotiations.

The integration of scientists into the policy process had to take account of the decentralization in the process of making security policy within the United States which stems originally from the constitutional division of power between the legislative and executive branches. The multiplication of executive agencies with responsibilities in security affairs after the Second World War further fragmented the process. Given their nature as loose coalitions, in which local interests tend to predominate except during Presidential election years, American political parties have been able to make

[7]The best theoretical analysis of this process is: Thomas C. Schelling, *The Strategy of Conflict* (1960). For an excellent real world application of this theoretical framework see Fred Charles Iklé, *How Nations Negotiate* (1964).

[8]For general analyses of the introduction of scientists into the process of formulating and implementing security policy see Robert Gilpin, *American Scientists and Nuclear Weapons Policy* (1962) and Robert Gilpin and Christopher Wright (eds.), *Scientists and National Policy Making* (1964).

at most a modest contribution as unifying forces. The fact that different parties can control legislative and executive branches of the federal government, as they did from 1946 through 1948 and again from 1954 through 1960, adds to the fragmentation. As a consequence of all of these factors, the formulation of security policy within the United States is characterized by a process of bargaining which is not totally unlike that which occurs among sovereign states. To formulate a policy requires building a consensus adequate to secure its adoption.[9] Depending on the nature of the policy (for example, whether or not it requires funds for its implementation and the magnitude of the funds needed), the process of building a consensus might be confined to an executive department or even to a bureau within it, or it might extend far wider and include several executive agencies, the legislative branch, and segments of the general public. Because of the nature of this process, scientists could and would have to enter at a variety of points; and they did.

Necessary though this development was, it brought with it complicated problems. What would be the best formal arrangements within the structure of government to insure that technical data and scientific advice would be available when needed and that scientists would be heard and their voice would be accorded neither too little nor too much weight alongside and in combination with those of other expert and interested groups? On a different level, would problems of communication arise between scientists and nonscientists; and, if they did, how could they be overcome, keeping in mind that it would not always be easy or even possible to be aware of communication difficulties as they occur? Often only some later event would make such difficulties apparent. The problem of communication obviously would affect the nature of the arrangements made for the scientists in government. Finally, the way and the extent to which scientists were brought into the process of formulating and implementing security policy were important not only from

[9]This concept was first articulated and developed by Roger Hilsman. See his excellent articles: "Congressional-Executive Relations and the Foreign Policy Consensus," *The American Political Science Review*, Vol. LII, No. 3 (September 1958), pp. 725-44; and, "The Foreign Policy Consensus: An Interim Research Report," *The Journal of Conflict Resolution*, Vol. III, No. 4 (December 1959), pp. 361-82.

the viewpoint of insuring that decisions were made as rationally and efficiently as possible, but also from that of insuring that the elected civilian leaders actually remained in control of the policy processes and their output, since civilian control is one of the most fundamental values embodied in the American constitutional system. Thus, at the same time that the United States grappled with basic problems concerning its position in the international political system, it also struggled with important organizational problems concerning its own political system.

III
The Nuclear Test Ban Negotiations as a Case Study

The negotiations which culminated in the signature of the Moscow Treaty extended over a period of five years, from the summer of 1958 through the summer of 1963. They were conducted principally between the Soviet Union on one side and the United Kingdom and the United States on the other, although almost all states participated in one form or another. These negotiations provide case study material which is both engrossing and instructive. They illustrate—perhaps better than any other international negotiations which have been conducted since the end of the Second World War—how the United States has attempted to resolve the complicated issues relating to the formulation, implementation, and substance of security policy stemming from the emergence of nuclear weapons. They also offer sharp insights into the functioning of the international political system in the nuclear era and possible future developments.

First, with respect to *the process of formulating and implementing American security policy,* the negotiations provide another opportunity to test the consensus-building model and to gain further insights into the operation of this process. The negotiations also demonstrate in a concrete fashion the practical arrangements which have been made for bringing scientific data and scientists into the policy process. They show how scientists have exercised their roles within this process and the way in which they have interacted with nonscientists. They contain evidence concerning the ease or difficulty with which the two groups have been able to communicate. The record, therefore, provides a suitable basis for evaluating the arrangements that have progressively evolved with respect to these matters thus far and for suggesting possible alternatives.

Second, with respect to the *substance of American security policy,* the nuclear test ban negotiations provide a focal point for examining the development of American attitudes and policies toward the problem of obtaining security in a nuclear-missile age. They reveal the extent to which the United States was prepared for serious negotiations concerning arms control or disarmament and provide a basis for assessing the appropriateness of certain widely held American concepts concerning the most effective means of creating a less dangerous world.

Third, with respect to *the working of the international political system,* the test ban negotiations illustrate in a graphic manner the interaction between domestic events, national policies, and international occurrences. They offer a striking picture of diplomatic intercourse between a totalitarian state with tightly sealed policy-making and close controls over its mass media on the one hand, and two relatively open, pluralistic states on the other. The negotiations show the extent to which states which do not possess nuclear weapons can influence the policies of the nuclear states, even concerning nuclear weapons, and the modalities through which this influence can be exercised. In this connection, they provide a number of insights into the role of the United Nations in the contemporary international political system. They also provide a wealth of data relevant to describing accurately the current state of the conflict between East and West and possibly suggest the contours of the future course of this struggle, which has been such an important and pervasive feature of the present period. Finally, the negotiations show how far mankind has gone in its efforts to harness the atom and illustrate clearly the difficulties which it faces in attempting to control the uses to which modern technology is put. Hopefully, a study of the record may lead to suggestions which could be useful in surmounting some of these difficulties.

Whether or not the Moscow Treaty will truly stand as a turning point in the nuclear age and more generally in the age of modern technology is dependent in varying degrees upon all of these factors. Admittedly American policy is only one variable in the equation, yet it is a crucially important variable. The substance of American policy cannot help but have a profound influence on the course of the future, and the substance of that policy will be shaped in important ways by the manner in which it is formulated and implemented. Obviously American security policy can only be conducted within the framework of the international system, and its effectiveness will partly depend upon how appropriate it is for this environment. For all these reasons, then, a detailed case study of United States policy in the nuclear test ban negotiations should help to determine if the Moscow Treaty should be regarded as, and can be made, a genuine turning point.

Chapter II

1957: La Mise en Scène

I

What Beginning?

Neither October 31, 1958, the opening date of the Conference on
the Discontinuance of Nuclear Weapon Tests, nor July 1, 1958, when
the Conference of Experts began—the conference which formulated the technical basis for the subsequent diplomatic talks—
is an appropriate starting point for an analysis of the nuclear test
ban negotiations. The negotiations, and American policy in them,
can be properly understood only when put in the context of earlier
events, particularly several occurring during 1957. For one thing,
the 1957 London session of the Subcommittee of the Disarmament
Commission of the United Nations was clearly a prelude to the
nuclear test ban negotiations; there is an important connection between the two, and the latter was in many ways a consequence of
the former. For another, certain conflicting international and domestic forces vitally affected American policy on the question of a test
ban; and, although it is difficult to fix a point in time when these
forces first emerged, their impact was strongly felt by 1957. Finally,
the formal arrangements for the participation of scientists in the
policy process within the United States government were signficantly
altered in 1957.

II

The Status of International Negotiations

The Confrontation at Lancaster House
The Subcommittee of the Disarmament Commission composed of
Canada, France, the USSR, the United Kingdom, and the United
States, held its most significant, and also its last, session at the
Lancaster House in London from March to September of 1957. As

14

a consequence of major policy reviews, both East and West came to the meeting with new proposals, and during the course of the session, they revised their policies still further.[1] Three developments during the London meetings in effect set the stage for the Geneva test ban negotiations.

The first of these developments was the announcement by the USSR on June 14 that it would agree to the establishment of a control system, including control posts on its own territory, on that of the United Kingdom and the United States, and in the Pacific Ocean, to monitor an agreement for the cessation of nuclear weapon tests.[2] Until that date the Soviet Union had always argued that no international control mechanism was necessary for this purpose. In the same announcement, the USSR also declared its willingness to accept a temporary suspension of tests for a period of two to three years. Previously the Soviet position had been that any agreement on suspension must be of unlimited duration. Both aspects of the announcement represented an important change from past Soviet positions. Ever since 1954 when the testing of nuclear weapons had become a matter of widespread public concern, the Soviet Union had sought to place itself in the forefront of the movement to prohibit further testing, although it had continued its own test program without interruption.[3] Starting in May 1955, the USSR had advanced a variety of proposals on the subject, and because of its insistence, this issue had been placed at the head of the agenda for the London session of the disarmament Subcommittee. In the Western view, however, prior to June 14 the Soviet positions offered no basis for constructive negotiations.

The West also altered its position on a test ban during the course of the London session, and this was the second development which contributed to the subsequent Geneva negotiations. Previously, the cessation of nuclear tests had been accorded relatively

[1]For detailed descriptions of the London session see Bernhard G. Bechhoefer, *Postwar Negotiations for Arms Control,* pp. 241-439, and Ciro E. Zoppo, *The Issue of Nuclear Test Cessation at the London Disarmament Conference of 1957: A Study in East-West Negotiation* (The RAND Corp., RM-2821-ARPA, 1961).

[2]UN Document DC/SC. 1/60.

[3]See Joseph L. Nogee, *Soviet Policy Towards International Control of Atomic Energy,* pp. 211-13.

low priority in Western proposals, and the Western states had taken the position that they could accept a ban on tests only if an adequate control mechanism was operative and the ban was part of a broader agreement covering other measures of disarmament as well. There were several reasons for the Western position. The most important was that Western military strategy depended on nuclear weapons to counter Soviet superiority in conventional forces. In addition, France, which was just beginning to develop nuclear weapons, was unwilling to have a test ban block its progress in this area, unless it were confident that the three nuclear powers were actually going to reduce their nuclear arsenals and perhaps also other components of their military power. The insistence on the establishment of a control system was, of course, an integral part of the Western position on disarmament.

At London, three changes were made in the Western position. First, the United States indicated at the outset that it was willing to accord a new priority to a test cessation; this measure could become an integral part of the initial stage of a disarmament agreement.[4] Secondly, on July 2, after the Soviet Union announced its willingness to accept an international control system, the four Western members of the Subcommittee stated that they would agree to a temporary suspension of testing while the control system was being established.[5] The following day, Harold Stassen, the American representative, mentioned ten months as the duration of the temporary suspension. Later, he offered to extend this period to twelve months, and to agree that there might be an additional suspension of another year. Thirdly, the Western powers hinted that they might accept a loosening of the tie between the test ban issue and other measures of disarmament, although the extent of this concession was not clear. In the end, the Western powers presented all of their first stage measures as an indivisible package, thus reducing the scope of the concession.[6]

This package—the provisions of which significantly would have allowed the transfer of nuclear weapons to non-nuclear powers— included measures for numerical limitation of armed forces and fixed reductions in armaments, safeguards against surprise attack,

[4]See UN Document DC/SC. 1/PV. 89, pp. 2-14.
[5]UN Document DC/SC. 1/59.
[6]UN Document DC/SC. 1/66.

limiting entry into outer space exclusively to objects designed for peaceful and scientific purposes, a cut-off on the production of fissionable materials for weapons purposes, and a test cessation. However, during the London session there were various indications in the press (especially following the review of American policy in May) that the United States was willing to treat questions relating to the production and testing of nuclear weapons as a separate issue.[7] Moreover, the only condition that Mr. Stassen listed for extending the temporary suspension of testing for a second year was that there should be progress "in relation to the cessation of production of fissionable material for weapons purposes."[8] In addition, he implied that the suspension would become permanent if a cut-off on production were achieved during the second year.

Thus, the gap between East and West on the question of a cessation of nuclear weapon tests had been narrowed considerably. However, important differences still remained. The Soviet Union was opposed to formally linking a test cessation with any other measure of disarmament. It was also unwilling to accept the extensive controls which the Western proposal would have required for supervising a cut-off on the production of fissionable materials for weapons.[9] In fairness, it should be pointed out that other states, such as Canada, also had some reservations about the extent of the proposed controls.[10]

The final development during the London session of the disarmament Subcommittee which had a bearing on the Geneva test ban negotiations was the introduction by the Western delegates of the idea of holding technical talks on control systems. As early as the opening meeting, Britain's Foreign Secretary, Selwyn Lloyd, suggested that the Subcommittee consider appointing technical working groups which would meet concurrently with the Subcommittee and explore the technical aspects of the various agenda items. This idea of having technical experts meet was an old favorite of Mr.

---

[7]See *New York Times,* June 1, 1957, p. 1.

[8]UN Document DC/SC. 1/PV. 149, p. 24.

[9]See Ambassador Zorin's statements in the Subcommittee on July 8 and August 27, 1957, UN Document DC/SC. 1/PV. 132, pp. 2-26; and DC/SC. 1/65/RPV. 1.

[10]See Bernhard G. Bechhoefer, *Postwar Negotiations for Arms Control,* p. 342.

Lloyd's, which he had raised several times previously in other con-texts. On May 6, the United Kingdom formally proposed "that a Committee of technical experts be established within the framework of the disarmament Sub-Committee, to consider possible methods of limiting nuclear test explosions and to investigate the requirements of effective supervision over an Agreement to limit such explo-sions."[11] This same suggestion was repeated in the July 2 response of the Western powers to the Soviet acceptance of the principle of international control, again by Selwyn Lloyd on July 17, and finally by Harold Stassen on August 21 when he announced the willingness of the United States to agree that the temporary suspension could be extended for a second year. The motivation for this suggestion was never made explicit. The British may have hoped that the proposed technical talks might precipitate broader political agree-ment. For the Americans, it was most likely a way of testing the reality of an essential aspect of the new Soviet position; that is, the declared Soviet willingness to accept a control system. The USSR, however, refused to consent to technical talks unless there were first an agreement on the period and the conditions of a test cessa-tion.[12] From the point of view of the Geneva negotiations, the im-portant thing was that the idea of technical talks was introduced and gained currency.

III

Conflicting Forces in Test Ban Policy Formulation

International Pressures

The encounter between the East and West at the conference table in London was only one factor in the formation of the American policy leading to the nuclear test ban negotiations. In diplomatic negotiations, the point and counterpoint of proposal and response often force adjustments of policy, but as a rule factors external to the negotiations play a greater role. Facts as understood by the policy-makers; their assumptions, philosophies and idiosyncrasies; the general policy framework; the working of national institutions as well as the many complex pressures exerted upon the policy-

[11]UN Document DC/SC. 1/56, p. 1.
[12]See Ambassador Zorin's statement, UN Document DC/SC. 1/PV. 136, pp. 2-15.

makers by individuals and groups in and outside the government, privately and through the mass media of communications; interventions of friendly governments in and outside international organizations; estimates of reactions of unfriendly governments—all these affect the content of a policy. Exact weighting of the relative influence of these factors is impossible in the case of the American test ban policy—as it is in most cases. For the purpose of this background, however, it may suffice to identify certain salient international and domestic forces which had a crucial impact on the policies pursued by the United States in the London session of the disarmament Subcommittee and thereafter. The principal issue for the American policy-maker during and after the London confrontation was whether and on what conditions the United States could accede to the Soviet demand and agree to taking the test ban negotiations out of the disarmament package with the resulting possibility that a test ban could come into effect without any assurance of nuclear or other disarmament.

One of the most important of the external pressures was the widespread public feeling against the testing of nuclear weapons. The motives for this worldwide attitude were mixed. For some, the issue provided a dramatic focal point for expressing their pacifist beliefs. Others, recalling Hiroshima and Nagasaki, were horrified by the frightful devastation which modern weapons could cause and feared the consequences of further technological developments. The fact that nuclear weapons had been used first and only against a nonwhite population linked the test ban issue with antiwhite and anticolonial attitudes. The problem of fallout, though, was probably the principal reason for the issue's arousing such a broad public response.

Public concern about radioactive fallout began to mount in 1954. On March 1 of that year the United States detonated a 15 megaton hydrogen bomb over the Bikini Atoll in the Marshall Islands.[13] The fallout from this explosion covered an unexpectedly

[13]For a detailed analysis of the public reaction to this shot see Earl H. Voss, *Nuclear Ambush: The Test Ban Trap* (1963), pp. 37-50. In general, Voss tends to belittle the danger from fallout. The United States' testing of nuclear weapons in a UN Trust Territory raised several political and legal issues. For analyses of these points see Harold Karan Jacobson, "Our 'Colonial' Problem in the Pacific," *Foreign Affairs,* Vol. XXXIX, No. 1 (October

large area of approximately 7,000 square miles. Some of the inhabitants of the American Trust Territory were endangered, and a Japanese fishing vessel, the *Fukurya Maru,* was contaminated. Shortly thereafter, a radioactive rain fell on Japan as a consequence of a Soviet hydrogen bomb test. People throughout the world were alarmed by these incidents and by the increasing quantity of radioactive material in the atmosphere. Later in March, 104 British Labor Members of Parliament signed a motion asking the United Nations to proclaim a ban on testing hydrogen weapons. The following month Prime Minister Nehru addressed a personal plea to the United States to end such tests. A few days after that, in a speech before the Indian Parliament, he proposed that the three nuclear powers should accept a "standstill agreement" on nuclear testing.

The limited extent of knowledge about fallout and its consequences—particularly the genetic effects—allowed a wide variety of estimates of the danger, and this in itself probably made the public alarm greater than it would have been had the dangers of fallout been known exactly. The United States government moved to quell these fears, but with little success. In February 1955, the Atomic Energy Commission published a report on this subject, but many discounted it on the ground that the source was an interested party. Later that year the United States and the United Kingdom proposed that the United Nations establish a scientific committee to study the effects of atomic radiation. This proposal was adopted unanimously, and the Committee was appointed in December 1955. However, it did not publish its first findings until June 1958.[14] Meanwhile, public concern about the effects of fallout grew, and Soviet tactics played on these fears.

During 1957 international opposition to the continued testing of nuclear weapons reached a high point. In March the Japanese

1960), pp. 56-66, at 59; Myers S. McDougal and Norbert A. Schlei, "The Hydrogen Bomb Tests in Perspective: Lawful Measures for Security," *The Yale Law Journal,* Vol. LXIV, No. 5 (April 1955), pp. 648-710; and, Emanuel Margolis, "The Hydrogen Bomb Experiments and International Law," *The Yale Law Journal,* Vol. LXIV, No. 5 (April 1955), pp. 629-47.

[14]UN, General Assembly, *Official Records* (13th Session), Supplement No. 17, "Report of the United Nations Scientific Committee on the Effects of Atomic Radiation."

government decided to send Professor Masateshi Matsushita, an eminent scientist, on a special mission to the USSR, the United Kingdom, and the United States, to urge a cessation of nuclear weapons tests. The following month, in a major address, Prime Minister Nehru renewed his appeal for a test ban, and he continued to urge such action throughout the year. Again in April the Labor Party in Britain, during a Parliamentary debate on the 1957 White Paper on Defense, moved that the government should be requested to take immediate initiative and put forward effective proposals for the abolition of hydrogen weapon tests through effective international agreement.[15] Later that month, eighteen of West Germany's leading nuclear physicists, including Professor Otto Hahn, the first to split the atom, signed a declaration that they would not participate in the construction or testing of nuclear weapons. On April 23 Dr. Albert Schweitzer issued an appeal through the Norwegian Nobel Committee which was broadcast in fifty countries, and received wide coverage elsewhere, asking that public opinion demand an end to nuclear tests. Within a few days his appeal was endorsed by the Pope, and on May 10 the West German Bundestag adopted a resolution, sponsored by the governing Christian Democratic Coalition, urging the three nuclear powers to temporarily suspend their tests, pending the negotiation of an arms control agreement.[16]

During the most active phase of the London session of the UN disarmament Subcommittee, these pressures subsided somewhat, but even then they remained at a high level. During June and July the Soviet Union gained some support in its efforts to have the International Labor Organization and the Economic and Social Council of the United Nations recommend a test ban, and in August the World Council of Churches urged an international accord to stop further testing, or if that proved impossible, unilateral action.

"The Disarmament General Assembly"

When the Subcommittee's failure became apparent, the pressures rose again, and they came to a head at the twelfth session of the UN General Assembly in the fall of 1957. It is significant that

[15]See U.K. House of Commons, *Debates,* April 16, 1957, 5th ser. vol. 568, col. 1758-1878; and, *ibid.,* 1929-2060.

[16]German Federal Republic, *Der Deutsche Bundestag, Verhandlungen,* 209. Sitzung, Mai 10, 1957, pp. 12051D-12138A.

that session has been dubbed the "Disarmament General Assembly."
In all, eleven different resolutions dealing with disarmament were
considered, as well as several amendments to them. Most of the
proposals, in one way or another, dealt with the question of testing. The USSR led off by proposing—along the lines of its London
announcement—that further tests of nuclear weapons be suspended
for a two to three year period starting January 1, 1958.[17] It also
proposed—as it had at the London meeting—that an international
commission should be created to supervise the test suspension, and
that control posts should be established on a basis of reciprocity
in the USSR, in the United Kingdom and its possessions, in the
United States, and in the Pacific Ocean areas, including Australia.
However, the Soviet Union eventually withdrew its draft in favor
of an Indian proposal. The Indian resolution would have asked the
nuclear powers to agree immediately to suspend tests and also
would have provided for the creation of a commission of experts
to recommend an adequate control system.[18] This resolution was
rejected by a vote of 24 to 34, with 20 abstentions. Pakistan and
Tunisia were the only countries from the African and Asian group
to vote with the West. The Assembly also rejected a Japanese proposal which was somewhat closer to the Western position. In the
end, the Assembly adopted, by a vote of 56 to 9, with 15 abstentions, a resolution sponsored by twenty-four powers, which in effect
endorsed the package proposal for a first stage disarmament agreement which the Western powers had presented during the closing
days of the London session.[19] This proposal included a test cessation as only one of several measures which presumably would occur
simultaneously.[20] In addition, as a consequence of an amendment
proposed by Norway and Pakistan, the resolution requested that the
disarmament Subcommittee appoint groups of experts to study the
technical aspects of monitoring disarmament agreements—an idea
also aired at London.

After the twenty-four power resolution had been introduced
in the Political Committee, and it was evident that it would probably be adopted there and in the plenary session, the Soviet Union

[17]UN Document A/3674 and Rev. 1.
[18]UN Document A/C. 1/L. 176 and Revs. 1, 2, and 4.
[19]General Assembly Resolution 1148 (XII).
[20]See *ibid.* §1(a).

announced that it would no longer participate in the Disarmament Commission or its Subcommittee.[21] The reason which the Soviet delegation gave for this position was that both bodies were composed in a one-sided fashion. The USSR was the only Communist country represented on the two organs. Nine of the twelve states on the Commission were members of the Western alliance system, and four of the five states on the Subcommittee were members of NATO. The fact that the twelfth Assembly was the first occasion, with one minor exception, since 1948 that the West—reportedly in response to a personal decision by Secretary Dulles—had insisted on the endorsement of its position on arms control despite Soviet opposition, may also have affected the Soviet stand. Generally, the practice had been to refer both sides' proposals to the Commission or the Subcommittee for further negotiations. The Western action in obtaining the backing for its position in the Assembly underscored the importance of the composition of the negotiating forum. However, it should be noted that the USSR had criticized the composition of the Commission and the Subcommittee from the opening of the Assembly session.

The Soviet Union proposed that the Disarmament Commission should be expanded to include the entire membership of the UN; and, although the Soviet representatives did not state this explicitly, they implied that such a body should conduct its affairs in public.[22] Alternatively, the USSR was willing to support proposals which would alter the composition of the Commission in the direction of parity between East and West. The West, on the other hand, even though it was willing to enlarge the Disarmament Commission, was unwilling to accept either solution favored by the Soviet Union. The net result was an impasse—although the Assembly voted to increase the membership of the Disarmament Commission, it did not significantly alter the disparity between East and West (sixteen of the twenty-five members belonged to Western alliances), and the Soviet Union stated that it would not participate in the new body either.

[21]UN, General Assembly, First Committee, *Official Records* (12th Session), p. 117.

[22]UN Document A/L. 230. See the statements by A. A. Gromyko and V. V. Kuznetsov: UN, General Assembly, Plenary Meetings, *Official Records* (12th Session), p. 34, and pp. 469-70.

The denouement was susceptible to varying interpretations. Bernhard Bechhoefer, in his authoritative account of the post-Second World War arms control negotiations, called the Assembly resolution endorsing the Western package proposal a "hollow victory" for the West.[23]

He asserted that:

> The Soviet refusal to participate further in the work of the Disarmament Commission was a logical and foreseeable consequence of the Western insistence on securing the United Nations endorsement of their August 29 proposals.[24]

It is also possible to argue, however, that the dispute about the composition of the Commission was independent of this action; that the USSR would not have agreed to participate in any body which would have been acceptable to the West at that time. In the narrow context of the test cessation issue, although the West enjoyed a temporary triumph, the resolution did not reduce the pressure for a nuclear test ban in any lasting way. In addition, the West found itself without any forum for continuing the negotiations, since *Hamlet* cannot be performed without the Prince of Denmark.

The Presidential Campaign

For those who had to set the course of American policy, particularly the Secretary of State and the President, this pressure was not merely an international phenomenon but a domestic one as well. Within the United States, discontinuing nuclear weapon tests became an important issue in the public debate in 1956, when during the Presidential campagin the Democratic nominee, Adlai E. Stevenson, suggested that the United States might unilaterally stop testing as the first step toward obtaining an agreement with the Soviet Union on this subject. Apparently the question of ceasing the testing of at least the largest nuclear weapons had been under study within the Administration since the spring of 1954 or per-

[23]*Postwar Negotiations for Arms Control*, p. 418.
[24]*Ibid.*, p. 425.

haps even earlier.[25] Mr. Stevenson's proposal therefore was not a totally new suggestion. President Eisenhower's response to the proposal was that to take such action outside of the context of a comprehensive, enforceable disarmament agreement would endanger the security of the United States. At the time, in the public image, the twin crises of Hungary and Suez seemed to support his position. The fact that the Chairman of the Council of Ministers of the USSR, Nikolai A. Bulganin, publicly endorsed Mr. Stevenson's suggestion probably did little to enhance its attractiveness, either to the Administration or to the American public.[26] However, as the Soviet posture became less bellicose in 1957, there was a resurgence of public concern about the effects of further testing.

Mr. Stevenson continued to press his position, and others joined him. The American Friends Service Committee and the American Unitarian Association both formally urged a test cessation, and they were joined by other religious groups. In several public appearances, Norman Thomas called for a monitored moratorium on further testing. Individual scientists and groups of scientists also took a stand. In February 1957, the Council of the Federation of American Scientists recommended that the Administration should "seek worldwide cessation of nuclear weapons tests without making this contingent on achieving more far-reaching goals in arms limitation."[27] In May and June over two thousand American scientists signed Linus Pauling's petition urging an immediate international agreement to stop the testing of nuclear bombs.[28] In public pronouncements, Dr. Pauling, winner of the 1954 Nobel prize for research in molecular chemistry, stressed the dangers of radioactive fallout resulting from nuclear testing.

Voices in the Congress

Various congressmen also urged that the United States should seek a test ban of some sort. In June Senator Mike Mansfield, a

[25]See Robert Gilpin, *American Scientists and Nuclear Weapons Policy*, p. 154; Thomas E. Murray, *Nuclear Policy for War and Peace* (1960), pp. 86-89; and Earl H. Voss, *Nuclear Ambush*, pp. 31-34.

[26]For the reaction of one Administration official see Lewis L. Strauss, *Men and Decisions* (1962), pp. 416-17.

[27]*Bulletin of the Atomic Scientists*, Vol. XIII, No. 4 (April 1957), p. 138.

[28]See *ibid.*, Vol. XIII, No. 7 (September 1957), pp. 264-66.

member of the Committee on Foreign Relations, proposed that a summit conference should be held on halting tests of large nuclear weapons. That same month, Representative Chet Holifield, Chairman of the Special Subcommittee on Radiation of the Joint Committee on Atomic Energy, recommended that the United States might unilaterally halt such tests to alleviate the problem of fallout. In July, Representative Sterling Cole, another member of the Special Subcommittee, made a similar proposal. The recommendations by Representatives Holifield and Cole—Democrat and Republican respectively—were especially noteworthy because they were made immediately after their Subcommittee had conducted an extensive public hearing on the dangers of radioactive fallout.[29] During the year, the Subcommittee on Disarmament of the Senate Committee on Foreign Relations explored the issue of a test ban, and in November, the Chairman, Hubert H. Humphrey, suggested in a letter to President Eisenhower that the United States should:

> . . . declare its willingness to negotiate separately on a ban on nuclear weapons tests for a 2-year period with the only condition being agreement on an effective inspection system with United Nations supervision to insure that the ban is being scrupulously observed.[30]

Although President Eisenhower's reply was noncommittal,[31] he obviously had to take these pressures into account. Thus, the Administration was being pushed by powerful international and domestic forces toward agreeing to some limited accord for the cessation of nuclear weapon tests.

New Tasks for Nuclear Weapons

However, other influential factors worked in a different direction. Although by this time the United States had abandoned "massive retaliation" as a conceptual basis for its military doctrine—if

[29]U.S. Congress, Joint Committee on Atomic Energy, Special Subcommittee on Radiation, *Hearings: The Nature of Radioactive Fallout and Its Effects on Man,* 3 parts, 85th Congress, 1st Session (1958).

[30]U.S. Congress, Senate, Committee on Foreign Relations, Subcommittee on Disarmament, *Control and Reduction of Armaments: Final Report,* 85th Congress, 2d Session (1958), p. 34.

[31]*Ibid.*

it indeed had ever accepted this concept in its bald outline[32]—it still relied heavily on nuclear weapons to deter Soviet expansionist moves. The Air Force, and within it the Strategic Air Command, continued to receive the largest share of the defense budget. Moreover, by 1957 nuclear weapons were also being thought of as important elements in the armament of American tactical forces. Thus, a test ban might inhibit developments of potential importance for both the strategic and tactical forces of the United States. This raised the fundamental issue of the effects of a nuclear test ban on the distribution of military power.

At the time, American scientists were working on the development of so-called "clean" weapons, which would produce little or no radioactive fallout. In general terms, since fission (the splitting of atoms) results in the release of radioactive products, while fusion (the joining together of atoms) does not, other things being equal, the radioactive fallout resulting from a nuclear weapon depends upon the relative extent to which fission and fusion processes contribute to the energy of the weapon.[33] Making a "clean" bomb therefore depends upon minimizing the proportion of the energy of the weapon derived from fission and maximizing that derived from fusion. Such weapons could be of special importance in defense against a nuclear-missile attack and in tactical situations. In addition, the scientists were attempting to improve the yield-to-weight ratio of nuclear weapons, a development which would have general utility, but which would probably have greater significance for the United States than for the Soviet Union, since in the immediate future Soviet missiles would have greater thrust and therefore greater carrying capacity.

This work was outlined in secret testimony before the Military Applications Subcommittee of the Joint Committee on Atomic Energy, which was headed by Senator Henry M. Jackson, on June

[32]Insufficient attention has been paid to the differences between John Foster Dulles' speech before the New York Council on Foreign Relations and his subsequent article, "Policy for Security and Peace," *Foreign Affairs,* Vol. XXXII, No. 3 (April 1954), pp. 353-64. In the latter, he stated a position which was not too different from that of many of his limited war or graduated deterrence critics, see especially pp. 358-59.

[33]See U.S. Department of Defense, Samuel Glasstone (ed.), *The Effects of Nuclear Weapons* (1962, revised edition), pp. 414 ff.

24, 1957, by three scientists from the Livermore Radiation Laboratory of the University of California, Ernest O. Lawrence, Mark M. Mills, and Edward Teller.[34] The members of the Subcommittee were particularly impressed with the concept of a neutron bomb which the scientists advanced. This weapon would have a relatively low yield and would have its greatest use in battlefield situations. It would be produced by tailoring the energy of a fusion explosion so that its primary product would be a burst of neutrons, instead of heat and blast. This burst would operate as a kind of death ray, doing almost no physical damage and leaving no contamination, but immediately destroying all life in the target area. Since this weapon would not produce fallout, there was no contradiction between the interest which certain Congressmen, such as Representative Holifield, displayed in it, and their position with reference to discontinuing tests of high yield, "dirty" weapons. The Subcommittee members arranged for the scientists to present their concept to President Eisenhower the following day. That the President was impressed can be seen by comparing his remarks on a test ban at his news conferences on June 19 and June 26.[35] On the latter occasion his support of an agreed cessation of further tests was a bit more cautious and qualified.

In addition to these factors, several policy-makers had the suspicion that the Soviet Union's demand that further testing be stopped was merely a continuation of its "ban the bomb" campaign. They thought that the Soviet Union would regard a test ban as a prelude to a prohibition of the use of nuclear weapons, and that the whole campaign was merely an effort to render ineffective the American superiority in nuclear weapons while preserving Soviet preponderance in conventional arms. There was sufficient evidence to give this interpretation some plausibility. During his opening statement in the General Assembly in September 1957, Soviet Foreign Minister, Andrei A. Gromyko, in listing the advantages of a temporary cessation of nuclear weapons tests, asserted that it would constitute "a first practical step towards the main goal—the absolute and unconditional prohibition of atomic and hydrogen

[34]See Charles J. V. Murphy, "Nuclear Inspection: A Near Miss," *Fortune,* Vol. LIX, No. 3 (March 1959), pp. 122-25, 155-62, at 156, and *New York Times,* June 25, 1957, p. 1, June 25, 1961, p. 1.

[35]See *New York Times,* June 20, 1957, p. 18, and June 27, 1957, p. 10.

weapons."[36] The same thought, in almost identical phraseology, was contained in the preamble to the draft resolution on this issue which the USSR submitted to the twelfth Assembly.[37]

For all of these reasons a number of high officials, such as Admiral Lewis L. Strauss, Chairman of the Atomic Energy Commission, several members of the Commission, and Secretary of Defense Charles E. Wilson, argued that a test cessation without other measures of arms control would be harmful to American security interests. However, some individuals in this group, for instance Commissioner Thomas E. Murray, would have been willing to have the United States forego testing high yield nuclear weapons in the interest of reducing the effects of fallout. The argument that no test ban could be considered unless it were linked with other measures of arms control was pressed forcefully within the Administration, and carried the day, but curiously it was not articulated clearly or effectively in public until a later time.

The NATO Interest

Significant international factors were pressing in a similar direction. The attitude of France has already been mentioned. On a more general level, the Western alliance was just as dependent upon American strategic nuclear power as was the United States. Moreover, in 1957 the North Atlantic Treaty Organization was in the midst of what proved to be a series of crises concerning its strategic doctrine. NATO strategy had always been based on the concept of the "sword" and the "shield"; the "sword" being the strategic forces of the United Kingdom and the United States, and the "shield," local forces within Europe. Although the local forces had never been brought up to a level which military planners considered adequate to counter the opposing Eastern forces, until the middle nineteen-fifties there had been general confidence that the superior strategic capability of the United States would deter an attack. With the growth of the USSR's strategic capacity, this confidence gradually began to wane. Many felt that the USSR could

[36]UN, General Assembly, Plenary Meetings, *Official Records* (12th Session), p. 33. See also V. V. Kuznetsov's statements in the Political Committee, UN, General Assembly, First Committee, *Official Records* (12th Session), pp. 97, 135.

[37]UN Document A/3674 and Rev. 1.

neutralize NATO's "sword," and that then Europe would be left with only a flimsy "shield."

Since the NATO powers, for a variety of reasons, appeared to be unwilling to raise the level of local forces—indeed, in 1957 there were even cutbacks—there was considerable groping for some method of restoring confidence. One idea was that arming the local forces with *tactical* nuclear weapons might make up for the gap in numbers, and the NATO Council authorized such action in December 1954. However, because the United States alone could make such weapons and because the Atomic Energy Act of 1954 prohibited the transfer of such weapons from American control, only American troops in Europe received such armaments. Another problem was that the tactical nuclear weapons then in existence, if used, could well contaminate large areas of Europe; hence the attractiveness of a neutron bomb.

A second idea for strengthening NATO was dispersing *strategic* capabilities among more NATO members.[38] NATO began to move in this direction in December 1957 when the NATO Council, consisting, for this meeting, of the heads of governments, decided to establish stocks of nuclear warheads in Europe and to put intermediate range ballistic missiles at the disposal of the Supreme Allied Commander. Again because of the provisions of the Atomic Energy Act, the warheads would remain in the control of American forces; the missiles, however, could be given to non-American troops.

Neither solution was totally satisfactory. Both left Europeans dependent on American willingness to use nuclear weapons, and many doubted even at that time that, short of an attack on the United States, an American President would actually take such a decision, even though at the December meeting President Eisenhower promised that he would do so. Therefore, the crisis concerning NATO strategy created pressures both for the development of clean weapons and for the dispersal of nuclear weapons, either by independent weapons programs, as in the case of France, or by transfer of knowledge or the actual weapons themselves. As early

[38]For cogent expressions of this proposal see Hans Speier, *German Rearmament and Atomic War* (1957), pp. 227-34, and Hans Speier, "Soviet Atomic Blackmail and the North Atlantic Alliance," *World Politics,* Vol. IX, No. 3 (April 1957), pp. 307-28.

as April 1957, Chancellor Konrad Adenauer declared that Germany should be allowed to have *tactical* nuclear weapons for its own defense.[39] During the year other NATO political leaders stated that all NATO forces should be so armed, and there was some discussion of the creation of a NATO *strategic* force. Secretary of State John Foster Dulles, in an article which was published in the October 1957 issue of *Foreign Affairs,* indicated that he was considering these possibilities.[40] On the twenty-fifth of that month in a joint statement President Eisenhower promised Prime Minister Macmillan that he would ask Congress to amend the Atomic Energy Act so as to permit a "close and fruitful collaboration of scientists and engineers of Great Britain, the United States, and other friendly countries."[41] These developments explain why the Western powers included in their first stage package proposal submitted to the London Disarmament Subcommittee on August 29, 1957, provisions which would have allowed the transfer of nuclear weapons.

To summarize the situation as it stood at the end of 1957, although there were powerful international and domestic pressures favoring an attempt to negotiate an arms control agreement covering only a cessation of nuclear weapons tests, there were also strong policy considerations pushing American policy-makers in a different direction. Presumably, the USSR's leaders were also subject to domestic and international pressures, but any analysis along these lines would be beyond the scope of this study. Suffice it to say that during 1957 Nikita S. Khrushchev seemed to be moving toward the consolidation of his power, Messrs. Kaganovich, Malenkov, Molotov, and Shepilov were dropped from their party and governmental posts as a result of a meeting of the Central Committee in late June, and Marshall Zhukov suffered the same fate in October and November. It was impossible to know the actual meaning of these events, but in the West they were widely interpreted as heralding a victory for the advocates of a moderate policy.

[39]Richard P. Stebbins, *The United States in World Affairs, 1957* (1957), p. 98.
[40]"Challenge and Response in United States Policy," *Foreign Affairs,* Vol. XXXVI, No. 1 (October 1957), pp. 25-43, at 30-33.
[41]U.S. Department of State *Bulletin,* Vol. XXXVII, No. 959 (November 11, 1957), p. 740.

IV

A New Base for Scientists in the White House

The Science Adviser and PSAC

Government organizations and procedures also affect the substance
of policy. Since key decision-makers cannot help but be influenced
by their immediate advisers, the question of access is crucial. Significantly, the formal arrangements for the participation of scientists
in the policy process within the United States government were
altered in late 1957, and a new group of scientists was given immediate access to the President. This change is an important element
of the background for the Geneva test ban negotiations.

The change actually came about as a response to two spectacu-
lar Soviet scientific feats. On October 4, as a part of its participation in the International Geophysical Year, the USSR launched the
first earth satellite, Sputnik I. About a month later, on November 3,
the Soviet Union launched the half-ton, dog-carrying Sputnik II.
These accomplishments were impressive evidence of Soviet scientific
capabilities. They also had ominous connotations, for they indicated
that the USSR led the West in the development of ballistic missiles.
Westerners were hardly reassured when the Soviet Union announced
on October 7 that it had successfully tested a powerful hydrogen
warhead of a new design. Soviet leaders emphasized that their missiles could easily carry such warheads.

In an effort to restore confidence in American capabilities,
President Eisenhower made a special telecast on November 7. After
recounting American military strength and scientific prowess, the
President admitted that there were certain deficiencies, and he proclaimed that science and technology would receive greater emphasis
in the future governmental programs. As a first step, he appointed
James R. Killian, Jr., President of the Massachusetts Institute of
Technology, as his Special Assistant for Science and Technology.
Several days later, the President announced that the membership
of the Science Advisory Committee of the Office of Defense Mo-
bilization (ODM) would be enlarged and that the Committee would
become a part of the White House Office on December 1. This
Committee, which consisted of nongovernment scientists sitting on
a part-time basis with certain government administrators serving
as consultants, had been appointed by President Truman in 1951.[42]

Dr. Killian had been a member of the group, and with the administrative change, he became its Chairman. In the past, however, the Committee had had access to the President only through the Director of ODM; now it was in a quite different position.

The effect of these decisions was to introduce a new group of scientists into the highest levels of the policy-making process within the United States.[43] Of course many scientists had had access to those levels previously, but in the mid-nineteen-fifties they had principally been those who were directly connected with the Atomic Energy Commission and the Department of Defense. Although the President's Science Advisory Committee (PSAC) contained a wide range of views, there were clearly some members who held opinions different from those which had previously been heard within the inner circles of the Eisenhower Administration.

Thus, when the issue of further testing of nuclear weapons came up again, as it was certain to, given the course of the past negotiations and the current of international and domestic pressures, the President would have scientists on his own staff to turn to for advice and would be confronted with new positions and viewpoints. With this development, the stage was set for the first act of the nuclear test ban negotiations.

[42]For a general description of the evolution of the role of scientific advisers in the policy process in the United States see J. Stefan Dupré and Sanford A. Lakoff, *Science and the Nation: Policy and Politics* (1962), pp. 64-77.

[43]The initial members of PSAC were Dr. Robert F. Bacher, Dr. William O. Baker, Dr. Lloyd V. Berkner, Dr. Hans A. Bethe, Dr. Detlev W. Bronk, Dr. James H. Doolittle, Dr. James B. Fisk, Dr. Caryl P. Haskins, Dr. James R. Killian, Jr., Dr. George B. Kistiakowsky, Dr. Edwin H. Land, Dr. Emanuel R. Piore, Dr. Edward M. Purcell, Dr. Isador I. Rabi, Dr. H. P. Robertson, Dr. Jerome B. Wiesner, Dr. Herbert York, and Dr. Jerrold R. Zacharias. All but seven of the eighteen were physicists. The seven who were not were Baker (physical chemistry), Bronk (physiology, biophysics), Doolittle (aviator), Haskins (physiology, genetics), Killian (administration), Kistiakowsky (chemistry), and Wiesner (electrical engineering). In Robert Gilpin's terms, the "finite containment school" scientists now had access to the Eisenhower Administration comparable to that which those of the "infinite containment school" had had (*American Scientists and Nuclear Weapons Policy,* pp. 176-77). Although his categorization can be criticized as oversimplified, the broad point in this case is certainly valid. For confirmation by a knowledgeable and sensitive journalist see Saville R. Davis, "Recent Policy Making in the United States Government," in Donald G. Brennan (ed.) *Arms Control, Disarmament and National Security* (1961), pp. 379-90, at 384-85.

Chapter III

The Conference of Experts

I

The Context—1958

The developments which began to take shape in 1957 continued their course with little change in the first half of 1958, and predetermined in large measure both the nature of the next negotiating forum and the subject matter for the negotiations.

Due to the refusal by the Soviet Union to accept the new composition of the United Nations Disarmament Commission, there was no agreed forum for continuing arms control and disarmament negotiations. In mid-February the Japanese government began to explore with other governments the possibility of convening a meeting of the Disarmament Commission, but this initiative was abandoned when on March 14, the USSR reiterated its refusal to participate in the Commission as long as the majority of its members belonged to Western military alliances. The impasse thus remained and could not be broken within the context of the decisions of the twelfth Assembly.

The pressure against the testing of nuclear weapons also continued unabated. Indeed, on the first day of 1958, the Afro-Asian Solidarity Conference, meeting in Cairo, adopted a declaration which among other things called for a cessation of further tests.[1] On January 13, Linus Pauling presented his petition urging an immediate accord to halt tests, now signed by more than nine thousand scientists from forty-three countries, to the Secretary General of the United Nations. On February 1, The Council of the Federation of American Scientists adopted a statement favoring a test ban which would cover even the smaller nuclear weapons and asserting that an appropriate control system could easily be established.[2]

[1]See *New York Times*, January 2, 1958, p. 2.
[2]*Bulletin of the Atomic Scientists*, Vol. XIV, No. 3 (March 1958), p. 125.

From the point of view of the American Administration, perhaps the most significant pressure was that engendered by Senator Hubert H. Humphrey's Subcommittee on Disarmament. This group held a series of hearings in February, March, and April, which will be considered in detail later, to explore the question of a nuclear test ban. Although the Subcommittee ostensibly approached the matter without a prior commitment to any position, at least some of the Senators clearly thought that the hearings should serve primarily to demonstrate the feasibility of developing a control mechanism for policing a test ban and also the wisdom of attempting to negotiate a separate agreement on this issue. The Chairman, Senator Humphrey, had, after all, written to the President urging such a course as early as November 1957. Senator Humphrey obtained strong support for his views in the hearings from Senators Stuart Symington, a former Secretary of the Air Force and a leading Congressional expert on military affairs, and Clinton Anderson, Vice-Chairman of the Joint Committee on Atomic Energy.

On the other hand, the forces which operated in the opposite direction also continued unabated. Some scientists and policymakers asserted that further testing would result in breakthroughs for "defensive" weapons, and in discoveries that would lead to important peacetime uses of nuclear energy. In the latter connection, the Atomic Energy Commission, which was consistently concerned lest a test ban impair weapons development, now also stressed the importance of its Project Plowshare, a continuing series of experiments designed to explore the peaceful uses of nuclear explosions for such purposes as building harbors or canals. It is important to realize that there has always been a significant link between the Plowshare experiments and the attempt to achieve "clean" bombs or neutron weapons, for using nuclear detonations as a means of excavation would be practical only if one could minimize the radioactivity resulting from the detonation. Planners in Project Plowshare have always counted on the availability of "clean" bombs.[3] Put in another fashion, the Plowshare experiments could have been in the very forefront of nuclear weapons

[3]See Arnold Kramish, *The Peaceful Atom in Foreign Policy* (1963), p. 123.

research since they involved minimizing the amount of fission products in nuclear explosions.

Edward Teller, at that time Associate Director of the University of California Radiation Laboratory, was the most forceful and articulate exponent of the case for further testing. Although he expounded his views in various forums, his most complete exposition was in a book entitled *Our Nuclear Future,*[4] which he wrote jointly with Albert Latter, a physicist employed by the RAND Corporation, an independent research organization supported principally by contracts from the Air Force. In their book, the two men minimized the danger of radioactive fallout, and argued the need for continued testing.

So far as the North Atlantic Treaty Organization was concerned, the events of early 1958 were a logical outgrowth of the decisions of the previous fall. In pursuance of these decisions atomic weapons were to be stocked on the territory of certain NATO countries, under the custody and control of United States military forces, to be turned over to NATO forces on the outbreak of hostilities at the direction of the President. Selected NATO countries were to be furnished missiles to which the atomic warheads might be attached, although the warheads would remain in American custody until the President authorized their transfer. Thus the actual use of the nuclear components of the weapon systems was to be dependent on an American decision.

The implementation of this plan was impossible under existing United States legislation. Consequently, the Atomic Energy Act of 1954 was amended on July 2, 1958.[5] The amended act authorized the transfer of the non-nuclear parts of atomic weapon systems and the communication of sufficient information to enable non-United States forces to handle atomic warheads, attach them to missiles, and monitor them prior to launching. The non-nuclear parts of atomic weapon systems could be transferred only to an individual nation and subject to the condition that "such transfer will not contribute significantly to that nation's atomic weapon design, development, or fabrication capability." Information could

[4]Edward Teller and Albert L. Latter, *Our Nuclear Future: Facts, Dangers, and Opportunities* (1958).
[5]Public Law 479, 85th Cong.; 72 Stat. 276 (1958).

be communicated either to a nation or to a regional defense organization such as NATO.

Another important innovation of the amended act was the authorization to transfer nuclear material for use in atomic weapons and non-nuclear parts of atomic weapons, and to communicate design information required for the fabrication of the nuclear core and assembly of the weapon. However, such cooperation could be undertaken only if the recipient nation had "made substantial progress in the development of atomic weapons."

Congress intended to limit the benefits of these provisions to the United Kingdom through this caveat. Although Congress clearly did not wish to encourage additional nations to achieve production capability, the caveat in a sense put a premium on developing independent production capability and may have served as a goad to the French nuclear weapons program. In addition, it probably added to General de Gaulle's bitterness toward the "Anglo-Saxons" at a time when, restored to power in the context of a military rebellion, the General began to shape a program for his Fifth Republic in which an independent *force de frappe* was to play a crucial role.

On July 3, the day after the amended act came into effect, the United States and the United Kingdom signed an Agreement for Cooperation.[6] This agreement authorized the communication of information concerning non-nuclear parts of atomic weapons systems and information concerning nuclear reactors for military purposes. It also authorized the transfer of a nuclear submarine propulsion unit with its nuclear fuel. The following year the agreement was amended and the United Kingdom was in effect authorized to receive all of the component parts of an atomic weapon except its fabricated core.[7] Agreements for cooperation concerning military applications of nuclear energy as permitted under the 1958 amendments were also signed with Canada, the Federal Republic of Germany, France, Greece, Italy, the Netherlands, and Turkey.[8]

[6]U.S. Department of State, *Treaties and Other International Acts Series* No. 4078 (1958).

[7]U.S. Department of State, *Treaties and Other International Acts Series* No. 4267 (1959).

[8]*Ibid.,* Nos. 4271, 4276, 4268, 4292, 4764, 4277, and 4278. A second agreement was signed with France in 1961: *ibid.,* No. 4876.

While their provisions varied, none provided for an extensive collaboration as did the Anglo-American accord.

During the spring of 1958, NATO planners laid the groundwork for the employment on NATO bases of medium and intermediate range ballistic missiles which would be equipped for nuclear warheads, and in June the first consignment of Redstone missiles was shipped to Europe for stationing in West Germany.[9] The first shipment of Thor missiles for delivery to the United Kingdom forces was received in September 1958. But these actions could hardly be called more than the implementation of the joint United States-United Kingdom communique of October 1957 and the NATO Council decision in December of that year. Moreover, they did not involve dispersing nuclear weapons capability to "nth countries." Whether or not they adequately anticipated the new role of continental Western Europe restored in its economic and political power, though, is another question.

Because of the nature of these decisions NATO continued to be plagued by a crisis concerning its strategic doctrine. Nothing had been done to raise the level of the Alliance's conventional forces and thus to increase its capability to defend itself without resort to nuclear weapons; little had been done to increase the participation of the continental allies in the general policy-making within NATO; and the defense of Europe by nuclear weapons continued to depend on either an American or a British decision to use such weapons—a situation which was to prove entirely unacceptable to France and which had already and would continue to cause considerable concern elsewhere on the continent. Furthermore, the nuclear weapons then available if employed in Europe would cause so much contamination that they would have limited usefulness in tactical situations. The crisis in military planning in NATO therefore created two pressures against the cessation of nuclear weapons tests. First, it tended to provide an added argument for the French program to develop an independent nuclear capability, which, given the legal and other inhibitions against the transfer of nuclear weapons, probably could not be achieved without testing. Secondly, it also provided an argument for the development of "clean" nuclear

[9]See *New York Times,* June 4, 1958, p. 13.

weapons, and possibly a neutron bomb, which presumably would also require continued tests.

In summary, in early 1958, American policy-makers were faced with roughly the same pressures and factors operating for and against the continued testing of nuclear weapons as they had been in 1957.

II

The Development of American Policy

The Correspondence Between Heads of States

In the months immediately preceding the Conference of Experts, American policy concerning the cessation of nuclear weapons tests was expressed principally in a series of exchanges of correspondence between President Eisenhower and the Chairman of the Council of Ministers of the USSR, Nikolai A. Bulganin until March 1958 and Nikita S. Khrushchev thereafter.

Within the United States government this exchange was treated primarily as an exercise in communications. The principal criterion determining what should be said appears to have been the estimated impact of a given position on public opinion. In the process, decisions were made which resulted in quite far-reaching and perhaps unforeseen consequences. American policy, as expressed in this exchange of letters, was not based on any considered and agreed position with respect to the interests of the United States, as was for instance the later decision to continue the 1958 American test series, nor was there any contingency planning concerning what the United States would do if certain of its proposals were adopted.

The exchange began with a letter which Chairman Bulganin sent to President Eisenhower on December 10, 1957.[10] In it, Bulganin dwelt at length on the dangers which he felt would result from dispersing nuclear weapons, and especially those which he foresaw if West Germany were to be armed with nuclear weapons. His comments were clearly aimed at the agenda of the NATO Council meeting. After reviewing the state of disarmament negotiations, he made a variety of proposals, of which the following were

[10]U.S. Department of State *Bulletin,* Vol. XXXVIII, No. 970 (January 27, 1958), pp. 127-30.

the most important for the issue of nuclear testing. First he suggested that the three nuclear powers should agree to stop further tests of nuclear weapons as of January 1, 1958, for a period of from two to three years. Secondly, he proposed that no nuclear weapons should be stationed in Germany, either the Eastern or the Western portion. He stated that if the Federal Republic of Germany and the Democratic Republic of Germany would agree neither to produce nuclear weapons nor to have them stationed on their territory, Czechoslovakia and Poland would also take similar action. Finally, Chairman Bulganin suggested that these matters could all be resolved at a summit conference, and he stated his willingness to have a personal meeting with President Eisenhower.

The President did not reply immediately, and his answer came in sections. Indirectly, he gave a partial answer through his proposals at the NATO Council meeting, which, as we have seen, eventually involved stationing nuclear warheads for missiles in Europe, including Western Germany, although these would remain under American control. In addition, on December 15, he stated the American position on nuclear testing in a letter addressed to Prime Minister Nehru.[11] The essence of his statement is contained in this excerpt:

> . . . I do not believe that we can accept a proposal to stop nuclear experiments as an isolated step, unaccompanied by any assurances that other measures—which would go to the heart of the problem—would follow. We are at a stage when testing is required particularly for the development of important defensive uses of these weapons. To stop these tests at this time, in the absence of knowledge that we can go on and achieve effective limitations on nuclear weapons production and other elements of armed strength, as well as a measure of assurance against surprise attack, is a sacrifice which we could not in prudence accept. To do so could increase rather than diminish the threat of aggression and war. I believe that bolder and more far-reaching measures are required. Specifically, I believe that any government which declares its desire to agree not to use nuclear weapons should, if they are sincere, be prepared to agree to bring an end to their pro-

[11]U.S. Department of State *Bulletin,* Vol. XXXVIII, No. 967 (January 6, 1958), pp. 17-18.

duction. Agreement to devote all future production of fissionable material to peaceful uses is, as I see it, the most important step that can be taken. Together with this we have proposed that we begin to transfer to peaceful uses, on a fair and equitable basis, fissionable material presently tied up in stocks of nuclear weapons.

It is difficult to measure the difference between President Eisenhower's statement and the Western position at the conclusion of the London session of the disarmament Subcommittee in August of the same year. The President implied in his letter that a test cessation might be a first step in a series of measures, but—as in the Western position in London—he clearly insisted on linking a test ban with an agreement for a cut-off on the production of weapons, and perhaps with an accord on transferring fissionable material from weapons stockpiles. The extent to which he contemplated links with other measures of disarmament was not clear.

Finally, on January 12, 1958, President Eisenhower sent a formal reply to Chairman Bulganin.[12] The only new element in this letter was the President's statement of his unwillingness to attend a summit meeting without proper preparatory work. He mentioned in particular the need for a meeting of Foreign Ministers, and repeated the suggestion that technical groups from East and West should meet together to discuss appropriate control mechanisms.

This reply can be properly understood only in the context of earlier events. President Eisenhower had been greatly encouraged by his first summit meeting with the Soviet leaders in Geneva in 1955. At least partly because of this euphoria, he was bitterly disappointed when the agreements in principle reached at Geneva dissolved into thin air. As a result, he became even more skeptical of Soviet motivation in seeking agreement with the West, and was determined that the 1955 experience should not be repeated.

Other letters were exchanged in February and March, but they were essentially restatements of points made in the original exchange. Perhaps the most important new element concerning the general positions of the two powers on arms control and disarmament measures related to another aspect of military activities. In a

[12]U.S. Department of State, Publication No. 7008, Historical Office, *Documents on Disarmament, 1945-1959.* (1960), 2 vols., Vol. II, pp. 932-41.

letter of March 3, Chairman Bulganin stated that the questions of limiting the uses of outer space to peaceful purposes and the liquidation of foreign military bases had to be considered together.[13] This point was also made in a proposal concerning outer space which the Soviet Union submitted on March 15 for consideration by the thirteenth General Assembly the following fall. In submitting this proposal, the Soviet Union stole a march on the United States, for although American spokesmen had said that some international action was necessary with respect to the use of outer space, the United States had not advanced any concrete proposal. Although these matters may seem rather remote from the issue of nuclear testing, they were relevant.

In considering military policy, and in thinking about arms control or disarmament, it is necessary to consider the means of delivering explosives as well as the explosives themselves. The revolution that has taken place in military technology since the outbreak of the Second World War has involved both of these aspects. Not only has the explosive power of weapons been increased vastly, but new carriers have also been invented which have greatly shortened the time that it takes for a weapon to reach its target. The developments with respect to carriers have had almost as frightening implications as those concerning explosives, for they have narrowed reaction times to dangerously short periods. The maximum warning time for a country under attack by intercontinental ballistic missiles would be about fifteen minutes. In such circumstances there would be little time for rational consideration. Decision-makers would have to respond quickly or risk the possibility of losing a substantial share of their forces. Since controlling the uses of outer space implied controlling the development of missiles as carriers of explosives, this issue concerned the other part of the revolution in military technology, and thus was relevant to attempts to deal with nuclear explosives.

The Debate About Linking a Test Ban with Other Measures of Arms Control

In March 1958, then, it was obvious that if there were to be any progress in arms control negotiations, compromises would

[13]U.S. Department of State *Bulletin,* Vol. XXXVIII, No. 982 (April 21, 1958), pp. 648-52.

have to be made. Some agreement would have to be reached concerning the negotiating forum, and the gap between the two substantive positions would have to be narrowed. So far as the American position was concerned, the question of linking a test ban agreement with an agreement on a production cut-off and other measures of arms control was subjected to intense scrutiny for the purpose of discovering whether some compromise might be possible. Although this debate occurred in many places, it was conducted in public principally before Senator Humphrey's Subcommittee on Disarmament.

On February 28, the opening day of the Subcommittee's hearings, Harold Stassen, whose resignation as Special Assistant to the President for Disarmament had only recently been accepted, advocated a test ban as a separate measure.[14] He argued that the control requirements for a test ban agreement were not very great and that such an agreement could therefore be negotiated with relative ease. He felt that a test ban agreement, in that it would do something to break the spiral of the arms race and would therefore hopefully have the effect of increasing confidence, might well be an important first step toward achieving other measures of arms control and disarmament. In subsequent sessions of the Subcommittee some of the problems of maintaining a link between a test ban and other measures of disarmament were brought out.

On March 12, for example, in response to questioning, Dr. Spofford English of the Atomic Energy Commission stated that to police a cut-off on the production of nuclear weapons in the Soviet Union three thousand to thirty-five hundred inspectors would have to be stationed on Soviet territory, and he asserted that under a cut-off agreement there could be no secret information with respect to nuclear energy.[15] In addition, the point was made several times in the hearings that there was no way of ascertaining with complete certainty the exact size and location of the stockpiles of nuclear weapons then in existence, since such weapons could be hidden

[14]U.S. Congress, Senate, Committee on Foreign Relations, Subcommittee on Disarmament, *Hearings: Control and Reduction of Armaments,* 85th Congress, 2d Session (1958), pp. 1335-64.

[15]*Ibid.,* pp. 1420, 1423. Jules Moch presented a much smaller estimate to the United Nations Subcommittee of the Disarmament Commission in 1957. See UN Document DC/SC. 1/PV. 131, pp. 11-15.

with relative ease. Thus, it would be almost impossible to police an agreement concerning the transfer of fissionable materials from weapons stockpiles if the object of such an agreement were the reduction and ultimate elimination of the stockpiles. One would never know what the starting point was.

On the other hand, the ease with which a test ban alone could be policed was brought out on several occasions. In his testimony, Harold Stassen estimated that eleven or twelve stations in the Soviet Union would be sufficient.[16] Later, Professor Harrison Brown, of the California Institute of Technology, estimated that only ten stations would be needed in the USSR, while Professor Jay Orear, of Columbia University, who had just completed a special study for Columbia University's Institute of War and Peace Studies,[17] held that twenty-five would be required.[18]

Whatever number one chose, it seemed clear that the control measures needed to police a test ban would not be very extensive. Thus the impression was given that linking a test ban with a production cut-off and possibly a transfer from stockpiles was irrational, in that it meant joining a measure which did not require very much control with others which required extensive control and concerning which, therefore, agreement was unlikely. Clearly, this was the impression that Senator Humphrey at least had sought to create.

In the hearings the various witnesses connected with the Atomic Energy Commission—the Chairman, Admiral Lewis L. Strauss; Commissioner W. F. Libby; Brigadier General Alfred D. Starbird; and Dr. Spofford G. English—all strongly defended the link. They argued that it was the production of nuclear weapons, not their testing that was dangerous for world peace. In addition, they held that the knowledge which would be derived from further testing would be of greater benefit to the defensive side in a future conflict and thus in their view would be more useful to the United States than to the Soviet Union. For some unexplained reason, they never made the obvious point that if a test ban were achieved without a production cut-off, the Soviet Union could continue to

[16]*Ibid.*, pp. 1351-52.
[17]See Seymour Melman (ed.), *Inspection for Disarmament* (1958), pp. 85-99.
[18]*Hearings: Control and Reduction of Armaments, supra* note 14, p. 1495.

enlarge its stockpile with the possibility that eventually it might equal or surpass that of the United States, thus wiping out this element of American superiority. Interestingly, no one from the Departments of State or Defense testified before the Subcommittee during these hearings. Therefore, the representatives of the Atomic Energy Commission were the only Administration witnesses. One could infer from the absence of the State Department spokesmen that Mr. Dulles was not very strongly interested in the issue at this time.

The Soviet Cessation of Testing

On balance, those who favored eliminating the link probably made the better case in public, but this was only one contributing factor in the evolution of American policy. A more important element—which, however, played on the same public sentiments— was a step taken by the USSR. On March 22, the Soviet Union concluded an extensive test series which it had begun the previous fall. This series had been conducted at an unprecedented rate, with two or more nuclear explosions sometimes being detonated in a single day. Professor Hans A. Bethe, a physicist from Cornell University, who for some time had headed the Atomic Energy Commission's scientific panel which reviewed the effects of Soviet nuclear weapons tests, alleged that the pace was determined so that the series would be completed before the United States began its planned 1958 tests.[19] As a consequence of the Soviet test series, radioactivity levels rose sharply in the spring of 1958. While the Soviet test series was in progress, it was largely kept secret within the USSR. After it was finished, however, on March 31, the Supreme Soviet adopted a decree resolving "to discontinue the testing of all types of atomic and hydrogen weapons in the Soviet Union."[20] The decree also contained an appeal to the other nuclear powers to follow a similar course and the warning that if they did not, the Soviet Union would feel free to resume its own testing program. Chairman Khrushchev restated the appeal on April 4 in a personal letter to President Eisenhower.

[19]*Ibid.*, p. 1545.
[20]U.S. Department of State, *Documents on Disarmament, 1945–1959,* Vol. II, p. 979.

The USSR's action won worldwide public acclaim and put the United States in a difficult position, especially since it was just about to begin an extensive test series. President Eisenhower's dismissal of the Soviet move, in his press conference of April 2, as a "gimmick" that should not be "taken seriously," only served to compound the situation.[21] A day earlier Secretary of State Dulles had admitted that the USSR had at least scored a "certain propaganda victory."[22]

It was probably extremely difficult for Mr. Dulles to make this admission. No Secretary of State enjoys admitting a propaganda defeat, and in this case the unpleasantness was compounded by the fact that Mr. Dulles had seen the problem coming, and had sought to avoid it. Only a few days previously he had argued within the Administration that the United States should itself unilaterally stop testing, presumably because he had been forewarned that the Soviet Union might take this initiative.[23] He argued his case principally in terms of the standing of the United States in world public opinion. His position was buttressed by his foreknowledge that a special panel of the President's Science Advisory Committee, which had been appointed in January 1958 and which was headed by Hans Bethe, would report its more or less unanimous view that a test ban could be policed and that to stop testing at some point in the near future would be in the best interests of the United States.

The Bethe Panel

The appointment of the so-called Bethe Panel was the result of a discussion of the question of nuclear testing at a National Security Council (NSC) meeting in early January. During the discussion Secretary of State Dulles made the point that the United States was suffering propaganda losses because of its nuclear testing programs and expressed his fear that the United Nations General Assembly might soon adopt a resolution condemning further testing, which he felt would prove extremely embarrassing to

[21]*New York Times,* April 3, 1958, p. 1.

[22]U.S. Department of State *Bulletin,* Vol. XXXVIII, No. 982 (April 21, 1958), p. 642.

[23]Charles J. V. Murphy, "Nuclear Inspection: A Near Miss," *Fortune,* Vol. LIX, No. 3 (March 1959), p. 122, at 160. See also Secretary Dulles' own account: U.S. Department of State *Bulletin,* Vol. XXXVIII, No. 982 (April 21, 1958), p. 642.

the United States. The President apparently shared his concerns. At this juncture, James R. Killian, Jr., the recently appointed Special Assistant for Science and Technology, whom the President had invited to attend the NSC meeting, offered to have the President's Science Advisory Committee conduct a study of the issues involved in banning nuclear weapon tests. In the late fall of 1957, at one of its first meetings in its new incarnation, PSAC had already begun a tentative exploration of some of the issues.

A few days after the NSC meeting Mr. Killian was directed to appoint the Panel.[24] In addition to Professor Bethe, the Panel contained one other member of PSAC, Dr. Herbert York, then Director of the University of California Radiation Laboratory at Livermore. The other members of the Panel were military officers or civilian employees of the government. All members of the Panel were actively involved in either the nuclear weapons development or test detection programs. Although seismologists were available to the Panel, no seismologist was a member, nor did the membership of PSAC include a seismologist. Ronald Spiers, a junior officer in Department of State, attended the sessions as an observer, but this was the only connection which the Department of State had. The Panel was asked to explore two questions: (1) what would be the effect of a nuclear test ban on American and Soviet weapons development programs; and (2) to what extent would it be possible to detect evasions of a nuclear test ban.

In Professor Bethe's view, at the outset, the majority of the Panel was highly skeptical of the advantages to be gained from a nuclear test ban. Eventually, however, the members of the Panel became persuaded that continued testing would ultimately result in the Soviet Union's narrowing the United States' lead in the development of more sophisticated nuclear weapons.[25] Professor Bethe probably held this view from the outset. In addition, unlike several

[24]The members of the Bethe Panel were Dr. Hans Bethe, Chairman; Dr. Harold Brown; Major General Richard Coiner, USAF; General Herbert Loper; Dr. Carson Mark; Mr. Doyle Northrup; Dr. Herbert Scoville, Jr.; Dr. Roderick Spence; Brig. General Alfred Starbird; Col. Lester Woodward, USAF; and Dr. Herbert York.

[25]The findings of the Bethe Panel have never been made public. It seems reasonable to assume, however, that they are reflected in Professor Bethe's testimony before the Humphrey Subcommittee on April 17; see

other members of the Panel, he felt that the additional benefits to be gained from further testing were minimal. To put his views in proper perspective, it should be recalled that in 1950, at the time of President Truman's controversial decision to proceed with the development of the hydrogen bomb, Professor Bethe, along with several other scientists, had signed a statement recommending that the United States government pledge never to use hydrogen weapons first, and that he had strongly recommended that the government make every effort to reach an agreement with the USSR concerning the control of nuclear weapons.[26] This had ranged him in that debate opposite Edward Teller, perhaps the most ardent advocate within the scientific community of the development of the hydrogen bomb.

Formulating the Initial American Response

Within the counsels of the Administration, apparently Chairman Strauss and Donald Quarles countered Mr. Dulles' position by arguing that important military advantages would be gained from the forthcoming test series, a view shared by members of PSAC, including Professor Bethe. In the end then it was decided not to try to take preemptive action against a possible Soviet initiative in this matter.

However, in the new setting the United States obviously had to make some response to the Soviet move, and to Chairman Khrushchev's letter of April 4. President Eisenhower's first reply, on April 8, was essentially a restatement of the general American position on arms control and disarmament issues, along with a repetition of the January 12 suggestion that technical experts from East and West should meet to discuss specific control measures.[27] It neither advanced the negotiations nor detracted from the Soviet Union's propaganda advantage.

Hearings, supra note 14, pp. 1526-47. In addition, the findings of the Bethe Panel have been analyzed in Robert Gilpin, *American Scientists and Nuclear Weapons Policy,* pp. 179-82; and in Charles J. V. Murphy, "Nuclear Inspection: A Near Miss," *supra* note 23.

[26]See "Let Us Pledge Not to Use the H-Bomb First," *Bulletin of the Atomic Scientists,* Vol. VI, No. 3 (March 1950), p. 75; and Hans A. Bethe, "The Hydrogen Bomb," *Bulletin of the Atomic Scientists,* Vol. VI, No. 4 (April 1950), pp. 99-104, 125.

[27]*Documents on Disarmament, 1945–1959,* Vol. II, pp. 982-85.

Apparently, Secretary Dulles drafted the letter himself. When the question was raised what would happen if the Soviet Union should accept the proposal for technical discussions, he averred that this was extremely unlikely, but that it was nevertheless a limited risk which he was willing to accept. He apparently felt that if the Soviet Union unexpectedly accepted the proposal, "the United States would have a fresh opportunity to pin the Kremlin down to either accepting an effective inspection system or rejecting it. The American propaganda position would benefit either way."[28]

On April 22, Chairman Khrushchev sent another letter to President Eisenhower.[29] The letter covered a range of points, but centered particularly on the issues of a test cessation and measures to guard against a surprise attack. With regard to the former, Khrushchev argued that no international controls would be necessary to detect violations of a test ban, but that in any case the Soviet Union had already agreed in principle to the establishment of such controls. In response to the suggestion for a meeting of technical experts, he asserted that it would be impossible for the experts to contribute to the solution of the problem of disarmament unless agreement had been reached between governments. To study the problem of control would simply delay matters. He also restated the Soviet positions concerning aerial inspection zones and controlling the uses of outer space.

Meanwhile, Professor Bethe had reported the conclusions of his Panel to the President, and the President's Science Advisory Committee had retired to Ramey Air Force Base in Puerto Rico to reconsider the American position concerning a test cessation in the light of the unilateral suspension by the USSR. They returned with the recommendation that the planned test series should be completed, but that after that, the United States could risk a test suspension.

President Eisenhower Suggests a Conference of Experts

President Eisenhower's reply, dated April 28, to Chairman Khrushchev's most recent missive, appears to have reflected this advice and also the mounting pressure for a test suspension.[30]

[28]Earl H. Voss, *Nuclear Ambush*, p. 177.
[29]*Documents on Disarmament, 1945–1959*, Vol. II, pp. 996-1004.
[30]*Documents on Disarmament, 1945–1959*, Vol. II, pp. 1006-7.

Though quite brief, it clearly implied that United States policy was in transition. The President repeated the suggestion for technical studies, but this time in the specific context of an agreement to suspend testing. This significant sentence came immediately after the suggestion for technical studies: "Studies of this kind are the necessary preliminaries to putting political decisions actually into effect." Although this was followed by the caveat that technical studies would of course be without prejudice to the positions of the two sides, it should have been clear that if the USSR agreed to have a meeting of experts, and the experts reached an agreed conclusion on a control system, reservations or no, diplomatic negotiations on a test ban agreement would be inevitable, and that these would be pursued separately from those on broader measures of arms control and disarmament.

This letter was drafted in the Department of State and signed by the President and dispatched without consulting the Department of Defense or the Atomic Energy Commission. Since the suggestion for technical talks had been a part of the American negotiating position since 1957, it was assumed—as it had been in the case of the April 8 letter—that there was no need for additional clearance. The immediate problem facing those who drafted the letter was to minimize the propaganda advantages which the Soviet Union had won, and at the same time, to permit the United States to continue its 1958 test series. The decision to continue this series of weapons tests was the only agreed decision within the Administration on the various issues involved. There were of course previous negotiating positions, but no formal consideration was given to the question of whether or not these were applicable to the current situation. The lack of consultation in the drafting of the President's reply prevented the development of an agreed position within the Administration about what the United States should and would do if the Soviet Union accepted his suggestion. The implications of the proposal were not thought through.

Much to the surprise of most American policy-makers, Chairman Khrushchev in his next letter to the President on May 9, after belittling the need for technical discussions, nevertheless agreed to the proposal.[31] Thus the Soviet Union now chose to accept a

[31]*Ibid.*, pp. 1036-41.

proposal which it had rejected or ignored ever since the London disarmament discussions and which reflected the Western emphasis on a control system as a prerequisite for any test ban agreement.

American policy-makers could only speculate on the motivation for this step by the Soviet Union. As they viewed it, several factors conceivably could have had some infleunce. Having just completed the test series which had advanced the Soviet weapons art, Soviet leaders may have decided that a test ban agreement might be worth exploring because it would prevent further American testing and development of American weapons and because it might provide relief for the Soviet economy by slowing down the arms race and perhaps leading to further disarmament measures which in turn might reduce the chance of a nuclear war. The prospect of continuing American superiority in nuclear weapons perhaps was less objectionable in the light of Soviet advances in other weapons areas, especially missiles. Moreover, the Soviet military apparently displayed little interest in developing tactical nuclear weapons for which continued testing would be required. Again, a generally accepted test ban agreement might help to resolve the "nth country" problem: both Germany and China might be less likely to obtain a nuclear arsenal. In addition, a recognized US-USSR-UK monopoly in nuclear weapons might point toward broader settlements among the three powers and a directorate-type sharing of power which has always seemed to appeal to the Soviet Union. The international pressures for a test ban mentioned earlier may have had some limited impact on the Soviet government, and the acceptance of President Eisenhower's proposal would obviously strengthen the image of the Soviet Union as being both reasonable and anxious to avoid further fallout pollution. To the extent that President Eisenhower's proposal may have indicated Western willingness to take the test ban out of the disarmament package as a concession to the Soviet view, and considering the character of the proposed forum, it may have appeared worthwhile to test the West's price in terms of a control system, or perhaps to try for an unpoliced ban. It was also possible to believe, however, that the Soviet leaders merely hoped to maneuver the West into a temporary test suspension, which could be used to cut the Western lead in the development of nuclear weapons.

A further exchange of letters between the two heads of states ensued, and ultimately it was agreed that the Conference of Experts should open on July 1 in Geneva and that the Conference should consist of two panels of experts, one composed of specialists from the United States, the United Kingdom, France, and Canada, and the other, of specialists from the Soviet Union, Czechoslovakia, Poland, and Rumania. There was no consensus as to whether or not agreement at the Conference would automatically commit governments to a test cessation; the USSR insisted that it would, but the United States insisted that it would not.

Through the exchange of correspondence a new negotiating forum was created. Significantly, East and West received equal representation: the concept of parity for which the Soviet Union had striven unsuccessfully in the United Nations and which the Western powers had rejected in the twelfth Assembly only a few months before, was now established. The Soviet Union apparently viewed parity in representation as essential not only as an assurance against being "outvoted" but also as a recognition of what it claimed to be the new power relationship requiring equality in negotiations between East and West.

Moreover, unlike the previous bodies for disarmament negotiations, the new forum was outside of the framework of the United Nations, a development which caused Secretary General Hammarskjöld great concern. As recently as April 2, the Secretary General had argued that controlled disarmament would only be possible through the instrumentality of the United Nations,[32] and as soon as the Conference of Experts appeared likely, he offered the United Nations' facilities and services. His offer was accepted and the Conference of Experts as well as the subsequent diplomatic negotiations were held at the European headquarters of the UN and were serviced by the UN Secretariat personnel. A personal representative of the Secretary General attended all of the formal meetings. Although the Secretary General's representative at times played an important role as an intermediary, there is no evidence that either he or the Secretary General influenced the basic course of the negotiations.

The establishment of the new negotiating forum outside the United Nations was a logical consequence of the Soviet Union's

[32]New York Times, April 3, 1958, p. 4.

refusal to negotiate in the UN Disarmament Commission as enlarged by the twelfth Assembly, and perhaps also of the endorsement by the same Assembly of the general Western position on disarmament. It is also true, however, that moving outside the United Nations' framework had certain attractions for the West. Even in 1958 some in the West were beginning to be apprehensive about the implications of the UN's expanded membership. Also, serious negotiations usually require some privacy, which presumably it would be more difficult to ensure in the UN. Finally, the problem of nuclear testing primarily concerned the three nuclear powers. Although it may have been argued that the prestige of the United Nations was adversely affected, it is difficult to identify any tangible repercussions of the fact that the new forum was not created by the UN or specifically approved by it. The General Assembly continued to concern itself with the disarmament problem in its subsequent sessions, and to attempt to affect the course of the negotiations.

One unique characteristic of the new negotiating forum deserves mention. International meetings of scientists arranged by scientific societies and institutions are, of course, a common occurrence. Another pattern is suggested by the 1955 and 1958 international conferences on the peaceful uses of nuclear energy, organized by the United Nations in Geneva, at which scientists as members of governmental delegations exchanged and disseminated technical information. Again, scientists have frequently served as advisers to governmental delegations in the United Nations and other bodies and at times have acted themselves as governmental delegates to technical international bodies and conferences. The 1958 Conference of Experts, however, represented the first instance in which a group of scientists, under the rubric of a technical investigation, was given an independent, specific negotiating task which proved, as will be seen, of paramount importance as a link in a chain of vital diplomatic negotiations.

Perhaps the implications of the new forum were not fully apparent to all persons concerned in the spring of 1958. But as a result of the modifications in the governmental positions mentioned earlier, the stage was set for the first phase of test ban negotiations.

III

Preparations for the Conference

The Western Panel of Experts

After the preliminary arrangements were settled, or at least underway, it was necessary for the four Western governments to agree
on the composition of the Western delegations. The Western panel
of experts was announced on June 20. It included three Americans:
Dr. James B. Fisk, then Vice-President of Bell Telephone Laboratories and a member of the President's Science Advisory Committee; Dr. Robert F. Bacher, a professor of physics at the California
Institute of Technology and a member of the President's Science
Advisory Committee; and Dr. Ernest O. Lawrence, the Director of
the University of California Radiation Laboratory. The other members of the panel were: Sir John Cockroft, a Fellow of the Royal
Society; Sir William Penney, also a Fellow of the Royal Society;
Professor Yves Rocard, the Director of the Laboratory of Physics,
Ecole normale supérieure de Paris; and Dr. Ormond Solandt, former
chairman of the Defense Research Board of Canada.

Dr. Fisk was appointed Chairman of the delegation. He was
a prominent physicist, who, like many other American senior
scientists, had had extensive administrative responsibilities for some
time. Except for two brief teaching assignments, and a period in
1947 and 1948 when he served as Director of Research for the
Atomic Energy Commission, he had spent most of his active career
with the Bell Telephone Laboratories, where he had been a Vice-
President since 1954. He had been a member of the Science Advisory Committee since its formation.

A number of advisers were also assigned to the Western delegation. Among the Americans in this group were: university scientists
including Professor Hans Bethe, who had headed the special PSAC
panel, a number of scientists from government agencies and from
the two laboratories which were involved in weapons development (the University of California Radiation Laboratory in Livermore and the Los Alamos Scientific Laboratory), and several of
the scientists responsible for the operation of the United States
nuclear test detection system, which had been in existence since
1947.[33] The Atomic Energy Commission was kept informed of
developments through Captain John H. Morse, Jr., who was a

Special Assistant to AEC's Chairman, Admiral Lewis L. Strauss. In addition, there were three officers from the Department of State: Donald Morris, a 28-year-old foreign affairs officer, who had joined the Department in June 1957; Ronald I. Spiers, the Officer in Charge of Disarmament Affairs, a Foreign Service Reserve Officer Class 4, who was 33, and who had joined the Department in 1955, after having spent five years with the Atomic Energy Commission; and Thomas B. Larson, 43, Chief of the Division of Research for the USSR and Eastern Europe, who as a Foreign Service Officer Class 3, held the highest rank. The fact that a person of as junior a rank as Class 4 was Officer in Charge of Disarmament Affairs reflects the scant attention given to such matters in the Department of State at that time.

In the selection of American scientists for service on the delegation an attempt was made to maintain some balance between the differing views in the scientific community on the wisdom of a test ban agreement. However, this was largely a balance within the center, for the scientists who took extreme positions on either side were not represented. AEC Chairman Lewis Strauss had recommended that Edward Teller be made a member of the Western delegation, but there was so much resistance to Dr. Teller that Strauss withdrew the suggestion, and instead recommended Dr. Lawrence.[34] James Killian recommended the other two American members of the Western delegation to President Eisenhower. Although Dr. Bacher was somewhat favorably disposed toward a nuclear test ban, he was certainly not as ardent an advocate as

[33]In addition to Professor Bethe, the other scientists were Harold Brown, Associate Director, Livermore Laboratory; Perry Byerly, Director, Seismographic Stations, University of California; Norman Haskel, Geophysics Research Directorate, Air Force, Cambridge Research Center; Spurgeon M. Keeny, Jr., Office of the Special Assistant to the President for Science and Technology; J. Carson Mark, Director, Theoretical Division, Los Alamos Scientific Laboratory; Doyle Northrup, Technical Director, Office of Atomic Energy, Department of Defense; George B. Olmstead, Assistant Technical Director, Office of Atomic Energy, Department of Defense; Carl F. Romney, Assistant Technical Director, Office of Atomic Energy, Department of Defense; Herbert Scoville, Jr., Consultant, President's Science Advisory Committee; and Anthony L. Turkevich, Enrico Fermi Institute for Nuclear Studies, University of Chicago.

[34]Earl H. Voss, *Nuclear Ambush,* p. 182.

Hans Bethe, much less Linus Pauling. Dr. Fisk, the Chairman, was regarded as being "neutral" on the issue.

This neatly contrived balance may have been upset somewhat by the fact that Dr. Lawrence became seriously ill during the course of the Conference. On the other hand, the other Livermore scientists on the delegation maintained frequent cable and telephonic contact with Edward Teller in California.

The effort to obtain a balanced representation may be taken in the first place as an indication of an awareness on the part of the American policy-makers that for a variety of factors, which will be discussed later, the technical investigation of the Conference would in fact require exercise of judgment which would or could be affected by the personal views of the scientists. In a delegation acting under governmental instructions the effect of personal views can be minimized if not eliminated. Not so in this "technical" delegation which was to function with minimal instructions, and which nevertheless was to grapple with problems that could not be resolved by resorting exclusively to scientific facts and knowledge. That the Administration felt it necessary to seek balanced membership testified also to the deep division within the American scientific community regarding the wisdom of attempting to seek a test ban. Thirdly, the Administration may well have had in mind the need of ensuring widest possible support in the Congress and by the public generally for whatever conclusions would be reached by the Conference.

Unlike the American members, the two British scientists, members of the Western delegation, as well as the British scientific advisors, all held official government positions. They were connected with the Atomic Energy Authority, the United Kingdom counterpart of the US Atomic Energy Commission, and their selection does not appear to have been affected by their personal views on the desirability of a test ban.

The Eastern Panel of Experts

The Eastern panel of experts should be listed for purposes of comparison. It included Yevgeni K. Fedorov, a corresponding member of the Academy of Sciences of the USSR; N. N. Semenov, an academician; I. Ye. Tamm, an academician; M. A. Sadovsky, a corresponding member of the Academy of Sciences of the USSR;

O. I. Leypunsky, a professor and doctor of physical-mathematical sciences; I. P. Pasechnik, a scientific collaborator of the Academy of Sciences of the USSR; K. Ye. Gubkin, a scientific collaborator of the Academy of Sciences of the USSR; and Semen K. Tsarapkin, chief of the section of international organizations, and member of the Collegium of the Soviet Ministry of Foreign Affairs. In addition, scientists from Czechoslovakia, Poland, and Rumania were also included.

Dr. Fedorov, who served as Chairman and thus was Dr. Fisk's counterpart, was a geophysicist and had been a member of the Communist party since 1938. Since 1955 he had been Director of the Institute for Applied Geophysics of the Academy of Sciences of the USSR. He had been deeply involved in the Soviet sputnik program and had been a prominent Soviet representative in the International Geophysical Year. In 1958 he published a book entitled *Rockets and Artificial Earth Satellites in Investigation of the Upper Atmosphere* and the following year another entitled *Weather Control*. Interestingly, his earlier publications included *The Red Army: An Army of the People* (1944) and a novel, *Concerning the Russian Revolution, 1917–1921* (1939).

His scientific colleagues on the panel were an impressive group. Dr. Semenov was the USSR's first Nobel prize winner. Tamm, the only Soviet delegate who was not a member of the Communist party, was a distinguished physicist; however, his actual role in the Conference was relatively slight. Dr. Sadovsky was a seismologist who apparently had been concerned for some time with the Soviet Union's nuclear test detection system.

The inclusion of Mr. Tsarapkin, one of the USSR's leading diplomats, marked the most important difference from the composition of the American delegation, which had no diplomats among its members and included even among its advisors only junior diplomats. Fifty-two years of age, Tsarapkin had been a member of Soviet delegations to the United Nations since 1947, eventually becoming Secretary General of the delegation. During the Second World War, he had been Minister Counselor of the Soviet Embassy in Washington and he had represented the USSR at the Dumbarton Oaks and San Francisco Conferences. After the Conference of Experts he became the USSR's chief delegate in the test ban negotiations. He did not speak during the formal sessions of the

Conference of Experts, but it was obvious to the participants that he played a crucial role in determining the Eastern position. High ranking Polish and Czechoslovakian diplomats were also included in the Eastern panel.

The Technical Preparation of the American Delegation

Since the time between its appointment and the opening of the Conference of Experts was little more than five weeks, the American delegation had to rely for technical preparation principally on their personal knowledge and experience, the work and conclusions of the Bethe Panel, and previous studies conducted by such groups as the task forces which Harold Stassen had assembled during his tenure of office. It is not clear, however, to what extent this earlier work was actually available and how much it was taken into account. Because the problem of detecting nuclear weapons tests involved a number of disciplines, several Western delegates had to spend part of their time prior to the conference merely in attempting to learn enough about disciplines other than their own so that they could understand their colleagues.

Although the report of the Bethe Panel has never been made public, it is possible to make certain inferences concerning its nature. In general, it can be said the Panel concluded that large nuclear explosions on the surface of the earth and in the atmosphere and substratosphere could be detected fairly easily by the United States' own detection system, but that an international network of control stations and the use of airborne sampling techniques for the collection of radioactive debris would be necessary for the conclusive identification of such explosions and for the detection of low-yield tests.

There were two possible environments for testing nuclear weapons in which the United States had little or no experience— deep underground and at extremely high altitudes (above 30 to 50 kilometers, or above approximately 19 to 31 miles). The United States had detonated only one nuclear explosion deep underground, the Rainier 1.7 kiloton shot, fired in Nevada on September 10, 1957. This shot had been designed as an experiment to explore whether certain kinds of weapons could be tested without creating radioactive fallout. It had been set up on a short time schedule, and was not highly instrumented. Thus, knowledge about the explosion and its effects was limited. Although the purpose of the shot was not to measure detectability, because of the general interest in detectability the test had been announced in advance, and a number of seismological stations—seismic signals are the only known means for the detection of deep underground explosions when no radioactive debris escapes the earth's surface—had voluntarily, and without financial support from the government, attempted to detect it. The shot was detected by a number of seismological stations within a radius of approximately 650 miles and by two stations beyond that distance, the most distant of which was at College Station, Fairbanks, Alaska, approximately 2,350 miles from the test site. However, it was somewhat debatable whether the signal which was received at that station would actually have been noticed there and distinguished from those created by minor earthquakes, had not the test been announced in advance.[35]

The direction of the first motion of the signal produced by a disturbance was probably the most important piece of diagnostic information—at least it was the one that most American seismologists felt should be used—in distinguishing between nuclear explosions and minor earthquakes. In the case of an explosion the first motions in all directions from the event are compressions, which will be registered as outward movements, while in the case of an earthquake there are usually some rarefactions, which will be registered as inward movements.

It is worth viewing the recording of the Rainier shot at College Station (Fig. 1), to see how difficult is the problem of distinguishing explosions from earthquakes.

In any case, regardless of one's willingness to agree that explosions could be detected at great distances, it was clear that the Rainier shot had been detected at near stations and the tendency, at least in nonclassified studies, was to generalize and extrapolate from this single experiment.[36] Presumably, the Bethe Panel also followed this tendency.

On the basis of the Rainier experiment, the general under-

[35]See the testimony of Admiral Lewis Strauss: *Hearings: Control and Reduction of Armaments, supra* note 14, pp. 1584-87.

[36]See Seymour Melman (ed.), *Inspection for Disarmament*, pp. 88-93. See also Jay Orear's testimony before the Humphrey Subcommittee: *Hearings: Control and Reduction of Armaments, supra* note 14, pp. 1496-1500.

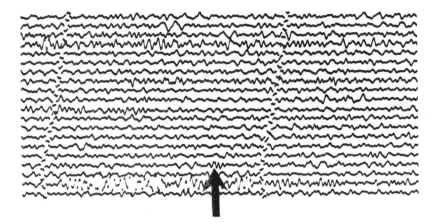

Fig. 1. Rainier seismic signal recorded at Fairbanks, Alaska.
A Coast and Geodetic Survey photograph.

standing was that even relatively small underground nuclear explosions could be detected, the exact magnitude depending upon the distance between control stations. The willingness of scientists to generalize on the basis of this one experiment varied greatly, depending on the individual's temperament, his basic predispositions, his office, and several other factors. Presumably, one factor was the way in which and persistence with which questions were asked. While a scientist in a laboratory might say that it was impossible to draw any general conclusion at this stage, the same individual might make some response when subjected to repeated questioning by government officials.

The range of answers that was possible was brought out clearly in June 1958 when the Senate Subcommittee on Disarmament published the replies of thirty-five seismologists, geophysicists, and geologists to a questionnaire on the detection of and inspection for underground nuclear explosions.[37] The report contained a mass of contradictory information. Some of the scientists replied unambiguously that underground explosions could be detected, others thought that *some* such explosions could, while still others held that it was impossible to make any general statement on the basis of

[37]U.S. Congress, Senate, Committee on Foreign Relations, Subcommittee on Disarmament, *Control and Reduction of Armaments: Detection of and Inspection for Underground Explosions: Replies from Seismologists to Subcommittee Questionnaire: Staff Study No. 10* (Comm. Print 1958).

existing knowledge. There was no agreement concerning the size of signals produced by explosions of various yields.

There was general agreement that on-site inspections would be necessary in some cases to determine whether an underground activity shown on a seismograph was an earthquake or a nuclear explosion, and in all cases to establish positive evidence that a nuclear explosion had taken place, since the only conclusive identification would be the discovery of radioactive debris. However, relatively little was known about the procedures which would be required in the case of an on-site inspection. Again, the Rainier shot was the only available experimental evidence. In that instance, even with foreknowledge of the location of the detonation, it had taken investigators more than two months to discover any radioactive materials evidencing the explosion.[38] Admittedly, this had been the first attempt of this nature, and the investigators had proceeded with great caution, but their experience was sufficient to indicate that the task would be difficult.

Prior to 1958, the United States had not detonated any nuclear weapons at high altitudes. (The Soviet Union may have.) Perhaps as a consequence, the Bethe Panel did not deal with testing in this environment.

There was still another area in which American technical preparation was relatively weak. Little thought had been given to ways in which nuclear explosions might be camouflaged and hidden.[39] There was not much experimental evidence, even with regard to fairly unsophisticated techniques such as shielding. Thus the Bethe Panel could not have done much more on this subject than to make certain hastily contrived assumptions and theoretical calculations.

The Problem of the Threshold

It was obvious to those who had studied the problem of detecting nuclear explosions that in the prevailing state of knowledge no feasible system would be capable of detecting and identifying all explosions in all environments. There would always be, de-

[38]See *Hearings: Control and Reduction of Armaments, supra* note 14, pp. 1366-68.

[39]See *ibid.*, p. 1486. Jay Orear made a few estimates, but they were extremely unsophisticated. See *ibid.*, pp. 1501-2; and Seymour Melman (ed.) *Inspection for Disarmament*, p. 96.

pending on the number of control stations and their equipment
and the rights of inspection, various thresholds beyond which under
certain circumstances evasion might be possible. Apparently, the
Bethe Panel made this point. However, neither that group nor the
Administration generally reached a conclusion concerning what
threshold would be compatible with American security interests;
that is, concerning what was the maximum yield explosion which
could be allowed to remain outside the absolute reach of the control system. Under the circumstances this was essentially a matter
of political judgment which called for the highest level decision,
taking into account all the relevant military as well as political
considerations.

Uncertainty about the threshold in large part accounted for
the varying estimates of the number of control posts which would
be needed in the USSR. Public estimates ranged from Professor
Harrison Brown's statement before the Humphrey Subcommittee
that ten would be sufficient, through Mr. Dulles' press conference
remark that more than twenty-four would be required,[40] to the
high estimate given by Professor Frank Press, a leading seismologist
at the California Institute of Technology, who stated that even
with one hundred stations in the USSR, some nuclear explosions of
2 kilotons or more might escape detection.[41]

In view of the then current interest in developing low yield
tactical nuclear weapons—especially the neutron bomb, the detonation of which would be difficult to detect—and because of the
scientific possibility of extrapolating data gained from small explosions, there was general agreement that the threshold would
have to be fairly low. Despite the urging of various scientists,
however, the Administration did not attempt to reach a decision
on a specific figure; instead this issue was dropped into the lap
of the American delegation in Geneva.

*Policy-Makers' Awareness of the State of Knowledge Concerning
the Detection of Nuclear Explosions*

It is important to ask how well United States policy-makers,
whose decisions were responsible for the convening of the Con-

[40]U.S. Department of State *Bulletin,* Vol. XXXVIII, No. 983 (April 28,
1958), p. 684.
[41]*New York Times,* May 1, 1958, p. 5.

ference of Experts, understood the state of knowledge with respect to the detection of nuclear explosions. It seems clear that they understood these matters in broad outline. Professor Bethe presented his conclusions to the National Security Council in early April,[42] and later that month testified before the Subcommittee on Disarmament. Of the forty-five minutes which the National Security Council spent discussing the issue, about forty were devoted to a discussion of the effects of a nuclear test ban on the relative military strength of the United States and the Soviet Union, and about five to a discussion of the problems of detection, although the fifteen-page report was equally divided between the two questions. Professor Bethe spent two hours and five minutes before the Subcommittee on Disarmament. Most of that time was spent on the issue of detection. In addition, the Subcommittee received testimony from several other scientists on this issue on other occasions.

Secretary of State Dulles' remarks in his news conferences indicate that in his case at least the scientists had made the point that no control system would give an absolute guarantee against evasion.[43] Indeed, it is widely reputed that members of the President's Science Advisory Committee were responsible for the acceptance by the Administration of the proposition that a less than absolute guarantee would provide adequate deterrence against evasion,[44] although this idea certainly must have fitted Mr. Dulles' predispositions, as the broad concept of deterrence played an extremely important role in his own thinking. The political leaders must also have understood that very little was known about testing nuclear weapons deep underground and at high altitudes. In view of subsequent events, however, it is less clear that they understood the scientific implications of this lack of knowledge; that it was difficult if not impossible to predict what future discoveries would yield. Perhaps no one who did not have an extensive background in science could understand this, and, indeed, even some scientists

[42]Charles J. V. Murphy, "Nuclear Inspection: A Near Miss," *supra* note 23, p. 124.

[43]See especially his remarks at his news conference of April 8, 1958, U.S. Department of State *Bulletin,* Vol. XXXVIII, No. 983 (April 28, 1958), pp. 682-83.

[44]See William R. Frye, "The Quest for Disarmament Since World War II," in Louis Henkin (ed.), *Arms Control: Issues for the Public* (1961) pp. 18-48, at 42.

occasionally tend to state their tentative conclusions as final answers. For the nonscientist, one confusing issue is that even the most tentative conclusions can be stated in what appear to be quantitatively precise terms. Since the space age was only a few months old, the whole concept of testing nuclear weapons at high altitudes may well have seemed more like science fiction than reality. Nor is it clear that American policy-makers were fully aware of the inability on the part of the scientists to say with any degree of accuracy what would happen if clever scientific minds were applied to the task of devising means of conducting clandestine tests of nuclear weapons. Whether the scientists did their best to emphasize these uncertainties and whether they were influenced in their presentation of the sketchy scientific facts by their own ideas regarding the wisdom of a test ban is also less than clear.

The Instructions Given to the American Delegation

The instructions which were given to the American members and advisors of the Western delegation to the Conference of Experts appear to have been minimal. In a press conference on June 10, Secretary of State Dulles described his instructions to the American experts in this manner:

> Our guidance to the United States experts, at least—I talked to them a few days ago and told them to look upon their job as a purely scientific technical job. They are to come to their own conclusions as to what is necessary to detect an explosion. Perhaps, in the light of the Soviet proposal, they may have to report on the evaluation of a lesser than complete detection system—bearing on the likelihood that there would be an evasion attempted. For example, it may be that they would say this system isn't 100 percent perfect but it is good enough that we would think that there would be a 75 percent chance that any evasion would be caught. They may have to make calculations of that sort. But we have given them complete authority to work on this matter as a purely scientific technical matter, to use their best judgment and report to us accordingly. I do not anticipate that there will be any need for political guidance.[45]

45U.S. Department of State *Bulletin,* Vol. XXXVIII, No. 992 (June 30, 1958), p. 1085.

Mr. Dulles was more painstaking in his private conversations than these remarks indicate. Terms of reference were drafted prior to the American experts' departure and a position paper was prepared by the Department of State and cleared with other interested departments. Nevertheless, in broad outline, Mr. Dulles' press conference remarks were a fairly accurate summary of the instructions. The American experts were given a great deal of freedom. They were merely told to seek some common understanding concerning the various techniques of detecting nuclear weapons tests, to analyze the capabilities and limitations of each technique, and to outline possible systems for policing a test cessation agreement. They were not told what role and status any report resulting from the Conference of Experts would have. As an entity the Administration obviously had no clear conception or expectations in this matter.

The general attitude reflected in these instructions or lack thereof partially explains why the advisers from the Department of State who were attached to the Western delegation had such relatively junior rank, in contrast to the Soviet delegation which included a senior diplomat as a full member. The assumption apparently was that the Conference of Experts would be purely a technical conference, and the Department of State adhered to this assumption throughout the Conference, for although the American delegation reported daily, it was never given fixed instructions nor told what position to take. A large number of the scientists in the American delegation also regarded their task as a purely technical one. Public opinion, however, certainly did not treat the Conference in this fashion. On the contrary, it was widely heralded in the public debate as an event of great political significance, as the prelude to a test ban agreement. That the public concept of the political nature and significance of the Conference was not far from reality was to be brought out by subsequent events.

One of the few political instructions which the American experts were given was that any control system must ultimately include mainland China.[46] The reason for this was that it was thought

46In the same press conference, Mr. Dulles made the following statement: "I would suppose that we would want to have—that the experts would feel we needed to have—inspection posts with some mobility not only in the Soviet Union but also on the mainland of China and other areas of that sort." *Ibid.*, p. 1085.

that control posts on mainland China would be necessary for the detection of certain explosions inside some border areas of the USSR. Moreover, without control posts in China, in view of the Sino-Soviet alliance, the Soviet Union might conduct clandestine explosions there. It was known that the Soviet Union had conducted certain underground tests in China, though these were assumed to be chemical explosions.[47] Because of the United States' position with respect to the recognition of the People's Republic of China, however, the experts were not permitted to refer to China, but instead had to insist on drafting a scheme for a "worldwide" system. As Mr. Dulles put it in a press conference: ". . . after the experts decide where it is necessary to have these posts, then there will have to be a political problem dealt with."[48] Apparently as of June 1958, he was not prepared to tackle this problem in the abstract. Considering the known views concerning Communist China of the Assistant Secretary of State for Far Eastern Affairs, Walter S. Robertson, and other influential political leaders, the problem would indeed be formidable.

Beyond this, the experts were, as Mr. Dulles said, "to come to their own conclusions." Thus the experts were asked to "decide where it is necessary to have these posts," to determine in general terms the number and location of the control posts without, however, being told what risks the United States was prepared to accept in view of the fact that a foolproof control system was not technically feasible. As the Conference unfolded—it will be seen shortly —other judgments with important political implications had to be made and Mr. Dulles' statement of instructions proved increasingly inadequate.

The United Kingdom Component

In addition to the Americans, the British were the only members of the Western panel to play an important role in the Conference of Experts. Like the Americans, the British scientists were given minimal political instructions. They were, however, urged to do all that they could to facilitate an agreement. They did not bring

[47]See *Hearings: Control and Reduction of Armaments, supra* note 14, p. 1546.

[48]U.S. Department of State *Bulletin,* Vol. XXXVIII, No. 992 (June 30, 1958), p. 1085.

a substantial body of independently obtained scientific information to Geneva. What information they had, they had gained from staff studies of the official Atomic Energy Authority, rather than from studies by panels of nongovernment scientists, such as had been used in the United States. The strength of the United Kingdom participation was mainly derived from the scientific competence and stature of the British scientists.

IV
The Conference

The External Environment

The Conference of Experts ran its course, on the whole, uninfluenced by external events. It was not that the world beyond the shores of Lake Geneva was static. On the contrary, East-West tension rose sharply during the period of the Conference. The principal cause was the crisis in the Middle East, which led eventually to military intervention by the United States and the United Kingdom. In the spiraling tension, the projected summit conference was at least postponed. The only encouraging development during the Conference of Experts was that on July 2, Chairman Khrushchev, in another letter to President Eisenhower, in a sense responding to the President's earlier general proposal, suggested that there should be a meeting at the expert level to consider practical aspects of the problem of developing guarantees against surprise attacks, and the United States agreed to this suggestion on July 31.[49] It later transpired, however, that the two governments were hopelessly at odds as to the nature of this meeting.

One other external event should also be mentioned. On July 2, the day after the Conference of Experts opened, Premier Charles de Gaulle stated in a letter to Chairman Khrushchev that France would not agree to a test ban unless it were accompanied by other measures of disarmament.[50] This communication made it clear that the French government, obviously determined to preserve its freedom to develop its own weapons program, was opposed to any loosening of the Western disarmament package.

[49]*Documents on Disarmament, 1945–1959,* Vol. II, pp. 1084-90.
[50]*New York Times,* July 3, 1958, p. 2.

The Agenda

As had become the fashion in East-West meetings, the Conference of Experts opened with an argument about the agenda. The argument stemmed from the Soviet desire to obtain a prior commitment that the ultimate objective of the Conference was a test ban,[51] and the contrary Western desire to limit the Conference to a technical analysis of the methods of monitoring a test ban.[52] The USSR had known what the Western position would be even before the opening of the Conference, among other reasons, because the United States Embassy in Moscow had delivered to the Soviet Foreign Ministry a list of the technical factors and special questions which the United States felt should be covered in the talks. Obviously, though, the submission of the list did not settle the issue, and at the very outset of the Conference the experts were faced with an essentially political issue. In this debate, Dr. Fedorov argued that national detection systems would actually be adequate to monitor a test ban, while Dr. Fisk, on the other hand, maintained that an international system would be required. Some East-West meetings, it will be recalled, have deadlocked on the agenda issue with political implications and have never reached the substantive problems. Unlike these confrontations, however, this controversy about the agenda was resolved fairly easily, and the solution was largely based on the Western position. After a brief recess, an agenda was adopted, and technical discussions began at the third meeting on July 4, 1958.

The Analysis of the Techniques of Detection

After a general exchange of views concerning the various methods of detecting nuclear explosions, the Experts examined in detail each of the four basic methods—recording acoustic and hydroacoustic waves, recording radio signals, collecting radioactive debris, and recording seismic signals. During this phase, the Conference was a curious cross between a diplomatic negotiation and an international scientific congress, with the latter aspect generally

---

[51]See Ye. K. Fedorov's opening statement: Conference of Experts Document EXP/NUC/PV. 1, p. 27. Hereafter all documents of the Conference of Experts and the Geneva Conference will be cited by their symbol only.

[52]See J. B. Fisk's opening statement, *ibid.*, p. 12.

predominating.[53] The objective was to write brief reports outlining the capabilities and limitations of each of the methods. This was mainly a matter of interpreting agreed theories and objective data. Nevertheless, the conclusions would have significance for national positions and policies, and this fact was always apparent.

The Western scientists tended to present more quantitative data, and their interpretations were, in general, more conservative than those of their Eastern counterparts. In a sense, this situation was a logical consequence of the respective political positions of the two sides; since the West was insistent upon the necessity of international control, it also had to bear the burden of proof of the necessity for such control. The Soviet scientists consistently took the position that the progress of science would make the task of detection easier. Although the Western scientists were unwilling to admit such a broad proposition in principle, interestingly, in each of the specific assessments of the four main techniques of detection, they were willing to admit a statement to the same general effect. Thus, the concluding paragraph in each subsection analyzing a particular technique, contained a sentence stating that the capabilities of that particular technique will most likely improve in the future.

One of the most significant features of the exchange between the Western and Eastern scientists concerning these matters was that it was incomplete. Neither side was willing to reveal the effectiveness of its national detection system, nor to divulge information about its weapons tests which might not be known by the other side. Therefore, the Eastern scientists generally presented their calculations in theoretical terms only, and when the Western scientists used concrete data, it was information about Western tests which had already been fairly widely publicized. It is impossible to know whether or not greater openness on both sides would have resulted in more clarity and certainty. Presumably neither side accepted conclusions which its private information contradicted.

There was one exception to this general pattern. Fairly late in the Conference, in an attempt to buttress an argument, Dr. Fedorov stated that during the current American test series in the Pacific,

---

[53]For detailed analyses of this aspect of the Conference see Ciro E. Zoppo, *Technical and Political Aspects of Arms Control Negotiations: The 1958 Experts Conference* (RAND Corp. 1962, Memorandum RM-3286-ARPA), and Earl H. Voss, *Nuclear Ambush*, pp. 183-203.

although the Atomic Energy Commission had announced only fourteen explosions, the USSR had detected thirty-two and he gave the time of each of the shots.[54] Although the United States task force in charge of the series had in fact planned and attempted to detonate thirty-two explosions, only thirty of these attempts had actually been successful. The Western scientists could only conclude therefore that the USSR had obtained its data through some technique other than those being discussed at the Conference. Conceivably the Soviet data could have been gained through monitoring the American communication network from Soviet ships stationed near the Pacific testing area. It goes without saying that Dr. Fedorov's presentation did little to advance the Soviet position. Moreover, the American scientists were convinced that certain American explosions of small nuclear weapons had not been detected in the Soviet Union.[55]

There was little controversy between East and West regarding two of the methods of detection, recording acoustic and hydroacoustic waves and recording radio signals. The other two, recording seismic waves and the collection of radioactive debris, however, were the source of some dispute.

The Collection of Radioactive Debris and the Dispute Concerning Overflights

There was a controversy as to whether the collection of radioactive debris from ground stations would be sufficient, or whether sampling techniques involving the use of aircraft would also be needed. This issue was important because radioactive debris is the only incontrovertible evidence that a nuclear explosion has occurred. The Soviet scientists maintained that collection points at ground stations would be sufficient for purposes of detection of nuclear explosions in violation of a test ban agreement,[56] while the Western scientists argued that in addition samples taken from the air were vitally necessary.[57] The problem can be stated this way: if the parties to a test ban were willing to allow aircraft to fly over

[54]EXP/NUC/PV. 22, pp. 4-5.
[55]See *New York Times,* August 1, 1958, p. 4.
[56]See EXP/NUC/PV. 8, p. 91; EXP/NUC/PV. 10, pp. 4, 26; EXP/NUC/PV. 12, p. 121.
[57]See EXP/NUC/PV. 9, pp. 4, 5, 11; EXP/NUC/PV. 10, p. 21; EXP/NUC/PV. 12, pp. 4-6; and EXP/NUC/PV. 14, pp. 41, 48-50.

their territories on certain occasions, they would gain a more sensitive, more precise and prompter means of detecting and identifying nuclear explosions. Exactly what the margins were, though, was difficult to determine. In reply to Dr. Fedorov's doubting request for information about explosions which were detected by aircraft but not by ground stations,[58] two Western scientists—employees of the Department of Defense—cited the cases of two "low kiloton" explosions in Nevada, but added that the really important issue was the speed of detection.[59] Everyone agreed that as a consequence of a test ban agreement both methods would become more effective, since the quantity of radioactive debris in the atmosphere would decrease, and the effects of a new explosion would therefore be more obvious.

Clearly this controversy involved an issue of basic political significance: the effectiveness of a system to monitor a test ban agreement on the one hand, and the degree to which signatory states would be required to open their territory on the other. Two years later the U-2 incident would show how sensitive the issue of overflight was. That the dispute had political implications was confirmed by the fact that when it was leaked to the press, presumably by some member of the Western panel, the Soviet delegation complained bitterly.[60] Ultimately, a compromise was worked out. It was agreed that sampling techniques involving the use of aircraft would be recommended. However, this agreement in principle was qualified in the following manner:

> To this end use should be made chiefly of the aircraft flights over the oceans made for the purpose of meterological observations.
> 10. In some cases use can be made of aircraft flights over the territories of the USA, the USSR, the UK and other countries to collect air samples for the purpose of checking on data obtained by the other methods of detection of nuclear explosions.
> The Experts consider that to accomplish this task it would be quite sufficient to make use of the aircraft of

[58]EXP/NUC/PV. 12, p. 121.
[59]See EXP/NUC/PV. 14, pp. 41, 48-50.
[60]See *New York Times,* July 13, 1958, p. 1, and EXP/NUC/PV. 12, p. 122.

the country being overflown and that in such cases it is sufficient that flights for the purpose specified should be made along routes laid down in advance. Representatives of the USSR, the USA, the UK or other States participating in the operation of the control system may be on board these aircraft in the capacity of observers.[61]

The Western scientists felt that because of the nature of this issue they had to refer the exact wording of the compromise formulation to Washington for approval, which was granted. This was the only instance in which this procedure was followed.

The Problem of Seismic Signals

Eastern and Western scientists were unable to agree on the effectiveness of the method of recording seismic signals. The reason for the difficulty was not clear. It may have stemmed partly from the fact that different scales for measuring seismic waves were used in Eastern and Western countries, and it was difficult to correlate the data measured by the two scales. In addition, the problem of estimating the seismic signal which would be produced by nuclear explosions of varying yields was a task of considerable intellectual difficulty, particularly in view of the fact that all of the calculations had to be extrapolations from a single point, the Rainier explosion. Whatever the cause, the controversy was extremely important, for the conclusions would determine many of the basic characteristics of the control network. Since underground nuclear explosions could only be detected through seismic waves, and since this was perhaps the least efficient of all the techniques, the figures accepted here would be of critical importance in determining the spacing and location of control posts. Moreover, since a major purpose of this technique was to distinguish earthquakes from nuclear explosions, the assessment of the capability for accomplishing this purpose would vitally affect the number of on-site inspections which would be required. The Soviet scientists were consistently more optimistic than their Western counterparts. The Americans attempted to buttress their position by citing the

[61]"Report of the Conference of Experts to Study the Methods of Detecting Violations of a Possible Agreement on the Suspension of Nuclear Tests, August 21, 1958," in U.S. Department of State Publication, No. 7258, *Geneva Conference on the Discontinuance of Nuclear Weapon Tests* (hereafter cited as *Geneva Conference*), pp. 271-310, at 277.

Rainier experiment, but Dr. Fedorov and other Soviet specialists countered by arguing the need to introduce theoretical considerations and data from TNT explosions. In the end, a compromise was reached, and as a consequence, the conclusions concerning this technique were considerably more optimistic than the original American presentation,[62] although they were not inconsistent with the Rainier data.

Detection of Explosions at High Altitudes

As indicated earlier, the United States had not detonated any nuclear weapons at high altitudes prior to 1958 and thus the Western scientists had no empirical foundation for any position. Both sides recognized this lack of experimental data with respect to the problem of detecting nuclear explosions conducted at high altitudes. The report made it clear that the Experts' conclusions in this area were based on purely theoretical considerations. Moreover, in contrast to the situation with respect to the surface, atmospheric, and underground explosions, the control system recommended by the Experts did not include any specific techniques for the detection and identification of nuclear explosions at high altitudes.

Camouflaging and Concealing Nuclear Explosions

During the course of the Conference very little attention was given to the ways in which a state which was determined to violate a test ban agreement might attempt to conceal or disguise nuclear explosions. Hans Bethe presented a paper in which he purported to prove that it would not be possible to "decouple" an underground explosion so that no or significantly weakened seismic waves would be produced.[63] Richard Latter, of the RAND Corporation, and Doyle Northrup, of the Department of Defense, discussed the possibility of shielding nuclear explosions so that their effects would be greatly reduced, and Harold Brown, of the University of California Radiation Laboratory, pointed out a number of techniques which might be used to make the identification of some nuclear explosions extremely difficult if not impossible. Soviet delegates tended to denigrate these presentations. Although the

---

[62]Compare EXP/NUC/PV. 12, pp. 67-85, and "Report of the Conference of Experts," *Geneva Conference,* pp. 277-79.

[63]See EXP/NUC/PV. 14, pp. 57-85.

points raised by Drs. Latter, Northrup, and Brown found their way into the Experts' report, they were mentioned only in passing and quite incidentally.

In these matters, as in the case of deep underground explosions, the scientists were working without the benefit of much empirical data. Their calculations were largely theoretical. This had the effect of making it difficult if not impossible for either side to prove its points conclusively.

The Elaboration of a System

After an analysis of each of the various techniques for detecting and identifying nuclear explosions had been completed, the next point on the agenda of the Conference of Experts was to examine these techniques in combination, with a view to considering what kind of system could be established for monitoring a test ban agreement. Formulating a system was partly a matter of deduction from the previously agreed conclusions concerning each of the various techniques—of applying the agreed formulae. However, various choices also had to be made. Perhaps the most important concerned the threshold—how sensitive should the system be, what yield explosions should the system be designed to detect and identify, and with what degree of assurance? Deductions as to the character of the system would depend on the answer to this question.

Even after the threshold had been established, there were other choices to be made. An equation containing several variables allows flexibility in fixing its components, and designing a control system involved manipulation of such an equation with a considerable degree of discretion; for example, increasing the number of fixed control posts would tend to reduce the need for on-site inspections. Elaboration of a system depended to some extent upon assumptions about unknown factors, especially the level of background noise throughout the world which would interfere with reception by the various techniques and thus reduce their reliability. Finally, assumptions had to be made about the competence, efficiency, and reliability of the personnel who would operate the system. For example, one could compensate for presumed low level technical competence by more elaborate mechanisms or by mechanical redundancy. In making these choices the American scientists, and apparently the entire Western delegation, were completely on their own; their instructions provided no guidance.

When the discussion of this agenda item opened, Dr. Fedorov immediately tabled a proposal for a control system involving from 100 to 110 control stations.[64] All of the technical bases for this proposal were not immediately made clear; however, several assumptions and calculations underlying it were brought out by both the Soviet and Western scientists in the subsequent debates. Apparently the acoustic method—a relatively efficient method of detecting nuclear explosions in the atmosphere—was used in establishing distances between control posts and thus determining their number. In addition, the Soviet proposal relied considerably on the existing net of seismic stations for distinguishing earthquakes from underground nuclear explosions and purported to use other aspects of seismic signals than first motion for purposes of detection and identification.

Neither approach was acceptable to the West. The Western scientists felt that the seismic method should determine the location of control posts. They held that existing seismic stations could be used to supplement the international control system, but could not serve as its basic components. For one thing, the Western scientists were doubtful about the adequacy of the equipment of existing seismic stations. In addition, since reversing the polarity of a seismograph can be accomplished fairly easily by merely switching some wires and the sign of first motion is thereby obscured and a compression made to appear a rarefaction, they were unwilling to rely on seismic stations which were completely manned by the personnel of a possible violator state. Nor were the Western scientists willing to accept other criteria than first motion, which they felt was the only method that had been proved.

The Soviet scientists never gave a flat estimate of the capabilities of the system which they proposed, what yield explosions it would detect and identify. But given Mr. Tsarapkin's presence on the Eastern delegation—if nothing else—the threshold on which the proposal was based was presumably politically acceptable to the USSR. At one point the Western scientists estimated that the system by itself would have the following capability of detecting and identifying underground nuclear explosions of various yields: 5

[64]EXP/NUC/PV. 22, pp. 3-31.

percent of those which had a yield of 1 kiloton; 50 percent of those which had a yield of 5 kilotons; and 90 percent of those which had a yield of 20 kilotons.[65]

Obviously, the Western panel could not just simply reject this proposal, but had to introduce a counter proposal. The task of elaborating a system for the West to propose was assigned to two young American scientists: Harold Brown of the University of California Radiation Laboratory and Richard Latter. The former, a child prodigy who had received his Ph. D. in physics while still 21, was at the time 29. His colleague was 35. They used the seismic method—the principal means of detecting underground nuclear explosions and a technique for which the most effective range is somewhat less than that of the acoustic method—as the determinant of distances between control posts. They postulated that the criteria for determining the threshold of the system would be observation of the sign of first motion on seismographs at five stations of the international control system. On the basis of these assumptions, and positing that the system should have a 90 percent capability of detecting and identifying underground explosions with a yield of 1 kiloton, they concluded that approximately 650 control stations would be needed.

Some of the Brown-Latter assumptions and calculations were outlined at the same meeting at which the Soviet proposal was introduced, and they were developed in more detail and the conclusion about the number of control posts needed was presented in subsequent sessions. Although the exact number of control posts which would be required in the Soviet Union was never specified, it was obvious that it would be fairly large. Without formally rejecting the Western presentation—which the Americans insisted was not a proposal—Dr. Fedorov made it obvious that such a control system would be unacceptable to the USSR.

After several sessions, on Tuesday, August 5, Sir William Penney of the United Kingdom, reading an agreed Western position, introduced a third system.[66] It was based on the same type of analysis as the system which the West had introduced previously; however, the threshold was raised. In this case with approximately

[65]EXP/NUC/PV. 26, p. 26.
[66]Ibid., pp. 26-35.

170 land-based control posts and several ships, the system was estimated to have a "good probability" of detecting and identifying nuclear explosions with yields down to one kiloton in the atmosphere and in the open ocean and also a "good probability" of recording seismic signals from deep underground nuclear explosions equivalent to one kiloton. In the latter case, it was assumed that there would be some difficulty in distinguishing the signals generated by explosions from those generated by earthquakes, and that this difficulty would increase significantly as one moved down from five kilotons to one kiloton. It was estimated that the system would be able to "identify as being of natural origin about 90 percent of the continental earthquakes, whose signals are equivalent to 5 kilotons, and a small percentage of continental earthquakes equivalent to 1 kiloton."[67] Since the system had relatively little capability with respect to subkiloton explosions, it was thought that it would probably not have been able to detect experiments involving the development of a neutron bomb.

At the same meeting, Dr. Fisk suggested that the experts might adopt a report which would list all three systems, outlining the capabilities and limitations of each.[68] Dr. Fedorov, however, made it apparent that the Eastern panel would only consider agreeing to a report which listed one system. Obviously a report which listed *one* system would have many more political implications and much greater political impact than one which listed several, and would be much more of a commitment so far as subsequent negotiations were concerned.

Six days elapsed before the next formal meeting. Dr. Fisk tried desperately to obtain a judgment from Washington as to whether or not the control system presented by Sir William would present an acceptable risk to the United States, but he could not obtain this assurance. Meanwhile, in Geneva there were three informal meetings, at which records were not kept. On Monday, August 11, the two sides promptly agreed to recommend to their governments a control system generally patterned after that which had been outlined by Sir William Penney. It was probably during this period that a number of the Western scientists were made

[67]*Geneva Conference,* p. 290.
[68]EXP/NUC/PV. 26, p. 61.

aware of the political implications of their efforts. Many of them appear not to have realized at the outset that what they did would become the basis for subsequent diplomatic negotiations. Even at this point, all of them may not have fully grasped all of the implications of their situation, but they must at least have been conscious of them to some extent. In any case, from this day on, and for the next three years, the figure of from 170 to 180 land and sea control posts became the fixed basis for negotiations.

There were a number of other matters which had to be settled once agreement had been reached on the broad outlines of a system. Dr. Fedorov sought to include in the Report of the Conference of Experts recommendations on the staffing of the control posts and the phasing of their establishment. He ventured the opinion that one or two controllers from "the other side"—that is, from the Western powers in control posts in the USSR and other communist countries and vice versa—would be sufficient to insure the proper functioning of a control post,[69] and that the control posts should be established first on the territories of the United States, the Soviet Union, the United Kingdom, Australia, Africa, and the Pacific Ocean area.[70] The Western scientists ruled out discussion of both of these proposals on the ground that they involved "political" rather than technical issues. The Report of the Conference of Experts merely stated that approximately thirty persons would be required to man a control post,[71] and it only specified the number of control posts that would be required on each continent and generally on islands and ships on the high seas, without mentioning specific countries.[72] The Experts also considered and reached detailed agreement on the specific equipment to be installed at each control post.

On-Site Inspection

The final matter discussed by the Experts was the problem of on-site inspections. Originally, the Western scientists advanced the

[69]EXP/NUC/PV. 23, p. 41.

[70]EXP/NUC/PV. 22, p. 31.

[71]"Report of the Conference of Experts to Study the Methods of Detecting Violations of a Possible Agreement on the Suspension of Nuclear Tests," *Geneva Conference*, p. 288.

[72]*Ibid.*

concept that inspections should be initiated by automatic criteria—any suspicious and unexplained signal of a given magnitude—and that there should be an elaborate mechanism for conducting such inspections.[73] For a variety of reasons—principally Soviet objections and lack of time and data—the Western scientists did not follow this initial presentation with detailed proposals. Consequently, the section in the Experts' Report dealing with the problem of on-site inspections is quite brief and contains few detailed directives.[74] As a result, it was possible to have a good deal of technical argument in the subsequent negotiations. The section on on-site inspections estimated that there would be from 20 to 100 earthquakes a year which would be undistinguishable on the basis of their seismic signals from deep underground nuclear explosions of about 5 kiloton yield, and it also stated that:

> When the control posts detect an event which cannot be identified by the international control organ and which could be suspected of being a nuclear explosion, the international control organ can send an inspection group to the site of this event in order to determine whether a nuclear explosion had taken place or not.[75]

This could be interpreted as a mandate for compulsory on-site inspection in the case of all unidentified events.

V

An Agreed Report: A Hopeful Sign?

Concluding Communiques

With the agreement on this point, except for matters involving the drafting and style of the report, the Conference of Experts had concluded its work. These matters were handled expeditiously, and on August 21 the Conference held its final session. The Conference then issued a public communique; the report itself was not pub-

---

[73]See the presentation by Robert F. Bacher: EXP/NUC/PV. 22, pp. 36-50.

[74]"Report of the Conference of Experts to Study the Methods of Detecting Violations of a Possible Agreement on the Suspension of Nuclear Tests," *Geneva Conference*, pp. 289-90.

[75]*Ibid.*, p. 289.

lished for several days after the conclusion of the Conference. Public attention probably focused most on these words in the communique:

> The Conference adopted an agreed conclusion regarding the technical equipment of the control system necessary for the detection and identification of nuclear explosions. The Conference reached the conclusion that it is technically feasible to set up, with certain capabilities and limitations, a workable and effective control system for the detections of violations of a possible agreement on the world-wide cessation of nuclear weapons tests.[76]

Probably most people tended to read this as saying—controls for a test ban are technically feasible. But was this an accurate representation of the work of the Conference?

In Geneva, among the Western delegations at least, there was a feeling of satisfaction that a difficult task had been completed. In the world at large, there was widespread public expectation that an arms control agreement might actually be in the offing. Dr. Fisk issued a communique which summed up the feeling of at least the American participants:

> The Conference of Experts has completed its work. We on the Western side are gratified that the task set for this Conference, which began its work seven weeks ago, has been successfully accomplished.
>
> That task was to seek a common understanding of the technical problems involved in the detection and identification of nuclear explosions. We have now reached such a common understanding, which is embodied in the report we have just agreed upon, and which we are now transmitting to our Governments. My colleagues and I are hopeful that this report, which carefully examines and sets forth the capabilities and limitations of present methods of detecting nuclear explosions, will prove helpful to all of our Governments in their future consideration of this important subject.
>
> As scientists we have sought to establish the facts pertinent to our subject and to draw from them sound and logical conclusions regarding a system of control.[77]

[76]*Documents on Disarmament, 1945–1959,* Vol. II, p. 1091.
[77]U.S. Department of State *Bulletin,* Vol. XXXIX, No. 1004 (September 22, 1958), p. 452.

But had their role simply been that of scientists attempting to establish the facts, and were Dr. Fisk's modesty, on the one hand, and optimism, on the other, warranted? Had not the scientists engaged in a role of extremely great political importance? And how happy should one be with a document which in fixed terms stated matters concerning which there was very little empirical data? It is one thing to have a scientific paper proved incorrect, but what would happen if an internationally agreed to document was proved incorrect?

Perhaps the basic question, however, was what would the United States do now in the light of this unexpected denouement. Even though at the outset the United States did not have any clear expectations in terms of broad strategy about the purpose of the Conference of Experts, now that there was an agreed report some fundamental decisions would surely have to be taken.

PART II

THE CONFERENCE ON THE DISCONTINUANCE OF NUCLEAR WEAPON TESTS

Chapter IV

The Opening of the
Diplomatic Negotiations

I

The Eisenhower Proposal

The Conclusion of the Conference of Experts

As the Conference of Experts drew to a close, it became apparent to the participants, and to the outside world as well, that it would result in a report accepted by the scientists of both East and West. Drs. Fisk and Penney informed President Eisenhower and Prime Minister Macmillan of the probable nature of the agreement several days before the conclusion of the Conference, and the American press began to forecast the outcome as early as August 10, 1958.[1]

This development would clearly call for new policy decisions, especially by the United States. Since the United States had proposed the Conference, and since American diplomats and politicians had consistently argued that the principal obstacle to disarmament was lack of agreement on controls, the United States bore a special onus for making the next move.

The Committee of Principals

The task of preparing the American response devolved upon a small group of officials within the Administration who had major responsibilities in the fields of foreign policy and national security. This group had met informally during the first half of 1958 in connection with the preparations for the Conference of Experts. Later, when negotiations for a nuclear test ban became an actual prospect, it came to be called the Committee of Principals. The Secretary of State, the Secretary of Defense, the Director of the Central Intelligence Agency, the Chairman of the Atomic Energy

[1]See *New York Times,* August 10, 1958, IV, p. 6.

Commission, and the Special Assistant to the President for Science and Technology were regular members of the Committee. In addition, the Special Assistant to the President for National Security Affairs was what might be described as an ex officio "nonvoting" member, and the Director of the United States Information Agency attended occasional sessions.

Whether an individual's role in a group such as the Committee of Principals is determined principally by his title and position within the Administration or by his own personal views is a moot point and in any case obviously varies with the individual, the strength of his convictions and personality, his experience, and the issue under consideration. It is obvious though that policies emerging from such committees are always a montage of departmental and agency viewpoints admixed with personal attitudes. Therefore, it is important to list the individuals who were involved. Under the Eisenhower Administration the Committee of Principals consisted of: John Foster Dulles, until he was replaced by Christian Herter in April 1959; Neil H. McElroy, until he was replaced as Secretary of Defense by Thomas S. Gates in December 1959; CIA Director Allan W. Dulles; John A. McCone, who succeeded Lewis L. Strauss as Chairman of the AEC in July 1958; Dr. James R. Killian, Jr., until he was replaced as the President's Special Assistant for Science and Technology by Dr. George Kistiakowsky in July 1959; Gordon Gray, who succeeded Robert Cutler as Special Assistant for National Security Affairs in July 1958; and, occasionally, USIA Director George V. Allen, or their deputies. When the Kennedy Administration assumed power in January 1961, the personnel of the Committee of Principals was changed to Dean Rusk, Robert S. McNamara, Allan W. Dulles, Glenn T. Seaborg, Dr. Jerome B. Wiesner, McGeorge Bundy, and, occasionally, Edward R. Murrow, or their deputies.

During the first three and a half years of the diplomatic negotiations, the Committee of Principals held somewhat more than thirty formal meetings. Although American policy relating to the negotiations was generally developed at a lower, "working," level, especially in the so-called Interdepartmental Working Group, the members of which came from the same departments and agencies as were represented on the Committee of Principals, this policy usually was at least discussed by the Committee of Principals before being approved by the President. In those instances in which it reached a decision, the Committee usually made a definite recommendation to the President. Decisions in the Committee of Principals were always the result of agreement, rather than voting. If it proved impossible to obtain agreement in the Committee, the issue could be taken to the President for resolution; however, this was seldom done. Although the Committee was sharply divided on a number of issues during the Eisenhower Administration, there were strong pressures against raising disputes to the Presidential level. To take a strong position necessitating a submission to the President would have risked alienating individuals whose collaboration was essential for the matter at hand and also in other vital endeavours. In such circumstances, an individual must regard an issue as being of particular importance before he will risk the possible consequences of elevating the dispute to the highest level. Moreover, in this case there was another inhibition. President Eisenhower strongly preferred to receive an agreed recommendation. At times, when he was confronted with conflicting views, he would call for further study and discussion to see if the dispute could not be resolved. Under the Kennedy Administration, the Committee of Principals was much more united, and it also received firm Presidential directives. Thus, in both administrations, the device of appeal was seldom used.

President Eisenhower's Statement of August 22

When this group began to formulate the American response to the anticipated successful conclusion of the Conference of Experts, Secretary of State Dulles was in New York at the Emergency Special Session of the General Assembly which met from August 8 until August 21, 1958, to consider the crisis in the Middle East. He was represented in the discussions by the Under Secretary, Christian Herter.

Although no brief formulation can adequately portray several complex positions, the viewpoints expressed in the Committee of Principals can be summarized in the following fashion. The Department of State strongly felt that the United States should take the lead in proposing negotiations for a test ban. The reasons for this varied with individuals. It was partly a matter of wanting to respond to and capitalize on public pressures; to put the United States in a favorable light before public opinion. To put it negatively, the Department of State wished to avoid being placed in the position that it had been in the spring when the USSR unilaterally suspended nuclear testing. Another motivation was a desire to explore and follow up a seemingly favorable first step toward a measure of arms control. Put in simplest fashion, this meant exploring Soviet intentions (calling the USSR's bluff, if that is what it was) or, more hopefully, proceeding with constructive negotiations. Mr. Dulles himself inclined toward nuclear test ban negotiations as he viewed the changing role of nuclear weapons in military strategy and the developing "nth country problem." Although not at all sanguine about Soviet intentions or the outcome, he seemed to favor exploring arrangements, including a test ban, which might ultimately offer some assurance, not only against a deliberate nuclear attack but also against accident and miscalculation which could unleash nuclear war. The wish to exploit the agreement at the Conference of Experts for a move toward arms control was particularly strong in the American scientific community, and it no doubt had an impact on the President's Science Advisory Committee and was expressed by the Special Assistant for Science and Technology. In addition, many scientists were deeply troubled by the problem of fallout. The Central Intelligence Agency favored any move which might introduce more openness into Soviet society. The Atomic Energy Commission and the Department of Defense, however, were convinced that a test ban, as an isolated measure of arms control, would endanger American security.[2]

Beyond the basic disagreement on the wisdom of a test ban, there was also a disagreement as to whether the United States should continue testing nuclear weapons while the negotiations were in progress. The principal protagonists in this dispute were the Department of State, which argued that the United States should cease testing the day that the negotiations began, and the Department

---

[2]Robert Gilpin argues that the fact that John A. McCone replaced Lewis Strauss as the head of the AEC on July 1, 1958, "removed from the policy debate a strong opponent of a nuclear test ban," (*American Scientists and Nuclear Weapons Policy,* p. 199). Even though Mr. McCone may have opposed a nuclear test ban less than Admiral Strauss, neither he nor the AEC favored a test ban as an isolated measure of arms control in these discussions.

of Defense and the Atomic Energy Commission, which held that testing should continue until the coming into force of a treaty. A compromise solution involving a moratorium covering only atmospheric testing was mooted for a while, but ultimately abandoned on the ground that such a move would not be properly understood by public opinion.

After consensus had been achieved within the Administration, on August 21, the Joint Committee on Atomic Energy was informed of the action which the United States planned to take. Although the members of the Committee could present their views, it was then so late that they could not alter the course of American policy.[3]

Allied views were also a factor. Perhaps the French view was the most important; at least it was the most clearly formulated and was argued with the greatest force. France was determined to push ahead with its plans for the development of an independent nuclear capability, and, as a consequence, continued to oppose a test ban as an isolated measure of arms control. Foreign Minister Maurice Couve de Murville reiterated the French position to President Eisenhower on August 21. In essence, the United States chose to downgrade seriously or perhaps even to ignore the French position.

The American response to the successful conclusion of the Conference of Experts—specifically President Eisenhower's statement of August 22—was a product of this melange of views. After it was drafted in Washington, the statement was taken to New York for Mr. Dulles' approval and then was released to the public. It was also immediately transmitted to the Soviet Foreign Ministry. The statement proposed the inauguration of negotiations for a test ban treaty and also defined the initial American negotiating position. The most important part of the statement was contained in the following paragraphs:

> The United States, taking account of the Geneva conclusions, is prepared to proceed promptly to negotiate an agreement with other nations which have tested nuclear weapons for the suspension of nuclear weapons tests and the actual establishment of an international control system on the basis of the experts' report.

[3]Robert Gilpin, *American Scientists and Nuclear Weapons Policy,* p. 199.

If this is accepted in principle by the other nations which have tested nuclear weapons, then in order to facilitate the detailed negotiations the United States is prepared, unless testing is resumed by the Soviet Union, to withhold further testing on its part of atomic and hydrogen weapons for a period of one year from the beginning of the negotiations.

As part of the agreement to be negotiated, and on a basis of reciprocity, the United States would be further prepared to suspend the testing of nuclear weapons on a year-by-year basis subject to a determination at the beginning of each year: (A) the agreed inspection system is installed and working effectively; and (B) satisfactory progress is being made in reaching agreement on and implementing major and substantial arms control measures such as the United States has long sought. The agreement should also deal with the problem of detonations for peaceful purposes, as distinct from weapons tests.

Our negotiators will be instructed and ready by October 31 this year to open negotiations with other similarly instructed negotiators.

As the United States has frequently made clear, the suspension of testing of atomic and hydrogen weapons is not, in itself, a measure of disarmament or a limitation of armament. An agreement in this respect is significant if it leads to other and more substantial agreements relating to limitation and reduction of fissionable material for weapons and to other essential phases of disarmament. It is in this hope that the United States makes this proposal.[4]

The British statement which was issued almost simultaneously was similar.[5] The October 31 date for the opening of diplomatic negotiations and the inauguration of the one-year moratorium meant that the United States would have over two months to continue the test series which was then in progress. However, if the USSR accepted the Western invitation to engage in diplomatic negotiations, the United States was pledged not to test nuclear weapons in any environment for a period of twelve months after October 30. This decision to engage in a moratorium prior to the achievement of a test ban treaty proved to be crucially important, and some

[4]*Geneva Conference*, p. 311.
[5]See *ibid.*, pp. 311-13.

have argued woefully misguided.[6] The rationale for the decision, which was developed mainly by the Department of State, was that such action was necessary because of the pressure of public opinion and to create the most propitious atmosphere for the diplomatic negotiations. The opposition of the Atomic Energy Commission and the Department of Defense to the decision was partly mollified by limiting the moratorium to twelve months.

The implied suggestion that detonations for peaceful purposes should be dealt with separately in the agreement, while safeguarding the American Project Plowshare, would pose difficult problems of discrimination. How could the purpose of an explosion be determined and how would it be possible to be certain that a device allegedly designed to produce a huge natural cavity would not also have military applications?

Perhaps the most important part of the statement concerned the conditions under which the United States—and the United Kingdom also—would be willing to cease testing nuclear weapons. The United States held to its earlier position that a test ban could only be regarded as one of several measures of arms control or disarmament, and as in earlier proposals, the United States sought to enforce this link by making the test cessation conditional on progress in other fields. In essence, President Eisenhower's statement was very similar to that which Harold Stassen had made on August 21, 1957, before the London session of the UN Disarmament Subcommittee.[7] The only differences were, first, that since the technical talks which Mr. Stassen had called for had already occurred, they could no longer be listed as a condition for extending the test cessation for a second twelve month period. Secondly, Mr. Stassen had implied that the only condition for making the test cessation permanent would be the achievement of a production cut-off, in addition of course to the condition that the test ban monitoring system be functioning effectively. President Eisenhower's statement opened up the possibility of several conditions. In some ways the American position as stated by President Eisenhower could be interpreted as indicating a lesser propensity to negotiate on the test

[6]See Robert Gilpin, *American Scientists and Nuclear Weapons Policy*, pp. 219-20; and, Thomas E. Murray, *Nuclear Policy for War and Peace*, pp. 93-96.

[7]See *supra* p. 18.

ban issue than could be inferred from Mr. Stassen's statement two years earlier.

The requirement that a test cessation be conditional on achieving progress in other fields of arms control or disarmament was inserted in President Eisenhower's statement at the insistence of the Department of Defense and the Atomic Energy Commission. The Department of State did not favor this position, but agreed to it in the process of mutual accommodation.

Why the requirement was stated so vaguely, however, rather than in terms of specific disarmament measures, is not clear. Perhaps the vagueness was a negotiating tactic, a device for gaining bargaining strength and maintaining flexibility. The vagueness may also have stemmed from the fact that by this time the difficulties involved in linking a test cessation with a production cut-off and possibly with a requirement for the transfer of fissionable materials from weapons stockpiles were widely recognized, and there were therefore cogent arguments against maintaining this particular link. Rather than substitute some other measure immediately, it may have seemed wiser to await the outcome of other developments then in progress relating to arms control and disarmament. At that time, a technical conference concerning measures for the prevention of surprise attack was a distinct possibility. Also, the question of the uses of outer space was scheduled for discussion at the thirteenth session of the General Assembly, which would open in September. Both of these discussions would deal in some fashion with the launching of missiles, among other things. It was thought that controlling the launching of missiles would require control measures of roughly comparable scope to those needed to monitor a test cessation;[8] and controlling technological developments with respect to delivery vehicles on the one hand and warheads on the other might be regarded as equivalent measures. Consequently, some may have hoped that a link between missile controls and a controlled test ban could be established.

There are also two other possible explanations for the vagueness of the link. It may have stemmed from inability to reach agreement within the Administration or from a lack of preparation.

[8]See Seymour Melman (ed.), *Inspection for Disarmament,* pp. 18-25, and *passim.*

Perhaps it was both. Assuming that there were strong arguments against the old position, discovering alternative measures of arms control with which a test ban could be linked would require a considerable amount of analysis. If a test ban alone would prove disadvantageous to the security interests of the United States, what other measures of arms control might serve as adequate compensation? What types of controls would these measures require? These were questions which could not be answered simply, or without detailed analyses of the technical as well as of the political and military aspects, and at that time the United States government was ill-equipped to conduct such analyses. Mr. Stassen's staff had largely been dispersed even before his resignation in February 1958. It is true that other offices had responsibility for American policy concerning arms control and disarmament; within the Department of State, the Office of the Special Assistant for Disarmament and Atomic Energy Affairs, and within the Department of Defense, the Office of International Security Affairs. However, both of these offices had relatively small staffs, and, as their titles indicated, they also had other responsibilities. In addition, many of the personnel were directly involved in the Conference of Experts. Thus, there was hardly any manpower available for broad planning. Moreover, there was no group which could do technical analyses quickly and on a continuing basis. Mr. Stassen had relied on task forces comprised principally of nongovernmental experts, and if the appointment of the Bethe Panel was indicative of a policy, it appeared as if this technique would be continued. There seemed to be no alternative, since the Department of State did not have any technically qualified scientists among its personnel, and since the staff of the Special Assistant to the President for Science and Technology was quite small and the Science Advisory Committee was only a part-time group. However, the device of convening a special panel is relatively cumbersome, and it is not likely to be utilized unless a problem is clearly identified. Although cooperation of scientists in private employment is clearly indispensable, the panel of this type does not lend itself to systematic advance planning aimed at exploring a variety of longer range contingencies. The vagueness in the American position therefore probably was the result of disagreement on the old link and inability to conceive of a new one.

The Holifield Dissent

The subtleties of President Eisenhower's statement, though, were largely ignored in public discussion in the United States. In the public view, the statement was generally regarded as an unambiguous invitation to negotiate a test ban. There was, however, at least one exception to the general euphoria. On August 22, shortly after the President's statement was released, Representative Chet Holifield read two statements into the *Congressional Record*. After generally expressing his approval, he went on to say that he was "gravely troubled" by the inclusion of the principle that a test cessation would be dependent on progress being made in other areas of arms control.[9] He pointed out that the statement was "unclear" and "susceptible of different interpretations," and asserted that if the condition were maintained he had "little hope for the completion of a nuclear testing agreement." He continued:

> I regret that I must state that the inclusion of the "one package" requirement as a contingency for nuclear weapon test cessation on a step-by-step basis casts a reflection on the sincerity of the President's statement. It seems to be a tragic continuation of the futile and abortive Dulles philosophy which has failed to establish, in world opinion, our sincerity in the search for world peace.
> It is this fatal lack of vision, this holding back, this being dragged into the future which is killing our influence throughout the world.

His statement was about as harsh a criticism of American policy as could be imagined. Interestingly, none of the major American newspapers or wireservices reported it. The Tass correspondent, however, noticed it and it was reported in *Pravda*.[10]

II

Interim Sparring

The Bombardment on Quemoy and Matsu

In the interval between the issuance of President Eisenhower's statement of August 22 and the opening of the Geneva test ban

[9]*Congressional Record,* Vol. 104, Part 15, p. 19245.
[10]August 25, 1958, p. 4.

negotiations on October 31, all interested parties sparred for position. Chronologically, the first relevant event was Communist China's commencement on August 23 of heavy bombardment of the offshore island groups of Quemoy and Matsu. On that day the islands were hit by some fifty thousand shells within a period of two hours. The crisis which this action touched off continued until late October.

It is impossible to know whether or not the Chinese Communist action was in any way related to the developments concerning a test ban. The People's Republic of China had for some time been engaged in a military build-up in the Fukien Province opposite Taiwan, and an increasing number of air and naval clashes between the Communists and the Nationalists occurred during the late summer. The Chinese Nationalist government had declared a state of emergency on Taiwan as early as August 7. It is therefore conceivable that the bombardment was unrelated to the events in Geneva and Washington.

On the other hand, the People's Republic of China would be affected by a test ban. The Conference of Experts had after all proposed a global system of control posts. Moreover, a test ban might affect Communist China's ability to develop an independent nuclear capability in the same sense that it might have an impact on France's program. If the three nuclear powers agreed to a test ban, public opinion throughout the world would probably strongly oppose any attempt by other states to test nuclear weapons. The three nuclear powers presumably would also have a strong interest in seeing that other states did not test because it might upset the delicate balance of trust and calculation of advantage on which a test cessation would rest. Thus, a test ban conceivably could freeze the situation in Eastern Asia in which Communist China would continue to face nuclear equipped American forces without having such weapons of its own.

Communist China and the USSR apparently had discussed the question of the former's obtaining a nuclear capability from time to time.[11] The Chinese have claimed that the two governments signed an agreement on October 15, 1957, relating to new technol-

[11]See Alice Langley Hsieh, *Communist China's Strategy in the Nuclear Era* (1962).

ogy.[12] The Chinese claim that the terms of this agreement obligated the USSR to provide the People's Republic of China with a sample of an atomic bomb and technical data relating to its manufacture. The USSR has neither confirmed nor denied the existence of this agreement. If in fact such an agreement existed, it is significant that it was signed after the breakdown of the London negotiations. The Soviet Union may well have agreed to sign the agreement only after it became clear that the prospects of obtaining a test ban at that point were rather remote.

Immediately prior to the bombardment of the off-shore islands, Nikita Khrushchev visited Peking from July 31 to August 3 and held extensive talks with Mao Tse-tung. Soviet Defense Minister R. Y. Malinovsky and his Chinese counterpart, Marshall Peng Teh-huai were present at the discussions. Rumors circulated in the West that the USSR had promised to supply its ally with nuclear weapons.[13] If such matters were discussed at these meetings, in the light of subsequent developments and Chinese claims about the 1957 agreement, it seems more likely that in return for assistance in developing a nuclear capability, the USSR insisted on gaining some control over China's military establishment.[14] Whether or not it was at these meetings, it is fairly clear that the USSR made such a demand sometime in 1958. Once the possibility of a test ban increased, as it did with the progress of the Conference of Experts, Soviet leaders may well have reasoned that they should proceed cautiously with the implementation of the 1957 agreement. The Chinese, on the other hand, probably saw a test ban and the degree of East-West détente that it would imply, as an obstacle to their gaining an independent nuclear capability, and to achieving their broader political objectives.

For these reasons, the timing of the Chinese bombardment of the off-shore islands is of particular interest, as is the reluctance with which the USSR supported the action. The Chinese move was certainly an expression of independence from the USSR, and

[12]This Chinese claim is discussed in detail in Alice Langley Hsieh, "The Sino-Soviet Nuclear Dialogue: 1963," *Journal of Conflict Resolution*, Vol. VIII, No. 2 (June 1964), pp. 99-115, at 110-14.

[13]Richard P. Stebbins, *The United States in World Affairs, 1958* (1959), p. 315.

[14]See Alice Langley Hsieh, *supra* note 12, at 111-13.

it also may well have been a warning of opposition to a test ban, and more broadly to an East-West détente.

Regardless of its motivation, however, the action by Communist China would certainly have had implications for the test ban negotiations. Among other things it strengthened the forces in the United States which opposed the recognition of Communist China, and thus would complicate the problem of bringing that state into any agreement which might be negotiated.

The Initial Soviet Reaction

The first official reaction by the USSR to President Eisenhower's August 22 statement was an interview which Chairman Khrushchev gave to a *Pravda* correspondent, which was published on August 29.[15] In this interview, Chairman Khrushchev asserted that:

> The statements of the United States and United Kingdom governments show that these Governments are continuing to seek every possible loop-hole in order to avoid an immediate discontinuance of nuclear tests. This becomes especially clear if we consider the reservations and manifestly far-fetched conditions which the Governments of the Western Powers attach to their proposals.

He objected to the fact that the initial suspension would be limited to one year. "It is obvious to everyone . . . that such a brief suspension of tests is completely meaningless, since one year is precisely the time required for preparing the next series of tests." To the extent that it would require at least a year of preparation for the United States and the United Kingdom to carry out test series as extensive as those conducted in 1958, his time estimate was correct.

He also objected to the two requirements which the Western powers listed as conditions for extending the moratorium on testing. He considered the requirement that a control system should be "installed and working effectively" was "an artificial one, since it has long been known that modern science guarantees the possibility of detecting any nuclear explosions and therefore control over the observance of an agreement on the discontinuance of tests is

[15]UN Document A/3904, pp. 3-9.

readily feasible." Did he mean to say that an international network
of control stations was not necessary, that existent national systems
were sufficient? Chairman Khrushchev's amplification of this statement compounded the ambiguity. He argued that "the conclusions of
the conference of experts fully confirm the correctness of the point
of view which the Soviet government has always maintained on this
question and demonstrate the falseness of the position of the Western
Powers." But he then went on to say that the Soviet government
agreed with all of "the conclusions and recommendations in the report of the conference concerning a system of control. . . ." The
exact implications of these statements were far from clear, and a
doubting mind on the Western side could with little difficulty interpret them as being most evasive.

Chairman Khrushchev also attacked the other requirement concerning "satisfactory progress" with respect to other measures of arms
control:

> But as everyone knows that it is the Governments of the
> Western Powers and those Governments alone which, by
> persistently adhering to a policy based on an armaments
> race and atomic blackmail, have year after year frustrated
> the achievement of agreement on matters of disarmament.
> In view of this situation, how is it possible to believe
> that they really want a discontinuance of tests when they
> put forward such a condition?

Again, anyone convinced of the basic reasonableness of the Western
position over the years with respect to disarmament and arms control, could easily regard his remarks as ominous.

Despite his harsh comments, Chairman Khrushchev agreed that
the negotiations should start October 31. However, he proposed that
the negotiations should be held in Geneva, rather than in New York
as the Western powers had suggested. He also proposed that the negotiations should be limited to two or three weeks. Finally, he flatly
stated that the USSR was "completely unable to accept the reservations and conditions which the Western powers attach to their statement of readiness to participate in the negotiations, since to accept
them would be to foredoom the negotiations to failure."

The following day, the Soviet Foreign Ministry sent a note to the
American Embassy in Moscow accepting the proposal that negotia-

tions should begin October 31 and repeating Chairman Khrushchev's suggestions with respect to the place and duration of the negotiations.[16] The Chairman's interview with the *Pravda* correspondent was attached. For the next two months, the USSR and the United States argued, through various exchanges of notes and statements, about the nature of the forthcoming negotiations.[17] In these exchanges, the USSR suggested that the conference should be at the level of Ministers of Foreign Affairs and also sought to limit its duration. A time limitation would have created a public expectation that agreement could be reached promptly, and presumably would have subjected the Western delegations to considerable public pressure. The Soviet government would not have been subjected to corresponding pressure from its own public opinion in view of its control over its domestic mass media and public spokesmen. Both Soviet suggestions were refused. The Soviet Union also continued to protest the requirements which the Western powers listed for extending the moratorium and to argue that the purpose of the conference should be "to conclude an agreement on the permanent discontinuance of atomic and hydrogen weapons tests . . . and to establish an appropriate control system for the enforcement of such an agreement." The Western powers, on the other hand, refused to drop their conditions, and always referred to the forthcoming conference as "the meeting on suspension of nuclear tests and establishment of an international control system." These differences were never entirely resolved.

Continued Testing of Nuclear Weapons

As these exchanges went on, both sides also maneuvered to gain advantages in nuclear weapons development. With at least a temporary cut-off date on further testing in prospect, where the development race would end became an important consideration, both in reality and in a symbolic sense. The United States and the United Kingdom test series were pressed forward. Additional shots, originally planned for a later period, were added to the American series then in progress. The effort came to be dubbed "Operation Deadline." In his interview with the *Pravda* correspondent, Chairman Khrush-

[16]*Ibid.*, p. 2.
[17]See UN Documents 3940, 3956, and 3973; and U.S. Department of State *Bulletin,* Vol. XXXIX, No. 1005 (September 29, 1958), p. 503.

chev said that because of the continued testing by the United States and the United Kingdom, the USSR was released from the obligation which it had unilaterally assumed the previous March, and on September 30, the Soviet Union in fact resumed testing. Between that date and October 25, the USSR conducted fourteen explosions. Seven of these were in the megaton range. These tests were probably designed both to advance the USSR's knowledge of nuclear weapons, and for their psychological effects. The Soviet resumption of testing would clearly put the West under a certain pressure by making a test ban agreement appear more desirable. It might also intimidate the uncommitted who in turn would increase the pressure on the West for a test ban.

On October 7, Foreign Minister Gromyko, extending the concept of East-West parity to a new sphere, asserted that the USSR had the right to continue testing until it had matched the number of tests conducted by the United States and the United Kingdom since March 31, the date on which the Supreme Soviet had adopted the decree resolving to discontinue testing in the Soviet Union. His statement had ominous implications for the possibility of establishing a moratorium at the beginning of the negotiations, for it was almost inconceivable that the USSR could match the number of Western tests by October 31. Nonetheless, the Western powers continued to plan that their testing would cease by October 31, and the last American shot was detonated shortly before midnight on October 30. As of that date, according to a later official American tabulation, the United States had set off 174 announced nuclear detonations, the United Kingdom, 21, and the USSR, 53.[18] Neither the United States nor the USSR had announced all of their shots. Of the American announced shots, 66 had been conducted in 1958. The Soviet Union had detonated 23 of its announced shots in that year.

The Thirteenth General Assembly: Arena for Sparring

The General Assembly of the United Nations, which opened its thirteenth session on September 16, was another arena for East-West sparring in the period immediately preceding the Geneva test ban negotiations. Several subjects relating to disarmament and arms

[18]U.S. Department of Defense, *The Effects of Nuclear Weapons*, pp. 671-81.

control were on the agenda, and the discussion and action on these subjects in the Assembly had direct and indirect implications for the forthcoming Geneva conference.

Although the provisional agenda of the thirteenth General Assembly included a general item entitled, "The Question of Disarmament," on September 15, the day before the Assembly opened, the USSR proposed that a specific item, "The Discontinuance of Atomic and Hydrogen Weapons Tests," should be added to the agenda.[19] In its supporting memorandum, the USSR stressed its view:

> . . . that the question of the discontinuance of atomic and hydrogen weapons tests should be separated from the general disarmament programme and resolved independently and at once, and that it should not be linked with other disarmament problems on which substantial differences exist among the States.

Clearly, one motivation for the Soviet action was again to bring pressure to bear before the opening of the Geneva Conference against the Western insistence on linking a test ban with other measures of disarmament.

One other part of the Soviet memorandum is also of special significance. It contained the statement that "consideration and positive solution" of the problem "would constitute the first important step towards the complete prohibition of atomic and hydrogen weapons," and then went on to say that it would also "create favourable conditions for the solution of other important disarmament problems." Obviously the USSR and the Western powers had somewhat different expectations and hopes concerning the consequences of a nuclear test ban. The USSR seems to have hoped that the most important consequences of a test ban would be a prohibition on the use of nuclear weapons, which the Soviet Union had advocated over the years. The effect of such a prohibition would of course have been to neutralize the American nuclear superiority. The Western powers on the other hand—insofar as such broad generalizations are possible —appear to have had in mind other measures of arms control and disarmament. These and other differences between the two sides were delineated and exposed in the course of the ensuing debate in the Assembly.

[19]UN Document A/3915, p. 1.

When the Assembly's Political Committee held its first meeting on October 8, Ambassador Zorin maintained that the question of nuclear testing should be discussed first and settled before other questions relating to disarmament were brought up.[20] As supporting arguments, he cited the urgency of the issue, the need to affect "the course and outcome of the Geneva negotiations," and the ineffectiveness—demonstrated in his view in past sessions—of combining all disarmament items in one discussion. Ambassador Lodge, on the other hand, argued for a combined discussion, maintaining that the issues "were interrelated."[21] He allowed, however, that delegates would "be free to discuss the items separately and in any order they wished." The issue of whether a link should be maintained between the test ban and other steps toward disarmament thus arose again in a procedural-tactical context at the very outset of the proceedings. After three days' debate, the Committee adopted an American compromise proposal, which provided that all items relating to disarmament should be discussed together in a general debate, but that the decision on the priority of consideration of draft resolutions should be postponed until the conclusion of the general debate.

For all practical purposes, the General Assembly's handling of the test ban issue and all other questions relating to disarmament was completed before the Geneva negotiations were really underway. The Political Committee concluded its work on these matters on November 4, and that same day the plenary session adopted the resolutions which the Committee recommended. In both forums, resolutions relating to the cessation of nuclear testing were voted on first. The Political Committee voted on these resolutions on October 31, the day the Geneva negotiations opened. In a sense then, the Assembly's action can be regarded as an adjunct to negotiations which were conducted outside of the United Nations. Certainly, most of the Member States, and especially the participants in the Geneva negotiations, regarded the Assembly proceedings in this light.

In all, six resolutions relating to nuclear testing were submitted to the Political Committee. Both India and the USSR submitted resolutions on October 5. The Soviet draft, after repeating in the preamble the opinion often expressed by Soviet spokesmen that a

[20]UN, General Assembly, First Committee, *Official Records* (13th Session), p. 3.
[21]*Ibid.*, p. 4.

cessation of nuclear tests would be a first important step "towards the total prohibition of atomic and hydrogen weapons," called upon all states to halt nuclear tests, recommended that the nuclear powers "enter into negotiations with a view to the conclusion of an appropriate agreement between them," and called upon all states "to accede to that agreement."[22] Since the draft resolution made no mention of controls, it could be regarded—like the Western statements of August 22—as a retrogression from an earlier position, that is from the position the Soviet Union had taken in 1957 during the London session of the Disarmament Subcommittee and the twelfth Assembly.

There is also another interesting aspect of the Soviet proposal. One of the hoped-for effects of a test ban would be that it would serve to prevent the dispersion of nuclear weapons; that it would ease the so-called "nth country problem." Concern about this problem was probably one of the motivations for Soviet policy on nuclear weapons testing. To the extent that such a brief draft could provide an indication of the USSR's attitude, it seemed to imply that the rest of the world should go along with whatever the three nuclear powers decided regarding a test ban.

The Indian resolution also called for an immediate suspension of the testing of nuclear weapons.[23] However, the cessation was envisaged as a transitional step "pending an agreement at the forthcoming conference among the States concerned in respect to the technical arrangements considered necessary to ensure the observance of the discontinuance of such tests." The "nth country problem" was handled by requesting the participants in the Geneva negotiations to report back to the General Assembly so that it could take steps to extend the agreement to all other states, which meanwhile were requested not to test.

Since both resolutions called for an immediate and essentially unconditional cessation of tests, they were unacceptable to the Western powers. Therefore, on October 10 the United States together with sixteen other countries—all of which were involved in NATO, SEATO, ANZUS, or OAS—tabled an alternative proposal.[24] It first urged the parties to the Geneva negotiations to "make every effort to reach an early agreement on the suspension

[22]UN Documents A/L. 247 and A/C. 1/L. 203 and Corr. 1 and Rev. 1.
[23]UN Documents A/L. 246 and A/C. 1/L. 202.
[24]UN Document A/C. 1/L. 205.

of nuclear tests under effective international control." Then, perhaps as a concession to the other side, and certainly as a concession to the pressure of world opinion, it urged the parties to the negotiations not to test nuclear weapons *while the negotiations were in progress.* This could involve a longer suspension than had been envisaged in President Eisenhower's August 22 statements, but it was not as extensive a commitment as one not to test "pending an agreement," the formulation embodied in the Indian proposal. The seventeen-power resolution also called attention to the importance of the forthcoming technical conference on surprise attack. It lauded the effectiveness of the technical approach to negotiations and expressed the hope that it would contribute to the creation of "a balanced and effectively controlled world-wide system of disarmament." The resolution provided that the UN should render assistance to the Geneva negotiations and asked the parties to the negotiations to keep the world organization informed. Interestingly, the draft resolution contained no provision relating to the "nth country problem."

There were two major attempts during the course of the Political Committee's consideration of these matters to discover some compromise which might lead to a unanimous decision. India, in company with thirteen other countries—including Pakistan, which was also a sponsor of the seventeen-power resolution—submitted a modified version of its resolution.[25] The principal changes were to urge a cessation of nuclear weapons tests "until agreement is reached," rather than pending an agreement, and to insert mention of controls. Even as modified, however, the resolution was unacceptable to the United States and the United Kingdom.

France also opposed the Indian resolution for the same reasons motivating the two Western nuclear powers as well as for other reasons, the most important of which concerned the resolution's treatment of the "nth country problem." French delegate Jules Moch stated that France would only agree to discontinue its nuclear weapons development program if "the 'atomic powers' should immediately cease to increase and begin to reduce their stockpiles under international control."[26] Perhaps the French attitude explains

[25]UN Document A/C. 1/L. 202/Rev. 1.
[26]UN, General Assembly, First Committee, *Official Records* (13th Session), p. 63.

why the seventeen-power resolution skirted this problem. Significantly, France was not one of the seventeen sponsoring powers, and when that resolution was put to the vote, France abstained.

Austria, Japan, and Sweden offered the other compromise proposal.[27] Their draft resolution merely expressed the hope that the Geneva negotiations would be successful, asked the parties to the negotiations to report whatever agreement might result from the negotiations to the Assembly, and asked the Secretary General to provide such assistance as the Geneva conference might request.

After a long procedural wrangle about the order in which the resolutions should be voted, it was decided (45-25 with 11 abstentions) to give priority to the seventeen-power proposal reflecting the Western view, which was adopted by a vote of 49 to 9 with 11 abstentions. Only the Soviet bloc opposed the resolution. The compromise proposal submitted by Austria, Japan, and Sweden was voted on immediately thereafter and adopted by a vote of 52 to 9 with 10 abstentions. Only the first operative paragraph of the revised Indian resolution was voted on, and it was rejected 36 to 26, with 19 abstentions. The remainder of the proposal was withdrawn, as was the entire Soviet proposal. In the plenary session the seventeen-power resolution was adopted 49 to 9 with 22 abstentions, and the resolution submitted by Austria, Japan, and Sweden was approved 55 to 9, with 12 abstentions.[28] The revised Indian proposal, which was reintroduced, was rejected, 27 to 41, with 13 abstentions.[29]

The other draft resolution relating to nuclear testing which the General Assembly considered dealt solely with the dispersion of nuclear weapons capability.[30] It was proposed by Ireland. After asserting that such a dispersion would aggravate international tension and make it more difficult to attain general disarmament, the resolution provided for the creation of an *ad hoc* committee to study the dangers inherent in this course and to recommend appropriate measures for averting these dangers. Only the paragraph containing the assertion was put to a vote, and it was adopted 37 to 0, with 44

[27]UN Document A/C. 1/L. 213.
[28]UN, General Assembly Resolutions 1252 A and B (XIII).
[29]UN, General Assembly, Plenary Meetings, *Official Records* (13th Session), p. 430.
[30]UN Document A/C. 1/L. 206.

abstentions, including France, the United Kingdom, and the United States. After this vote, the resolution was withdrawn.

In addition to the resolutions relating to nuclear testing, three other resolutions concerning arms control and disarmament were considered by the Assembly. One of these was a Soviet proposal which recommended that France, the USSR, the United Kingdom, and the United States should reduce their military budgets by from ten to fifteen percent and devote some part of the savings to economic development projects.[31] This proposal was rejected in the Political Committee by a vote of 10 to 39, with 32 abstentions. The other two resolutions were both sponsored by India and Yugoslavia. One gave the Assembly's blessing to the forthcoming technical talks concerning surprise attack.[32] The other provided for the reconstitution of the Disarmament Commission so that it would include all UN Member States.[33] Both resolutions were adopted without opposition; there were, however, a few abstentions in each case.

One other issue on the agenda of the thirteenth Assembly had implications for the Geneva negotiations, the Peaceful Use of Outer Space. Whether or not and under what conditions the development of missiles was controlled would have implications for the control or development of nuclear explosives. It will be recalled that the USSR requested the inclusion of an agenda item on this subject as early as March 1958. However, at that time, and in the original proposal which it submitted to the Assembly, the Soviet Union insisted that the question of a ban on the use of outer space for military purposes must be linked with "the elimination of foreign military bases on the territories of other States, primarily in Europe, the Near and Middle East and North Africa."[34] In other words, the Soviet Union took the position that it would only renounce its head start with respect to the development of ballistic missiles with intercontinental range, if the United States dismantled most of its military bases abroad. There is a striking parallel between the Soviet attitude with respect to the control of missiles, an area of weaponry in which it seemed to be ahead, and the United States attitude

[31] UN Document A/C. 1/L. 204.
[32] UN Document A/C. 1/L. 211.
[33] UN Documents A/C. 1/L. 210 and Rev. 1 and 2.
[34] UN Document A/C. 1/L. 219.

toward the control of nuclear explosives, an area of weaponry in which it held the lead. It is interesting and perhaps significant that the Soviet proposal did not mention bases in Eastern Asia. Perhaps this implied a willingness by the USSR to have American power used to check that of the People's Republic of China in East Asia. In any case, the link between the control of missiles and the elimination of overseas bases was completely unacceptable to the United States and the USSR was fully aware of this.

The Western twenty-power proposal on this issue was modest.[35] It merely called for the creation of an *ad hoc* committee with a broad mandate to explore the question of the peaceful uses of outer space.

Eventually the USSR agreed to drop the condition that work toward the elimination of foreign bases must accompany that concerning limiting the uses of outer space.[36] Nevertheless, the Soviet Union and the United States could not agree on the composition of the *ad hoc* committee; the Soviet Union insisted on parity of representation between East and West, a concept which the United States refused to accept. In the end, the Assembly adopted a revised version of the twenty-power proposal which provided for the creation of an *ad hoc* committee of eighteen—three from the Soviet bloc, twelve affiliated with the Western alliance system, and three neutrals—and the USSR announced that it would refuse to participate in the new body.[37] In view of this refusal, if any work were to be done prior to the next session of the General Assembly in the fall of 1959, when the composition of the *ad hoc* committee could again be reviewed, it would have to be done in the technical conference on measures to prevent a surprise attack. This conference, it should be noted, would be composed—by agreement of all concerned, including the United States—on the basis of parity.

If the thirteenth session of the General Assembly can be regarded as a preliminary round to the Geneva negotiations, the United States and the West emerged with a slight lead. At least the Assembly had been kept from going on record as favoring an unconditional cessation of nuclear testing, and thus prejudging the outcome

[35]UN Document A/C. 1/L. 220.
[36]UN Document A/C. 1/L. 219/Rev. 1.
[37]UN, General Assembly, Plenary Meetings, *Official Records* (13th Session), p. 616.

of the Geneva talks. On the other hand, the United States had backed a proposal calling for a suspension of nuclear testing as long as the negotiations continued, which was different and went somewhat further than President Eisenhower's statement of August 22. One analyst has argued that this resolution later became an important obstacle to the United States resuming testing after the expiration of the initial twelve months' moratorium.[38]

The origin of the inconsistency between the President's statement and the United States support of the UN resolution is not clear. At least three alternative explanations are possible. The inconsistency may have been a conscious concession, considered and agreed in Washington by the governmental agencies concerned, perhaps in response to pressures from friendly delegations reported to the State Department by the United States delegation to the Assembly.[39] As such it may have been agreed to by the AEC and the Department of Defense without much thought of the consequences because no one expected the negotiations to last as long as a year. Again, the inconsistency may have resulted from a failure in the coordination between the United States delegation on one hand, and the Department of State and other agencies of the government on the other. Finally, it may have reflected an effort by some individuals within the United States government to use the United Nations as an instrument in bureaucratic infighting for the purpose of forcing an adjustment in the American position against the opposition of their colleagues. Since the Department of State contained the highest proportion of individuals favoring an intensive exploration of test ban possibilities, and since it was in the best position to control the American stand in the UN, the last interpretation has a degree of plausibility. Incidents of this sort occur when policy objectives are not clearly articulated and when disagreements among the governmental agencies concerned are glossed over in general policy statements which do not provide sufficient guidance in new

[38]Earl H. Voss, *Nuclear Ambush,* p. 284.

[39]As a matter of law the delegation receives instructions from the President through the Secretary of State. In practice, the instructions are formulated in the Department of State which is also responsible for clearance with other agencies concerned. Not infrequently, the delegation suggests to the Department that its instructions be modified.

tactical developments, such as the situation in the General Assembly, requiring specific and prompt action.

The fact that the discussion of limiting the development of missiles would be confined to the forthcoming technical conference on measures against surprise attack was another significant outcome of the thirteenth session of the Assembly.

Domestic Sparring

As this maneuvering for position was in progress on the international level, there was also considerable sparring on the domestic level within the United States. Although no simple description is adequate, perhaps the best way of briefly describing what happened would be to say that the individuals who questioned the wisdom of a test ban, having been somewhat nonplussed by the events of the summer, sought to bring their views to the fore.

Perhaps the most significant effort of this group was an article by Professor Henry A. Kissinger entitled "Nuclear Testing and the Problem of Peace," which appeared in the October 1958 issue of *Foreign Affairs*. It was the lead article, and that issue of the magazine was published in late September, coincidentally with the opening of the thirteenth session of the General Assembly. During the debate in the First Committee, Soviet bloc delegates cited the article as proof that the United States was not really interested in a test ban.[40] Similar Soviet attempts to impugn American motives on the basis of citations from the public debate became a common feature of the Geneva negotiations. Doubtlessly, this was a negotiating and propaganda device. However, it may also have been more than that. In the early fall of 1958, any shrewd analysis of the American position would have to take account of the views which Mr. Kissinger expressed. On the basis of his book, *Nuclear Weapons and Foreign Policy,* published in 1957, he was a widely respected authority, and it was clear that his views would receive at least a respectful if not a sympathetic hearing by a number of influential people within and outside of the government.

Mr. Kissinger asserted that when the Conference of Experts had concluded that it was technically feasible to detect nuclear weapon tests, the United States had been forced "to make a critical

[40]UN, General Assembly, First Committee, *Official Records* (13th Session), pp. 16, 20 and 34.

policy decision, although only its technical aspects had been fully
explored."[41] He then went on to question whether a complete suspension of nuclear testing was desirable. He argued that the United
States "should deal with the health hazard by ending tests which
produce appreciable fallout," but that it "should agree to a complete ban only as part of a general disarmament agreement which
includes conventional weapons." He described the technical difficulties and uncertainties which were involved in detecting and identifying nuclear explosions and pointed out that these would be
compounded in the case of a closed society, such as the USSR. He
also illustrated how difficult it might be to obtain credible evidence
of a violation of a test ban agreement and raised the fundamental
question of what action the United States could and would take
if a violation occurred, a problem which was unresolved when the
American delegation went to Geneva and which was to plague
American representatives in the Geneva negotiations. He raised the
possibility that the Soviet Union "might use a temporary cessation
to prepare tests of superior weapons," an interesting thought which
raised serious questions about the wisdom of accepting a moratorium
before a treaty was signed. His basic arguments, however, concerned
the wisdom of a test ban agreement from the point of view of
American military policy. He made the point that a ban on nuclear
testing might well lead to a prohibition of the use of nuclear weapons
and argued that unless the United States and the West generally
were willing to increase substantially their conventional forces (or
unless Soviet bloc conventional forces were decreased), such a prohibition would cripple the defenses of the West. He maintained that
advances in the development of nuclear weapons would benefit the
West. Finally, Mr. Kissinger analyzed the strategic problems which
confronted NATO and suggested that they could be solved through
the development of a NATO nuclear striking force. As a policy for
the Geneva negotiations, Mr. Kissinger suggested that the United
States:

> . . . should invite the Soviet Union to join a U.N. commit-
> tee which would immediately set a maximum dosage of
> permissible fall-out from testing well below the level

[41]Henry A. Kissinger, "Nuclear Testing and the Problem of Peace,"
Foreign Affairs, Vol. XXXVII, No. 1 (October 1958), pp. 1-18, at 2.

brought about by recent tests. The U.N. committee should then assign a quota to the United States and its allies and another to the Soviet bloc on a 50 - 50 basis. (Since most of the potential 'fourth' Powers are in the West, this would be a considerable concession to the U.S.S.R.) For two years all Powers would agree to register with the U.N. all tests which involve fall-out and both sides would agree not to exceed their quota. During those two years the quota would be progressively reduced, ultimately to zero. Afterwards, unless there were by then a general disarmament agreement, nations would remain free to conduct surface tests of 'clean' weapons, underground tests and tests in outer space, so long as they did not cause fall-out. Technical experts from both sides would agree on an adequate inspection system, which would be relatively simple.[42]

It is impossible to state the extent to which Mr. Kissinger's article reflected or influenced the views of individuals in responsible positions; certainly the initial American position in the Geneva negotiations bore little resemblance to his recommendations. However, his article was a persuasive statement of the doubts which some felt about the wisdom of a comprehensive test ban as a single measure of arms control or disarmament. It served as a rallying point for individuals who shared these concerns. Thus the article was both a symbol of the fact that the argument within the United States about the course of American policy concerning this issue was far from settled and also an instrument in this continuing battle.

The Surprise Attack Conference

Even though chronologically it occurred after the Geneva negotiations opened, the technical conference on surprise attack—formally known as "The Conference of Experts for the Study of Possible Measures Which Might Be Helpful in Preventing Surprise Attack"—which met from November 10 to December 18, 1958, must also be viewed as an element in the background of the test ban negotiations. The Conference recessed after six weeks with no concrete achievements mainly because the two sides failed to agree on its purposes.[43] The United States sought to discuss methods of con-

---

[42]*Ibid.,* p. 16.

[43]For a more extensive analysis of the technical conference on surprise attack see: Bernhard G. Bechhoefer, *Postwar Negotiations for Arms Control,* pp. 464-88. See also the report of the Conference: UN Document A/4078.

trolling missiles, long-range aircraft, tactical aircraft, ground forces, missile-launching submarines, other naval forces, and other possible instruments of surprise attack, and in that order. The USSR, on the other hand, sought to discuss such matters as the creation of zones of inspection and the reduction of military forces in Europe, including the denuclearization of Germany. The USSR refused to discuss the items which the United States raised on the ground that such discussion would involve divulging secret information which would be useful to the West without giving the Soviet Union any compensating advantages in return. In addition, Soviet delegates said that the USSR would not agree to discuss the establishment of controls on missiles until nuclear weapons had been banned. The American delegates, in contrast, who viewed this conference as another Conference of Experts, refused to discuss the matters raised by the USSR on the ground that they involved "political" issues not appropriate for consideration in a technical conference.

In essence, the two sides were concerned about different problems. So far as American policy in the Geneva test ban negotiations was concerned, the first essential implication of this denouement was that the USSR probably would not negotiate for controls on missiles—on means of delivery of nuclear weapons—except in the context of a board agreement covering several measures of arms control or disarmament. In other words, the concession which the USSR made on this point at the thirteenth session of the General Assembly would not hold up in a more concrete negotiating situation than the Assembly, and the USSR still insisted on maintaining a link between controlling missiles and other measures of arms control. A second implication was the underscoring of the USSR's concern about the possibility of the German Federal Republic's obtaining access to nuclear weapons. Putting it in a different way, the conference emphasized that the USSR was concerned about a very specific "nth country problem."

The Opening Atmosphere

Despite the optimistic expectations arising from the agreement at the Conference of Experts, the real setting for the Geneva Conference was still the unrelieved Cold War atmosphere of deep distrust and mutual suspicion in which the motives of the other side were constantly questioned and scrutinized, with every doubt invariably resolved against rather than in favour of the other side's good faith. Despite the generally recognized dangers of a nuclear catastrophe, the atmosphere was clearly not conducive to decisions involving the risks entailed in an immediate diminution of national power, in return for longer range benefits conditioned more or less on the continuing good faith of the other side. On entering the negotiations, the Soviet Union appeared to aim at obtaining an immediate, permanent, and far-reaching commitment from the West, with minimum control machinery. The United States, while apparently willing to give a qualified commitment, demanded guarantees against evasion which would lift the "iron curtain" substantially and which could not be frustrated unilaterally, and perhaps also further measures of arms control. Both sides appeared to question each other's sincerity in desiring to give any genuine commitment with respect to a test ban. The Soviet Union sought to find confirmation of its suspicions in the open public debate continuing in the United States on the wisdom of the test ban; the Western suspicions on the other hand fed on the unrestrained resort to propaganda by the Soviet Union's indiscriminately seeking to generate pressures on the West. As the negotiations opened, this pervading atmosphere made it exceedingly difficult for the two sides to cut through the underbrush of tactical and propaganda positions developed in the preliminary sparring and to start real negotiations. All in all, the setting was not auspicious.

III

The Initial Phase of the Geneva Negotiations

The Selection and Preparation of the American Delegation
As soon as the USSR agreed in its note of August 30 that negotiations concerning a test ban agreement should begin on October 31, and while the preconference maneuvering for position was in progress, the United States began preparations for the opening of the talks. The first step was the appointment of a delegation. James J. Wadsworth was chosen as the U.S. representative, with the personal rank of Ambassador. Prior to 1953, he had been engaged in the management of various business enterprises and had held a variety of public offices, including membership in the New York State Assembly from 1931 to 1941. When the new adminis-

tration took over in 1953, President Eisenhower appointed Mr. Wadsworth, a Republican, to the office of deputy representative of the United States to the United Nations with the rank of Ambassador. In this capacity he had participated in various negotiations involving arms control and disarmament and nuclear energy. However, by self-admission, he was not in any sense a technical expert in the subject matter of the test ban negotiations. In fact, during the course of the conference he sometimes emphasized that he did not understand the technical intricacies which were involved. Ambassador Wadsworth's greatest strength was his skill in advocacy and his personal relationships. Robert F. Bacher, a member of the President's Science Advisory Committee and one of the Western delegates at the Conference of Experts, was chosen as his deputy. In addition, the American delegation included: senior advisors from the Department of State, the Department of Defense, and the Atomic Energy Commission; two Congressional advisors, Senator Albert Gore, with Senator Hubert H. Humphrey as his alternate (both Democrats); Senator Bourke B. Hickenlooper (Republican); and a number of special advisors.[44]

Unlike the Conference of Experts, which consisted of Eastern and Western panels, the Geneva negotiations would be comprised of delegations from the three nuclear powers, the USSR, the United Kingdom, and the United States. In practice, however, as the Soviet representatives constantly pointed out, there were only two sides. The two Western delegations hardly ever differed in the public sessions of the Geneva talks. The principal British delegate was David Ormsby-Gore, the Minister of State for Foreign Affairs. He

[44]The advisers to the American delegation were: Charles C. Stelle, Department of State; Alfonzo P. Fox, Lt. Gen., USA (retired), Deputy Assistant Secretary of Defense for International Security Affairs; George M. Kavanaugh, Atomic Energy Commission; all titled senior advisers; and Vincent Baker, Department of State; Robert G. Baraz, Department of State; Stephen Benedict, USIA; Hans Bethe, PSAC; Darcey Brent, Department of State; Harold Brown, Atomic Energy Commission; Charles E. Collett, Col., USAF, Department of Defense; Spurgeon M. Keeny, Jr., Office of the Special Assistant to the President for Science and Technology; Richard Latter, RAND Corporation; Doyle L. Northrup, Department of Defense; David H. Popper, American Consulate General, Geneva; Luther Reid, Department of State; Malcolm Toon, Department of State; Paul Toussaint, Department of State; Henry S. Villard, American Consulate General, Geneva; and Secretary of the Delegation, Virgil L. Moore, American Consulate General, Geneva.

had been a delegate at the 1957 London session of the UN Sub-committee of the Disarmament Commission. The British delegation included several others from the Foreign Office, but interestingly no ranking scientists or high level officials from the Atomic Energy Authority or the Ministry of Defense.

As has already been mentioned, Ambassador Semen K. Tsarapkin was appointed as the chief Soviet delegate.[45] Yevgeni K. Fedorov was his principal technical assistant. Dr. Fedorov had been the Chairman of the Eastern panel at the Conference of Experts and Mr. Tsarapkin had been a member of the panel. The Soviet delegation also included additional scientists and other diplomats who had had previous experience in disarmament negotiations. The composition of the Soviet delegation reflected a consistent Soviet policy of generally continuing to use the same diplomatic and scientific personnel in disarmament negotiations. This policy has facilitated continuity and has avoided the laborious process of "educating" new persons. The American practice, followed by both the Republican and Democratic administrations, has been in striking contrast: new personalities, frequently lacking any related knowledge or experience, have been regularly placed in responsible negotiating or policy-making positions requiring almost instant action.

In the relatively short time available after its appointment, the American delegation and other officials prepared a position paper which ultimately was approved by the Committee of Principals. This paper, which was about ten pages in length, reiterated the basic elements of the August 22 statement, which became the core of the American negotiating position. The paper outlined the major issues which could be anticipated and formulated an American position on each of these. It was in no sense a draft treaty. Many issues were covered only generally and some hardly at all. The progress in other areas of arms control that would be required if the test moratorium were to be extended was not defined, any more than in the President's statement of August 22. A variety of technical problems were not worked out. Interestingly, the position paper suggested that the United States might, at some appropriate stage in the negotiations, introduce the concept that the treaty should only cover explosions above a certain yield level. In pre-

[45]See *supra* p. 57.

paring the paper, the scientists and the Department of State personnel tended to work separately on different problems and without a great deal of interchange.

Whether or not the position paper constituted adequate preparation is a difficult question, and one which can be examined better at a later stage, after the actual negotiations have been reviewed. It is necessary though at this point to consider why the preparations were not more extensive. Partly, it was again a matter of time. Less than two months elapsed between the time that the delegation was appointed and the time that they had to depart for Geneva. In addition, the lack of detail in the position paper was partly a matter of tactics; it was thought that the American position should be developed in the context of the Soviet position as expressed in the negotiations, and in any case there was the general maxim of not displaying one's hand too early in the game. Further, the nature of the American preparation was related to the interim sparring that went on in this period. Since it takes two to reach an agreement, the seriousness with which one views one's task is partly a function of one's perception of the seriousness of the opposite party. Viewing the course of events, an American justifiably could have some reservations about Soviet intentions. Finally, it must be said that American preparation was not more advanced because certain key officials were unwilling to do more and, above all, because it would have been difficult to get agreement in the Committee of Principals on a more precise document. The cleavages concerning the wisdom of various courses among the individuals and agencies represented on the Committee were too great to allow more than an agreement on broad and rather vague principles. Of course, these difficulties could have been resolved by directive from the President, but they were not.

Opening Controversies

As has already been mentioned, there was also something less than full agreement between East and West on the objective of the Geneva negotiations. The debate about this continued until the last hour. The final note on the subject was sent from the Soviet Foreign Ministry to the American Embassy and face to face controversy occurred the moment the conference opened.

It took an informal, off-the-record meeting lasting three hours, on Saturday, November 1, 1958, to achieve agreement on the title of the conference. Even after that the parties disputed the meaning of the title, "The Conference on the Discontinuance of Nuclear Weapon Tests." The United States held that discontinuance meant "suspension" while the Soviet Union interpreted it as meaning essentially "cessation."[46] There was more to the dispute than mere semantics, a basic issue was at stake, the question of whether a test cessation would or would not be permanent and unconditional, and both sides sought to have the title reflect their position.

There were also other procedural differences at an early stage. The USSR wanted the meetings to be open, but ultimately agreed to the Western proposal that they should be closed.[47] The Soviet Union also suggested that the Conference should grant hearings to representatives from nongovernmental organizations.[48] Mr. Tsarapkin advanced this as a general suggestion and made a specific proposal that the representatives from the Committee for a Sane Nuclear Policy—an international group with membership in several Western countries which strongly opposed the testing of nuclear weapons—should be heard. The Western powers refused to accept the Soviet proposal, arguing that representatives of nongovernmental organizations could make their views known to the various delegations separately.

Through both proposals the Soviet Union sought to use worldwide public pressure against the testing of nuclear weapons as a way of influencing the Western position in the negotiations. Although the Conference decided not to grant hearings to these representatives the Soviet delegation felt free not only to talk to them but—despite the agreed procedure—to hold formal press conferences as well, obviously in order further to stimulate public pressures. In practice, even though the Soviet Union accepted the Western position that the Conference should be private—that is, that attendance should be limited to the representatives of the three nuclear powers and the Secretary General of the United Nations, that the records of the meetings should not be published until the participating states agreed, and that only brief communiques should

[46]GEN/DNT/PV. 2, pp. 3-4.
[47]GEN/DNT/PV. 1, p. 8.
[48]GEN/DNT/PV. 7, p. 3.

be issued—the Soviet Union continued to play for the support of public opinion.

For example, at the first meeting of the Conference the Soviet Union submitted a short draft treaty (which will be analyzed in more detail later) providing for an immediate, permanent and unconditional cessation of nuclear weapons tests.[49] Within a few days, the Soviet delegation to the United Nations gave the text of the proposal to the press, and it was subsequently published in a number of Western papers, although not in Soviet papers. Sharp Western protests in the Conference provoked first a defense of the action by Mr. Tsarapkin, and then the interesting statement, made, as he put it, purely of his "own volition, that the Soviet delegation has not handed the text of the draft agreement to anyone."[50] Thus, despite an action for which his government could be held accountable, he sought to safeguard his own personal reputation with his negotiating partners.

Subsequently, the Western delegations also sought to rally public opinion to their side, and thereby to buttress their position in the Conference. In fact, Western techniques may even have been somewhat more sophisticated, leaks to the press were made with considerably more subtlety. Two points, however, must be made. The first is that the USSR initiated the practice, and in a most blatant fashion. The second is that the play for public opinion was necessarily confined almost entirely to efforts to influence opinion in Western and uncommitted countries. Because of the rigid controls of the press in communist countries, their citizens could read only what their governments approved. Some Western radio broadcasts may have reached citizens of these countries, but the effects were clearly negligible. Thus, although both sides had a more or less equal opportunity to influence people in uncommitted areas, the battle for "home opinion" was quite unequal. Moreover, the principal Soviet policy-makers needed to be concerned about the "home opinion" much less than the Western governments. The USSR could seek to undermine the strength of the Western delegations, while the West did not have the same opportunity. For the West, this part of the battle had to be defined principally in terms of

49GEN/DNT/1.
50GEN/DNT/7, p. 10.

countering Soviet efforts. In negotiations involving an issue charged with as many emotional implications as that of nuclear testing, this difference was quite important.

Continued Soviet Testing of Nuclear Weapons

Although these Soviet efforts to play upon public opinion in the opening stages of the Geneva negotiations may have put the Western powers under some constraint, another Soviet action was even more bothersome to them. On October 30, the Soviet Foreign Ministry issued a statement on the "Question of the Cessation of Nuclear Tests," which was transmitted to the Secretary General of the United Nations the following day, the day that the Geneva Conference opened.[51] The statement asserted, as Foreign Minister Gromyko had done previously, that because of the continued testing of nuclear weapons by the Western powers after the USSR had unilaterally renounced further testing on March 31, and because of the unacceptable nature of the Western proposal for a one-year suspension of further tests, the USSR had the right to continue testing until it had completed as many experiments as the United States and the United Kingdom combined had undertaken since March 31. The statement went on to say:

> This is just the line of action the Soviet Government will pursue, in its concern for the security of the Soviet people, so long as the Governments of the United States and the United Kingdom will persist in wrecking agreement and raising repeated obstacles to an agreement on the immediate stopping of the tests of atomic and hydrogen weapons for all time.

On November 7, the United States Atomic Energy Commission announced that the USSR had detonated two "relatively low-yield" devices in Siberia on November 1 and November 3; that is, after the Geneva negotiations had opened. The USSR's previous shots that fall had been conducted at a different proving ground. In addition, the November shots were at a different height from the immediately preceding series. The new shots seemed to be tests of

[51]UN Document A/3973.
[52]See Richard P. Stebbins, *The United States in World Affairs, 1958,* p. 78.

relatively unsophisticated weapons.[52] They may well have been planned principally for their psychological effect.

Immediately after the AEC's announcement, President Eisenhower issued a statement in which he said that although the Soviet action relieved the United States of its unilateral obligation, under his proposal of August 22, not to conduct further tests, it would continue the suspension "for the time being," and he "understood that the United Kingdom would also."

The Western delegations also raised the issue of the Soviet tests in the Geneva Conference on November 7. Although Mr. Tsarapkin replied immediately, over two weeks later, on November 29, he read a formal declaration, which probably should be considered the USSR's official reply.[53] The declaration essentially restated the October 30 statement of the Soviet Foreign Ministry. It asserted the right of the USSR to continue testing, and then said: "This is exactly what the Soviet Government is doing, since it is concerned about its country's security." However, after November 7, 1958, neither side announced a nuclear explosion on Soviet territory, until the USSR publicly abrogated the moratorium in the fall of 1961, and there is no publicly available evidence that the Soviet Union conducted tests during this period.[54]

There are several unanswered questions concerning the episode. For example, why did the Soviet Union not announce the tests, or why did the United States wait until November 7 to make its announcement? Were the two shots attempts to test the efficiency of the Western national detection systems? The most plausible interpretation seems to be that the Soviet action was a warning that the USSR would not be bound by any cut-off date unilaterally proclaimed by the West and also an attempt to bully the Western governments into agreeing to the Soviet version of a test ban through playing on Western anxieties concerning the relative state of weapons development and on the widespread public fear of the consequences

---

[53]GEN/DNT/15, pp. 3-11.

[54]Earl H. Voss, however, maintains that "the Defense Department finally recognized that clandestine testing probably had been occurring in the Soviet Union." (*Nuclear Ambush,* p. 512.) It is difficult to know how to evaluate his conclusion. It seems clear that some suspicious seismic signals were recorded during this period, but these obviously did not constitute incontrovertible evidence of clandestine nuclear detonations.

of further testing. If this was the Soviet goal, the action did not succeed. Nor did it result, on the other hand, in widespread public condemnation of the USSR for testing after the opening of the Conference.

The Controversy Concerning the Agenda

The basic conflict between the two sides manifested itself in the controversy over the agenda of the Geneva Conference. The dispute about the agenda began during the opening session and continued to occupy the Conference for three weeks. Finally, on November 21, the Conference implicitly dropped the idea of attempting to reach agreement on an agenda, and launched into a substantive discussion without any formal agenda.

In reality, the discussion on the agenda was a substantive discussion, for it involved attempts on both sides to influence the outcome under the guise of settling mere procedural issues. The essential issue at stake was whether the discussion of a control organization would precede, accompany or follow the conclusion of an agreement on the cessation of nuclear weapons tests. The Soviet proposal—mirroring those that it had advanced since the very first post-Second World War negotiations on arms control and disarmament—was that the first item on the agenda should be "Conclusion of an agreement on the cessation, by States possessing atomic and hydrogen weapons, of tests with such weapons."[55] After that, according to the Soviet proposal, the Conference would approve provisions concerning the control organization to monitor such an agreement. The Conference would finally prepare a report to be submitted to the participating governments and the Security Council and General Assembly of the United Nations. In the Western view—again resembling Western reactions in the past—such an agenda could well result in an unmonitored test ban, since the obligation not to test would be adopted prior to agreement on the control system. In any case, the Soviet agenda would have the effect of making it difficult to condition the cessation of testing on the establishment and effective operation of a control system and on progress in other areas of arms control or disarmament.

In the agenda proposed by the United States, the order of the first two items was reversed, and, in addition, the agreement on the

[55]GEN/DNT/PV. 2, p. 5.

"discontinuance of nuclear weapons tests" would not be adopted until the Conference had decided on interim measures to bring the agreement and control system into operation.[56] Mr. Tsarapkin initially took the attitude that to proceed in this fashion would be "tantamount to talking about pointless matters, since it is proposed to create a control system before any agreement is reached about what is to be controlled."[57] He added that the nature of the control system would depend on the nature of the agreement concerning the cessation of the tests, and then asserted that a one-year moratorium would be an insufficient period of time even to establish a control system. He argued that the conditional moratorium proposed in President Eisenhower's August 22 statement was a way of creating loopholes so that the Western powers could resume their testing programs.

Both sides offered revised versions of their proposals.[58] The revisions were all in the direction of formulations which would allow simultaneous discussion of the nature of the agreement and the nature of the control system, although the Soviet proposals were always somewhat ambiguous in this regard. In the end, however, once the quest for an agenda was abandoned, this was in fact the procedure which the Conference followed. In terms of distance from opening positions, ignoring the question of whether or not these were justifiable, the outcome represented probably a greater concession on the part of the USSR than on the part of the West.

The Initial Soviet Proposal

The same issues that were involved in the dispute about the agenda arose in the discussion of the draft treaty which the Soviet Union tabled during the opening session of the Conference. The proposal was both brief and simple. Its provisions were:

> The Government of the Union of Soviet Socialist Republics, the Government of the United Kingdom of Great Britain and Northern Ireland and the Government of the United States of America,
> Pursuing the aim of putting a check to the nuclear

[56]*Ibid.*, p. 11.
[57]*Ibid.*, p. 19.
[58]See GEN/DNT/PV. 7, pp. 11-12, 17-18; GEN/DNT/PV. 9, pp. 3-4; and, GEN/DNT/PV. 4, p. 4.

armaments race and to the further improvement and creation of new, even more destructive types of these weapons of mass destruction,

Endeavouring to take a practical step towards the 'urgent objective of prohibiting atomic weapons and eliminating them from national armaments,' as indicated by the United Nations,

Being moved by the desire to eliminate forever the danger to the life and health of the population of all countries of the world resulting from experimental explosions of nuclear weapons,

Have decided to conclude for these purposes the present Agreement and have appointed as their plenipotentiaries . . . who, having exchanged their full powers, found in good and due form, have agreed as follows:

Article 1

The Governments of the Union of Soviet Socialist Republics, the United Kingdom of Great Britain and Northern Ireland and the United States of America solemnly undertake not to carry out any tests of atomic and hydrogen weapons of any type from the date on which the present Agreement is signed.

Article 2

The three Governments undertake to promote the assumption by all other States in the world of an undertaking not to carry out tests of atomic and hydrogen weapons of any type.

Article 3

For the purposes of keeping observation on the fulfillment of the undertaking contained in Article 1 of this Agreement, the States Parties to this Agreement shall institute machinery for control.

The above-mentioned control machinery shall have at its disposal a network of control posts set up in accordance with the recommendations of the Geneva Conference of Experts.

Article 4

The Governments of the Union of Soviet Socialist Republics, the United Kingdom of Great Britain and Northern Ireland and the United States of America agree to the installation on their territories and also—in the case of the United States of America and the United Kingdom of Great Britain and Northern Ireland—on the territories of their possessions and trust territories, of an agreed number of control posts.

Article 5
This Agreement shall continue indefinitely and shall enter into force immediately after it has been signed.[59]

This proposal paralleled the Soviet suggestions for the agenda of the Conference, and also the Soviet draft resolution submitted to the thirteenth session of the General Assembly. It also resembled tactics often previously employed by the USSR. It would have resulted in the signatory states signing an agreement not to test nuclear weapons at a point when they had achieved only a vague agreement in principle on the nature of a control system. This draft treaty, in combination with the Soviet actions at the thirteenth session of the General Assembly, and the Soviet proposal with respect to the agenda of the Geneva Conference, clearly made many in the West wary of Soviet intentions and doubtful about the Soviet willingness actually to accept a control system. The Soviet position therefore served to strengthen the fears and also the hand of those within the United States who questioned the wisdom of a test ban. It also made those who favored a test ban somewhat reluctant, at this stage, to press their position with vigor. In the opening days of the Conference, it was difficult to argue that concessions should be made to the Soviet position in the interest and hope of reaching an agreement. Whether the initial Soviet position would have been different if President Eisenhower's statement of August 22 had been more acceptable to the USSR is an interesting subject of speculation. If the Conference of Experts could be interpreted as a concession to the West on the part of the USSR, the August 22 statement contained no compensating concessions to the Soviet position. Whether the statement was wise from the point of view of American security interests is one question. Its impact on the USSR is a separate, although related, question.

The Soviet draft treaty has a number of other interesting aspects. First, no mention was made of other measures of disarmament. Secondly, there was no mention of possible sanctions against

[59]GEN/DNT/1.

a violation of the agreement. Thirdly, it was confined to the three nuclear powers. Fourthly, it attacked the "nth country problem" by fiat, so to speak. The only possible implication of Article 2 would have been that the United States, the United Kingdom and the USSR would have been obligated in some way to see that their allies and neutral states too should agree not to conduct nuclear weapons tests. Immediately, this meant France and China and possibly at a later date, West Germany. Finally, since the "agreement" would have gone into effect immediately upon signature, so far as the United States was concerned, it would have circumvented the requirement of consent by the Senate to ratification. No doubt, the choice of the word "agreement" was intentional.

Although the Western delegates raised most of these points in the debate, their criticisms centered on the vagueness of the provisions concerning control in the draft agreement. The initial Soviet response was that the problem of control had been settled by the Conference of Experts—the report of that Conference contained recommendations for a control system with which the USSR agreed—and that a separate document could be prepared containing the "technical details relating to the control system."[60] The Western powers regarded this as an inadequate reply since it did not provide for the tight connection that they desired to see established between the obligation not to test and the establishment and effective operation of a control system.

On a more fundamental level, the Soviet response raised a problem which was to become increasingly troublesome for the Western powers during the course of the negotiations. The question concerned the status and significance of the report of the Conference of Experts. To what extent was it the basis for the Geneva Conference? Was it the final formulation of the control system, or merely an initial recommendation? To what extent could the system recommended in the report be supplemented or altered without destroying the basis for the negotiations? It will be recalled that the Western panel had refused to discuss a number of issues at the Conference of Experts on the ground that they were political. How should these matters now be treated? In addition, the report of the

[60]GEN/DNT/PV. 2, p. 31.

Conference of Experts contained no recommendations concerning a system for the detection of nuclear explosions at high altitudes. Just as the Western states lacked a clear conception at the outset concerning the function of the Conference of Experts, when the Geneva negotiations began, they were uncertain about the status which they were willing to assign to the report. But while the Soviet proposal raised this problem, it did not do so in a critical fashion, and at this stage not much attention was devoted to the issue.

Senator Gore's Reaction

Senator Albert Gore, who was a member of both the Joint Congressional Committee on Atomic Energy and the Senate Committee on Foreign Relations, and who had been appointed as a Congressional Adviser to the United States delegation, attended the Geneva negotiations for a week during the early period when attention was focused on the controversy about the agenda and on the Soviet draft agreement. The experience left him profoundly disturbed. On his return to Washington in mid-November, he voiced his concerns publicly,[61] and also sent a private memorandum to President Eisenhower. In Senator Gore's view, the USSR's actions relating to the Conference, including the draft agreement which it had tabled, were ample grounds for suspicions of Soviet motives. He doubted that the USSR was actually willing to accept adequate control measures, and he had concluded that the USSR's ambition was merely to weaken United States deterrent strength, and particularly to inhibit the development of tactical nuclear weapons. Moreover, he felt that the USSR was winning widespread public sympathy by its behavior and that the Western position was not being properly understood. The conclusion that the Western position was incapable of receiving widespread public support was implicit in his argument.

He proposed that the West should adopt a new position. In his memorandum to the President he suggested that the President should:

[61]See his signed article in *New York Herald Tribune,* November 16, 1958, and also the accounts in *New York Times,* November 16, 1958, p. 1, and November 18, 1958, p. 1.

. . . announce the unconditional and unilateral cessation of all nuclear tests in the earth's atmosphere for a specific period, say three years, ask similar action by other nuclear powers and suggest that the Geneva Conference proceed immediately to negotiate a treaty among the nuclear powers for a permanent stoppage of atmospheric tests.[62]

His public recommendations were similar. Both publicly and privately he argued that stopping atmospheric tests would eliminate most of the danger of radioactive fallout. He also asserted that existing national detection systems had demonstrated their effectiveness in detecting atmospheric tests. This was a most interesting assertion in view of the official American insistence then and later on an international control system. Of course, at this point the official American position was not addressed to the question of a ban limited to atmospheric tests. After an atmospheric ban was signed, Senator Gore felt that the conference could go on to explore the more complex questions of inspection and control involved in a total ban. Senator Gore thought that shifting the United States position in this way would make it more attractive to public opinion and might possibly lay the groundwork for a successful conference in Geneva, or, at least, mitigate or save the United States from blame for its failure.

It is impossible to know whether Senator Gore's experiences at the Geneva Conference spawned these ideas or whether his experiences merely reinforced views which he had previously held. Certainly the ideas had been expressed before in the debate which had gone on within the United States. However, Senator Gore's expression of his ideas at this point was crucially important, and probably exerted some pressure on the USSR—if it was interested in a comprehensive test ban—to modify the Soviet position so that it would be more acceptable to the West. At the same time, Senator Gore's opinions also cast doubt upon the extent to which the efforts of the American delegation in Geneva would be supported within the United States, and particularly within the Senate, which would have to consent to the ratification of any treaty. Mr. Tsar-

[62]Memorandum for President Eisenhower from Albert Gore, U.S.S., November 19, 1958.

apkin, citing the reports of Senator Gore's statements, raised these doubts in the Geneva Conference.[63]

However, there is no evidence that the Senator's actions provoked a formal reappraisal within the Eisenhower Administration of the American position at this time. The Administration had in a sense considered the possibility of a partial ban when the moratorium decision was made and had rejected it on the ground that stopping tests in only some environments would be misunderstood by public opinion. Moreover, it was thought that the USSR was only interested in a comprehensive test ban. Finally, many in the Department of State strongly wanted the world to experience the establishment and operation of an international control system, and it could be argued that the likelihood of this occurring would be less if Senator Gore's suggestion were adopted. In the same vein, one of the gains that the CIA saw resulting from a test ban was that it would "open up" the USSR.

Just as Americans could be concerned about the USSR's motivations, Soviet analysts could with some justification have reservations about the American position. A casual reading of the popular press would have revealed the deep division within the United States about the wisdom of discontinuing tests of nuclear weapons. In view of this, as was suggested earlier, the August 22 statements of the Western powers could be interpreted as not indicating a serious intention to negotiate a test ban agreement. Senator Gore's statement could have had the effect of reinforcing the reservations which Soviet analysts might have had. Although it is impossible to weigh accurately the advantages and costs which would accrue to each side, it is probably true that the USSR would not benefit as much from a partial test ban as it would from a total cessation of nuclear weapons tests. It was the United States, not the Soviet Union, which expressed great interest in the development of tactical nuclear weapons and in testing such devices underground. Putting it in a different way, American military leaders viewed tactical nuclear weapons as a way of compensating for the USSR's superior strength in conventional forces. Because of this superiority the USSR showed little interest in tactical nuclear weapons. Thus, probably neither the opening position of the Western powers in

[63]GEN/DNT/PV. 10, pp. 8-9.

the Geneva negotiations—that is, the August 22 statements—nor Senator Gore's suggested alternative were very appealing to the USSR, and by mid-November, Soviet leaders, if they had any intrinsic interest in the problem, could—perhaps justifiably—begin to question whether the United States would accept an agreement which would also be acceptable to the USSR. If, on the other hand, the Soviet elite was merely interested in using the negotiations as a device to inhibit the weapons development programs of the West, they could interpret the course of events as indicating a need for some concessions to prolong the discussions.

The Soviet Concession

Since the opening positions of the two sides seemed basically incompatible, the initial task of the negotiators was to see if the gap between the two could be narrowed so that there would at least be a chance of reaching an agreement. In essence, this is what happened in the Geneva Conference during the period from the opening on October 31, 1958, until the second recess began on March 19, 1959, or during the first seventy-two meetings of the Conference.

The process actually began even before the attempt to reach an agreement on an agenda was abandoned. Starting at the fifth meeting, on November 6, the Western representatives began to outline their concept of a control organization. Mr. Ormsby-Gore led off by outlining his conception of the general functions of a control organization.[64] A week later, following the announcement that the USSR had continued testing after October 31, the United States tabled a "Working Paper Outlining a Treaty on Discontinuance of Nuclear Weapon Test Explosions Including Establishment of an Effective Control Organization."[65] As in the August 22 statement, the duration of the obligation not to test nuclear weapons was made conditional on satisfactory progress in the establishment and effective operation of a detection and identification system and on satisfactory progress "in reaching disarmament objectives to be agreed."

Perhaps in response to the description of the control organiza-

[64]GEN/DNT/PV. 5, pp. 4-5.
[65]GEN/DNT/PV. 8, pp. 5-8.

tion which was contained in these working papers and the verbal explanations which accompanied their presentation, or perhaps as a reaction to Senator Gore's statements, or maybe as an independently planned tactic, on November 29 Mr. Tsarapkin read a Declaration in which *inter alia* the Soviet government announced its willingness to have the basic provisions regarding control embodied in the text of the test ban agreement.[66] The Declaration in its entirety was a curious mixture. It started out as a defense of the USSR's continued testing of nuclear weapons, shifted to an attack on the position of the Western powers in the Geneva negotiations, mentioned, almost in passing, the new Soviet willingness to have one document instead of two, and concluded with the submission of a revised version of the draft agreement which the Soviet Union had introduced the day that the negotiations had begun. The most basic change was the insertion of a new article stating that the provisions for a control system would be attached to the agreement as a protocol which would enter into force simultaneously with the agreement. In addition, the final article now stated that the agreement would enter into force immediately after it had been "ratified" by the parties "in accordance with their constitutional procedures." However, the obligation not to test would start on the date that the agreement was signed. Apart from these changes, the draft agreement was identical with the original version. Nevertheless, the basic concession was sufficient to narrow the gap considerably between the Soviet position and that of the West. The USSR had again agreed that control was necessary as a part of any test ban agreement, and it was at least back to its 1957 position concerning this matter. With this concession, the actual negotiations began.

What Parties to the Treaty?

One week later, on December 6, 1958, the Conference adopted Article I of a Treaty on the Discontinuance of Nuclear Weapon Tests. Three more articles were adopted before the Conference adjourned on December 19 for a brief Christmas recess, and another three were adopted before the second recess began on March 19, 1959. These agreed articles dealt in part with noncontroversial for-

[66]GEN/DNT/PV. 15, pp. 3-11.

malities, such as the registration of the treaty with the United Nations. Other parts, however, concerned more basic issues.

Perhaps more important than the number of agreed articles was that both sides began to exchange views in detail on their concepts of a test ban treaty and a control organization, and to narrow their differences. In this respect, the Conference was unlike any other postwar political negotiations on disarmament.

One of the first issues to be explored and settled was whether or not states other than the three nuclear powers would be allowed to adhere to the agreement and to have membership in the control organization. It will be recalled that the Soviet draft treaty mentioned only the three nuclear powers. The Western powers, on the other hand, from the outset envisaged a more inclusive organization. The issue arose concretely first in the discussion of Article I; should it read, "Each of the Parties to this Treaty agrees . . ." as in the American draft,[67] or should it read, "The Governments of the Union of Soviet Socialist Republics, the United Kingdom of Great Britain and Northern Ireland and the United States of America solemnly undertake . . .", as in the Soviet version. Several issues were involved:

1) the degree of security which would result from the system depending on how many and which states were included;

2) methods of handling the "nth country problem";

3) the distribution of political power within the control organization; and

4) the timing of the test ban.

For the Western powers the first, or first two, aspects seemed to be the most important. The problem of China apparently loomed large in their considerations, although the United States delegation, like the American experts at Geneva a few months earlier, was under instructions not to mention the People's Republic of China.[68] Nonetheless, it was widely known that the USSR had conducted explosions—apparently employing TNT—on the territory of the People's Republic of China. Moreover, the ability to detect nuclear

---

[67]GEN/DNT/12.

[68]See the exchange between Senators Gore and Humphrey: U.S. Congress, Senate, Committee on Foreign Relations, Subcommittee on Disarmament, *Hearings: Disarmament and Foreign Policy,* 86th Congress, 2d Session (1959), p. 10.

tests in the USSR depended to some extent upon having control posts on mainland China. The USSR, on the other hand, seemed to be mainly concerned about the last issue, the timing of the test ban. It agreed to the Western phraseology only after it had received assurances from the Western powers that including other states would not cause a delay, that the treaty would enter into force as soon as it had been ratified by the USSR, the United Kingdom, and the United States.[69] Presumably, the original Soviet stand was at least partly motivated by the known opposition of France to a test ban.

The same issues were involved—and were settled in a similar way—in the discussion of Article II, which obligated the parties to the treaty to establish a Control Organization and to cooperate with it.

The "nth country problem" also came up in connection with the Soviet proposal that the treaty should contain an article binding the USSR, the United Kingdom and the United States to "promote the assumption by all other States in the world of an undertaking not to carry out tests of atomic and hydrogen weapons of any type."[70] This had been article two in the original Soviet proposal. Significantly, Mr. Ormsby-Gore's question whether the treaty would be abrogated if, despite the best efforts of the signatory states, another state conducted a nuclear weapons test, went unanswered.[71] The Western powers argued that they could not accept an obligation of this nature. In part, it violated Western concepts of cooperation among sovereign states. Further, the Western powers too were bothered by the position of France. So far as this phase of the Conference was concerned, the "nth country problem" was handled by agreeing to mention it in the preamble, agreeing that the Control Organization should be open to other states and that there should be an article on accession by other states, and agreeing to this rather mild commitment in Article I, "to refrain from causing, encouraging, or in any way participating in, the carrying out of nuclear test explosions anywhere." In essence, what was ruled out was aiding another state to conduct a nuclear test explosion by

[69]GEN/DNT/PV. 20, p. 6.
[70]GEN/DNT/1, p. 25.
[71]See Tsarapkin's vague statement: GEN/DNT/PV. 4, p. 16.

giving it technical or material assistance. The transfer of nuclear weapons for stockpile purposes, an important issue with respect to NATO, was not ruled out.

Differing Concepts Concerning a Control Organization

More profound differences between the two sides developed as they began to discuss the structure and nature of the proposed Control Organization. The Western powers envisaged an organization which would consist of a small executive body or commission composed of the three nuclear powers and a few other states, a conference which would include all parties to the treaty, an internationally staffed detection and identification system including the basic components recommended by the Conference of Experts and certain other features, and a chief executive officer.[72] In the Western view, the Control Organization should, with only a few exceptions, either operate automatically on the basis of pre-established technical criteria or on the basis of some form of majority voting.

The original Soviet concept of the Control Organization was quite different.[73] The detailed proposal which the USSR tabled had no provisions for a conference or a chief executive officer. The central headquarters of the detection and identification system would be staffed on the basis of parity between East and West, and control posts would be manned by the citizens of the territories where they were located, except that there would be one "controller" from the other side. All important decisions would require the agreement of the USSR, the United Kingdom, and the United States.

An even more fundamental difference between the positions of the two sides concerned what action the Control Organization might take in the event of a suspected violation. The USSR argued that if one of the three nuclear powers—and implicitly any state—refused to allow an investigation of a suspicious event, the only conceivable action would be for the Commission to report this disagreement to the states which were parties to the treaty and to the Security Council of the United Nations.[74] Although the Western

---

[72]See GEN/DNT/PV. 5, pp. 4-5; GEN/DNT/PV. 8, pp. 5-8; GEN/-DNT/PV. 13, pp. 4-5; GEN/DNT/PV. 17, pp. 5-9; GEN/DNT/13; and GEN/DNT/22.

[73]GEN/DNT/19, pp. 16-18.

[74]See GEN/DNT/PV. 13, pp. 19-20; and, GEN/DNT/PV. 24, pp. 6-7.

delegates were always somewhat vague about their expectations, they made it clear that the Soviet position was unacceptable, and implicitly seemed to demand that the Control Organization should be able to obtain incontrovertible evidence that a nuclear explosion had occurred.[75] In the case of a suspected underground explosion, this would have meant an on-site inspection, the only means of obtaining definite proof. The Western position seemed to reflect some uncertainty about the problem.

Taken at face value, the two different conceptions reflected different interests and fears, and paralleled the broad approach of the two sides toward international organization. The West wanted to avoid creating a Control Organization which the East could obstruct and the East wanted to avoid creating an international organization which the West might use against the interests and opposition of the East. In essence, the opening positions of the two sides on these matters were such that they were obviously unacceptable to the other.

Some progress was made, however, prior to the Christmas recess, in reducing the distance between the two positions. After the Western powers had stated several times that the chief executive officer would be responsible to the Commission and would generally act under its directives,[76] and that some decisions of the Commission would require the agreement of the three nuclear powers,[77] the USSR accepted this formulation of Article III, which was suggested by Mr. Ormsby-Gore:

> The Control Organization established under Article 2 of this Treaty shall consist of: a Control Commission, hereinafter referred to as 'the Commission'; a Detection and Identification System, hereinafter referred to as 'the System'; a Chief Executive Officer, hereinafter referred to as 'the Administrator'; and a Conference of Parties to the Treaty, hereinafter referred to as 'the Conference'.[78]

In particular, the USSR sought and received Mr. Ormsby-Gore's assurance that the Administrator could not initiate an on-site in-

[75]See GEN/DNT/PV. 13, p. 12.
[76]See GEN/DNT/PV. 22, pp. 13, 22, and 28; GEN/DNT/PV. 23, pp. 23-24; and GEN/DNT/PV. 24, pp. 31-32.
[77]See GEN/DNT/PV. 21, pp. 5-6.
[78]GEN/DNT/PV. 24, p. 31.

spection of a suspicious but undetermined underground event without a specific directive from the Commission.[79] The Conference also agreed on a text of Article IV, which specified that the Commission should consist of the USSR, the United Kingdom, and the United States as permanent members and four states elected for two-year terms by the Conference.

The most basic differences, however, remained unresolved when the Conference recessed on December 19, 1958, and even some of the apparent agreements were in actuality merely formulations which concealed wide disagreements. For example, even though it was agreed that there should be an Administrator, his powers remained undefined, and although it was agreed that the Commission should consist of seven states, the principles which should govern the selection of the four elected members and the voting procedures of the Commission were not determined.

Differences on Other Issues

There were other differences between East and West, which had been apparent even before the opening of the Geneva negotiations, concerning the link between a test ban treaty and other measures of disarmament and also the duration of the Treaty. Mr. Tsarapkin kept pressing the Western delegates for an indication of what specific measures in other areas of arms control would be required for the continuance of the test moratorium.[80] The Western delegates, however, were only able to say that the specific measures would have to be accepted by the Conference and that eventually they would submit a detailed paper. That was the extent of their instructions. Mr. Tsarapkin also repeatedly made the point that the USSR would only agree to a permanent cessation of nuclear tests, not a temporary and conditional cessation as suggested in the Western proposals.[81]

Even so, as East-West conferences go, the Geneva Conference had an unusual record of achievement when the first recess began on December 19, 1958.

---

[79]See GEN/DNT/PV. 23, pp. 16-20 and 23-24.
[80]GEN/DNT/PV. 4, p. 26; and GEN/DNT/PV. 6, pp. 18, 19.
[81]GEN/DNT/PV. 3, pp. 10, 12, 13; GEN/DNT/PV. 4, p. 9; GEN/-DNT/PV. 10, p. 7; and GEN/DNT/PV. 15, p. 7.

IV

A Major Reverse and Some Lesser Advances

The New Data

When the Conference resumed on January 5, 1959, the American delegation requested that a brief informal meeting should be held immediately prior to the formal session. At that time, Mr. Wadsworth informed Mr. Tsarapkin, and through him the Soviet government, that during the underground tests which had been held in Nevada in October 1958, new data had been obtained which indicated that it would be more difficult to identify underground nuclear explosions than had previously been believed. In other words the conclusions of the Conference of Experts now seemed to be excessively optimistic in the light of further experimental evidence. Specifically, the United States government now believed that:

> a) The method for distinguishing earthquakes from explosions by the direction of first motion is less effective than previously estimated.
>
> b) The number of earthquakes per year equivalent to a given yield is about double that previously estimated.[82]

In practical terms, if the new data were valid, it would mean either that the capability of the system proposed by the Geneva Conference of Experts to detect and identify underground nuclear explosions would not be as great as had been expected—roughly the threshold would be raised from 5 to 20 kilotons—or that to obtain the same capability, a greater number of control stations and on-site inspections would be required. In the informal session Ambassador Wadsworth introduced the information and requested that it be considered. Later, in the formal session, he merely introduced it. That same day, the President's Science Advisory Committee released a public statement which contained similar information, although it had considerably less technical detail.[83] The Department of Defense issued a more detailed release on January 16, 1959.[84]

The implications of this action were devastating. Reflecting on

[82]GEN/DNT/25.
[83]*Documents on Disarmament, 1945–1959*, Vol. II, p. 1335.
[84]Earl H. Voss, *Nuclear Ambush*, pp. 255-56.

his experiences as a negotiator on arms control and disarmament measures in his book published in 1962, James Wadsworth wrote that "it spread a pall over the negotiations from which they never completely recovered."[85] For the opponents of a test ban treaty in the West, the new data provided convincing proof of the wisdom of their position. On the other hand, the Soviet Union could interpret the new data as an indication that the West was now raising the ante in terms of opening up the USSR, and Mr. Tsarapkin charged that the data had been introduced to justify sending ten times as many on-site inspection groups as the Conference of Experts had contemplated. The stark outline in which the new data was presented, and the fact that it was not accompanied by a definite proposal for action allowed all parties to draw whatever inferences they might.

Why then, in the face of these obvious implications, did the United States submit the data in such raw form? Why did it not request an adjournment of the Conference during which the data could be properly evaluated from the technical viewpoint and, what is perhaps even more important, concrete proposals could be elaborated for the necessary modification of the detection and identification system?

There are several answers. In the first place, President Eisenhower's immediate reaction on being informed of the new data (which will be treated in more detail later) was that the United States government must tell the "truth" to its negotiating partners and the American public. Secondly, it would have been impossible to keep the new data secret. Many seismograms yield data for the public domain. Moreover, the scientists and politicians opposing a test ban obviously perceived the value of the new data as powerful ammunition in support of their cause, and they could have leaked it through Congressional or other channels with even more serious consequences on the Geneva Conference.[86] Since past experience had shown that the Administration was not willing or able to control interventions of this sort—and they were encouraged from Congressional quarters—there was little risk involved for the persons concerned. Another and perhaps more important reason for the

[85]James J. Wadsworth, *The Price of Peace* (1962), p. 24.
[86]See Wadsworth's frank statement in this regard GEN/DNT/PV. 50, p. 16.

hasty submission may have been the conclusion reached by several within the Department of State that it would have been impossible to obtain agreement within the government on reasonable proposals to accompany the submission of the new data. Mr. Dulles, who had become increasingly convinced of the advantages of a controlled test ban, although skeptical of Russian motives, was taken aback by the new data. It will be recalled that the American delegation was never given concrete guidance on the threshold problem so that apparently there was no agreed policy on the subject which could now be reviewed in the light of the new knowledge and all other relevant technical and political-military considerations. Under the circumstances, any proposals based on the new data on which an agreement could have been reached among the agencies concerned through regular process of coordination would probably have called for such far-reaching modifications of the scheme developed by the Conference of Experts that their submission in Geneva might well have spelled the doom of any further negotiations. And Mr. Dulles was not prepared to take a strong stand and bring the matter before the President. Hence, the decision to submit the new data in unevaluated form appeared to be the least of several evils.

Viewing it from a slightly different perspective, the new data is a reflection on the rather casual way in which crucial decisions were taken in the United States in the spring and summer of 1958. At that time, as was shown earlier, it was a matter of common knowledge, at least among American scientists, that the conclusions with respect to detection and identification of underground explosions rested on extrapolations from one case. In an environment where there had been just one less case, high altitude, the Conference of Experts had refused to make a recommendation.

In Geneva, during the formal session on January 5 in which the new data was offered, Mr. Wadsworth suggested that the Conference should appoint an *ad hoc* working group of technical experts to discuss the problem of high altitude detection.[87] He recalled the absence in the Report of the Conference of Experts of a recommendation concerning this environment, and asserted that this gap had to be closed. He went on to say that he believed that

[87]GEN/DNT/PV. 29, p. 17.

"good use" could be made of such groups "in getting forward with our negotiations." Mr. Tsarapkin's response was lightning quick:

> Mr. Wadsworth's last remarks with regard to high-altitude explosions . . . only confirm our view that we should not at this Conference depart from the starting point which we have already taken as the basis for our discussion, that is to say, the conclusions worked out by the meeting of experts at Geneva last summer.[88]

Obviously, both men had the problem of the new data in mind. Two days later, Mr. Wadsworth formally proposed that the Conference should convene a technical working group to study the implications of the new data.[89] Mr. Tsarapkin's immediate response was negative.[90] He argued that to convene a technical working group would merely delay the progress of the Conference, that new information could always be discovered, and that political negotiations had to have a fixed basis, in this case the Report of the Conference of Experts. He asserted that after the Control Organization was established, it could take steps to cope with the new data but that in the present form the "preliminary and hastily prepared document" did not call for study. Moreover, he affirmed the belief, often stated by Soviet scientists at the Conference of Experts, that the progress of science would make the process of detection and identification of nuclear explosions easier rather than more difficult.

Roughly, this is where the controversy stood when the second recess began on March 19, 1959. The United States outlined the various alternative ways in which the Conference might attempt to cope with the new data, but its basic proposal continued to be that an *ad hoc* technical working group should be convened.[91] The Soviet Union, on the other hand, continued to deprecate and refuse any consideration of this proposal.

The Darkening Atmosphere

Meanwhile, the atmosphere surrounding the Geneva Conference darkened. Within the United States, domestic opposition to the

[88]*Ibid.*
[89]GEN/DNT/PV. 31, p. 7.
[90]*Ibid.*, pp. 8-13, 22-26.
[91]See GEN/DNT/PV. 52, pp. 4-8.

test ban increased. After the new data was released, various congressmen and administration officials spoke out against a comprehensive test ban as an isolated measure of arms control. Some of these had taken this position from the outset, and they asserted that the new data confirmed the wisdom of their position. Others apparently changed their position on the basis of the new data. And there was silence at the White House.

In Geneva, the speeches became more acrimonious. Both the USSR and the United States issued statements from their national capitals blaming the other for the impasse.[92] While four articles had been adopted in the first twenty-eight meetings of the Conference, none was adopted from the twenty-ninth until the seventy-second, and then, on the last day before the recess, three articles were hastily accepted.[93]

The Conference continued to discuss the various issues relating to the nature of the Control Organization, but the differences between the two positions seemed to be even more implacable than they had been before the Christmas recess.

Dropping the Link

The atmosphere, however, was brightened somewhat when on January 19, 1959, Mr. Wadsworth opened the thirty-seventh session of the Conference by announcing that the United States would "no longer insist that the duration of the treaty be made conditional upon progress in other fields of disarmament."[94] Mr. Ormsby-Gore made a similar statement immediately thereafter. In other words, "the link" had been formally dropped.

Obviously, before this action could occur in Geneva, the Committee of Principals had to agree to new instructions for the American delegation. Certain key Congressmen were also involved in the reformulation of the American position, although the issue was basically decided within the Administration. In this intra-administration struggle, the Department of Defense and the Atomic Energy Commission continued to insist on the wisdom of maintaining "the link." Secretary of State Dulles, in opposition, argued that insistence

---

[92]*Documents on Disarmament, 1945–1959,* Vol. II, pp. 1339-45.
[93]GEN/DNT/PV. 72, *passim.*
[94]GEN/DNT/PV. 37, p. 6.

on the link was muddying the waters, harming the public image of the United States by making it more difficult to prove to public opinion that the Soviet Union was really unwilling to accept adequate control measures—a fact which in his view had been established by Soviet actions since the Conference of Experts and particularly by the nature of Soviet participation in the diplomatic conference thus far. The President decided in Mr. Dulles' favor. Perhaps one reason that AEC and Department of Defense officials did not strenuously object to this decision to "drop the link" and to negotiate for a separate test ban treaty was their feeling that it was unlikely that an adequate treaty could actually be achieved in any event. This could explain the paradox that at a time when the disclosure of the new data had lessened even further the value of a test ban treaty in the eyes of the individuals who had insisted on "the link," those same individuals acquiesced in dropping the link.

As is invariably the case when a controversial issue is considered within the United States government, the debate on the link "radiated" beyond the governmental chambers. The arguments in support of dropping the link, made for internal consumption, minimized the value of the link from the American viewpoint and the import of these arguments was, of course, not lost on the USSR. This made it more difficult for the United States delegation in Geneva to present the abandonment of the link as a real and important Western concession. Nevertheless, after the Western announcement of this concession, the outlook for the negotiations appeared to improve slightly. Two days later, the USSR stated its willingness to allow more than two foreign "controllers" at control posts,[95] and eventually suggested the number of four or five.[96] The Western powers, on their part, developed their concept of an "international staff" so that it allowed the possibility of citizens of countries which were allied with and friendly to the host country serving at control posts there as part of the foreign contingent.[97] In addition, they agreed that the administrative staff would be comprised completely of host country nationals. The differences between the two sides on the composition of the Commission and

[95]GEN/DNT/PV. 39, p. 10.
[96]GEN/DNT/PV. 47, p. 3.
[97]GEN/DNT/PV. 42, pp. 29-31.

on that organ's voting procedures were also narrowed somewhat. But no move was made toward settlement of the basic question of whether or not the Control Organization would be able to take action against the wishes of one of the three nuclear powers. Nor was significant progress made with respect to a variety of other subsidiary issues.

The West Tables an Article on Duration

Throughout this phase of the Conference the Soviet Union constantly brought up the question of the duration of the treaty. Finally, on March 10, 1959, the United States tabled this article:

> This Treaty shall remain in force indefinitely subject to the inherent right of a Party to withdraw and be relieved of obligations hereunder if the provisions of the Treaty and its Annexes, including those providing for the timely installation and effective operation of the control system, are not being fulfilled and observed.[98]

A party would have an "inherent" right to withdraw and be relieved of its obligations (it is not clear whether necessarily with immediate effect with respect to all obligations) if the treaty provisions, including the control system provisions, were not fulfilled, or were violated by another party or presumably also by an organ set up under the treaty. The violations which would give rise to the right to withdraw were not defined; nor was there a provision for an automatic termination of the treaty in case of certain treaty violations. Thus the determination of the existence of the circumstances warranting withdrawal was left to each party but presumably would have to be made in good faith.

In his book, Ambassador Wadsworth viewed this article as a built-in "three-way stretch" girdle of support for the continuation of the treaty. If one of the three nuclear powers parties to the treaty were to refuse cooperation in any way—in the development and maintenance of the control system or in observing other financial, political, or technical provisions of the treaty—either of the other two could withdraw; this right, he argued, would constitute a strong deterrence against any violation at least as long as the continuation

98GEN/DNT/PV. 70, p. 3.

of the treaty was considered in the national interest by all the powers concerned.[99]

The Soviet Union, of course, had already had considerable evidence that the United States did not intend to limit the test cessation to a twelve-month period. At the thirteenth session of the General Assembly, the American delegation had voted for a resolution urging that the moratorium should continue as long as the negotiations continued.[100] And in January 1959, President Eisenhower, in his budget message, pointedly refrained from asking for funds for the conduct of nuclear weapons tests during the fiscal year 1960.[101] However, by tabling the article on duration the United States formally accepted the Soviet position that a test ban treaty should be of indeterminate duration.

Two sessions later, at the last meeting before the Easter recess, the Soviet Union accepted this article. It also accepted an article proposed by the United Kingdom authorizing negotiation of agreements between the Control Organization on one hand and the United Nations and any future disarmament body on the other, and a United States proposal relating to the periodic review of the control system. The former article was a purely formal matter, although it did have implications for the relationship between the Control Organization and the United Nations. The latter article was somewhat more significant in that it provided for a mandatory review of the effectiveness of the system two years after the coming into force of the treaty and the possibility of annual reviews thereafter.[102] In a sense, this provision could be interpreted as a response to the "new data," since it indicated the possibility of changes in the detection and identification system proposed by the Conference of Experts, which was to be embodied in the treaty.

To sum up the outcome of this opening stage of the Geneva Conference, the two sides dropped conditions which were obviously unacceptable to the other. The Western concessions concerning the link with other measures of disarmament and the duration of the treaty could—at least in terms of the negotiations—be regarded as

[99]James J. Wadsworth, *The Price of Peace,* pp. 70-71.
[100]See UN, General Assembly, Plenary Meetings, *Official Records* (13th Session), pp. 421, 430.
[101]*New York Times,* January 20, 1959, pp. 1, 21.
[102]See GEN/DNT/44.

the equivalent of the Soviet willingness to accept a Control Organization and some system of control, and to have one treaty instead of two. On the other hand, when the Conference began its Easter recess on the afternoon of March 19, many basic differences concerning the nature of the Control Organization remained unresolved. Indeed, the progress which had been made in this area since January 5 was almost imperceptible. Moreover, the USSR continued adamantly to oppose the convocation of a technical working group to examine the new data. Whether or not the Conference was on balance nearer to a treaty than it had been at the time of the first recess was debatable. In any case, there were now two broad areas of controversy: one relating to technical data, going to the very basis of the negotiations, and the other relating to the Control Organization. Chapters V through VIII will deal with the former, Chapter IX with the latter.

Chapter V

Formulating A New Western Position

I

The Shifting Technological Base

Although the information which the United States submitted to the Geneva Conference on January 5, 1959, and the statement which the President's Science Advisory Committee released that same day gave some indication of how the progress of science and technology had affected some of the conclusions of the Conference of Experts, they did not portray the full magnitude of the problem. To see the issues from the point of view of the American policy-makers, it is necessary first to consider in detail certain aspects of the United States 1958 nuclear weapon test series which, as was seen earlier, ended on October 30, the day before the opening of the diplomatic negotiations.

Hardtack I and Argus: New Data

For one thing, neither the information submitted to the Conference nor the PSAC statement indicated that the United States now realized that it was possible to test nuclear devices at high altitudes and had some understanding of the consequences of this possibility. During its 1958 test series the United States had detonated five nuclear devices at high altitudes. On August 1 and August 12, 1958, before the conclusion of the Conference of Experts, as a part of the Hardtack I series, two nuclear devices with yields in the megaton range were detonated in the vicinity of Johnston Island in the Pacific Ocean, the first—Teak—at an altitude of nearly fifty miles, and the second—Orange—at an altitude of nearly twenty-seven miles.[1] On August 27 and 30 and September 6, three more

[1] U.S. Department of Defense, *The Effects of Nuclear Weapons, 1962,* pp. 50-52.

145

devices having yields from 1 to 3 kilotons were fired in the South Atlantic at an altitude of about three hundred miles. These three shots were called the Argus Operation. They were not weapons testing shots—but rather experiments designed to provide information on trapping electrically charged particles in the earth's magnetic field—and therefore yielded only a limited amount of data which was relevant for a test ban control system.

These high altitude shots were not made public until March 19, 1959, when an article concerning them appeared in the *New York Times*. Although many scientists who knew about the tests favored announcing them and publishing some of the measurements, Deputy Secretary of Defense Donald A. Quarles expressed disappointment about the leak which had resulted in the story in the *Times*.[2] In the same statement, Mr. Quarles also denied that the tests had any relevance for East-West negotiations then in progress.

In fact, however, the Johnston Island and Argus tests made extremely obvious the need to fill in the gap which was caused by the failure of the Conference of Experts to recommend control measures for high altitudes and outer space. This need was further underscored on January 2, 1959, when the USSR fired "Lunik I," an earth satellite aimed in the direction of the moon, which went into permanent orbit around the sun, becoming the first artificial planet. Consequently, the President's Science Advisory Committee appointed a panel, headed by Professor Wolfgang K. H. Panofsky of Stanford University, to consider what control mechanisms would be required to fill this gap.

The data gained from the high altitude tests also affected the test ban negotiations in another way. They indicated that nuclear explosions at high altitudes might interfere with certain radio and radar frequencies and thus inhibit military communications and warning systems. They also yielded data which indicated that the released neutrons from high altitude blasts could possibly be used to detonate incoming enemy warheads, and thus obviate the need for physical contact by an anti-missile missile. The tests, though, merely raised these possibilities, they did not confirm them. Thus, they created pressures among persons in the military establishment

[2]*New York Times,* March 20, 1959, p. 10.

and scientists interested in weapons development for further testing at high altitudes.

Some have argued that this was the overall effect of the 1958 test series. Writing in 1960 former AEC Commissioner Thomas E. Murray stated:

> Furthermore, the elaborate series of "small" tests which we rushed through at the Nevada Proving Ground in September and October 1958 to beat the moratorium deadline amply testified to the fact that the technology of lower and especially fractional kiloton weapons was still far from being adequately developed . . . the imperative objectives of our test program had not nearly been achieved.[3]

Among other things, the neutron weapon was not developed. However, significant advances were made with respect to certain weapon systems, for example, the Davey Crocket, a tactical nuclear weapon which could be carried by a small vehicle or a man. The extent to which one interpreted the 1958 test series as indicating a need for further testing depended really upon one's estimate of what advances could be made in nuclear weaponry and their utility.

Hardtack II: More New Data

The United States 1958 test series also included eight underground detonations. These shots were fired from September 21 through October 30 in Nevada as a part of the Hardtack II series. Of the eight, only two, the Logan 5-kiloton shot of October 16, 1958, and the Blanca 19-kiloton shot of October 30, 1958—the last shot fired by the United States prior to opening of the test ban negotiations on October 31—yielded sufficient data for meaningful analysis of detection capabilities. However, the Working Paper which the United States submitted to the Geneva Conference on January 5, 1959, also listed the Tamalpais 72-ton shot of October 8, 1958. American scientists used this shot in constructing their scaling law. The memorandum contained technical data only on the two principal shots. The PSAC statement did not contain any technical data. The American public first received the technical data in a Department of Defense press release of January 16.

[3]*Nuclear Policy for War and Peace*, pp. 94-95.

In the West, the intensity of underground disturbances—thus of earthquakes and explosions—is measured on a logarithmic scale, commonly called the Gutenberg-Richter scale. Recorded earthquakes range from −1.50 to 8.50 on this scale. The farther down the scale one goes, that is, the smaller the size of the signal, the more earthquakes there are. The estimate of the intensity of an underground disturbance is arrived at by averaging the signals received at several seismological stations. Because of the process of averaging, and for other reasons, the estimate of an underground disturbance was normally given with the reservation that there may be an error of plus or minus a specific amount which varies inversely with the magnitude on the Gutenberg-Richter scale. At the time of of the Conference of Experts in the summer of 1958, the magnitude of the Rainier 1.7 kiloton shot was believed to be 4.25. Since in the range from 4.1 to 5 the margin of error could be as high as plus or minus .4, the magnitude of the Rainier shot should be understood as 4.25 ± .4. It should also be noted that the first public paper on the Rainier shot estimated its magnitude as 4.6.[4] In calibrating the Blanca and Logan shots it was discovered that the seven seismic stations near the event with adequate equipment which had recorded the Rainier shot gave anomalously large magnitudes, 5.0 to 4.6 respectively. Three stations within the same radius had not recorded Rainier at all, but this fact had been disregarded in the computation of its magnitude. Using seventeen stations, ten of which (including the seven that recorded Rainier) were permanent stations, and seven other specially established temporary stations, the magnitude of the Blanca and Logan shots was estimated to be 4.8 and 4.4 respectively. Extrapolating from this data, American scientists concluded that the magnitude of the Rainier shot had been estimated incorrectly; that it should have been estimated as 4.06 ± .4 rather than 4.25 ± .4. Since seismologists knew that there were several times as many earthquakes of magnitude 4.06 as there were of magnitude 4.25, the new estimate of the Rainier magnitude meant that the problem of distinguishing between earthquakes and underground nuclear explosions would be considerably more difficult than it had been thought to be at the

[4]G. W. Johnson and others, "The Underground Nuclear Detonation of September 19, 1957, Rainier, Operation Plumbbob," (February 4, 1958).

time of the Conference of Experts. Extrapolating and constructing a formula—now on the basis of three points instead of one— American scientists estimated that for any given yield there would be several times as many unidentified events. The implication of this would be that unless the technology of detection could be improved either the threshold of detection would have to be raised or the number of control posts or on-site inspections drastically increased. The President's Science Advisory Committee examined the new estimate of the seismic magnitude of the Rainier shot and approved it. Later, however, some members of PSAC came to feel that the Committee had not exercised its responsibilities with sufficient care and had acted too hastily.

The Blanca and Logan shots also produced smaller signs of first motion than had been anticipated. Consequently, American scientists evaluating the data concluded that:

> . . . the first motion must exceed the background noise of natural unrest of the earth, by at least a factor of 3 to 1 instead of the previous estimate of 2 to 1 if the direction of first motion is to be reliably determined.[5]

PSAC also approved this conclusion. In other words, if a factor of only 2 to 1 were used, which had been the basis on which the Conference of Experts had estimated the probability of detecting first motion, the compression or the upmotion caused by a nuclear explosion might be confused with background noise and only the subsequent swing of the seismogram, the rarefaction or downmotion might be noticed. Interestingly some scientists had always felt that the factor of 2 to 1 was too small.

Baldly, the implication of the new conclusions was that the detection of nuclear explosions deep underground would not be as easy as it had been thought and that the conclusions of the Conference of Experts concerning the size of explosion which could be detected were much too optimistic.

How much the effectiveness of the control system was denigrated by these new conclusions was not clear. The Working Paper which the United States submitted to the Geneva Conference on January 5, 1959, stated that:

[5]U.S. Department of Defense, Press Release, January 16, 1959.

> . . . the annual number of unidentified continental earth-
> quakes equivalent to 5 KT or larger will be greater than
> that previously estimated by a factor of 10 or more.[6]

The statement released by PSAC the same day contained a similar estimate. Thus the conclusion of the Conference of Experts that there would be from 20 to 100 earthquakes which would be indistinguishable on the basis of their seismic signals from nuclear explosions of about 5 kiloton yield, would have to be raised to from 200 to 1,000. However, in testimony before the Senate Subcommittee on Disarmament on January 28, 1959, Dr. Carl Romney, an Air Force seismologist, who had headed the panel which had evaluated both the Hardtack II data and the original Rainier data stated that it was more nearly a factor of 15, and that the number of unidentified events equivalent to a nuclear explosion of 5 kiloton yield would probably be from 700 to 3,000, 100 to 600 of which would occur within the USSR and mainland China.[7]

The evaluations of the data gained in the 1958 test series began to be available in late November 1958 and were analyzed first by government scientists. The last stages of the initial analysis were actually completed shortly after Thanksgiving Day in Geneva and the results of this preliminary analysis were presented to Messrs. Ormsby-Gore and Wadsworth in a one-hour briefing session. At that stage, neither the two diplomats nor the scientists making the presentation felt that the information was very significant. The scientists regarded the new conclusions as being within the realm of experimental error.

This estimate would soon change, however, or at least others would take a different view. The next step in the evaluation was the convocation of a special panel and then the review by PSAC. As the evaluation proceeded, the implications for the test ban negotiations seemed to be increasingly ominous, and it was decided that another special panel should be appointed to consider whether or not there was any way in which the capability of the control system recommended by the Conference of Experts could be improved and hopefully restored to the original estimate. The panel was

[6]GEN/DNT/25.

[7]U.S. Congress, Senate, Committee on Foreign Relations, Subcommittee on Disarmament, *Hearings: Disarmament and Foreign Policy,* 86th Congress, 2d Session (1959), p. 29.

to consider whether or not this could be done, first within the framework of existing technology, and secondly through a program of
research in seismology. On December 28, 1958, the President's
Special Assistant for Science and Technology, James R. Killian,
appointed Lloyd Berkner, the President of Associated Universities,
Inc., as Chairman of the Panel on Seismic Improvement.[8] Although
the Working Paper which the United States submitted to the Geneva
Conference and the PSAC statement mentioned that the data from
the 1958 test series was still being evaluated, neither mentioned
the appointment of the Berkner Panel. The first public mention of
this Panel occurred February 11, 1959.[9]

Decoupling: A New Theory

During this same period another technological development
occurred which would have an even more profound effect on the
course of the Geneva negotiations, the discovery of the decoupling
theory. Edward Teller, who after the death of Ernest O. Lawrence
had become Director of the University of California Radiation
Laboratory at Livermore, had always had grave doubts about the
wisdom of a test ban. He felt that the further development of nuclear weapons would significantly and principally benefit the West.
He also deeply distrusted the Soviet Union. The book, *Our Nuclear
Future,* which he had written with Albert Latter and which was
published in early 1958, contained the following passage:

> If an agreement were made to discontinue the tests, the
> United States would surely keep such an agreement. The
> very social and political structure of our country excludes

[8]The other members of the Panel were Professor Hugo Benioff,
California Institute of Technology; Professor Hans Bethe, Cornell University;
Professor W. Maurice Ewing, Columbia University; Dr. John Gerrard, Texas
Instruments, Inc.; Professor David T. Griggs, University of California at
Los Angeles; Mr. Jack H. Hamilton, The Geotechnical Corporation; Dr.
Julius P. Molnar, Sandia Corporation; Dr. Walter H. Munk, Scripps Institute of Oceanography; Dr. Jack E. Oliver, Columbia University; Professor
Frank Press, California Institute of Technology; Dr. Carl F. Romney, Department of Defense; Dr. Kenneth Street, Jr., Lawrence Radiation Laboratory, University of California; Professor John W. Tukey, Princeton University. The group included eight geophysicists, three physicists, one nuclear
chemist, one mechanical engineer, and one mathematician, specializing in
statistics.

[9]*New York Times,* February 12, 1959, pp. 1, 3.

the possibility that many people would collaborate in breaking an international undertaking. Whether Russia would or would not keep such an agreement would depend on the ingenuity of the Russians, on their willingness to make economic sacrifices, and on their honesty. Of these three factors we can have a firm opinion about the first. The Russians are certainly ingenious enough to devise secret methods of testing. As to the other questions, whether the Russians will want to invest the effort and whether they will be bound by their word, we feel that each man is entitled to his own opinion. According to past experience, an agreement to stop tests may well be followed by secret and successful tests behind the iron curtain.[10]

In addition, Dr. Teller was convinced that no control system could give absolute assurance against violations, and that it would be especially difficult to devise an effective control system in an area such as that of nuclear weaponry where technological change was occurring at such a rapid pace. Both in *Our Nuclear Future* and in an article which he had published in *Foreign Affairs* in January 1958, he had expressed the opinion:

In a more general way we may ask the question: Is it wise to make agreements which honesty will respect, but dishonesty can circumvent? Shall we put a free, democratic government at a disadvantage compared to the absolute power of a dictatorship? Shall we introduce prohibition in a new form, just to give rise to bootlegging on a much greater scale? It is almost certain that in the competition between prohibition and bootlegging, the bootlegger will win.[11]

These attitudes—having little to do with science or technology, it should be noted—made him a firmly convinced opponent of efforts to draft a test ban agreement with the Soviet Union.

After the conclusion of the Conference of Experts, Dr. Teller began to speculate about the effectiveness of the control system which had been recommended, and he asked some of the scientists at the University of California Livermore Laboratory—now named

[10]*Our Nuclear Future, Facts, Dangers, and Opportunities* (New York: Criterion Books 1958), p. 140.

[11]*Ibid.*, pp. 140-41; and "Alternatives for Security," *Foreign Affairs,* Vol. XXXVI, No. 2 (January 1958), p. 204.

the Lawrence Radiation Laboratory—and at the RAND Corporation to consider whether or not there might be ways in which a clever violator could evade detection. The President's Science Advisory Committee was scheduled to visit the Lawrence Laboratory in January 1959, and Dr. Teller hoped to be able to present to them a convincing case that the recommended control system was unsatisfactory. The scientists developed a number of ideas involving such possibilities as exploding a nuclear device in a mountain, in a large porous container resembling an egg shell, or in an expandable container fashioned like a lung. There were also other schemes, some quite fanciful. None of the ideas seemed very practical, or to be more than mere possibilities. Nevertheless, Dr. Teller had decided to present them to the members of PSAC.

Shortly before the PSAC meeting, Albert Latter of the RAND Corporation reexamined a possible means of concealing explosions which had been considered at the Conference of Experts, setting them off in large cavities. Hans Bethe had presented a paper on this subject at the Conference and had concluded that it would be impossible to muffle the seismic signals from nuclear explosions in this manner. Doing paper and pencil theoretical analysis, Latter concluded, not that Bethe's calculations had been wrong, but that in certain instances they were irrelevant. Latter's conclusion (without going into technical details) was that if the cavity were sufficiently large in relation to the size of the explosion so that the medium surrounding the hole would remain elastic under pressure, it would be possible to decouple or muffle nuclear explosions. His estimate was that it would be possible to decouple by a factor of several hundred, however, by January 1959 he had not completed all of his work, and his argument could be presented only in semi-quantitative terms.

Albert Latter's theory was technically so convincing that Dr. Teller and his colleagues decided that it would be the only paper on concealment presented to the President's Science Advisory Committee. The members of PSAC, including Hans Bethe, recognized the importance of the theory, and in general terms immediately accepted its validity.[12] Now it appeared that the conclusions

[12]Edward Teller & Allen Brown, *The Legacy of Hiroshima* (1962), p. 196.

of the Conference of Experts might be obsolete for another reason beyond the new empirical data which had been gained from the 1958 test series.

After Albert Latter's presentation, some scientists, especially Professor David T. Griggs, of the University of California at Los Angeles, began to argue that the mandate of the Berkner Panel should be expanded to include consideration of the possibility of the concealment of tests as well as the implications of the new data. Eventually, in the latter part of February 1959, at the decision of Drs. Fisk and Killian, this was done. At this stage, only the scientists who were involved knew about the possibility of decoupling. Dr. Latter's first paper on the subject was not published for circulation within the government until March 30, 1959, and it was not declassified until October 20, 1959.[13] It was only given public release on December 22, 1959. One of the reasons for not making the theory public sooner was the fear that to do so would in effect tell the Soviet Union how to evade the control system. However, as a consequence of this secrecy, the public debate in the United States about the wisdom of a test ban treaty suffered. Scientists and politicians who were worried about the effectiveness of the control system had to base their public arguments on the data gained from the 1958 test series, even though they were actually much more concerned about the possible degrading effect of the decoupling theory. Since this argument could not be stated, their opponents conversely could not attempt to meet it.

II

Confusion and Controversy
Within the United States

"Betrayal by Science?"

The immediate result in the United States of the revelation—or for most Americans, the partial revelation—that the technological assumptions on which the recommendations of the Conference of Experts had been based were no longer valid, was first to engender considerable confusion and perhaps a feeling of having been betrayed by science, and secondly to reopen the debate, which had

[13]A. L. Latter, *A Method of Concealing Underground Nuclear Explosions* (RAND Corp. RM-2347-AFT, 1959).

been relatively quiescent during the opening days of the diplomatic negotiations, concerning the wisdom of a test ban.

One account has it that when President Eisenhower was informed of the evaluation of the 1958 test series he "was furious, and 'blew his stack.' "[14] Others were also bitterly disappointed. Yet it was not at all inconsistent with the history of science that subsequent experiments should modify earlier conclusions and hypotheses.

As has already been mentioned, President Eisenhower's more reflective reaction to the new data was that scientific facts could not and should not be hidden, and that the government must tell the American people and the other states participating in the test ban negotiations what the scientific facts were. Eventually he came to feel that being confronted with the new data would be a good test of the USSR's intentions, since Soviet scientists could check on their validity. Thus the President dismissed the argument, raised by some individuals within the Administration, that to introduce the new data into the negotiations would open the United States to charges of duplicity.

Since the matter was relatively technical, it is far from certain how many nonscientists fully understood the significance of the new data, and its limitations. For example, President Eisenhower's attitude indicated a certain lack of understanding on his part. While it is true that formulae based on three cases are probably more reliable than those based on one, there could be no certainty that with more experiments the conclusions would not have to be modified further. Moreover, as has been seen, the new conclusions were based on a rather complicated and—it will emerge—somewhat debatable process of reasoning. Actually, later, after having conducted further deep underground nuclear tests, the United States would again revise its conclusions concerning these matters. Moreover, the Rainier, Logan, and Blanca shots were all conducted in the same location and in the same geological medium, tuff, or volcanic rock. Whether or not the formula constructed on the basis of these shots would be applicable to nuclear explosions in other media was an open question.

[14]C. J. V. Murphy, "Nuclear Inspections: A Near Miss," *Fortune,* Vol. LIX, No. 3 (March 1959), p. 122 at 155.

Hans Bethe, in testimony before the Senate Subcommittee on Disarmament on February 2, 1959, repeated the point that he had made before the same forum the previous April, that the scientists badly needed more information.[15] For the moment, however, because of the moratorium on testing, it would be impossible to gain further information, and it was uncertain whether any nuclear detonations would be allowed if and when a test ban treaty went into effect. Although Foreign Minister Gromyko had stated in a speech delivered before the Supreme Soviet on December 25, 1958, that it might be possible for a test ban treaty to contain a provision allowing nuclear detonations for peaceful purposes, the conditions which he set—*inter alia* parity between East and West in the number of detonations, and complete internal and external examination of the device to be detonated—were quite rigorous and possibly unacceptable to the West.[16] Therefore, temporarily at least, scientists would have to work with the data that they had. But to regard these as incontrovertible facts was too simple a view.

Obviously it was even more difficult for those outside the Administration to interpret the new data. After the publication of the PSAC statement of January 5, 1959, the public press was filled with conflicting estimates by politicians, scientists and military figures. To clarify the situation—or to reinforce their members' predispositions—two Congressional committees began hearings on the matter. The Joint Committee on Atomic Energy held closed hearings and the Senate Subcommittee on Disarmament open hearings. Perhaps the earliest comprehensive exposition was the speech which Senator Hubert Humphrey gave on the Senate floor on January 20, 1959, seven days—it is interesting to note—before his Subcommittee opened its hearings.[17]

There was also disagreement about what effect the new conclusions would have on the test ban negotiations. Appearing before the Senate Subcommittee on Disarmament, on January 28, 1959, Philip J. Farley, Special Assistant to the Secretary of State for Disarmament and Atomic Energy, asserted in a prepared statement that:

[15]*Hearings: Disarmament and Foreign Policy, supra* note 7, at 167.
[16]*Pravda,* December 26, 1958, pp. 9-10. See also the proposal which the USSR tabled on February 23, 1959: GEN/DNT/32.
[17]*Congressional Record,* (1959), Vol. CV, Part 1, pp. 929-34.

This new information on the problem of detecting and identifying underground nuclear explosions has not had a significant impact on the negotiations as yet. It bears, of course, only on a limited part of the control system described last summer by the Geneva experts, and prospects are encouraging that ways will be found to maintain the full effectiveness of that system.

There has been an understandable initial Soviet suspicion of U.S. motives in transmitting and subsequently publishing the new data . . . . When our continuing studies of possible ways of overcoming these technical difficulties have reached the stage when they can be communicated in their turn to the Soviet Union, this may help persuade them of the probity of our intentions.

In the meanwhile, the Soviet Union finds this U.S. action a convenient progaganda weapon to replace the one we have just deprived them of by our recent decision not to insist on a treaty link between disarmament progress and nuclear testing.[18]

Others took a much more pessimistic view, and subsequent events would uphold their interpretation.

The Battle Rejoined

It was in this atmosphere of confusion that the controversy about the wisdom of a test ban flared again. Shortly after the release of the PSAC statement, Senator Gore pronounced that "events have sustained my position." To him the new seismic data indicated that an effective control system for all environments was impractical, at least at that point, and he repeated his suggestion for a partial test ban limited to atmospheric tests.[19] Other Congressmen rallied to his side.

In a speech delivered on January 21, AEC Chairman John A. McCone denied that the Commission was opposed to the Administration's policy of seeking a test ban with the Soviet Union. He then went on to say that the Commission supported any test suspension which could be "properly" policed, and which would give reasonable assurance against cheating.[20] Of course, the con-

[18]*Hearings: Disarmament and Foreign Policy, supra* note 7, pp. 33-34.
[19]*New York Times,* January 12, 1959, p. 14.
[20]*Ibid.,* January 22, 1959, p. 11.

troversy was whether or not a test ban could and would be "properly" policed. In the same speech, Mr. McCone indicated that the Commission was considering conducting tests late in the summer of 1959 relating to the peaceful uses of atomic energy. It was his interpretation that the current East-West moratorium was "no injunction against the Commission going ahead with such tests." Four days later the *New York Times* contained a story stating that the AEC had recommended to the President that a test ban be limited to atmospheric explosions.[21]

Somewhat later, Senator Frank Church, a member of the Committee on Foreign Relations, also made a similar proposal to the Acting Secretary of State.[22] He was supported on the Senate floor by Senators Dodd, Fulbright, Gore, and Gruening.

Partisans of different persuasions also raised their voices. In a public statement Hans Bethe asserted that it would still be possible to devise an effective control system,[23] and Senator Humphrey's exposition of January 20 had a fundamentally optimistic tone. A few days later, twenty-two prominent Americans, including Mrs. Franklin Delano Roosevelt, Norman Thomas, Norman Cousins, James B. Carey, Ralph Lapp, and Robert R. Nathan, sent a letter to President Eisenhower, Chairman Khrushchev, and Prime Minister Macmillan asking them to take steps to conclude a test ban treaty despite the fact that there might be a risk of cheating.[24] They averred that nations which could mobilize scientific talent and resources to develop hydrogen bombs and intercontinental ballistic missiles ought also to be able to devise "a workable inspection system to satisfy all reasonable requirements." After Mr. McCone's speech, a number of American scientists let it be known that they felt that plans for nuclear detonations for peaceful purposes should be postponed so as not to disrupt the Geneva negotiations.[25]

During this period, American policy seemed to lack certainty. When questions were raised concerning the implications of the new

[21]*Ibid.*, January 25, 1959, p. 1.
[22]See his letter of February 25, 1959, *Congressional Record* (1959), Vol. CV, Part 3, p. 3134.
[23]*New York Times,* January 14, 1959, p. 5.
[24]*Ibid.*, February 2, 1959, p. 22.
[25]*Ibid.*, March 4, 1959, p. 14.

data at Secretary of State Dulles' news conference on January 13, 1959, he replied that technical studies were in process; but, if necessary, alternatives such as that advocated by Senator Gore would be considered.[26] Other Department of State officials asserted that official American policy continued to be to seek an accord covering all tests. There were no comments from the White House.

Clearly this vagueness was partly attributable to the uncertainty concerning the technological facts. It was also the result of the reopening of the debate within the Administration concerning the wisdom of a test ban. Furthermore, at this crucial juncture, the voice of the Department of State in intra-administration counsels was severely weakened. In early 1959 Secretary of State Dulles' illness took a sharp turn for the worse, and on February 9, 1959, he went on medical leave. Christian Herter was appointed Acting Secretary of State. During his last days in office, Mr. Dulles was not as effective as he had been previously. One source has reported that he showed himself to be "impatient and changeable" with respect to a test ban and disarmament.[27] Some of his closest associates even felt that he wanted to break off the test ban negotiations. As an Acting Secretary, Mr. Herter did not have quite the same authority, and he was not appointed Secretary until April 22, 1959. Moreover, Mr. Dulles had had a particularly close relationship with the President, which few men could hope to duplicate.

The Report of the Berkner Panel: The Need for Further Research
Finally, on March 16, 1959, the findings of the Berkner Panel on Seismic Improvement were submitted to the President, and on March 31 the complete report was filed.[28] The two documents were not publicly released until June 12, 1959, the day that they were submitted to the Geneva Conference. However, fairly extensive accounts of the Panel's conclusions appeared in the *New*

[26]U.S. Department of State *Bulletin,* Vol. XL, No. 1023 (February 2, 1959), pp. 161-62.
[27]Sir Michael Wright, *Disarm and Verify: An Explanation of the Central Difficulties and of National Policies* (1964), p. 119. Sir Michael was a member of the United Kingdom delegation in the nuclear test ban negotiations from 1959 through 1961.
[28]*Geneva Conference,* pp. 335-39, 340-54.

York Times on March 8, 1959, and in an article in the March issue of *Fortune*.[29]

In the summary of its findings, the Berkner Panel first affirmed the substantial correctness of the original evaluation of the new data. However, it produced a new figure for the total number of unidentified earthquakes which would generate a seismic signal equivalent to that of a 5-kiloton explosion (see Table 1).

TABLE 1[30]

Estimated Annual Number of Unidentified
Worldwide Continental Earthquakes

	5KT and greater	10KT and greater	20KT and greater
Estimate—Geneva Conference of Experts—August 1958	20-100	—	—
Estimate—Geneva network and equipment on basis of Hardtack data—January 1959	1500	400	60
Estimate—Geneva network with improvements within the present state of technology on basis of Hardtack data—April 1959	300	40	15

This figure was greater than that suggested by the PSAC statement, but within the range mentioned by Dr. Carl Romney in his testimony before the Senate Subcommittee on Disarmament. The Berkner report stated that within the framework of existing technology it would be possible partially to restore the capability of the control system recommended by the Conference of Experts by increasing the number of seismometers at each control station from 10 to 100 and by using other criteria than first motion for identifying earthquakes. It also stated that with the advance of

[29]*New York Times,* March 8, 1959, p. 32; C. J. V. Murphy, "Nuclear Inspection: A Near Miss," *supra* note 14 at 162.

[30]From the "Findings of the Berkner Panel on Seismic Improvement," *Geneva Conference,* p. 337.

technology it would probably be possible to improve the capability of the Geneva system even more. Interestingly, this paralleled the claim of Soviet diplomats and scientists. The Panel emphasized the tentative nature of its estimates, the scanty data on which they were based, and the need for further research. The later report of the Berkner Panel was exclusively devoted to this last topic.

The Berkner Panel had invited Albert Latter to present his theories. By the time of his presentation he had made a firm estimate that by detonating a nuclear device in a large cavity it would be possible to reduce the seismic signal by a factor of 300. During the Panel's discussion, Hans Bethe estimated that the factor would be 700. However, the findings of the Berkner Panel merely stated "that decoupling techniques existed which could reduce the seismic signal by a factor of ten or more."[31] Perhaps the reason for this caution was the theoretical nature of Dr. Latter's calculations. The report emphasized the need for high explosive and nuclear shots to test these calculations empirically. Although Dr. Latter's theories seemed to be incontrovertible, even at this stage many scientists doubted that they actually could be applied. They questioned whether or not it would be possible to create a large spherical hole deep underground in which to detonate a nuclear device. For example, according to the theory, to decouple a 10-kiloton shot by a factor of 300, the shot would have to be detonated in a spherical hole 3,000 feet underground with a diameter of 360 feet. To many, this seemed like a formidable engineering feat, and even if feasible, an incredibly expensive task. Until there was some experimental evidence, however, neither side could prove its case. But whatever the reason for the discrepancy between the private governmental estimate of decoupling and public estimate in the Berkner report, the latter was such an understatement as to be grossly misleading.

As mentioned earlier, the "Report of the Berkner Panel on Seismic Improvement" was essentially a detailed statement of the need for a research program in this area. It stressed how little was known about the propagation of seismic waves and the limited amount of funds available for research. It also stated that: "The USSR in recent years has emphasized seismological research to

[31]*Ibid.,* p. 338.

such extent that the Soviets enjoy a position superior in many respects to our own."[32] Similar statements appeared in other places in the report. The report oulined a number of hypotheses and areas for research and recommended an initial program involving expenditures of more than $52,825,000 over a two-year period. For the moment, however, American policy-makers would have to act on the basis of the available data.

III
The British Seek the Lead

The Soviet Reaction

In formulating a new negotiating position, interpretations of the opponent state's behavior in the negotiations and estimates of its probable response to alternative courses are important factors—or should be if the task is conducted rationally—therefore it is necessary to consider the USSR's reaction to the presentation of the new data on January 5, 1959. As has already been mentioned, Mr. Tsarapkin's immediate response was violently negative.[33] He attacked the motives of the Western powers in submitting the new data, asserting that their real purpose was either to undermine the Conference or to open opportunities for Western intelligence operations. He ignored Mr. Ormsby-Gore's and Ambassador Wadsworth's rather candid replies that if the Western delegations attempted to suppress the information and it nevertheless became known, their positions would be untenable before Parliament, Congress, and public opinion, and that this would have an unfavorable impact on the Conference and on the possibility of a treaty being ratified.[34] Beyond casting aspersions on the motives of the Western powers, the Soviet position as espoused by Mr. Tsarapkin consisted of several assertions. He held that the negotiations had an agreed base in the report of the Conference of Experts and they must not depart from this base. He acknowledged that new technological developments would always occur, but that these would have to be handled by the Control Organization, not the Conference

[32]*Ibid.*, p. 341.
[33]Mr. Tsarapkin's comments may be found in GEN/DNT/PV. 29, pp. 14-15; PV. 31, pp. 20-28; PV. 32, pp. 22-24; PV. 41, pp. 8-10.
[34]See GEN/DNT/PV. 32, p. 24; and PV. 50, p. 16.

drafting the treaty. Finally, he maintained strongly that the progress of science would always result in greater rather than lesser capacity for detection.

Never once during the session of the Conference from January 5 to March 19, 1959, did Mr. Tsarapkin deal with the technical matters connected with the new data. The closest that he came to touching technical issues was on January 23, 1959, when he denied that the relevant sections of the report of the Conference of Experts had been based solely on one case, the Rainier shot. He claimed that the experience with high explosive detonations had also been taken into account. This was true, but the Rainier shot had been the point from which the effectiveness of the recommended control system had been calculated. Mr. Tsarapkin continually rejected the suggestion that a technical working group should be convened to consider the new data. His greatest concession was contained in a formal statement of the Soviet Foreign Ministry which he read on February 9 and which had appeared in the Soviet press the previous day. The statement declared that as soon as the Western powers completed their evaluation of the new data and submitted their conclusions to the Conference, the USSR would have its scientists make a "careful study" of those conclusions.[35] It then asserted that in any case this ought not to affect the course of the negotiations.

The only Soviet comment on the technical issues involved in the dispute was an article which appeared in *Pravda* January 20, 1959, signed by Y. V. Riznichenko and L. Brekhovski, two corresponding members of the USSR's Academy of Sciences, who had served as advisers to the Eastern delegation at the Conference of Experts.[36] They attempted to refute the American Working Paper submitted in Geneva on January 5, 1959.

First, like Mr. Tsarapkin, they denied that the calculations of the Conference of Experts had been based on the Rainier shot alone. Secondly, they pointed out that the seismographs used to measure the Logan and Blanca shots did not conform to the recommendations of the Conference of Experts. This was true, but at that date no existing or permanent station had seismographs which

[35]GEN/DNT/PV. 51, p. 4.

[36]*Pravda*, January 20, 1959, p. 6. A condensed version is printed in *The Current Digest of Soviet Press*, Vol. XI, No. 3 (February 25, 1959), pp. 23-24.

did conform to those specifications. Among other things, the Berkner Panel recommended that a station conforming to the Geneva standards should be established so that its capabilities could be properly understood.

The two Soviet scientists also asserted that the new estimates gave undue weight to the findings of the seven temporary stations which had been specially established to measure the Hardtack II series, and that these stations were less effective than the permanent ones. It will be recalled that the 1958 estimate of the magnitude of the Rainier shot had been based on the average of the signals received at seven permanent stations near the event and that three permanent stations within the same radius from the event did not receive any signal. The signals received at the latter three stations and the seven temporary stations from the Logan and Blanca shots led the American scientists to conclude that the estimate for Rainier was incorrect.

It was difficult for a nonscientist to judge whether or not the temporary stations were less effective than the permanent stations. Scientists presented conflicting views in the public debate. For example, in testimony before the Senate Subcommittee on Disarmament, Dr. Carl Romney said that the temporary stations "on the average gave better results" than the permanent stations because "the temporary stations had better equipment than the average of the permanent stations at the same distances," while a few days later Professor Bethe stated that the temporary stations "were not as good in general as the permanent stations."[37]

The Soviet statement criticized the American Working Paper for not taking into account the recordings of other stations in the United States, of which there were ninety, or of stations outside of the United States, in such areas as Sweden. At the time that the American Working Paper was composed, these recordings were not taken into account. They were not available. They were, however, considered by the American scientists at a later date. In addition, the American scientists sought to obtain recordings from the stations in the USSR, but their requests were spurned for almost a year. The Soviet scientists claimed that the data from the Blanca

[37]*Hearings: Disarmament and Foreign Policy, supra* note 7, pp. 18, 184.

shot were not relevant, since the cavity had blown out, thus releasing some of the energy. In fact, the cavity had caved in several seconds after the seismic effect had passed. Apparently the Soviet scientists were not aware of this.

Finally, the Soviet scientists asserted that the new estimate of the magnitude of the Rainier shot was "within the limits of experimental accuracy." This was true. It will be recalled that in the range of the signal resulting from the Rainier shot, estimates of seismic magnitude were usually qualified as being accurate $\pm.4$. The change was within this range.

The Soviet scientists concluded that there was no need to revise the conclusions of the Conference of Experts. Since Albert Latter's work with respect to decoupling was not public knowledge, the statement naturally contained no reference to it.

On January 28, 1959, Carl Romney, in an appearance before the Senate Subcommittee on Disarmament, criticized the statement of the two Soviet scientists and defended the American Working Paper. Ambassador Wadsworth echoed many of his statements in the Geneva Conference on February 11, 1959. Thus, a scientific controversy was touched off which remained a feature of the Geneva Conference throughout its course.

To be fully understood, the Soviet position needs to be seen in the light of a proposal, mentioned in Chapter IV, which the Western delegations had tabled shortly before the Christmas recess in December 1958. On December 16, the Western delegations tabled a draft version of Annex I of the treaty, dealing with the detection and identification system.[38] Among other things the Annex included provision for on-site inspection of all unidentified seismic events with an estimated yield of five kilotons or more and of twenty percent (selected on a random basis) of all unidentified seismic events with an estimated yield of less than five kilotons. In addition, any unidentified seismic event with an estimated equivalent yield of less than five kilotons which the data from the system indicated had an unusually high probability of being of nuclear origin would be inspected. In another section the Annex provided for the creation of a number of "inspection groups," personnel who would have the sole duty of carrying out on-site inspections.

[38]GEN/DNT/22.

On the basis of the figures in the summary of the findings of the Berkner Panel, the new data would have meant that the worldwide total of probable on-site inspections required by these provisions would have increased from 20 to 100 to more than 1500. Even with the improvements recommended by the Panel, the number still would have been more than 300. If the estimate which Dr. Carl Romney had expressed before the Senate Subcommittee on Disarmament were correct, and the Berkner Panel had accepted a figure for the gross total inside the range that he had mentioned, without improvements in the control system the new data would have meant that there would have to be at least from 100 to 600 on-site inspections annually on the territory of the USSR and main-land China. Whatever Soviet motivation may have been at this stage of the negotiations and regardless of the Soviet understanding of the technical validity of the new data, it is clear that acceptance of the Western interpretation would have involved opening up the USSR considerably more than had been envisaged under the orig-inal assumptions.

On January 30, 1959, the USSR submitted a list of actions by the Control Organization which would require unanimity of the three nuclear powers. The adoption of a decision to dispatch an on-site inspection group was included in this list, as was the "adop-tion of a decision . . . on the basis of the results of such investi-gations." Thus both questions relating to obtaining evidence of a violation by means of on-site inspections and those relating to the action to be taken if an on-site inspection yielded evidence of a violation would be subject to the veto.[39] It is probable that the USSR would have demanded a veto in these matters even if no new data had been discovered and submitted to the Conference. The USSR's desire to maintain absolute control over access to its territory is long-standing and well known. However, the implica-tions of the new data must at least have strengthened Soviet reluct-ance to allow on-site inspections to occur on a more or less auto-matic basis. On the other hand, the Soviet demand for a veto was clearly unacceptable to the West on the ground that it might block the Control Organization from obtaining incontrovertible evi-dence that a violation had occurred.

[39]GEN/DNT/PV. 46, p. 32.

Macmillan's Proposal for a Political Compromise: A Quota of On-Site Inspections

Dr. Fedorov, who continued to be a member of the Soviet delegation at this stage of the negotiations, discussed these problems with Mr. Ormsby-Gore during a private conversation sometime in early 1959. He intimated that it would be difficult for the Soviet Union to accept a treaty under which it could be subjected to an unlimited number of on-site inspections, and suggested that it would be easier for the USSR if it knew how many such inspections there might be each year.[40] He also suggested that one way of circumventing these difficulties would be to establish an annual quota for on-site inspections, and mentioned a range of figures that went from three or so to more than twenty. Mr. Ormsby-Gore reported this conversation to London, where it was studied and considered in detail.

Prime Minister Harold Macmillan visited the USSR from February 21 through March 3, 1959, and had extensive talks with Chairman Khrushchev. During the course of these conversations, either without having discussed the matter with the United States or despite American opposition,[41] the Prime Minister repeated Dr. Fedorov's suggestion for an annual quota of on-site inspections, mentioning a range of figures from three or five to more than twenty. This was the first of a series of British initiatives designed to keep the negotiations alive and to stimulate progress in them. At that time, Chairman Khrushchev apparently neither accepted nor rejected the proposal, although he clearly found it attractive.

Because of its implications for later developments, it is worth noting that the joint Anglo-Soviet communique issued at the conclusion of the talks between Prime Minister Macmillan and Chairman Khrushchev mentioned among other things the possibility of an agreement being reached on a limitation of both conventional and nuclear forces and weapons, under an appropriate inspection system, in an agreed area of Europe.[42] This concept was strongly

[40]See Ormsby-Gore's account, GEN/DNT/PV. 293, p. 10.
[41]For the conflicting reports see respectively T. E. Murray, *Nuclear Policy for War and Peace,* p. 104, and Sir Michael Wright, *Disarm and Verify,* p. 137.
[42]*New York Times,* March 4, 1959, p. 1.

opposed by NATO Headquarters, the Federal Republic of Germany, and the United States.

On March 5, two days after Prime Minister Macmillan had left Moscow, Senator Hubert H. Humphrey sent a memorandum to President Eisenhower, in which he advanced a proposal for a quota of on-site inspections very similar to that which had been discussed in Moscow.[43] President Eisenhower agreed that the proposal should be studied but refused to commit himself beyond that.

The Western Summit

By late March 1959, the stage was set for a major review of Western policy concerning the test ban negotiations. The Berkner Panel had completed its work, domestic opinion had had some time to congeal, and policy-makers had some sense of the Soviet reaction and position. On March 19, Ambassador Wadsworth proposed that the Conference be recessed until April 13, and Mr. Tsarapkin, though stating that the USSR was opposed to the suggestion, agreed.[44] That same day, Prime Minister Macmillan and Foreign Minister Selwyn Lloyd arrived in Washington for consultations with President Eisenhower and other American officials.

During the next five days many issues were discussed, including broader arms control and disarmament proposals, the Berlin crisis, and the prospects for a summit conference. With respect to these broader issues, it was agreed that a meeting of the foreign ministers of France, the USSR, the United Kingdom, and the United States should be convened in Geneva on May 11, 1959.

The two Western leaders also spent considerable time discussing the flagging Geneva negotiations. Prime Minister Macmillan mentioned his suggestion to Chairman Khrushchev for an annual quota of on-site inspections. In explaining his suggestion, the Prime Minister used a golfing analogy, as Selwyn Lloyd did later in discussing the matter before the House of Commons.[45] The Prime Minister said the quota would be like a bisque, a stroke or strokes which can be used when desired by the opponent of the person against whom it is given. Despite this reference to the President's

[43]Earl H. Voss, *Nuclear Ambush,* pp. 291-92.
[44]GEN/DNT/72, p. 17.
[45]U.K. House of Commons, *Debates,* April 27, 1959.

favorite sport, as in Moscow, Prime Minister Macmillan's suggestion was neither approved nor rejected.

Many of the discussions were held at Camp David and they ultimately included most of the Committee of Principals and their British counterparts. Mr. Dulles attended some of the conversations, but by that time he was greatly weakened. Ambassador Wadsworth, however, was not included in these meetings. Nor were Congressmen. In fact, it emerged in Mr. Wadsworth's testimony before the Senate Subcommittee on Disarmament on March 25 that at that point neither he nor the Senators had had access to the conclusions of the Berkner Panel, although they had been submitted to the President nine days earlier.[46] The Camp David talks, though, settled the course of future Western policy.

While the talks were in process pressures for and against a test ban continued to rage in the United States and abroad. Since Prime Minister Macmillan faced the prospect of a general election in the not too distant future, he no doubt was sensitive to the pressures in the United Kingdom. Unlike the situation in the United States, in the United Kingdom these pressures almost without exception favored efforts to achieve a test ban.[47] An important explanation for this is that British public opinion was much more fearful of nuclear war than was opinion within the United States, and rightly so, since the United Kingdom was much more vulnerable. A pointed example of the pressure exerted on the British government occurred immediately after the conclusion of the Prime Minister's trip to Washington. On March 30, some fifteen thousand British citizens rallied in London to urge British unilateral nuclear disarmament.[48]

The Senate Resolution

In an effort to put the debate within the United States in a proper context, and to strengthen the American negotiating position, and perhaps for other reasons as well, on March 27, Senator Humphrey

[46]U.S. Congress, Senate, Committee on Foreign Relations, Subcommittee on Disarmament, *Hearing: Geneva Test Ban Negotiations,* 86th Congress, 1st Session (1959), p. 20.

[47]For confirmation of this point by a British negotiator see Sir Michael Wright, *Disarm and Verify,* pp. 131, 135.

[48]*New York Times,* March 31, 1959, p. 8.

introduced a resolution supporting the United States efforts to negotiate a test ban including "an adequate inspection and control system."[49] Two days earlier, in explaining the purpose of the resolution to Ambassador Wadsworth, Senator Humphrey said:

> The idea behind this is that as the Soviet works its propaganda apparatus, it tries to make it seem every time we bring up another consideration that we are out either to delay this agreement, or to wreck the conference, or to precipitate some kind of crisis that will produce a stalemate.
>
> It would seem to me that since the policy of our Government is what you are attempting to do, namely, to negotiate an agreement, that it might be well to give some consideration to expressing as the sense of the Senate our genuine intent and good intentions.[50]

In keeping with this concept, the original resolution asked the President to request the Soviet government to transmit the resolution to the Soviet people, a provision which was subsequently dropped at the suggestion of the Department of State.

Whether or not Senator Humphrey's resolution served to nullify Soviet propaganda is questionable. It is true that after it was unanimously adopted on April 30, 1959, Ambassador Wadsworth could refer to it as indicating the sense of the Senate. However, the debate in the United States was really about what constituted "an adequate inspection and control system," and whether or not such a system was even possible. Those who had always questioned the wisdom of a test ban treaty for the United States now focused their criticisms on these issues.

A more important effect of the resolution may well have been that in the context of the domestic debate, its adoption made it more difficult for the Administration to break off the negotiations.[51] To do so might have seemed to defy the sense of the Senate. Establishing this inhibition may well have been Senator Humphrey's main motivation.

[49]*Congressional Record,* Vol. CV, Part 4 (1959), p. 5347.
[50]*Hearing: Geneva Test Ban Negotiations, supra* note 46, at 30.
[51]See Earl H. Voss, *Nuclear Ambush,* p. 298.

IV

The New Western Position

Eisenhower to Khrushchev: An Atmospheric Ban?

The tensions in American opinion were amply evident in the new Western position which emerged from the Camp David talks. The new Western position was expressed in a letter which President Eisenhower sent to Chairman Khrushchev on April 13, 1959, the day that the Geneva Conference reconvened. That same day Prime Minister Macmillan also sent a letter to Chairman Khrushchev endorsing the President's letter, and Ambassador Wadsworth introduced and expounded the President's proposals in Geneva.

The essence of the new Western position was to offer the Soviet Union two alternative courses. The President put it this way:

> If you are prepared to change your present position on the veto, on procedures for on-site inspection, and on early discussion of concrete measures for high altitude detection, we can of course proceed promptly in the hope of concluding the negotiation of a comprehensive agreement for suspension of nuclear weapons tests. If you are not yet ready to go this far, then I propose that we take the first and readily attainable step of an agreed suspension of nuclear weapons tests in the atmosphere up to 50 kilometers while the political and technical problems associated with control of underground and outer space tests are being resolved. If we could agree to such initial implementation of the first—and I must add the most important—phase of a test suspension agreement, our negotiators could continue to explore with new hope the political and technical problems involved in extending the agreement as quickly as possible to cover all nuclear weapons tests.[52]

In other words, the new Western position was that to obtain a comprehensive ban on the testing of nuclear weapons in all environments, the Soviet Union would have to agree to a variety of Western conditions, otherwise the West would only agree to an atmospheric test ban, which hopefully, however, would be the first phase of a more far-reaching agreement. The basis for the proposal for a phased treaty was a suggestion formally submitted to Sec-

[52]*Geneva Conference*, p. 355.

retary of State Dulles by AEC Chairman McCone on behalf of the members of the Commission in late January.[53] That it became an alternative choice offered to the Soviet Union rather than the single American position reflected the process of consensus-building within the Administration and between the Western allies. The Department of State and the British insisted on keeping open the possibility of a comprehensive test ban. For the moment, Prime Minister Macmillan's quota proposal was ignored.

It is interesting how the President's letter underplayed the problem of the new data. In Geneva, in Salle IX of the *Palais des Nations,* Ambassador Wadsworth was less reticent. He explicitly mentioned "technical discussion of . . . improvements which might be made in the system of underground detection," as a condition for continuing efforts to reach a comprehensive agreement.[54]

Ambassador Wadsworth also defined the alternative course of a phased treaty more precisely. The first phase agreement, as he outlined it, would prohibit atmospheric, and if the USSR were willing, underwater nuclear tests. It would be monitored by stationary control posts in the USSR, the United Kingdom, the United States, and the Pacific area, spaced in accordance with the recommendations of the Conference of Experts for nonseismic areas; that is, at distances of 1,700 kilometers. The system would also include routine and special aircraft sampling flights.

It will be recalled that several months earlier Senator Gore had asserted that an atmospheric test ban could be monitored by existing national detection systems. It is not clear why the United States was unwilling to adopt such a position at this point. Probably the principal reason was that no one within the Administration was willing to argue for it. The Department of State saw experience in operating a control system as one of the main benefits of a test ban agreement. The Central Intelligence Agency wanted to penetrate the veil of Soviet secrecy. And the Department of Defense and the Atomic Energy Commission sought as much assurance as they could get that an agreement would not be violated. Naturally the possibility of detecting clandestine explosions in the USSR would be greater with some control posts on Soviet territory than without any

[53]Earl H. Voss, *Nuclear Ambush,* p. 290.
[54]GEN/DNT/PV. 73, p. 5.

there, but how significant this difference would be is debatable.

The Western proposal for a phased agreement, as outlined by Ambassador Wadsworth also envisaged continuing negotiations within the framework of the Geneva Conference, or the Control Commission, toward extending the test ban to other environments and "joint" studies, research and possibly experiments concerning the technical problems which had arisen. The Preparatory Commission for the Control Organization might also be given responsibility for these activities.

Finally, Ambassador Wadsworth presented a fairly precise summary of the conclusions of the Berkner Panel.

Both within and outside the Geneva Conference the new Western position was widely interpreted as a victory for the position advocated by such individuals as AEC Chairman McCone, Senator Gore, and Thomas E. Murray. Depending on one's persuasion, the West had either finally awakened to the difficulties of control, or had at last revealed its underlying desire to continue developing nuclear weapons through testing in some environments. To a degree, both interpretations were accurate. Mr. Murray, in commenting on the proposal in his book in 1960, called it "one of the most sensible moves the Administration made," on the ground that it represented a "turning away from the chimera of an absolute fully policed test ban." He then went on to say that Chairman Khrushchev, recognizing the fact that the proposal "left an opening for the United States to acquire much-needed weapons capabilities in the tactical nuclear field, quickly rejected it."[55]

Both views, however, probably overestimated the importance of the Eisenhower and Macmillan letters. They represented only a new position, not a new policy, a limited move rather than a thought-out plan. The West still lacked a clear conception of where it was going, or indeed where it wanted to go. However, the new Western position did have the merit of forcing the participants in the negotiations and the onlookers to consider more seriously than they had previously the importance of the objective of reducing the hazards of radioactive fallout. It soon became apparent that the possibility of achieving this objective alone would not immediately be sufficient to induce an agreement.

[55]*Nuclear Policy for War and Peace*, p. 102.

Chapter VI

The Search for Technical Agreement

I

Some Initial Compromises

President Eisenhower's letter, or more properly the formulation of a new Western negotiating position and its communication to the Soviet Union, touched off a process best described as a search between East and West for agreement on the technical issues in dispute, which lasted throughout 1959, finally ending in seeming futility. A variety of issues were at stake: whether or not the test ban treaty would be comprehensive; the extent to which the new data and the changing technological base would be taken into account; eventually, the fate of the moratorium on testing; and, to some extent, the diffusion of nuclear capabilities. President Eisenhower's letter and Ambassador Wadsworth's presentation on April 13 raised the first two issues. Given the public debate on these matters in the United States, the moratorium was obviously an important element in the background, and since one of the putative objectives of the Conference was prevention of the spread of nuclear weapons capability, this issue was inevitably involved.

The USSR Protests NATO's Nuclear Plans

The first Soviet move after the communication of the new Western position concerned the last problem. On April 21, 1959, the Soviet Foreign Ministry delivered a note to the American Embassy in Moscow protesting against plans, reported in the Western press, for the provision of missiles to NATO countries and the stockpiling of nuclear warheads there.[1] As was described earlier, in December 1957 the NATO Council had decided that selected NATO countries were to be furnished missiles to which nuclear

[1] *Documents on Disarmament, 1945–1959*, Vol. II, pp. 1393-96.

warheads might be attached. Then the Atomic Energy Act had been amended in July 1958 to allow the transfer of nuclear warheads under certain specified conditions. These warheads were to remain in American custody until the President had decided that they could be used.

Under these terms an agreement was signed with the United Kingdom in 1958, and work was begun on the installation of bases in that country for Thor intermediate range rockets. A similar agreement was reached with Italy in March 1959, for the installation of Jupiter rockets, although in this case both the missiles and the warheads would remain under American control. The Western press was full of speculation that the NATO Command also had plans to establish similar bases in other NATO countries.

The Soviet note singled out Greece, Turkey, and the Federal Republic of Germany, and warned against the establishment of bases in these countries, especially in West Germany. It argued that no action should be taken in this sphere prior to the Foreign Ministers' meeting, since to do so would constrict and perhaps foreclose the possibility of agreement.

The West replied through a statement of the NATO Council issued on May 7, 1959, and a note from the American Embassy in Moscow to the Soviet Foreign Ministry dated the following day.[2] The essence of the Western position was to reiterate the public rationale of the December 1957 decisions; that is, that the USSR had prevented disarmament, and at the same time had introduced modern weapons into its armed forces, therefore, the West had no alternative but to take similar action.

On May 5 and 6, bilateral agreements were signed by the United States with Greece, the Federal Republic of Germany, the Netherlands, and Turkey under the provisions of the Atomic Energy Act of 1958 for the transfer to the latter countries of the non-nuclear components of nuclear weapons systems and knowledge about their use.[3] A similar agreement was signed with Canada on May 22, 1959.[4] At that time it was envisaged that intermediate range ballistic bases might be established in all of the countries

[2]*Ibid.*, pp. 1405-9.
[3]See U.S. Department of State, *Treaties and Other International Acts,* Nos. 4292, 4267, 4277, and 4278 (1959).
[4]*Ibid.*, No. 4271.

except West Germany, which according to the NATO plans then
in effect was only slated to receive Matador rockets with a range
of approximately six hundred miles. Eventually, only Turkey received IRBM's, under an arrangement agreed to in October 1959.
Nonetheless, the May agreements established the legal framework
for the transfer of nuclear weapon systems within the limitations of
the 1958 Atomic Energy Act.

To a certain extent the signing of these agreements at this
time merely represented the elaboration of previously agreed decisions. It may also have been an attempt by those who had strong
feelings in the matter, especially the United States Department of
Defense, the NATO Command, and policy-makers in the Federal
Republic of Germany, to make it difficult for the Foreign Ministers
of the four powers to adopt a plan for nuclear or general disengagement in Central Europe at their forthcoming meeting. These
issues were relevant to the Geneva Conference since they dealt with
the diffusion of nuclear weapons, one of the issues supposedly at
stake in the Conference.

*Chairman Khrushchev's Formal Reply: "No" to Eisenhower, "Yes"
to Macmillan*

The first direct Soviet reply to the new Western position came
on April 23, 1959, in letters from Chairman Khrushchev to President Eisenhower and Prime Minister Macmillan.[5] First, Khrushchev
rejected the possibility of an atmospheric test ban. He argued that
the aim of a test ban should be "to halt the nuclear arms race, or
at the very least, to prevent the creation of new and ever more
destructive types of atomic and hydrogen weapons." Since an
atmospheric ban would allow testing in other environments, in his
view, it would not achieve this goal. Although they evaluated it
differently, in the United States, the opponents of a test ban treaty
also clearly recognized this possibility. Khrushchev further asserted
that nuclear weapons tests in the high atmosphere would cause fallout. He claimed that the purpose of the Conference should continue
to be "to conclude an agreement providing for a cessation of all
forms of nuclear weapon tests—in the atmosphere, underground,
under water, and at high altitudes."

[5]*Geneva Conference*, pp. 356-60.

Khrushchev then suggested that it might be possible to surmount the difficulties in which the test ban negotiations were currently enmeshed by adopting Prime Minister Macmillan's proposal for an annual quota of on-site inspections. He elaborated that not many on-site inspections would be required and that they would have to be "founded . . . on objective instrument readings." It was his view that the mere possibility that an on-site inspection would be conducted would be sufficient to deter a potential violator.

Four days later, in the Geneva Conference, Mr. Tsarapkin submitted a formal proposal embodying Chairman Khrushchev's proposal,[6] and in the next few sessions he elaborated its meaning and ramifications. He stated that if the instruments registered a suspicious event in a given location according to predetermined criteria, the opposite side could request an on-site inspection and an inspection group would be dispatched: there would be no question of voting in the Control Commission.[7] Thus he seemed to say that the Soviet demand for a veto on on-site inspections would be dropped, if the quota proposal were accepted. Mr. Tsarapkin also stated that the size of the quota—which would have to be a "small number"—for the territories of each of the three nuclear powers would have to be fixed by agreement among them. He ruled out the possibility of fixing the quota as a set percentage of the number of unidentified events registered on seismographs.[8] Or, as he put it to his partners in the Conference, agreement will be impossible "if you are going to talk of thousands of earth tremors a year and fix a certain percentage." Later, he asserted that it would not be necessary to consider the new seismic data prior to the adoption of the quota proposal.[9]

Toward More Scientific Data: Projects Vela and Cowboy

Meanwhile, the United States moved to consider more seriously than it previously had the technical problems involved in detecting and identifying nuclear explosions. On April 23, 1959, the same day that Chairman Khrushchev dispatched his letters to President

[6]GEN/DNT/PV. 83, pp. 3-11.
[7]GEN/DNT/PV. 84, pp. 10-11; PV. 85, p. 4.
[8]GEN/DNT/PV. 84, p. 8.
[9]GEN/DNT/PV. 85, p. 6.

Eisenhower and Prime Minister Macmillan, Dr. Killian, Special Assistant to the President for Science and Technology, Chairman McCone of the AEC, and Deputy Secretary of Defense Quarles met to discuss the reports of the Panofsky Panel, which had considered problems of high altitude detection, and the Berkner Panel, which had examined problems of seismic detection.[10] They decided that the Department of Defense should assume overall responsibility for implementing the research programs recommended by these two panels and that it should receive support from the Atomic Energy Commission and the National Aeronautics and Space Administration.

In the next few months various advisory groups within the Department of Defense began a number of preliminary studies, and then the Air Force Technical Applications Center prepared specific proposals for research. In August various supervisory committees were established. Finally, on September 2, 1959, the Secretary of Defense assigned responsibility for overseeing the research—subsequently named Project Vela—to the Advanced Research Projects Agency of the Department of Defense, and the first work order was issued one month later.

During the next two years the project was expanded to full dimensions. It was divided into three aspects: Veia Uniform, dealing with underground nuclear tests; Vela Sierra, relating to monitoring nuclear tests in space from ground bases; and Vela Hotel, concerning monitoring nuclear tests in space by satellite-borne instrumentation. Various governmental and nongovernmental organizations were involved under contracts let in 1960 and 1961, and $10,000,000 was made available for the project during fiscal year 1960. From the outset it was envisaged that both conventional and nuclear explosions would be involved, and because of this the AEC was given a prominent role. Nuclear explosions were obviously desirable from a technical standpoint: without them, theories relating to detection could not be completely tested, and since it would be some time before the project would advance to the stage in which nuclear explosions would be crucial, the planners of Vela

[10]U.S. Congress, Joint Committee on Atomic Energy, *Summary-Analysis of Hearings: Developments in the Field of Detection and Identification of Nuclear Explosions (Project Vela) and Relationship to Test Ban Negotiations,* 87th Congress, 2nd Session (Comm. Print. 1962), p. 12.

simply ignored the question of whether or not such explosions would be politically feasible.

Curiously, the first public announcement of Project Vela was made May 7, 1960, well after the program was underway.[11]

A second project, concerning decoupling, was inaugurated somewhat earlier. As soon as they were presented, Albert Latter's theoretical calculations invited empirical testing. The Atomic Energy Commission agreed to fund such work and assigned operational responsibility to the University of California's Lawrence Radiation Laboratory at Livermore. The RAND Corporation would also participate in the analysis of the data. These arrangements were discussed before Congressional Committees in June 1959. A series of ten or more underground chemical explosions was planned under the code name Project Cowboy and the first of these was conducted in a salt mine in Winnfield, Louisiana, on December 17, 1959, before Project Vela was even seriously under way. Thus the United States moved faster to examine through empirical tests whether or not the seismic effects of underground nuclear explosions could be muffled than it did to consider in the same way whether or not the effectiveness of the control system recommended by the Conference of Experts could be improved.

An important reason for the difference in the speed with which the two projects got underway was the fact that several policy-makers felt that if the decoupling theory proved valid a ban on testing nuclear weapons underground would probably be out of the question. In addition, Project Vela was much more complicated than Project Cowboy and required considerably larger expenditures of funds. Further, most aspects of Project Vela would be executed by nongovernmental agencies, often universities. Drafting and letting contracts is time consuming, and the rhythm of academic life seldom allows the rapid commitment of large scale resources to meet external requirements. Finally, housing Project Vela within the Department of Defense meant that the responsibility for proving that a test ban could be adequately monitored was given to an agency which was less than enthusiastic about the wisdom of a test ban and which had as its basic responsibility the overwhelming

[11]See President Eisenhower's Statement: U.S. Department of State, *Documents on Disarmament, 1960* (1961), pp. 86-87.

and pressing task of developing and maintaining the military capacity of the United States. When priorities were established, as they inevitably were, the latter fact was especially important.

Many Senators and scientists complained about the slowness with which Project Vela was implemented. Even Earl H. Voss, who was not among the most enthusiastic supporters of the test ban negotiations, commented in his book *Nuclear Ambush* that the project "obviously was not being pushed full speed ahead."[12]

Divided Counsel: A "Political" or "Scientific" Question?

Regardless of the West's state of technical preparedness, negotiations were in progress and Chairman Khrushchev's missives called for a reply. Among other things, the USSR appeared to be gaining propaganda benefits from the seeming shift in the Western position from advocacy of a comprehensive test ban to support for an atmospheric ban, a point stressed in Chairman Khrushchev's letters. In an attempt to counter this, the White House issued a statement on April 27, 1959, asserting that the United States continued to desire a complete test ban, but the Soviet Union thus far had "been unwilling to accept the control which would make such agreement possible."[13] If the statement had any effect at all, however, it altered the situation only slightly.

Thus on the one hand there was continued pressure by public opinion for a comprehensive test ban. Opposed to this were the arguments that such a ban could not be enforced. These contradictory pressures clashed in the formulation of the next Western move. Chairman Khrushchev's proposal for a predetermined quota of on-site inspections caused deep divisions within the United States Administration. The Atomic Energy Commission, and especially its Chairman, John A. McCone, strongly opposed the concept, arguing that a test ban including such a provision would not provide adequate safeguards for American security. The Department of State, on the other hand, gave the proposal a qualified endorsement. In addition, the British favored it; indeed, they in a sense had originated it.

In the Committee of Principals, Mr. McCone took the attitude

---

[12]Earl H. Voss, *Nuclear Ambush,* p. 445.
[13]*Documents on Disarmament, 1945–1959,* Vol. II, p. 1402.

that this issue was "technical," not "political," and therefore the judgment of the technically qualified experts ought to prevail. The Department of State, on the other hand, took the opposite view. In reality, both technical and political judgments were intertwined. The crucial issues involved the size of detonation which one wished to detect and the degree of assurance which one sought that such detonations were detected; in other words the old threshold problem, which had never been resolved. Such issues were partly "technical" in that they involved estimates of the capability of the proposed control network, but they were also political, in that they involved judgments about the level of acceptable risk, and weighing the risks of a less than perfect test ban against the risks of a world without a test ban. Varying estimates of the trustworthiness of the Soviet Union also entered the picture. As in the past, these issues were not settled, but a new Western position was formulated which was more or less acceptable to all of the parties involved.

The Western Response to Khrushchev: Further on the Inspection Quota

The formal Western response was expressed in letters from President Eisenhower and Prime Minister Macmillan to Chairman Khrushchev dated May 5, 1959.[14] The letters narrowed the differences between East and West to a slight degree. Both Western leaders agreed to "explore," through their representatives in Geneva, the Soviet proposal for an annual quota of on-site inspections on the territories of the three nuclear powers. In particular, the Western leaders argued that questions relating to the criteria for initiating on-site inspections, timely access to areas where unidentified events occurred, and the relationship between the detection capability of the control system and the size of the quota, needed clarification. President Eisenhower also mentioned his feeling that broader problems concerning the operation of the Control Organization and system should be settled. Both Western leaders reiterated their desire for a comprehensive test ban, but went on to say that this was dependent upon the USSR's agreeing to the appropriate control measures, and both repeated the earlier suggestion for a phased agreement starting with an atmospheric ban. President Eisenhower

[14]*Geneva Conference*, pp. 360-63.

wrote that the West would welcome a technical discussion by scientists to consider the feasibility of immediately extending the atmospheric ban to high altitudes and outer space.

Since the report of the Conference of Experts contained no recommendations for control measures at high altitudes and in outer space, obviously some technical decisions would have to be made for these environments. How well prepared the West was to embark on such decisions was debatable. For experimental data, there were the results of the 1958 Johnston Island and Argus shots. These data had been analyzed by the Panofsky Panel and certain tentative conclusions had been drawn. However, the first contract under Project Vela Sierra and Vela Hotel was not let until September 1960, and it would be at least another year before concrete results would be available. Apparently, though, no one on the Committee of Principals within the United States or in the West generally seriously questioned the wisdom of calling for technical talks at this time.

Interestingly neither President Eisenhower nor Prime Minister Macmillan mentioned the new seismic data in their letters to Chairman Khrushchev, bringing it in only inferentially, by requiring that the quota have some relationship to the detection capability of the control system. In the Geneva Conference the Western negotiators were again more explicit on this point, and openly insisted that the new data had to be considered.[15] Mr. Tsarapkin, on the other hand, was equally adamant, maintaining that the technical basis of the negotiations had been established by the Conference of Experts and that these questions could not be reopened. He argued that:

> There can be no doubt that either side could, if it wanted, submit at any time endless so-called new scientific data, which might differ widely in their nature according to the purpose pursued by the experimental scientists in that field. Those who wanted to prove at any cost how difficult it is to detect and identify nuclear explosions would prepare their experiments correspondingly. There are scientists who support this kind of view. We all know that there are certain such scientists in the United States also. It is sufficient to mention, for instance, Dr. Teller.[16]

[15]See GEN/DNT/PV. 88 and PV. 89, *passim*.
[16]GEN/DNT/PV. 89, p. 19.

The USSR's position continued to be that the Treaty had to be negotiated on the basis of the recommendations of the Conference of Experts, which it held the three governments had "accepted"; that the Control Commission could consider new technical developments; and that the Periodic Review Article amply provided for revisions in the control system.

The USSR also took the same attitude with respect to control measures for the detection of nuclear tests at high altitudes and in outer space. Mr. Tsarapkin maintained that the report of the Conference of Experts did contain certain conclusions and that these were sufficient. He also repeated and elaborated his statement made January 8, 1959, that the USSR would be willing to launch artificial earth satellites and to establish ground stations to receive signals from the satellites for purposes of control in these environments.[17] The technical details, he argued, could be worked out by the Preparatory Commission or the Control Commission. In his view, it would be diversionary to become enmeshed in a discussion of such technical details during the course of the political negotiations. It might also set a precedent in terms of going beyond the work of the Conference of Experts prior to the signature of a test ban treaty.

This was where matters stood on May 8, 1959, when the Geneva Conference recessed. The West requested the recess on the ground that the Foreign Ministers of France, the USSR, the United Kingdom, and the United States were scheduled to meet the following Monday, May 11, 1959, and they might hopefully resolve some of the issues which divided the Conference in the course of their meeting.

II

Technical Working Group I

From Diplomats to Scientists: Getting Ready for Technical Working Group I

Certain of these issues were indeed resolved at the Foreign Ministers' meeting—or it would be more accurate to say during the Foreign Ministers' meeting. On May 14, 1959, three days after

[17]GEN/DNT/PV. 89, pp. 25-26.

the meeting opened, Chairman Khrushchev replied to President Eisenhower and Prime Minister Macmillan.[18] Basically the letters were restatements of the Soviet position; however, there was one important exception. The Chairman agreed that there should be a brief "technical discussion of concrete measures as to methods of detecting nuclear explosions at high altitudes on the basis of the conclusion of the Geneva meeting of experts, for the purpose of including such methods in the system of control." The Foreign Ministers confirmed this agreement.

The terms of reference of the technical discussion—or of Technical Working Group I (TWG I) as it ultimately was called —were left to be worked out at the Geneva Conference after it reconvened on June 8, 1959. This proved to be a disputatious task, and one which took the better part of six meetings. The terms of reference were not finally approved until June 15, 1959. Several issues were involved; all probably more important in terms of their implications with respect to the controversial and still unresolved problem of detecting and identifying underground tests and the American new seismic data than in their own right.

Chairman Khrushchev implicitly, and Foreign Minister Gromyko directly, both again refused to consider the new data and insisted that the negotiations had to be based on the conclusions of the Conference of Experts. The West on the other hand continued to insist that the new data had to be considered. On June 12, 1959, the United States finally introduced the findings and report of the Berkner Panel into the Geneva Conference.[19] Having failed to obtain agreement through the Foreign Ministers, the United States now apparently hoped to force a modification in the Soviet position through a more open confrontation. Mr. Tsarapkin's immediate response was that the conclusions of the Berkner Panel had been "broadly known" to the USSR "since last March from the magazine *Fortune.*"[20]

The dispute about the terms of reference of Technical Working Group I should be viewed in the light of this continuing controversy. First, the two sides were divided as to whether or not the report of

[18]*Geneva Conference,* pp. 363-67.
[19]GEN/DNT/PV. 94, pp. 24-31.
[20]*Ibid.,* p. 32.

the Conference of Experts should be mentioned. The Western powers finally reluctantly agreed that it should be. Secondly, there was a controversy concerning whether TWG I should discuss only which instruments should be used for detection, as the USSR argued, or more broadly evaluate the possible techniques of detection and identification, as the West insisted. In this case the Western position was accepted. Thirdly, the two sides differed about whether or not the tentative theoretical evaluations concerning the effectiveness of various techniques contained in the report of the Conference of Experts could be changed; the Soviet Union argued that they could not, and the Western powers that they could. A related issue was whether or not the data from the United States 1958 tests could be considered. Mr. Tsarapkin eventually agreed that the new material could be considered, and the larger issue was solved in a compromise fashion, as can be seen from the terms of reference:

> The technical working group should assess the capabilities and limitations of possible techniques for the detection and identification of nuclear explosions at high altitudes (more than 30 to 50 kilometers) above the earth and, on the basis of discussions and conclusions of the Geneva conference of experts, recommend techniques and instrumentation for consideration by the Conference for incorporation in the Detection and Identification System.[21]

Fifthly, the Soviet Union sought to expand the terms of reference of Technical Working Group I so that it would also be directed to consider the problem of determining criteria for on-site inspections in the case of suspected underground nuclear explosions. The Western powers refused this proposal on the ground that different technical specialties were involved and, more importantly, they felt that the question of criteria could not be examined without considering the new seismic data. Finally, the Soviet Union won Western agreement that the Technical Working Group should report to the Conference on June 29, 1959, one week after it was convened, which proved to be an impossibly short time. Even though TWG I extended beyond this deadline, the scientists had an incredible, almost around the clock, working day during the Conference, as they did each time that they met during the test ban negotiations.

[21]GEN/DNT/PV. 95, p. 13.

Once agreement had been reached on the terms of reference, it was necessary to assemble delegations to participate in the technical discussions. A British delegation of three scientists in government employ was quickly assembled.[22] None of the three had attended the Conference previously. The Soviet delegation was headed by Dr. Fedorov, who had chaired the Eastern panel at the Conference of Experts and had stayed in Geneva for the opening stages of the political negotiations. Two others of the seven-member Soviet delegation had also served on the Eastern panel at the Conference of Experts, M. A. Sadovsky and O. I. Leypunsky.[23]

In the United States, several scientists had been approached on a tentative basis earlier. PSAC and the Office of the Science Adviser served as the bodies which recommended nominations to the President and the Department of State. On Tuesday the sixteenth, those selected were informed that they should fly to Geneva that Thursday and be ready for the opening of the discussions the following Monday. Wolfgang K. H. Panofsky, Director of the High Energy Physics Laboratory at Stanford University, who had headed the Panel of the President's Science Advisory Committee which had examined this subject, was chosen as the Chairman of the American delegation.[24] In creating the delegation, an attempt was made—as it had been with respect to the Conference of Experts—to maintain balance between the conflicting points of view among scientists concerning the wisdom of a test ban, and those with extreme positions were not included. Of the nine men appointed to the delegation, only two, Richard Latter and Spurgeon Keeny had at-

[22]H. R. Hulme, I. Maddock, and R. Press.

[23]The other members of the Soviet delegation were J. L. Alpert, A. I. Ustyumenko, O. A. Grinevsky, and S. N. Vernov. There is reason for believing that Grinevsky was not a scientist but a political representative.

[24]The other members of the delegation were: Sterling Colgate, Lawrence Radiation Laboratory, University of California; Allen F. Donovan, Director, Astrovehicles Laboratory, Space Technology Laboratory, Los Angeles, California; Allen Graves, Lawrence Radiation Laboratory, University of California; Spurgeon Keeny, Jr., Technical Assistant, Office of Special Assistant to the President for Science and Technology; Richard Latter, Chief, Physics Division, RAND Corporation, Santa Monica, California; Col. Dent L. Lay, Assistant Director, Technical Operations Division, Advanced Research Projects Agency, Department of Defense; Allen M. Petersen, Head, Propagation Laboratory, Stanford Research Institute, Menlo Park, California; and Kenneth M. Watson, Professor of Physics, University of California at Berkeley.

tended the Conference of Experts. The former (like his brother Albert) was a RAND Corporation physicist and the latter, a technical assistant in the Office of the Special Assistant to the President for Science and Technology. In addition, the delegation included Allen Graves, a physicist on leave from the Lawrence Radiation Laboratory, who had been attending the political negotiations as the representative of the Atomic Energy Commission.

Professor Panofsky was actually intercepted in the midst of a cross-country trip with his wife and five children. His destination, though, was Geneva, where he planned to spend a year at CERN, the *Organisation européenne pour la recherche nucléaire*. He left his family, hurried to Washington—he was the only nonofficial member of the delegation to go there prior to departure for Europe—where he had a fifteen-minute conference with the Secretary of State, and then went on to Geneva, arriving somewhat later than the rest of the American delegation, and after the first meeting of Technical Working Group I.

Many of the members of the American delegation had been members of Professor Panofsky's Panel on the detection of nuclear explosions at high altitudes and in outer space, and this was the only preparation that the group had to work with. The Panel had met about eight or nine times in the winter of 1958-59. Each meeting lasted about a day, and the Panel members did various pieces of work in the interim periods. Dr. Killian had attended most of the meetings, and representatives of the Department of Defense and Atomic Energy Commission were members of the Panel. The Department of State, however, was not represented, and generally speaking the group had very little politicial guidance. Again, the scientists were not told what threshold of detection would be the maximum risk that the United States could accept. In this instance, in contrast to the Conference of Experts and a later technical working group, the questions of identification· and "objective criteria" were carefully avoided. The scientists were not told how much money the United States would be willing to invest in a detection and identification system, nor were they told how much to assume that an evader would be willing to spend to mask his action. Thus there were no cost figures. This was the case despite the fact that the report of the Panofsky Panel had contained an approximate assessment of the cost of conducting clandestine nuclear explosions in space using various methods, and of the cost of various detection systems. The scientists were not given any guidance concerning the basis for choice between various alternative techniques. They were merely given the data from the 1958 test series and asked to evaluate the capabilities and limitations of various techniques for detection and identification and to elaborate a possible system. Secretary of State Herter did not expand these instructions very much in his brief conference with Professor Panofsky. Just as in the case of the Conference of Experts various crucial problems were left for the scientists to decide.

Nor were these matters settled when the American delegation assembled in Geneva. The scientists spent most of the weekend brushing up on their technical preparation. Ambassador Wadsworth was reluctant to become involved in technical discussions, and in any case, could not make fundamental politicial decisions. A junior State Department member of the American delegation at the Geneva Conference was assigned to the scientists, but he did not fully understand the technical issues, nor did he attend all of the meetings of Technical Working Group I. During the course of the negotiations the scientists found it completely impossible to obtain political guidance. In other words, the United States treated Technical Working Group I, as it had the Conference of Experts, as a purely technical session which the scientists should work at by themselves.

TWG I: Toward an Adjustment in the Scientific Base

Technical Working Group I began with an argument between East and West concerning the agenda, which in several respects repeated the controversy about its terms of reference. Dr. Fedorov proposed a draft agenda which virtually would have limited the discussion to the elaboration of matters treated by the Conference of Experts.[25] The West on the other hand preferred a broader definition of TWG I's tasks, and eventually won its point. However, the controversy continued to plague the technical discussions. Throughout TWG I the Soviet scientists tended to take the report of the Conference of Experts as a fixed document, binding the various states. They were willing to accept only evaluations which confirmed or upgraded the assessments arrived at then, and fought

25GEN/DNT/TWG I, PV.1, pp. 12-15.

any attempts to demonstrate that these assessments were too optimistic.

As in the Conference of Experts, the burden of proof tended to rest with the West since it was the Western powers which had demanded that the technical discussion be held. The Western scientists presented the bulk of the data, and it seems fairly clear that the Soviet scientists withheld considerable data which would have been useful to the discussions. This is not to say that the West made all of the data which it had available, but merely to say that it made considerably more available. Throughout the discussions, the Western scientists pressed for quantitative assessments. The Soviet scientists preferred more general formulations. The Western scientists sought to point out how violators might attempt to avoid detection. The Soviet scientists made light of these suggestions and often appeared not to have previously considered the possibilities. The Western scientists sought to indicate that although something was known about the signals of nuclear explosions at high altitudes and in outer space, very little was known about the natural background with which such signals had to compete. None of the devices which were discussed as instruments of detection existed at that time, although some of their component parts were technically proved. The Western scientists introduced data from the United States 1958 test series but argued that only the Teak and Orange shots were directly relevant and that these were conducted at relatively low altitudes. They maintained that further empirical data might invalidate their theoretical conclusions, making them appear either too optimistic or too pessimistic. The Soviet scientists argued as they had in the past that the progress of science as a whole could only result in improvements in the ability to detect and identify nuclear explosions at high altitudes.

In testimony before the Joint Committee on Atomic Energy about a year later, Professor Panofsky summed up the position and difficulties of the Western scientists.

> We all realize that the Russians have very little interest in the technical reliability of control procedures because clandestine testing is essentially impossible in any of the Western countries. They do, however, have a very substantial interest in maintaining the secrecy of their country, and therefore in reducing the degree of access demanded

by the control system. Hence, it is always in their interest to minimize the extent of the control system; in order to do this the tendency is to view the performance of the control system in the best possible light. Any critical evaluation of the performance of the system, therefore, always rests upon the shoulders of the Western delegations. In turn, this makes the performance of the negotiations very arduous for the Western technical delegates since in many cases the facts which have to form the basis for a critical assessment have not been developed prior to negotiations.[26]

The differences between the Western and Soviet scientists in these matters were even more acute during the sessions of Technical Working Group I than they had been during the Conference of Experts. No doubt, both sides, and especially the Western scientists, constantly had the controversial history of the report produced in that meeting in mind.

Following the pattern of the Conference of Experts, and the agenda, the report of Technical Working Group I was divided into two basic sections. The first section contained a general discussion of techniques for detecting nuclear explosions at high altitudes. It was divided into two subsections; the first, dealing with detection by means of apparatus installed in artificial earth and solar satellites; and the second, dealing with detection by means of apparatus installed at ground-based control posts. The second half of the report contained recommendations for consideration by the political Conference concerning the techniques and instruments which might be incorporated in the Detection and Identification System. In this section, in contrast to the report of the Conference of Experts, alternatives were spelled out in certain areas and the choices left to others.

Other than the problems which arose from the broad differences of approach mentioned above, drafting the first part of the report was relatively noncontroversial. The only deep difference appeared to be caused by differing technical experiences; the orbit

[26]U.S. Congress, Joint Committee on Atomic Energy, Special Subcommittee on Radiation and the Subcommittee on Research and Development, *Hearings: Technical Aspects of Detection and Inspection Controls of a Nuclear Weapons Test Ban,* 86th Congress, 2d Session (1960), pp. 38-39.

of Soviet satellites had been such as to gather little information on the Van Allen radiation belt, and as a consequence the Soviet scientists were less inclined to take this feature of the atmosphere into account than the Western scientists. In general, both sides had very little empirical data on the level of background radiation in the atmosphere.

Not surprisingly it proved less easy to agree on recommendations for control systems, which was after all the core of the issue. Indeed, it is difficult to see why the attempt to arrive at joint assessments was necessary, except as an effort to erect an agreed point of departure for the recommendations. In formulating the recommendations, the scientists were in effect engaging in political negotiations, though the subject matter was technical and scientific. The American scientists were clearly considerably more aware of this than they had been a year earlier at the Conference of Experts.[27] However, their political instructions were not any more complete than they had been in the previous instance. In the absence of instructions on such vital matters as threshold and cost, the American scientists tended to push for the maximum. For example, one of the problems of detection of nuclear explosions at high altitudes was the danger of false alarms; the danger that the control system might indicate that a nuclear explosion had occurred when actually none had. The Americans sought to minimize this possibility as much as possible through redundancy (having overlapping systems) and other methods; their target was a system that would not produce more than one false alarm every one hundred years. The Soviet scientists on the other hand were inclined to make more modest demands on the recommended system, but ultimately generally agreed to the American position.

The same pressure to provide for all possible contingencies led the American scientists to argue the need for a system of satellites in orbit around the sun, so that there would be no blind spots behind the sun or the moon. This recommendation, to which the

[27]For example, during the Conference Panofsky said to Fedorov: "I am more than happy to negotiate on matters of recommendations where political judgment is involved, where we must reach an agreement in order to have an agreed report concerning what steps are to be taken, but I cannot negotiate on the question of the modification of scientific facts." GEN/DNT/-HAT/PV. 16, p. 46.

Soviet scientists were opposed and which would have involved substantial cost, was phrased in optional terms. Interestingly, after the conclusion of Technical Working Group I, with the advantage of further research, the American scientists also became less interested in the system of solar satellites.[28] They eventually concluded that the costs and difficulties of conducting clandestine nuclear explosions behind the sun or the moon would be so great that it was highly unlikely that any violator would take such action.

In all, ten methods of detection were considered, and techniques involving all but one of these were recommended for inclusion in the Detection and Identification System. The one which was not recommended was a ground-based technique, backscatter radar. After over a week of irrelevant, and at times spurious technical argument, Dr. Fedorov stated that the Soviet scientists could not agree to recommend backscatter radar because it could "also be used for purposes having nothing to do with the control of high-altitude explosions."[29] Although the American scientists were reluctant to admit that backscatter radar is an effective means of observing the launching of missiles, nevertheless, on the basis of the Argus experiments, the American scientists believed it to be an extremely useful means of detecting nuclear explosions at high altitudes. Failure to include it in the Detection and Identification System would result in an uncovered "hole" in the system under certain conditions in the area from 50 to 100 kilometers and a "half-covered hole" from 100 to 1,000 kilometers. The report merely stated that the Technical Working Group had been unable to come to an accord on this matter. That under certain circumstances there would be a "hole" in the system was not mentioned in the report.

This provides an example of the difficulty which the scientists had in obtaining political guidance. When it appeared certain that there would be an impasse on the question of whether or not to recommend backscatter radar in the control system, the American scientists felt that the most constructive move would be to agree to disagree. This being a political decision, the delegation sought guidance, but found it extremely difficult to convey the nature of the

[28]See Panofsky's comments before the Joint Committee on Atomic Energy, *Hearings: Technical Aspects . . . of a Nuclear Weapons Test Ban, supra* note 26, p. 47.

[29]GEN/DNT/HAT/PV. 17, p. 81.

problem to the diplomats and politicians in Geneva and Washington. In the end, the scientists had to take the decision on their own responsibility.

In formulating the recommendations the Western scientists sought to be as specific as possible, for instance listing the exact number of satellites required and their orbits. The Soviet scientists preferred more general formulations, and at one point suggested that matters involving a choice between various alternatives should be left to the Control Commission. Professor Panofsky refused to do this, on the ground that decisions on such issues should be the prerogative of the diplomatic Conference.[30] In some instances he was willing to leave the choice between alternatives for subsequent decision, although in more specific terms than the Soviet scientists preferred, but he argued that the diplomatic Conference had to decide how the decisions should be made. The reason for the insistence of the American scientists on being specific was their awareness of the tentative agreement reached in the Geneva Conference that major changes in the detection and identification system would require the unanimity of the three nuclear powers.[31]

The problem of identifying the violator after a nuclear explosion at high altitudes had been detected by the control system was not discussed in Technical Working Group I. Nor did the group discuss criteria for establishing evidence of detection. As had been mentioned, these issues had been carefully avoided by the politicians and diplomats in their discussions with the scientists. Technically, there is no way the violator could be identified unless the control system also had available to it information on missile launchings. Had the system been established, either some agreement would have had to have been reached on this point, or in the case of a detection of a nuclear explosion, states would have had to base their decision concerning what action to take on their unilateral intelligence systems. Since the duration article provided that the treaty could be terminated by unilateral action, this would be feasible. However, in all of the other environments the Western powers demanded incontrovertible evidence identifying the violator.

One might ask if such evidence was necessary in other en-

[30]GEN/DNT/HAT/PV. 14, p. 71.
[31]See *Hearings: Technical Aspects . . . of a Nuclear Weapons Test Ban, supra* note 26, p. 40.

vironments, why not at high altitudes? Or, if not necessary at high altitudes, then why was it necessary for atmospheric, underwater, and underground explosions? Presumably the reason was that for identification it would have been necessary to have controls over another element of weaponry, the launching of missiles. But, to establish positive identification in the case of underground explosions, on-site inspections are required, which might also reveal other aspects of military strength.

Whether or not the system recommended by Technical Working Group I would have provided sufficient safeguards against the possibility of clandestine nuclear explosions in outer space was a matter of judgment. First, there was the "hole" in the system at low altitudes under certain conditions caused by the failure to recommend the backscatter radar technique. Secondly, there was the problem of identification. Finally, and perhaps most importantly, at extremely high altitudes—above 5,000,000 miles—it would only be possible to detect nuclear explosions through the soft or thermal X-ray technique, and shielding would appreciably reduce the effectiveness of this technique. Thus, if a violator were willing to spend sufficient resources to put a nuclear device, the necessary instrumentation, and a shield into outer space, and were patient enough to wait some time for the results, he could conduct undetected nuclear weapon tests.

Whether or not the possibility that a state might conduct undetected clandestine nuclear explosions in outer space constituted a serious risk was subject to debate. Professor Panofsky, in testimony before the Joint Committee on Atomic Energy expressed this opinion:

> From the purely technical point of view, it appears likely that, given arbitrarily high incentives on the part of the violator, it will always be possible to devise an essentially undetectable means of carrying out the violation. I believe, however, that before that point is reached, there is the question of whether there really is sufficient incentive either for the violator to carry out tests under these extreme conditions or for the detecting system to be expanded to the maximum possible degree.[32]

[32]*Hearings: Technical Aspects . . . of a Nuclear Weapons Test Ban,* *supra* note 26, p. 37.

On the other hand, Dr. Byron P. Leonard, of the Space Technology Laboratory, during the same hearing asserted, "It is really no trick at all to run tests outside of the X-ray detection circle . . ."[33] Edward Teller expressed the same view in a syndicated newspaper article, "Testing in space provides a loophole through which one could drive a herd of wild elephants."[34] Again, all three scientists used the same technical data; where they differed was in their estimate of the necessary degree of security or in the threshold of detectability below which American security interests would be endangered. This was a political judgment involving an assessment of the intentions of other states, one's willingness to bear monetary and other costs involved in any type of detection system, and one's willingness to accept risks. Yet these were decisions on which the American scientists at Technical Working Group I, as their predecessors at the Conference of Experts, received little guidance from either United States politicians or diplomats.

TWG I Reports to the Diplomatic Conference

Technical Working Group I adopted its report on the morning of Friday, July 10, 1959. That afternoon the report was presented to the diplomatic Conference. Both sides argued that the results of the Technical Working Group supported their position with respect to the report of the Conference of Experts.[35] In the Soviet view, the report of TWG I confirmed the findings of the earlier report, and proved that the progress of science made detection easier, while in the Western view it was conclusive evidence of the importance of looking at new data, and also proved that the demand to do this was not grounded on obstructionist motives.

The Conference agreed to release the report of Technical Working Group I immediately. This was in contrast to the situation with respect to the report of the Conference of Experts, which had first been submitted to the governments concerned and then released.

The next move with respect to the problems discussed by Technical Working Group I came one month later, on August 10,

[33]*Ibid.*, p. 345.
[34]*Houston Post,* August 16, 1960.
[35]See GEN/DNT/PV. 109, *passim.*

1959, when Mr. Tsarapkin announced that the USSR agreed to "the inclusion of the methods and instrumentation recommended . . . for the detection of high-altitude nuclear explosions in the system of control over the cessation of nuclear tests."[36] That same day, the British delegate, Sir Michael Wright, stated that his government accepted the report "as a correct technical assessment of possible techniques for the detection and identification of high-altitude nuclear explosions in the light of scientific knowledge available at the time of the Working Group's session."[37] He added that his government was prepared to take part in discussions regarding the embodiment in the treaty of provisions on high-altitude controls, in the light of the recommendations contained in the report."

It was obvious that Ambassador Wadsworth, at this point, had no instructions on the issue. On August 26, 1959, however, following Sir Michael Wright's phraseology, he stated that the United States accepted "the report as a correct technical assessment of the capabilities and limitations of possible techniques for the detection and identification of high-altitude nuclear explosions in the light of presently available scientific knowledge."[38] He also said that the United States was studying the "complex problems of timing and scope" that would be involved in preparing treaty language for a high-altitude detection system "that would be established" on the basis of "the report of TWG I." However, the United States did not discuss its proposals concerning this matter in broad outline until March 29, 1961,[39] nearly two years later, and it did not submit specific treaty language until April 18, 1961.[40]

The basic reason for the delay was the inability of the United States Administration to agree on the degree of risk that the United States could reasonably accept; again, it was the threshold problem. The demands of the Atomic Energy Commission and, to a lesser extent, of the Department of Defense, were considerably higher than those of the Department of State or the President's Science Advisory

[36]GEN/DNT/PV. 121, p. 10.
[37]Ibid., p. 13.
[38]GEN/DNT/PV. 127, p. 4.
[39]See GEN/DNT/PV. 280, pp. 3-7.
[40]Geneva Conference, pp. 508-9.

Committee. A related reason was the high cost of the complete high altitude system. Few were willing to countenance this cost. Thus the United States put itself in the uncomfortable position of insisting on the one hand that the "loophole" associated with the lack of high altitude coverage was sufficient reason to be an impediment toward concluding a nuclear test ban treaty, while on the other hand it did not appear to regard the "loophole" as being of sufficient importance to be willing to pay the money to plug it. Significantly, when treaty language was finally proposed, with the advantage of data gained from Vela Sierra and Vela Hotel, the United States asked for a system which was somewhat more modest and consequently considerably less expensive than that which had been recommended by Technical Working Group I. Eventually, when the United States signed the Moscow Treaty, which relied on national detection systems, it agreed to a ban on testing at high altitudes and in outer space before basic elements in its own national control system were operative.

The subsequent history of the action with respect to the report of Technical Working Group I, raises again the question of why the Western powers insisted on calling the meeting. Certainly the Western governments did not learn anything from the discussions that they could not have learned from private consultations with their own scientists. The extent of knowledge was limited, and there were risks in doing anything such as making formal recommendations for a control system that might tend to "freeze" the situation. Formulating recommendations involved political choices, which the United States government was unprepared or unable or unwilling to make at that time and for more than a year and a half after the report of TWG I was filed. Perhaps some American officials hoped that the technical discussions would in some way solve the problem for them. If they did, they both overestimated and misunderstood the qualities and powers of science. In fact, however, the Technical Working Group I did set a precedent for reconsidering matters discussed by the Conference of Experts, and perhaps this was its principal function for the West. In addition, of course, when the United States eventually decided to accept some of the recommendations of TWG I, the Soviet Union was already on record as having done so.

The Diplomatic Conference Inches Along

The Geneva Conference had been in session during the meetings of Technical Working Group I and it continued in session until August 26, 1959. The meetings, however, appeared to be mainly exercises in marking time. Neither side substantially modified its position. The Western powers continued to insist that the new data had to be considered, and the USSR continued to refuse to take this action. Mr. Tsarapkin constantly referred to the report of the Conference of Experts as "the basis" for the negotiations, while Ambassador Wadsworth held that it was merely "an agreed statement of the best scientific opinion available as of mid-1958."[41]

The USSR's position, though, was clarified somewhat when on June 19, 1959, Mr. Tsarapkin gave a more detailed response to the findings of the Berkner Panel.[42] It was essentially negative. First of all, he alleged that to act on the recommendations of the Berkner Panel would mean that a test ban would be delayed for many years. He pointed out that no one could confidently predict how the suggestion for putting seismographs in deep holes would work out, since this technique was largely unexplored. He also objected to the suggestion of unmanned stations placed at considerably closer intervals than had been recommended at the Conference of Experts. He alleged that they would create opportunities for espionage since men would have to install the stations and check their operation.

The Soviet position was further clarified on July 9, 1959, when Mr. Tsarapkin submitted a draft article on on-site inspection.[43] As he had asserted previously in response to Western questioning, the terms of the article did not require the unanimous agreement of the three nuclear powers for the dispatch of an inspection team and the inspection teams could go anywhere that the instruments indicated that an unidentified event had occurred. From the Western point of view, an unexpected feature of the proposal was that the three nuclear powers would each be subject to an equal number of inspections. Actually the proposal advanced the negotiations very little, for the most crucial element, the number of on-site inspections that

[41]GEN/DNT/PV. 99, p. 10.
[42]*Ibid.*, pp. 14-16.
[43]GEN/DNT/PV. 108, pp. 3-4.

would be allowed annually, was not specified; the draft merely contained a blank space. The USSR did not formally submit a definite figure until more than a year later. However, the day before Ambassador Tsarapkin submitted the draft article, Soviet First Deputy Premier Frol R. Koslov told Michigan's Governor G. Mennen Williams that the USSR might accept as many as three on-site inspections each year,[44] which is the figure that the Soviet Union ultimately proposed on July 26, 1960. Soviet representatives also mentioned the figure three in informal conversations in Geneva in the summer of 1959.

The West assumed that a much larger number would be needed, and the ensuing argument between East and West concerning whether the quota should be "politically determined," as the USSR insisted, or "scientifically determined," as the United States and the United Kingdom insisted, was in reality principally an argument about numbers. At the time very little was known about the frequency of small earthquakes and the knowledge about the relationship between the seismological signals transmitted by underground nuclear explosions and earthquakes was at best sketchy. If one accepted the estimate of unidentified events contained in the report of the Conference of Experts, the figure of three on-site inspections annually in the USSR would not be completely unreasonable even though such a small figure would pose practical difficulties. However, the West felt that in view of the new data such a figure would be clearly insufficient. At the same time, the West was not prepared to submit a specific figure, and actually did not make a definite proposal until February 11, 1960. Then it merely suggested that a fixed percentage of unidentified events should be eligible for inspection. In fact, no one knew how many unidentified events there would be. In these terms, the Western demand that the Conference consider the new data and agree that the quota of on-site inspections should be scientifically determined were really demands to get pegs on which to base claims for a larger number of inspections. The United States position also reflected the Atomic Energy Commission's insistence that this was a "technical" matter on which its views should have precedence. In somewhat different terms, the question of the number of on-site inspections again raised the

[44]*New York Times*, July 9, 1959, p. 3.

troublesome problem of the threshold. What risk could and should the United States take?

The debate on these matters continued throughout this phase of the Conference. Perhaps the most lively session occurred on July 1, when the American delegation was accompanied by the Chairman of the Atomic Energy Commission, John A. McCone, and a group of Congressional observers.[45] Both sides were at their belligerent best. Exactly what purpose this episode served is difficult to fathom.

The Ending of Soviet Nuclear Assistance to Communist China

Actually, the most important events for the course of the negotiations at this stage occurred elsewhere. Perhaps the most important of these was that the USSR appears to have decided to discontinue assisting Communist China develop a nuclear capacity. The Chinese have charged that on June 20, 1959, "The Soviet Government unilaterally tore up the agreement on new technology for national defense concluded between China and the Soviet Union on October 15, 1957, and refused to provide China with a sample of an atomic bomb and technical data concerning its manufacture."[46] If this charge is true, and the USSR has not denied it, such a decision on the part of the Soviet Union had important implications for the prospects of a test ban. Like the United States, the Soviet Union apparently found it impossible to engage in a complete transfer of nuclear weapons to other states. One can only speculate about the reasons for this, but it seems plausible to assume that the USSR wanted to avoid creation of situations which might allow it to become involved in nuclear war by the actions of an ally. No doubt the USSR was also concerned about its present and potential relationship with the ally in question. China's acquisition of a nuclear capability would strengthen that state in relation to the USSR. If these were the Soviet concerns, at this point a test ban may well have assumed greater importance for the USSR.

45GEN/DNT/PV. 106.
46"Statement of the Chinese Government, July 31, 1963," *Jen-min Jih-pao,* July 31, 1963, as quoted in Alice Langley Hsieh, "The Sino-Soviet Nuclear Dialogue: 1963," *Journal of Conflict Resolution,* Vol. VIII, No. 2 (June 1964), pp. 99-115, at 111.

The American Decision to Continue the Moratorium

At that time, however, the West was ignorant of these developments. For the United States, the most crucial decision that had to be taken during this period was whether or not, in the light of the impasse in the negotiations, the one-year moratorium on testing of nuclear weapons offered by President Eisenhower in his initial proposal for the Conference should be continued. Although this was related to the question of whether or not the negotiations should be continued, the two issues were considered to be separable. That the issue of the moratorium had to be decided shows the limited significance of President Eisenhower's statement, made in November 1958 when he revealed that the Soviet Union had continued to test after the opening of the diplomatic conference, that the United States would no longer consider itself bound by its pledge to forego testing.

Even though there was a specific point at which a decision in this matter supposedly was made, like so many important decisions in the course of these negotiations—and perhaps generally—by that time prior decisions and other events almost forced the choice. Alternatives were first narrowed in the discussions and decisions relating to the Federal Budget for fiscal year 1960. As has already been mentioned, the Administration decided not to ask for funds for the testing of nuclear weapons during that period. Chairman McCone and General Starbird of the Atomic Energy Commission explained the nature and ramifications of the decisions within the Administration—which Congress in due course confirmed—in testimony before the House Committee on Appropriations on June 23, 1959. They stated that the Administration had decided to request only sufficient funds to maintain the test sites on a standby basis "except for limited tunnel construction at the Nevada test site to provide an underground test readiness capability should weapons tests be resumed."[47] In the Pacific Test area, the AEC envisaged employing fewer people and spending less money than was normally spent in periods between test series; the objective was only to retard and prevent the inevitable deterioration resulting from the climate. The work on the tunnels in Nevada was in part designed to obtain

---

[47]U.S. Congress, House of Representatives, Appropriations Committee, *Hearings: Atomic Energy Commission Appropriations for 1960*, 86th Congress, 1st Session (1959), p. 72.

information from past tests. In addition, the program was designed
to give decision-makers some flexibility. If no construction were
undertaken, it would take nearly a year from the time that a decision
was taken to resume testing until it could be executed.[48] As it was,
because of the extensive nature of the 1958 test series and the
budgetary decisions for fiscal 1960, the United States probably could
not have resumed testing nuclear weapons on a significant and
meaningful scale in 1959, and probably not even in the first half
of 1960.

A second factor narrowing the range of alternatives was that
in the summer of 1959 a new round of East-West negotiations
came into prospect. The Foreign Ministers of France, the USSR,
the United Kingdom and the United States resumed their negotiations in Geneva on July 13 and continued in session until August
5. Among other things they agreed that a Ten-Nation Disarmament
Committee should be established outside the framework of the
United Nations and on the basis of parity between East and West.
Thus, they finally conceded what the Soviet Union had demanded at
the twelfth session of the General Assembly in 1957. They agreed
that the Committee should meet sometime in 1960 and that it should
report to the UN Disarmament Commission. In anticipation of this
development, the Administration established a committee under the
chairmanship of Charles A. Coolidge, a Boston attorney and a
former Assistant Secretary of Defense, to reexamine and reevaluate
the American position with respect to disarmament. The Administration again chose to rely on an "outsider" and a generalist for
a reexamination and reformulation of its basic disarmament position.
A related development was that in mid-July, President Eisenhower
decided that he would invite Chairman Khrushchev to visit the
United States and that he would agree to return the visit. Khrushchev's trip was scheduled to coincide with the opening of the
fourteenth General Assembly of the United Nations in September.

Prior to his trip, Khrushchev made two important pronouncements with respect to the test ban negotiations. On August 11 he
stated that the USSR would accept a pledge not to be the first
nation to resume testing nuclear weapons.[49] At about the same time,

[48]See *ibid.*, p. 168.
[49]*New York Times*, August 11, 1959, p. 1.

an article was submitted under his name for publication in *Foreign Affairs*. Although it was not published until early September, decision-makers were aware of its contents somewhat earlier. In the article he stated that the progress in the test ban negotiations justified "the hope that an agreement on the discontinuation of nuclear weapon tests will shortly be reached."[50] He went on to state that such an agreement "would be an important step on the way to the solution of the disarmament problem and the banning of nuclear weapons in general." Among other things, the statement revealed the verbal constancy of the Soviet objective of eliminating nuclear weapons.

Thus when the Committee of Principals discussed whether or not to continue the moratorium there was really little choice. The United States was not in a position to inaugurate a significant test series. To end the moratorium might jeopardize the test ban talks and might also foreclose the possibility of fruitful negotiations on broader issues. In any case, the United States would be subjected to criticism on these grounds, and since the General Assembly was about to open, critics would have ample access to a worldwide forum. In the light of Chairman Khrushchev's pronouncement about the Soviet position, the United States could be particularly vulnerable.

The advice of the Committee of Principals and the decision of the President was first that the United States should ask for a six-week recess in the Geneva negotiations which would coincide with Chairman Khrushchev's visit to the United States and the opening of the General Assembly, and secondly that the United States should continue its unilateral suspension of nuclear weapons tests through the current calendar year. The latter aspect of this decision was made public in a statement released by the Department of State on August 26, the day the Conference recessed.[51]

The United Kingdom took a somewhat different line. On August 27 the Foreign Office announced that the United Kingdom would not resume nuclear weapons tests as long as "useful discussions" were under way looking toward an agreement.

[50]"On Peaceful Coexistence," *Foreign Affairs*, Vol. XXXVIII, No. 1 (October 1959), pp. 1-18, at 10.
[51]*Geneva Conference*, p. 375.

The following day the Soviet Government released its statement on the matter. The statement was in accord with Chairman Khrushchev's earlier pronouncement. It stated that the Council of Ministers had resolved:

> Not to resume nuclear tests in the Soviet Union if the Western Powers do not resume testing of atomic and hydrogen weapons. Only in the case of resumption by them of nuclear weapons tests will the Soviet Union be free from this pledge.[52]

If all three governments acted according to their pledges, the moratorium would continue through 1959, and in view of the Soviet and British positions, there would be strong pressure to continue it even longer. At this point, the Soviet Union had in reality what it had always asked for, an unpoliced test ban.

On the East River and at Camp David

Actually, because of the British election, the Geneva Conference did not resume until October 27. Meanwhile, the question of a test ban was considered and debated in other forums, both as a separate issue and in the context of broader measures of disarmament. In particular, the matter was discussed in private meetings between President Eisenhower and Chairman Khrushchev and their advisers at Camp David and in public on the bank of the East River in the General Assembly of the United Nations. On the surface, none of the discussions appeared to advance the negotiations.

Chairman Khrushchev stole the headlines on September 19 when, during the course of his appearance before the United Nations, he offered a proposal for General and Complete Disarmament."[53] By the terms of this proposal all states "should divest themselves of the means of waging war" within a period of four years; they would be permitted to retain only those forces required for internal security. If the Western powers were not prepared to accept this, Khrushchev offered an alternative proposal for partial measures

[52]*Ibid.*, p. 377.
[53]UN General Assembly, Plenary Meetings, *Official Records* (14th Session), pp. 31-38. See also UN Document A/4219.

of disarmament. Interestingly, a test ban was not included in either suggestion. However, during the course of his address, he stated that the question of a test ban was "acute and eminently ripe for solution," and asserted that negotiations on broader measures of disarmament should not delay progress on this matter. He also repeated the pledge that the USSR would not "resume nuclear explosions in its country if the Western Powers do not resume the testing of atomic and hydrogen weapons."

Actually, British Foreign Minister Selwyn Lloyd had outlined a comprehensive plan for disarmament the previous day, but because it was phrased in less dramatic terms, it received much less public attention.[54] His was a gradual scheme, which included a test ban as an integral first step.

The General Assembly did not begin to consider either proposal in detail or other matters relating to disarmament until October 9. In the interim, Chairman Khrushchev and President Eisenhower held their tête à tête at Camp David. The two leaders discussed the test ban talks fleetingly and Secretary of State Herter and Foreign Minister Gromyko also considered the matter.[55] Apparently all that happened was that both sides expounded their positions. In retrospect, however, it appears that the Soviet leadership became convinced of the American determination that the new seismic data would have to be considered before the United States would agree to a comprehensive test ban.

Back in the General Assembly both the Soviet and British disarmament schemes were mooted, and eventually a resolution was unanimously adopted which referred both, as well as other suggestions, to the new Ten-Nation Disarmament Committee.[56]

In addition, the Assembly discussed the questions of banning nuclear tests and preventing the dispersion of nuclear weapons both in general terms and specifically with respect to the proposed French tests in the Sahara. In contrast to the previous session, neither the USSR nor the United States submitted draft resolutions. The pre-

[54]UN General Assembly, Plenary Meetings, *Official Records,* (14th Session), pp. 21-26. See also UN Document A/C. 1/820.

[55]See Secretary of State Herter's comment at his news conference of October 6, 1959: U.S. Department of State *Bulletin,* Vol. XLI, No. 1061 (October 26, 1959), p. 578.

[56]UN General Assembly Resolution 1378 (XIV).

vious year each protagonist had submitted draft resolutions with the obvious motivation of gaining support for their respective positions and strengthening their hands at the negotiating table. Now, however, the two superpowers seemed content to leave the matter for private talks, and it was the smaller powers who were attempting to use the Assembly. They felt strongly about the general issue and were particularly concerned about the proposed French nuclear tests. The strength of their sentiment can be explained in various terms. For one thing, nuclear weapons were glaring evidence of the disparity between their power and that of the superpowers. Thus the issue became mixed with the traditional small state-large state controversy. For another, they regarded testing, with the resultant contamination of the atmosphere all over the world, as a flagrant violation of their moral and legal rights. Their ire at the French plans stemmed from general concern about the "nth country" problem, and also from specific concern about the implications of the dispersion of nuclear weapons for their own relative strength and future plans. In addition, the fact that the French planned to test nuclear weapons in a colonial territory which was in the midst of an active revolt joined the issue with anticolonial sentiments and the anticolonial movement.

In August, India had requested that the issue of the suspension of nuclear and thermonuclear tests be included in the agenda, and after the Assembly opened it submitted a draft resolution. Subsequently, twenty-three other states, all of which except Cuba and Yugoslavia were from Africa and Asia, joined in sponsoring a version of India's proposal. Austria, Japan, and Sweden also submitted a draft resolution. Both resolutions expressed the hope that the states participating in the Geneva Conference would soon reach an agreement and that they would continue the present voluntary moratorium.[57] In addition, the twenty-four power resolution appealed to other states to desist from testing. In explaining the United States position, Ambassador Lodge asserted that the American objective was "the ending of nuclear weapons tests under an agreement providing effective international control," and he argued that

[57]See UN General Assembly Resolutions 1402 A (XIV) and 1402 B (XIV).

"an indefinite continuation of a voluntary uncontrolled suspension of tests would not contribute to that objective."[58]

Both resolutions were enthusiastically supported by the Soviet bloc. The United States and the United Kingdom voted for the resolution which had been submitted by Austria, Japan, and Sweden, which was adopted by a vote of 76 to 0, with 2 abstentions, but abstained on the twenty-four-power resolution, which was adopted by a vote of 60 to 1, with 20 abstentions. The representatives of the United States and the United Kingdom never explained specifically why they took different action in the two instances, but clearly the position of France and the way that state was affected was a factor.

France abstained from voting on the three-power resolution and opposed the twenty-four-power draft. Its opposition was even more pronounced in the case of those resolutions which dealt with the dispersion of nuclear weapons. One, submitted by Ireland, asked the newly created Ten-Nation Disarmament Committee to examine the feasibility of an international agreement including appropriate inspection and control provisions which would provide that the nuclear powers would refrain from giving control of nuclear weapons to non-nuclear powers, and that the latter would refrain from manufacturing nuclear weapons.[59] In other words, what was envisaged was a freezing of the nuclear club. The resolution probably did not contravene the NATO stockpile concept then in effect. It was adopted by a vote of 70 to 0, with 12 abstentions. The Soviet block, Peru, the Republic of China, and France abstained. Interestingly, all those states which abstained argued, basically, that the resolution was not sufficiently comprehensive, that this problem could only be handled in the context of other measures of arms control. The Soviet Union argued that the resolution was meaningless as long as states could station nuclear weapons outside of their territory, an obvious reference to United States policy in NATO and elsewhere.[60] France argued that it would only be just to

[58]UN General Assembly, First Committee, *Official Records* (14th Session), p. 178.

[59]UN General Assembly Resolution 1380 (XIV).

[60]UN General Assembly, First Committee, *Official Records* (14th Session), pp. 161-62.

take action against the dispersion of nuclear weapons in the context of broader measures leading to nuclear disarmament.[61] Their positions had interesting implications for the Geneva Conference, since easing the "nth country" problem was one of the putative advantages of the test ban.

The other resolutions considered by the Assembly on the subject of the dispersion of nuclear weapons dealt with France directly. In August, Morocco had asked that the question of the proposed French tests in the Sahara be inscribed on the agenda, and the day that the debate on this item opened twenty-two African and Asian states submitted a draft resolution specifically asking France to refrain from conducting its planned tests.[62] During the course of the debate Italy and the United Kingdom submitted a substitute resolution, which merely would have requested France to take account of the views expressed in the debate and expressed the hope that France would associate itself with whatever arrangements were worked out in Geneva for the discontinuance of nuclear weapons tests.[63] Although the Western powers generally supported this resolution, the African and Asian group and the Soviet bloc did not, and it was rejected in the First Committee by a vote of 24 to 38 with 20 abstentions. Both the First Committee and the Assembly adopted a slightly modified version of the twenty-two-power draft. In the plenary session the vote was 51 to 16 with 15 abstentions. The United Kingdom and the United States both voted against the resolution, as did France.

During the course of the debate Ambassador Lodge emphasized that the United States "had no technical information about the French experiment."[64] The French delegate, Jules Moch, stated in extremely clear terms that France would abandon its planned tests only if the three original nuclear powers "agreed to halt, under international control, the production of fissionable materials for military purposes, to begin the reconversion of their stockpiles and

[61]UN General Assembly, Plenary Meetings, *Official Records* (14th Session), pp. 581-82.

[62]UN Document A/C. 1/L. 238 and Add. 1 and Rev. 1.

[63]UN Document A/C. 1/L. 239 and Add. 1.

[64]UN General Assembly, First Committee, *Official Records* (14th Session), p. 110.

to do away with nuclear weapons carriers—in short, to give up their *de facto* monopoly."[65]

In the same debate, the Soviet delegate asserted that "the French nuclear test would not contribute to the success of the Geneva talks."[66] This statement was made immediately after he had repeated Khrushchev's pledge that:

> Only in the event of the resumption of nuclear weapons tests by the Western Powers, would the USSR be released from the obligation which it had taken upon itself.

The point that he did not clarify was whether or not the USSR would regard nuclear tests by France as the resumption of tests by the Western Powers. The debate indicated clearly how difficult the "nth country" problem would be, and the serious implications that the problem had for the test ban negotiations.

Presidential Politics

At the same time that these events were occurring, the entire test ban issue was becoming involved in the political maneuverings associated with the forthcoming Presidential election in the United States. On October 25, in a radio interview, Governor Nelson A. Rockefeller, a prominent aspirant for the Republican nomination, stated that he felt that the United States should resume testing nuclear weapons underground.[67] Five days later, Senator Hubert H. Humphrey, a Democratic hopeful, in a speech in Pontiac, Michigan, announced his position on the issue.[68] He favored extending the moratorium for one year. He advocated trying to negotiate a controlled agreement banning nuclear weapon tests in the atmosphere, at high altitudes, and underwater, and tests of weapons of five kilotons yield or more underground. He also proposed that a two-year moratorium should be established on tests of weapons of lesser yields. This period would be used to test Soviet good faith on inspection and for research to improve detection capabilities relating to low yield underground explosions.

[65]*Ibid.,* p. 93.
[66]*Ibid.,* p. 113.
[67]*New York Times,* October 26, 1959, p. 1.
[68]*Ibid.,* October 31, 1959, p. 3.

III

Technical Working Group II

The Resumption of the Geneva Conference: Another Mission for the Scientists

The Geneva Conference resumed on October 27. For a week there was no change in the position of either side. The United States continued to insist that the new seismic data had to be considered, and the USSR, with equal adamancy, continued to refuse. Tones were moderate, but that was the only evidence of the spirit of Camp David. On November 2, Ambassador Wadsworth indicated that, if there were no change in the Soviet position, the United States would begin a unilateral presentation of the technical situation, as Americans understood it.[69]

Mr. Tsarapkin—at least for the record—interpreted this as a threat to deadlock and possibly terminate the conference. Nevertheless (or perhaps, as a result), the following day, he proposed that the conference convene a technical working group to draft agreed criteria for the dispatch of on-site inspection terms and allowed that the "new seismic data" could be examined and considered within this context.[70] In making his proposal he pointed out that the Foreign Ministers had agreed some time ago that the question of criteria would have to be considered. He also proclaimed that the USSR could not agree to any revision of the Geneva Experts' report, which it viewed as the "agreed scientific and technical basis for drafting the treaty."[71] Finally, he questioned what the objectives of the Western powers were, if, as they claimed, they did not seek to increase the number of control posts or inspections.

Although the shift in the Soviet position, publicly announced as a concession to the spirit of Camp David, meant that the deadlock was broken, three weeks elapsed before the Conference could agree on terms of reference for Technical Working Group II (TWG II). Agreement was finally achieved on November 24, the day that most of the experts arrived in Geneva, and the day before they formally began their work. The central controversies concerned the status of the report of the Conference of Experts and

[69]GEN/DNT/PV. 131, *passim.*
[70]GEN/DNT/PV. 132, pp. 16-18.
[71]*Ibid.,* p. 13.

the freedom to be given the scientists in considering the new seismic data. Although the compromise formulation did not mention the new seismic data, the United States felt that it was worded so that they could be considered.[72]

> The Technical Working Group of Experts shall consider the question of the use of objective instrument readings in connexion with the selection of an event which cannot be identified by the international control organ and which could be suspected of being a nuclear explosion, in order to determine a basis for initiating on-site inspections. As part of their work, the experts, proceeding from the discussions and the conclusions of the Geneva Conference of Experts, shall consider all data and studies relevant to the detection and identification of seismic events and shall consider possible improvements of the techniques and instrumentation.[73]

In addition, at Soviet insistence, the terms of reference included the requirement that the Group should report to the Conference by December 11; that is, in about two and a half weeks.

The note of optimism generated by this agreement was furthered by an event which occurred at about the same time outside of the framework of the Geneva Conference. After many years of disputation, on December 1, 1959, twelve states including France, the USSR, the United Kingdom, and the United States, after a brief negotiation of less than seven weeks, signed the Antarctica Treaty.[74] Among other things, the Treaty provided for the demilitarization of Antarctica, with full unilateral rights of inspection, and for a ban on nuclear explosions and the dumping of radioactive wastes there. During this same period the United States and the USSR also reached agreement on the composition of the United Nations Committee on the Peaceful Uses of Outer Space. Previously, the Soviet bloc had boycotted the Committee because of disagreement on this issue. Observers began to proclaim that perhaps the meeting *à deux* between Chairman Khrushchev and President Eisen-

[72]See GEN/DNT/PV. 137, p. 14.

[73]GEN/DNT/PV. 137, p. 14.

[74]For a brief account of the negotiations and the issues involved see Howard J. Taubenfeld, "A Treaty for Antarctica," *International Conciliation,* Vol. 531 (January 1961), pp. 245-322.

hower had significantly altered the climate and atmosphere of international politics.

TWG II: Differences of Motivation and Expectation

Even within the Geneva negotiations significant progress was made. On November 30 the three powers reached agreement on Annex III to the draft treaty, setting forth the functions of the Preparatory Commission, and on December 14 the Soviet Union tabled a major compromise package proposal concerning a number of unresolved issues relating to the Control Organization.

Whether or not the Western participants in Technical Working Group II were optimistic concerning their tasks, though, was another matter. In fact, it is far from certain that they, or the Western politicians and diplomats to whom they were responsible, had a very clear concept of what the optimum or even expected outcome of this meeting would be. No one seriously expected the Soviet Union to accept the new Western assessment of the capabilities of the control system proposed by the Conference of Experts. Yet the basic instruction given to the American delegation, which was headed by James B. Fisk and included a number of other scientists who had previously been involved in one way or another in the negotiations,[75] was to attempt to straighten out the technical situation.

In a press conference on November 12, Secretary of State Herter said that the United States sought the meeting "so that from the scientific point of view we would have a common understanding

[75]The United States delegation consisted of: James B. Fisk, chairman, Executive Vice President, Bell Telephone Laboratories; Hans A. Bethe, Professor, Cornell University; Harold Brown, Associate Director, Livermore Laboratory; Richard Foose, Stanford Research Institute; Richard L. Garwin, International Business Machines Corporation; Spurgeon Keeny, Jr., Technical Assistant, Office of the Special Assistant to the President for Science and Technology; Albert Latter, Physics Division, RAND Corporation, Santa Monica, California; J. Carson Mark, Director, Theoretical Division, Los Alamos Scientific Laboratory; Jack E. Oliver, Lamont Geological Observatory; Wolfgang K. H. Panofsky, Director, High Energy Physics Laboratory, Stanford University; Frank Press, Director, Seismological Laboratory, California Institute of Technology; Carl F. Romney, Assistant Technical Director, Office of Atomic Energy, Department of Defense; John Tukey, Princeton University; Anthony L. Turkevich, Enrico Fermi Institute for Nuclear Studies, University of Chicago.

as to what existing instruments were capable of doing from the point of view of detecting."[76] Twelve days later, in another press conference, he described the purpose of the technical working group as being to examine all available data and "to determine whether or not existing technological instrumentation is adequate to detect all types of underground tests or only some underground tests, and what kind, and what improvements are likely to be made in the instrumentation itself."[77] He allowed that the scientists might not agree and even envisaged the possibility of separate reports. Secretary Herter then went on to say that it would be difficult for the United States to agree to a comprehensive test ban "if our scientists, in their objective judgment, felt that the instrumentation that might be available was not good enough to be an effective deterrent from the point of view of inspection."[78] His comments indicate the range of expectations which was possible for one individual. Given the different perspectives of other individuals, one can easily see the melange of views which was involved in any discussion of this issue by the Committee of Principals.

In a sense, the American insistence on holding Technical Working Group II was a product of the divergence of opinion within the United States government and of the inability of the government to reach a decision on the basic political issues of what risks it would be willing to accept. Those who questioned the wisdom of attempting to negotiate a comprehensive test ban could see the working group as an opportunity to embarrass the Soviet Union; the disagreement which they expected to result would serve as a justification for shifting to an attempt to negotiate a partial test ban or even as a rationale for breaking off the negotiations. On the other hand, the proponents of a comprehensive test ban could see the technical working group as a device for keeping the negotiations going and could hope that some solutions to the technical problems would emerge, either from the meeting with the Eastern scientists or from time and research. Somewhat later, in describing his expectations before the Subcommittee on Disarmament, Philip J. Farley of the Department of State said: "It was,

[76]U.S. Department of State *Bulletin,* Vol. XLI, No. 1066 (November 30, 1959), p. 785.
[77]*Ibid.,* Vol. XLI, No. 1068 (December 14, 1959), p. 863.
[78]*Ibid.,* p. 865.

of course, our hope that the facts would be looked at there, that answers would be found that would provide a technical basis for concluding a comprehensive agreement."[79] For both groups and for those who were not strongly identified with either, the technical working group could serve as an excuse for avoiding decisions on the basic issue concerning the degree of risk that the United States could tolerate.

The Soviet Union viewed its agreement to hold Technical Working Group II as a fundamental concession to the West. Thus the Soviet scientists, who were again headed by Dr. Fedorov,[80] apparently had no firm instructions in a positive sense as to what should emerge from the discussions. They did, however, as will become apparent, have firm instructions as to what should not emerge. In essence, they could not agree to any joint report which would make the problem of detecting and identifying nuclear explosions appear to be more difficult than it had seemed at the time of the Conference of Experts in 1958.

As in the case of the previous technical negotiations, there was no special preparation for the American delegation. The Chairman was briefed by the Secretary of State, but the other scientists went directly to Geneva. Their technical preparation consisted of the knowledge which they had as a result of their individual work and their past experience in matters relating to the negotiations. The Vela Project was just getting underway, and so far as the data gained from Hardtack II was concerned, there had been little further analysis of it during 1959, after the preparation of the document which the United States submitted to the Conference on January 5.[81]

Again, following the pattern of other sessions, Technical Working Group II opened with a disagreement about the agenda. The

[79]U.S. Congress, Senate, Committee on Foreign Relations, Subcommittee on Disarmament, *Hearing: Technical Problems and the Geneva Test Ban Negotiations,* 86th Congress, 2d Session (1960), p. 19.

[80]The other Soviet scientists were K. Y. Gubkin, V. I. Keilis-Borok, D. R. Pashchnik, Y. V. Riznichenko, M. A. Sadovsky, V. Shustov, and A. I. Ustyumenko.

[81]See the testimony of Wolfgang K. H. Panofsky before the Joint Committee on Atomic Energy: *Hearings: Technical Aspects . . . of a Nuclear Weapons Test Ban, supra* note 26, p. 69.

controversy really derived from the ambiguity of the terms of reference. The central issue, although it was not stated this baldly at that time, was whether or not TWG II should reevaluate the capability of the control system recommended by the Conference of Experts. In the Western view this was the essential function of the discussions. On the other hand, this was one of the things to which the Soviet scientists could not agree. Although a compromise formulation for the agenda was achieved in an informal meeting, it essentially glossed over the problem, and this fundamental disagreement continued to plague the discussions.[82]

Where Science Ends and Politics Begin

Although the basic reason for the Soviet refusal to agree to a reevaluation of the Experts' control system was to avoid undercutting the USSR's negotiating posture, the Soviet scientists adduced technical and philosophical reasons to support their position. Dr. Fedorov argued that even with the data gained from the Hardtack II experiments, because the data were still extremely limited, any estimate of the capability of the control system would be, as it had been in 1958, conjectural in nature; that the capability could only be properly assessed when the control system was in operation.[83] He also, as will be shown, attacked the validity of the new data. The Western position, on the other hand, was that the assessment had to be as up-to-date as possible. This position was advanced as having no political motivation; as being simply a demand that the Working Group should provide the governments concerned with, as Dr. Fisk put it, "a sound basis for taking the decision which they must take."[84] In the discussions, Dr. Fisk repeatedly asserted, at times almost plaintively:

[82]See the agenda GEN/DNT/TWG. 2/PV. 2, p. 3. For the different way in which this agenda was interpreted by the two sides see: GEN/DNT/-TWG. 2/PV. 8, p. 37; GEN/DNT/PV. 11, p. 77; GEN/DNT/PV. 13, pp. 58-60; GEN/DNT/TWG. 2/PV. 16, pp. 93-95. Panofsky commented on this problem in his testimony before the Joint Committee on Atomic Energy, *Hearings: Technical Aspects . . . of a Nuclear Weapons Test Ban, supra* note 26, p. 64.

[83]He made this point in several of the exchanges cited above. See also GEN/DNT/TWG. 2/PV. 10, p. 42, and GEN/DNT/TWG. 2/PV. 18, p. 31.

[84]GEN/DNT/TWG. 2/PV. 13, pp. 58-60.

> I assure Mr. Fedorov once again that our sole purpose in these meetings is to set the scientific and technical facts straight. . . . Our motives are purely technical, and the spirit of our proposals is scientific.[85]

But regardless of how the Western scientists perceived their motivations, their position had fundamental political ramifications. This was particularly true in that the majority among them at that time thought that the decoupling theory involved a much more serious degradation of the control system recommended by the Conference of Experts than the new seismic data and a degradation for which they could see no effective remedy. The implications of this were ominous when coupled with such statements as that made by Secretary of State Herter at his press conference the day before the Working Group began its sessions. Both in the discussions in the Working Group and in the Conference, Soviet delegates alleged that the West was motivated by a desire to prove that a comprehensive test ban could not be adequately monitored.[86] The fact that after the discussions were over the United States sent the USSR part of the terms of reference of the American delegation to TWG II may or may not have convinced Soviet leaders that this was not the American goal.

From their actions, it is easy to infer that the Soviet delegation had political instructions and guidance. They apparently could not agree to: anything that would indicate that the control system recommended by the Conference of Experts was less effective than the original estimate; anything that would imply that control over a comprehensive test ban would be impossible; or anything that would imply that there should be a greater number of control posts or on-site inspections in the USSR than originally had been thought necessary.

While the United States scientists did not have political instructions in the same sense, there were clearly political limits on their actions, although these may well have been self-imposed.[87]

---

[85]GEN/DNT/TWG. 2/PV. 12, pp. 36, 37-40.

[86]See for example, Fedorov's statement in the Working Group and Tsarapkin's statement later in the Conference: GEN/DNT/TWG. 2/PV. 19, p. 92, and GEN/DNT/PV. 148, p. 7.

[87]Gilpin puts it even more bluntly, "Little did the American scientists realize, however, that the Russian scientists were actually no more political

The American scientists were clearly aware of how important the concept and issue of control over arms control agreements were to the United States. As a group, they were also much more aware of the legal and political ramifications of any document that might emerge from their discussions than the American delegation to the Conference of Experts had been. The American scientists also now had a conception of Soviet behavior which led them to believe that in formulating any joint document everything should be developed in as much detail as possible. They felt that if it were not, there would be disputes subsequently and, moreover, once an agreement was signed, nothing new could be added. As a consequence of these factors, in evaluating and analyzing data, the American scientists felt that they had to be, as Dr. Fisk told the Conference, "as careful and as conservative as we could."[88]

At times, as a result of these factors the American posture became almost grotesque. For example, in a discussion of instrumentation Hans Bethe made this statement:

> We believe that the experts in 1958 knew quite well about instruments, but we believe that we now know even better about them. We do not believe that the experts of the control commission will know any better than we know.[89]

To argue in abutting sentences that knowledge had changed, but would not change again, posed certain logical complications, at the least.

On the other hand, because of the political position of their state, the Soviet scientists had to be as optimistic as they could. Dr. Fedorov typified their attitude at one of the final meetings, during a discussion of formulating criteria for the initiation of on-site inspections, when he asked, "What kind of scientists are we if we cannot find a solution for such a problem?"[90]

There was also another difference between the nature of the

than they." (*American Scientists and Nuclear Weapons Policy*, p. 243). Although this may be true in terms of the end effect of the action of each group, there were important differences in method and style, which should not be ignored.

[88]GEN/DNT/TWG. 2/PV. 20, p. 4.
[89]GEN/DNT/TWG. 2/PV. 12, p. 16.
[90]GEN/DNT/TWG. 2/PV. 19, p. 91.

participation of the American and Soviet scientists in the Technical Working Group. The United States delegation presented by far the bulk of the empirical data which was considered. The Soviet contribution was principally in the nature of critical analysis.[91] There is no way of knowing how open either side was in terms of presenting data, or whether or not all of the available data were put before the Group. During the course of the discussions the United States did submit a vast quantity of data, and the USSR did make available seismograms with signals recorded during the Hardtack series. Dr. Fedorov stated that the USSR had not carried out any underground nuclear explosions and thus could not supply data beyond that which it had gathered on American tests.[92]

In terms of formal participation, the British scientists, who were again headed by Sir William Penney,[93] played only a nominal role. Because of their limited experience, they could not add much empirical data. At that time the United Kingdom had not detonated a nuclear device underground. On the few occasions on which he spoke, Sir William Penney emphasized the importance of a test ban and, consequently, of attempting to reach agreement within the Working Group. This reflected both his personal preferences and the official attitude of the United Kingdom.

On the Hardtack II Data: An Uncomfortable Uncertainty

Carl Romney, a seismologist with the United States Air Force, made the first technical presentation in Working Group II.[94] In it, he expounded the American analysis of the Hardtack II data. Although he presented more technical details, his basic conclusions were identical with those contained in the January 5 Working Paper; that is, that the magnitude of Rainier had been estimated incorrectly and consequently that there were many more earthquakes of equivalent size, and that first motion was more difficult to detect than it had previously been thought. The decoupling theory was

---

[91]See Panofsky's comment, *Hearing: Technical Problems and the Geneva Test Ban Negotiations, supra* note 79, pp. 35-36.

[92]GEN/DNT/TWG. 2/PV. 3, pp. 103-5.

[93]The other British delegates were H. R. Hulme, I. Maddock, F. Panton, and J. W. Wright.

[94]GEN/DNT/TWG. 2/PV. 1., pp. 22-56.

not presented until a week later, at the seventh meeting of the Working Group.[95]

The immediate Soviet response to both presentations was of a legalistic character. With respect to the Hardtack II data, the Soviet scientists argued that since the instrumentation used was not identical with that which had been recommended in the report of the Conference of Experts, no implications could be drawn for the recommended control system. With respect to the decoupling theory, Dr. Fedorov questioned whether it could be considered under any item of the agenda.[96] After Hans Bethe and Albert Latter had presented the theory, he caustically commented that:

> . . . the contribution to our work which Dr. Latter tried to make in his report is quite similar to the contribution that he made previously to this problem; I mean the book that he published on the subject along with Dr. Teller.[97]

Later in the conference, he would mention the book, *Our Nuclear Future*, in even more bitter terms.

When the Soviet scientists began to comment on the substance of the issues, they did so by way of the presentation of formal papers which countered and contradicted the American findings. The American scientists professed to be puzzled and upset by the disagreement. At the tenth meeting Wolfgang Panofsky commented:

> It just should not occur that objective examination and a full exchange of seismic data should lead our Soviet colleagues to one conclusion while the conclusions of our own seismologists are different.[98]

At the following meeting Frank Press repeated the same sentiment and then offered the explanation and recommended solution which most of the American scientists seemed to favor:

> As scientists we know that given the same basic data we should be able to arrive at similar conclusions, and yet

[95]GEN/DNT/TWG. 2/PV. 7, pp. 58-110.
[96]*Ibid.*, pp. 55-56.
[97]*Ibid.*, p. 111.
[98]GEN/DNT/TWG. 2/PV. 10, p. 4.

we have not been able to. This can only be because the communication and interchange between us has been imperfect. The only way to make progress, to resolve these differences, is to improve the communication, to study the data jointly step by step.[99]

The solution, the American scientists thought, would be small informal meetings, and they began arguing for such meetings at an early stage in the conference. The Soviet scientists, however, did not agree to this procedure until the final week of the meetings.

Even after the informal sessions, several fundamental disagreements remained, although some differences were eliminated and others narrowed. With respect to the Hardtack II data, the Soviet scientists tended to concentrate their attention and criticisms on the problem of measuring seismic magnitude. They made a number of what can be termed procedural criticisms. They were critical of the fact that less than thirty of the seismological stations in the United States which had recorded Logan and Blanca had had seismographs which were sufficiently calibrated so that magnitude could be measured. They also criticized the fact that the American scientists gave them one relevant seismogram for study as late as December 14, during the sixteenth meeting of the Working Group.

Their more fundamental substantive criticisms centered on the statistical methods used in the computation of seismic magnitudes and on the use of magnitude scales. To deal with the issue of statistical methods first, the relevant empirical data were widely scattered. The question was whether in the computation of averages all of the figures should be used, as the Americans insisted, or whether the extremes and certain other figures should be excluded as the Russians argued. The second issue involved the question of how to relate two different scales of measurement. Some American scientists felt that what their Soviet counterparts did in this matter was unscientific and dishonest.[100]

There is evidence, however, that a number of American scientists felt rather uncomfortable with respect to the whole problem of measuring the seismic magnitude of nuclear explosions because

[99]GEN/DNT/TWG. 2/PV. 11, pp. 87-90.
[100]See Romney's comment before the Disarmament Subcommittee, *Hearing: Technical Problems and the Geneva Test Ban Negotiations, supra* note 79, p. 38.

of the great uncertainties involved. Wolfgang Panofsky put it suc-
cinctly in testimony in April 1960 before the Joint Committee on
Atomic Energy when he stated that:

> . . . the matter is greatly beclouded by the inaccuracy of
> our seismic information concerning earthwide occurrence
> of small earthquakes. Specifically, a body of information
> on the frequency of occurrence of small earthquakes
> exists only for California and New Zealand, and going
> from this information to worldwide estimates, and particu-
> larly to estimates for the Soviet Union, involves many un-
> certainties; these uncertainties are in fact considerably
> larger than change in the situation created by the new
> data of the Hardtack series. This issue is, therefore, not an
> important new consideration, and it now appears that
> probably its importance has been overemphasized in the
> United States.[101]

Because of these facts, many of the American scientists participating in TWG II concluded that the question of the number of on-
site inspections required was essentially a political issue, as the
USSR maintained. During the meetings of the Working Group,
on several occasions Dr. Fisk sought to emphasize that the American delegation did not consider this aspect of the Hardtack II
data the most important element.

Nevertheless, the differences between the Soviet scientists and
the American scientists with respect to the problem of measuring
seismic magnitude led the former to interpret the Hardtack II
data as indicating that there would be *fewer* earthquakes which
would give signals equivalent to any given size nuclear explosion
rather than more, as the Americans felt would be the case.[102]

Rather than their revised estimate of the seismic magnitude
of the Rainier shot, the American scientists tended to stress instead
the fact that the Hardtack II data indicated that because of background noise it would be much more difficult than had been thought
to detect the sign of first motion. They now estimated that the
ratio of signal to noise would have to be greater than had previously been thought for the compressional first motion to be

[101]*Hearings: Technical Aspects . . . of a Nuclear Weapons Test Ban,*
supra note 26, p. 65.
[102]See *Geneva Conference,* pp. 392-93.

detected, that is, for it not to appear as a rarefaction. In other words, first motion would only be useful for detecting substantially higher yields than had been estimated at the Conference of Experts. Here, the principal Soviet criticism was that the instrumentation used in the Hardtack II test series was not identical with that recommended by the Conference of Experts. The Americans countered by arguing that, although the Soviet charge was true, valid extrapolations could be made.

In the course of the argument, in the second week of the meeting it was discovered that the Russian and English versions of the report of the Conference of Experts were different, and that the differences would allow different interpretations of what instrumental characteristics with respect to magnification and response the Experts had recommended.[103] The differing interpretations led the scientists from the two sides to feel that the Conference of Experts had recommended instruments which would conform to those that they had used in their national stations. This episode underscores the importance of proper translation in negotiations.

The American scientists were nonetheless convinced that their interpretation was the correct one; that instruments constructed on the basis of their interpretation would be the most efficacious in detecting first motion; and that the instruments used during the Hardtack II test series fell within the category recommended by the Experts. To prove their point, as soon as the difference was discovered they designed a seismograph based on the Soviet interpretation of the specifications and had it built. On December 9 it was installed on a pier at a location in Oklahoma alongside an instrument similar to those used in the Hardtack II series. In the first eight hours of operation there was a small earthquake, and a comparison of the signals received on the two instruments clearly indicated that the instrument based on the Soviet interpretation was considerably less effective in detecting the sign of the first motion.[104] Despite this evidence, however, the Soviet scientists continued to

[103]See Panofsky's comment before the Joint Committee on Atomic Energy: *Hearings: Technical Aspects . . . of a Nuclear Weapons Test Ban, supra* note 26, pp. 67-68. The only American scientist fluent in Russian at the Conference of Experts, Turkevich, left the meeting before the final texts of the report were prepared.

[104]See Romney's presentation, GEN/DNT/TWG. 2/PV. 17, pp. 91-96.

maintain that because the instruments used in the Hardtack II series did not conform exactly to those recommended by the Conference of Experts, the data recorded by them were not relevant.[105]

On Decoupling: "Deeply Embarrassed"

Hans Bethe and Albert Latter presented the decoupling theory during the second week of the meeting. Later, Professor Bethe referred to the task as a "doubtful honor" and said that he felt "deeply embarrassed in so doing because it implied that we considered the Russians capable of cheating on such a massive scale."[106] His views of the Russian character provide an interesting contrast with those expressed by Edward Teller and Albert Latter in their book. For a variety of reasons, Professor Bethe was a logical person to be involved in the task. He had presented the relevant material at the Conference of Experts, and in the course of the discussion he had to admit that his original calculations were "not correct."[107] It was also tactically expedient to have him share in the presentation, since he, in contrast to Albert Latter, was known as a proponent of a test ban.

Most American scientists who participated in the Working Group agreed with Professor Bethe's comment that "the Russians seemed stunned by the theory of the big hole."[108] At first they attempted to develop counter theoretical arguments, but after various formal confrontations and informal meetings, they admitted the theoretical validity of Albert Latter's calculations concerning decoupling. They maintained, however, that there was no proof that the theory would work in practice, and, of course, at that time there was very little empirical proof. The British, who had been informed of the theory of decoupling in the summer, had conducted a limited series of experiments involving detonating small charges of TNT in cavities, and they presented the results of these experiments, which tended to confirm the theory, to the Working Group.[109] The first explosion in Project Cowboy was detonated on

[105]See *Geneva Conference,* pp. 393-94.
[106]"The Case for Ending Nuclear Tests," *Headline Series,* No. 145 (January-February 1961), p. 17.
[107]GEN/DNT/TWG. 2/PV. 8, p. 47.
[108]"The Case for Ending Nuclear Tests," *supra* note 106, p. 17.
[109]GEN/DNT/TWG. 2/PV. 11, pp. 32-37.

December 17, 1959, the day before the Working Group recessed, and the project was not discussed during the session.

The question of the feasibility of constructing cavities of sufficient size to allow the decoupled detonation of fairly large sized weapons was not discussed either, although the United States was prepared to go into this matter in some detail. In the fall of 1959 the Atomic Energy Commission had become concerned with this issue and had discovered that petroleum companies used large underground cavities for storing their materials. In October the Philips Petroleum Company had been commissioned to undertake certain feasibility studies, and the individual responsible for this work was brought to Geneva for the week of December 7. His work, however, was confined to assisting Albert Latter and others.

On the On-Site Inspection: à Quoi Bon?

During the course of 1959 another element of doubt, in addition to the implications of the Hardtack II data and the decoupling theory, had arisen in the American scientific community. Starting in April 1958 scientists at the University of California Radiation Laboratory at Livermore had become concerned about the matter of on-site inspection, and after preliminary discussions with geologists and geophysicists, and exploratory studies, the Laboratory let a contract to the Stanford Research Institute for the conduct of studies of the problem of on-site inspection during the Hardtack II test series. These studies indicated that the problem of conducting an on-site inspection would be quite difficult, and that the chance of actually obtaining radioactive debris and thus identifying a clandestine underground explosion would be relatively small. The American delegation was given freedom to introduce or to withhold this issue. Eventually, the delegation decided to introduce the issue, but not to stress it, and perhaps thereby detract from what they considered the more important degradations of the control system caused by the Hardtack II data and the decoupling theory.[110] Dr. Fisk mentioned the problem in the plenary session,[111] the reports

[110]Earl H. Voss has interpreted this, we think wrongly, as a deliberate attempt to gloss over the difficult problem of on-site inspection (*Nuclear Ambush*, p. 347). In his book he virtually accuses American scientists of attempting to mislead the American public on the issue of on-site inspections.
[111]GEN/DNT/TWG. 2/PV. 8, pp. 76-77.

on the work were introduced as an annex to the records of the conference,[112] and the project director from the Stanford Research Institute communicated his findings to Dr. Fedorov in a private meeting. The only Soviet response was a brief denial of the American analysis and interpretation.[113] The issue was not mentioned in any of the formal reports of Technical Working Group II.

On Improving the Control System: What Conclusions from Scientific Data?

Along with their presentation of the Hardtack II data, the decoupling theory and the information relating to on-site inspection, the American scientists also presented their thoughts concerning possible improvements in the control system recommended by the Conference of Experts. They concerned both instrumental matters and improved diagnostic techniques. Interestingly, one of the more significant of these improvements was discovered by Albert Latter during the meetings of the Technical Working Group and was immediately presented at the next-to-the-last meeting.[114] On these matters, there was considerable agreement between the Soviet and Western scientists.

What disagreement there was, concerned what practical conclusions to draw from the technical facts. This was illustrated by the attempts of Dr. Fedorov at the conclusion of each American presentation to elicit a formal proposal or recommendation for the use of new instruments or techniques. The American response was invariably that the state of knowledge was not sufficient to allow definite formulations, but that the presentations indicated lines of further inquiry. After one such exchange, Dr. Fedorov exclaimed, ". . . this is not a congress of seismologists. . . . What we are interested in here . . . is how this scientific contribution can be used in practice to improve the control system. . . ."[115] The American scientists, however, were determined not to become involved in the elaboration of any formal texts which their scientific data and understandings could not fully support

[112]GEN/DNT/TWG. 2/PV. 9/Add. 1.
[113]GEN/DNT/TWG. 2/PV. 11, pp. 51-61.
[114]GEN/DNT/TWG. 2/PV. 20, pp. 31-36.
[115]GEN/DNT/TWG. 2/PV. 4, p. 82.

Despite this disagreement, the Technical Working Group was able to produce an agreed report regarding possible improvements of techniques and instrumentation.[116] In keeping with their general positions, in the preparation of this report the American scientists sought to be much more specific than the Soviet scientists.

On Criteria for On-Site Inspection: Can One Agree Without Agreement on Data?

The final substantive item on the agenda of Technical Working Group II was the formulation of objective criteria which could serve as a basis for the initiation of on-site inspections. From the outset, the American position was that there was no point in attempting to discuss this matter until there was agreement on the technical data; for example, on the effectiveness of first motion as a diagnostic technique. As it developed, the discussion of criteria began without agreement on the technical data. Indeed, there was no agreement on the data at the time that the conference adjourned.

The Soviet scientists led off at the eighth meeting on December 3 by tabling a draft proposal relating to criteria.[117] The Americans objected to this proposal, first because they felt that it contained a number of judgments which were concerned with matters beyond the purview of the technical working group.[118] For example, it assumed that there would be a quota of on-site inspections and that data from national seismic stations would play an important role. Moreover, it also contained stipulations on the circumstances under which on-site inspections should be discontinued. Among other things, the Soviet draft provided that if the epicenter of an unidentified event were located in a densely populated area, or if its depth of focus were beyond technological possibilities, it would be considered to be an earthquake. The American scientists felt that both of these involved political, rather than technical, considerations. However, the more important American objections to the Soviet criteria were of a technical nature. The American scientists felt that the Soviet criteria would have resulted in clandestine nuclear explosions being categorized as earthquakes: in par-

[116]*Geneva Conference,* pp. 386-88.
[117]GEN/DNT/TWG. 2/PV. 8, pp. 87-92.
[118]See Fisk's comments: GEN/DNT/TWG. 2/PV. 13, p. 22.

ticular, they argued that the Blanca and Logan experiments would have been so classified.[119]

The American proposal on criteria was introduced on December 11.[120] Soviet objections to this proposal were equally as strong as the American objections to the Soviet draft. Dr. Fedorov commented that the criteria proposed by the United States scientists turned the principle of selection "topsy turvy," the result would be "that from the total number of recorded events the greater part of them will remain open to suspicion [and thus eligible for on-site inspection] and the smaller part would be free from suspicion."[121] He asserted that this was contrary to the conclusions of the Conference of Experts. The Americans agreed with his conclusions, but argued that with the present state of knowledge, they could not go farther. In the context of this debate, Dr. Fedorov remarked that science had solved more complicated problems and ought to be able to solve this one. He went on to assert that ". . . the purpose we have as scientists is to try to help our political officers to identify suspicious events."[122] Dr. Fisk rejoined, ". . . science is not the servant of political expediency."[123]

The American draft did list various types of auxiliary information, which it was stated might develop into criteria "to establish an event as natural in origin" at some later time after further research. Wolfgang Panofsky again summed up this problem a few months later in his testimony before the Joint Committee on Atomic Energy:

> The principal problem is that these methods are potentially useful, but within the present state of knowledge there is no way of evaluating quantitatively how useful they could be nor is it possible to write specific recommendations under which they could be used by unskilled operators. In the hands of skilled seismologists, even at

[119]See Fisk's comments: GEN/DNT/TWG. 2/PV. 12, pp. 57-66; and *Hearing: Technical Problems and the Geneva Test Ban Negotiations, supra* note 79, p. 7. See also Panofsky's comments before the Joint Committee on Atomic Energy: *Hearings: Technical Aspects . . . of a Nuclear Weapons Test Ban, supra* note 26, p. 72.

[120]GEN/DNT/TWG. 2/PV. 14, pp. 3-21.

[121]GEN/DNT/TWG. 2/PV. 15, pp. 27-30.

[122]GEN/DNT/TWG. 2/PV. 19, p. 76.

[123]*Ibid.*, p. 81.

the present the use of some of these methods might very well improve the judgment which can be exercised in distinguishing earthquakes from explosions.[124]

As his comments indicate, in addition to being worried about the state of knowledge and the legal and political status of their report, the American scientists were concerned about the technical competence of the personnel that would staff the control posts, and they tended to assume, probably rightly, a relatively low level of competence.[125]

Although both sides made some compromises, the differences in approach proved irreconcilable, and Technical Working Group II failed to agree on criteria for initiating on-site inspections. Interestingly, the Soviet scientists did not include their proposed criteria in their report to the Conference. Whether or not the Soviet criteria were intended as a serious proposal or as a bargaining position was moot. The Soviet proposal was logically defensible only in the light of the Soviet criticisms of the measurements of the Hardtack II series, and especially the criticism of the instruments which had been used.

Although submission of an agreed report to the Geneva Conference seemed to be out of the question in view of the basic divisions between the Eastern and Western scientists, all three groups of scientists, for their own reasons, strongly wanted an agreed report, and an attempt was made. Dr. Fisk even suggested the possibility of reconvening the Working Group in January 1960 after a Christmas recess,[126] but in the last analysis the scientists recognized that their differences could not be resolved by further meetings.

The attempt to write an agreed report was complicated by the fact that the scientists knew that the report of Technical Working Group I had been given immediate public release and they were concerned about the effect of any report on public opinion. In

---

[124]*Hearings: Technical Aspects . . . of a Nuclear Weapons Test Ban,* *supra* note 26, p. 70.

[125]See also Panofsky's comments before the Subcommittee of the Committee on Foreign Relations, *Hearing: Technical Problems and the Geneva Test Ban Negotiations, supra* note 79, pp. 9-10.

[126]GEN/DNT/TWG. 2/PV. 20, p. 62.

addition, neither side wanted to have a report prejudge issues which were still in contention in the Conference. The American objections to the Soviet proposals on criteria have already been mentioned. Similarly, the Soviet scientists objected to American proposals relating to experimental explosions designed to yield data that would be helpful in improving the control system.[127]

In the end, the many divisions proved insurmountable. The scientists could agree only on a brief procedural report to which four annexes were attached.[128] The first of these contained the agreed recommendations on improvements, and the remaining three, the separate views of the three delegations. The British report basically agreed with the American conclusions, except in the matter of magnitude and the number of equivalent earthquakes.

IV

Deadlock

Scientists Disagree: Back to the Diplomats
Technical Working Group II recessed after twenty-one meetings at 9:20 p.m. on Friday, December 18. The following afternoon the report and the annexes were presented to the diplomatic Conference.[129] The meeting was acrimonious. Dr. Fedorov's statement, which Dr. Fisk subsequently labeled "incorrect, distorted, and misleading,"[130] attacked the scientific integrity of the American delegation, among other things. The American scientists were deeply distressed by this,[131] and by the general denouement. In addition to the substantive issues at stake, many of them felt that in the process of the discussion personal relationships with Soviet scientists, carefully built up over a number of years, had been jeopardized.

The outcome of Technical Working Group II meant that the search for agreement between East and West on a technical level had failed. The closing speeches of the diplomatic representatives

[127]GEN/DNT/TWG. 2/PV. 21, p. 6.
[128]See *Geneva Conference,* pp. 384-413.
[129]GEN/DNT/PV. 150.
[130]*Ibid.,* p. 16.
[131]See the comments by Panofsky and Fisk, *Hearing: Technical Problems and the Geneva Test Ban Negotiations, supra* note 79, pp. 13, 35.

in the Conference, indicated that each side saw the other's action as precluding agreement and revealed the prevailing mutual suspicions concerning motivations. Mr. Tsarapkin went so far as to charge that there were forces trying to prevent the conclusion of a comprehensive agreement. The West clearly felt that the USSR was evading the issue of control.

Perhaps the British delegate, Sir Michael Wright, sounded the most optimistic note. He argued that the principal difficulties were caused "by the comparative scarcity of firm experimental data and by the lack of time thus far for research directed to our special problems."[132] He expressed the opinion that a solution might well be found through research, "jointly undertaken." For the moment, however, the negotiations had reached an impasse.

[132]*Ibid.,* p. 22.

Chapter VII

The Search for Political Compromise

I

Revamping the Western Position

The failure of Technical Working Group II to achieve agreement marked the conclusion of one phase in the Geneva Conference. The attempt to restore the agreed basis for the negotiations through the mechanism of technical talks had failed. If the negotiations were to be advanced, new mechanisms would have to be tried. Thus the failure of TWG II touched off an effort to by-pass the technical disagreement, which continued until the Geneva Conference adjourned *sine die* on January 29, 1962.

Although this effort was principally diplomatic in nature and was pursued mainly on a diplomatic level, it continued to have a large technical component. This was inevitable since the dispute concerned technical issues, but it was also a product of the Western attraction for the concept that political agreements could be achieved through efforts at the technical level. Rather than technical talks, hopes came to be pinned on technical research, conducted by the individual governments themselves and perhaps jointly. Research might yield ways of satisfying both the Soviet demand for a comprehensive treaty and the Western demand for "adequate control." Moreover, research was a neutral device. One could be for research, just as one could be for technical talks, regardless of one's position on the wisdom of a test ban treaty. By stressing research one could avoid political disputes and decisions. Signs of this developing attitude were already evident in the speeches of the Western delegates—especially Sir Michael Wright's—at the session of the Geneva Conference when Technical Working Group II reported. However, research would take time. Meanwhile, compromises would be necessary on the political level.

The Decision to Continue the Moratorium

The first decision that the United States had to take related to the moratorium on testing nuclear weapons. As will be recalled, in August the United States had announced that it would continue the voluntary suspension until December 31, 1959. The British had taken a different position; they had declared that they would continue the moratorium as long as the negotiations continued; therefore this issue did not arise for them.

In late December, President Eisenhower summoned a group of advisers to Augusta, Georgia, to discuss what action the United States should take. The failure of TWG II had strengthened the convictions and the case of those who questioned the wisdom of continuing the moratorium. They were now even more convinced that it would be difficult to detect and identify clandestine explosions of small nuclear weapons. The experience of TWG II had also served to underscore the reservations which many had about Soviet intentions. No one, however, went farther than to argue for a resumption of testing underground and possibly in outer space. That no one urged resuming atmospheric testing reflected both the extent to which public opinion, or fear of an adverse public reaction, could inhibit United States policy, and the conscience of American policy-makers.

On the other side, it was argued that broad East-West relationships were moving gradually toward a détente. General disarmament talks were to be resumed again for the first time since 1957 when the Ten-Nation Disarmament Committee would meet in Geneva in March 1960. Even though the Coolidge Committee had been unable to formulate a new American negotiating position, the United States looked forward to these talks. There were prospects for a summit meeting later in the spring or early summer, and it seemed likely that President Eisenhower would make a trip to the USSR sometime thereafter. Moreover, more progress had been made in the Geneva Conference than in any other arms control negotiation since the Second World War. By this time the three states had agreed to a preamble, seventeen articles, and an annex to a treaty, an unprecedented achievement.

To compound the matter, it was not at all clear what the effects of any given American policy would be on the Soviet Union; for example, whether continuing the moratorium would make the USSR more or less willing to negotiate.

The result was a compromise embodied in a declaration and inaction with regard to the substantive issues at stake. On December 29, 1959, President Eisenhower issued the following statement:

> Although we consider ourselves free to resume nuclear weapons testing, we shall not resume nuclear weapons tests without announcing our intention in advance of any resumption. During the period of voluntary suspension of nuclear weapons tests the United States will continue its active program of weapon research, development, and laboratory-type experimentation.[1]

He prefaced this statement by saying that the prospects for a test ban agreement had been injured by "the recent unwillingness of the politically guided Soviet experts to give serious scientific consideration to the effectiveness of seismic techniques for the detection of underground nuclear explosions," and he characterized the Soviet annex to the Technical Working Group II report as "intemperate and technically unsupportable." On the other hand, no decision was made to ready test sites, nor were budgetary allocations for such activities increased. Administration officials explained the President's statement to the press as a "bargaining maneuver."[2]

In his account of the negotiations, Sir Michael Wright has argued that by choosing the course that it did, the "Eisenhower Administration got the worst of both worlds."[3] He maintains that while the United States did not in fact resume testing, "the statement enabled the Russians to claim that the West had been the first to speak of resuming."

It is difficult to know how the Soviet Union interpreted the American decision. Although the Eisenhower statement was criticized in the Soviet press and in statements by Soviet officials, the criticism was relatively restrained, and on January 3, 1960, Chairman Khrushchev reiterated his pledge that the USSR would not resume testing nuclear weapons unless the West did. He repeated this pledge eleven days later in a speech before the Supreme Soviet of the USSR, and in so doing pointed out that any state

[1]*Geneva Conference,* p. 413.
[2]*New York Times,* December 30, 1959, p. 1.
[3]Sir Michael Wright, *Disarm and Verify,* p. 126.

that resumed testing nuclear weapons would find it difficult to reconcile its decision with the decisions of the United Nations.[4] In the same speech he acknowledged that it might be possible to camouflage some underground nuclear explosions and that others would be difficult to detect. Regardless of these difficulties though, he argued that if an agreement were signed, it would be fulfilled: "Should any side violate the obligations to which it has committed itself, the instigators of such violations will cover themselves with shame, and they will be condemned by people of the world." Curiously, a few days earlier, on December 30, 1959, *Pravda* charged that the United States had already violated the moratorium by setting off underground atomic explosions.

Chairman Khrushchev's Supreme Soviet speech also contained other elements of some significance for the test ban negotiations. Most notably, he gave figures on Soviet troop strength over the years, and proposed that the current total of 3,623,000 be reduced by a third. The Supreme Soviet promptly enacted legislation to implement this suggestion. In the West this move was alternatively interpreted as indicating either a desire for détente, or the modernization of the Soviet armed forces. To a certain extent, probably both interpretations had elements of validity. In any case, the move would mean that as their conventional capacity lessened, Soviet forces would become increasingly reliant on nuclear weapons. In a certain sense, Khrushchev's speech paralleled Dulles' massive retaliation pronouncement six years earlier. Indeed, Khrushchev spoke of the Soviet Union having sufficient modern weapons:

> . . . that should any madman launch an attack on our state or on other socialist states we would be able to literally wipe the country or countries which attack us off the face of the earth.[5]

Clearly, the Soviet Union was moving in the direction of adopting a doctrine of deterrence.

The United States' Proposal for a Phased Treaty

The decision about the moratorium was a relatively simple one. Formulating a new Western negotiating position in view of the

[4]*Documents on Disarmament, 1960,* pp. 4-15.
[5]*Documents on Disarmament, 1960,* p. 14.

outcome of Technical Working Group II was a more complex issue and one which required more time. In fact, the United States was unable to present a new position until February 11, 1960, over four weeks after the Geneva Conference had resumed. Meanwhile, the Conference lagged. Ambassador Wadsworth pointed out that the United States' position would have to be based on the conclusions of the American expert delegation to TWG II; any treaty which was not so based would clearly be rejected by the Senate.[6] Mr. Tsarapkin countered by pointing out that the scientific position advanced by the Western scientists would leave large numbers of events eligible for inspection, and then went on to say that the USSR might ease its concept of criteria defining events eligible for on-site inspection if the West would accept the Soviet proposal for an annual quota of on-site inspections.[7] The West would have to agree to the quota concept, however, before the criteria could be formulated. He pointed out that the Control Commission would be able to conduct research, and that improvements in the capability of the detection and identification system presumably would result. He also argued that in any case there would be no on-site inspections until the control system was completely installed; that is, for a year or two after the treaty entered into force. Several days later, though, Mr. Tsarapkin allowed that the real problem with violations, if indeed there would be a problem, would relate to underground explosions, that a violator would not attempt to test in other less covert environments.[8]

Finally, on February 11, the United States tabled a new negotiating position. Although the terms of the American proposal were not publicly released until after their presentation in Geneva, they were in large measure revealed and discussed in the press and other mass media long before their presentation to the Conference. In part, this was inevitable, since the new American proposal was derived rather logically from past American positions, particularly President Eisenhower's suggestions of April 13, 1959, and from the outcome of Technical Working Group II. That the new proposal was telegraphed in advance was also the result, though, of the American decentralized processes of decision-making.

[6]GEN/DNT/PV. 152, pp. 4-5, 20.
[7]*Ibid.,* pp. 8, 12, 19.
[8]GEN/DNT/PV. 168, p. 19.

The American proposal was presented verbally; no treaty language was tabled.[9] In essence, it provided for a phased treaty, testing nuclear weapons would be prohibited in those environments where in the American view control was feasible, and the prohibition would be extended as control could be extended. The proposal provided for the immediate prohibition of testing in the atmosphere, underwater, "in outer space up to the greatest height with respect to which agreement can be reached on the installation of effective controls," and underground "down to the lowest limit of size or threshold" which the United States felt could be adequately controlled. As an illustration, and as a proposal, the United States suggested a threshold of magnitude 4.75 on the unified magnitude scale. With respect to on-site inspection, the United States presented two alternative schemes, depending on whether or not agreement could be reached on criteria. Both, however, envisaged actual inspection of only a fraction of the unidentified events, the choice to be determined by the "other side." Thus the proposal involved acceptance in principle of the concept of a numerical quota of on-site inspections. If agreement were reached on the criteria proposed by the American delegation to Technical Working Group II, thirty percent of all unidentified events would be subject to inspection, otherwise twenty percent of all events located by the system would be eligible. The United States estimated that with a threshold of magnitude 4.75 and with control posts initially only on the territories of the three nuclear powers, the application of either formula would result in about twenty on-site inspections in the Soviet Union in an average year. The United States also estimated that the number of comparable events in the United States and the United Kingdom together would be approximately the same. A higher threshold would result in fewer inspections, and a lower one in more. Ambassador Wadsworth stated that the United States would be willing to have the quota fixed in numerical rather than percentage terms, but in that instance the quota would have to be subject to revision at least annually and it should be determined by applying "the agreed percentage to the number of events which has actually occurred in the previous period." In presenting the new American position, Ambassador

[9]See GEN/DNT/PV. 170, pp. 3-9.

Wadsworth stressed the dynamic nature of the phasing concept, and proposed that the three countries institute a "program of joint research," with the aim of moving toward a comprehensive treaty as rapidly as possible. The results of the research would be introduced into the control system as rapidly as "they had reached a technologically useful state." This would allow the parties to the treaty to consider the extent to which each advance might permit moves toward a comprehensive treaty.

The new American proposal was an attempt to reset the requirement of "adequate" control, but at the same time to satisfy the Soviet demand that the number of on-site inspections be limited. In addition, since it implicitly allowed the possibility of testing some nuclear weapons, at least temporarily, it was satisfactory to those who had always felt, or had come to feel, that American security interests demanded this.

It was this last aspect which drew the most critical questions from Mr. Tsarapkin. He immediately asked whether or not the treaty would prohibit nuclear tests underground that would register below the 4.75 seismic magnitude threshold, and if it would not, if there would be a moratorium on such tests.[10] He also asked if all tests in outer space would be prohibited. After receiving Ambassador Wadsworth's negative replies, and hearing his admission of lack of full instructions concerning outer space, Mr. Tsarapkin charged that the new American proposal was an invitation to renew the nuclear arms race; that the nuclear powers would strive to improve their capabilities and that non-nuclear powers would attempt to gain nuclear status. Ambassador Wadsworth denied the second point by arguing that only the countries that were already nuclear powers had sufficiently advanced technology to create devices or weapons with low enough yields so as not to violate the threshold. Mr. Tsarapkin also criticized the concept of expressing the threshold in terms of seismic magnitude, arguing that, as Technical Working Group II had indicated, determination of magnitude was a controversial issue. Finally, he alleged that, American assertions to the contrary notwithstanding, an international control system was not necessary to detect those tests covered by the American proposal, but only for a comprehensive test ban. Although his remarks

10*Ibid.,* pp. 9-10.

were impromptu and did not constitute a formal Soviet reaction, they certainly presaged a less than warm reception for the American proposal.

II
Differences Narrow

The French Nuclear Tests

The formal Soviet reply did not come until several days later; meanwhile an event ocurred which had significant implications for the test ban negotiations, although its immediate effect was imperceptible. On February 13, 1960, refusing to heed the General Assembly's recommendations, France detonated an atomic device with an estimated yield of from 60 to 70 kilotons. Interestingly, this development was not mentioned in the Geneva Conference until March 2, and then only implicitly when Ambassador Wadsworth referred to what had previously always been called the "4th country problem," or the "nth country problem," as the "5th country problem." The Soviet Union did not mention the fact that France had tested a nuclear device until September 29.[11] By that time, France had detonated a second nuclear device, and it would detonate a third before the year was out. Clearly, with each passing day the "nth country" problem would become more difficult, and for that reason, the question of a test ban more complicated.

The Soviet Proposal for Temporary Criteria

On February 16, Mr. Tsarapkin presented the USSR's formal response to the American suggestion for a phased treaty.[12] In a rather moderate speech he labeled the suggestion "unacceptable" because the USSR favored a comprehensive treaty; but he went on to suggest that it might be possible to surmount the difficulties in which the Conference was enmeshed by exploring a concept which had been advanced by the United Kingdom on January 15, that is, to have temporary criteria for the initiation of on-site inspections. He then proposed temporary criteria which would apply for an initial period of from two to three years. These provided that an event would be eligible for inspection if it were localized on the

[11]GEN/DNT/PV. 248, p. 13.
[12]GEN/DNT/PV. 172, pp. 3-7.

basis of data from several surrounding stations within an area of approximately 200 square kilometers. If the control posts were situated only on one side of the event, as for example an event in a coastal area, a larger area would be allowed. An event would be ineligible for inspection if (1) its depth of focus were established as below 60 kilometers, (2) its epicentral location were established to be in the deep ocean and it were not accompanied by a hydro-acoustic signal, (3) it were established within 48 hours as the fore-shock of an earthquake, or (4) if it were established as the aftershock of an earthquake. Mr. Tsarapkin claimed that these criteria repre-sented the area of agreement between the Western and Soviet scientists, and in large measure they did, except that the concept of first motion was completely omitted. All events regardless of their seismic magnitude would be eligible for inspection, the actual number of inspections to be fixed according to the Soviet quota proposal, but the USSR continued to be unwilling to indicate any specific figure for a quota. During the period that the temporary criteria were in effect, Mr. Tsarapkin envisaged that the Soviet and Western scientists "would continue the joint study of the question of criteria" with the aim of agreeing upon a complete and more rigid set of criteria which would replace the temporary criteria. Thus the Soviet Union accepted the principle of "joint research," and this was confirmed in subsequent questioning. The following day Mr. Tsarapkin stated that the research program could begin immediately after the signature of the treaty—that is, before its coming into force—and that nuclear devices would not be required in the program, that chemical explosives would be sufficient.[13]

Even though Mr. Tsarapkin denied it, the Soviet proposal seemed to acknowledge some of the technical difficulties which the Western scientists had striven so painfully to present in Technical Working Group II. In any case, the two sides appeared to be moving closer to agreement, and on March 2, Ambassador Wads-worth pronounced the proposed Soviet criteria "generally acceptable technically."[14] The American reservation applied principally to the area of localization, which Ambassador Wadsworth argued was too small, but also to the identification of foreshock. In addition, he

[13]GEN/DNT/PV. 173, p. 8.
[14]GEN/DNT/PV. 180, p. 5.

maintained that the proposal would only be acceptable if some arrangement could be worked out so that if agreement were not reached on more rigid criteria during the initial period, the organization would not be left without criteria. However the divergence between East and West on broader issues was still great, and the greatest portion of Ambassador Wadsworth's speech was actually devoted to pointing these out. In sum, the United States continued to believe that with existing technology it would be impossible adequately to control low yield underground explosions, and thus that for the time being a comprehensive treaty was out of the question. The Soviet Union, on the other hand, continued to insist on a comprehensive treaty, and held to its position that on-site inspections could occur only within such a context.

The Soviet Proposal for a Phased Treaty and a Moratorium

The next attempt to narrow the gap between the two sides was also advanced by the Soviet Union, although its origins were more diffuse. On Saturday, March 19—just in time for the Sunday editions—Ambassador Tsarapkin announced that the USSR would be willing to conclude a treaty "on the cessation of all nuclear weapon tests in the atmosphere, in the oceans, and in outer space, and of all underground tests which produce seismic oscillations of magnitude 4.75 conventional units or above."[15] He stated that the Soviet government would also agree to the American proposal "to institute a programme of joint experiments by the Soviet Union, the United States, and the United Kingdom," with respect to unidentified events below magnitude 4.75 conventional units, "on the understanding that all parties to the treaty assume at the same time the obligation not to carry out during that period any nuclear weapons tests producing seismic oscillations of magnitude 4.75 conventional units or below." In other words, the partial treaty would have to be accompanied by a moratorium covering the tests which were not banned. Apparently the USSR felt that the moratorium should be part of the treaty. Senator Humphrey had made a similar suggestion several months previously in a speech in Pontiac, Michigan, and the idea was explored verbally in guarded fashion by the principal delegates to the Geneva Conference several

[15]GEN/DNT/PV. 188, p. 13.

days prior to the Soviet proposal.[16] Sir Michael Wright had indicated that he would advance the concept to the United Kingdom government.

The Soviet proposal was widely regarded as a major move. Coming as it did a few days after the opening session of the Ten-Nation Disarmament Committee, and with a summit meeting scheduled within two months, it could be interpreted as an attempt to secure a détente. On the other hand, it involved a continuation of the unpoliced moratorium.

Formulating a Western Response

The first Western response was to probe the precise meaning and implications of the Soviet proposal. Some questions were put to Mr. Tsarapkin immediately after he made the proposal. These were repeated in a more formal fashion and others were added at the next session of the Geneva Conference on Monday, March 21.[17] The first group of questions related to the "joint research programme" and the obligation to refrain from testing. They concerned the length of the program and whether or not the two aspects would be concurrent. Ambassador Wadsworth also asked what would happen at the end of the period, and specifically, "if, in the opinion of the scientists, the controls were still not completely effective, would the obligation not to test nevertheless persist?" Ambassador Wadsworth was also concerned about the scope of the research program, particularly whether it would be limited to the problem of criteria or would be broader.

A second group of questions concerned the number of on-site inspections and the threshold of magnitude. Ambassador Wadsworth asked if the Soviet Union accepted the Western proposal to use the unified magnitude scale. He also asked if the Soviet Union accepted the threshold of magnitude 4.75 and if there would be a quota for inspections above the threshold, below the threshold, or for the entire range. A related query concerned the Soviet attitude toward the American proposal for simplified criteria.

A third area of questions concerned high altitude and outer

---

[16]See the interchanges between Tsarapkin and Popper (US), GEN/-DNT/PV. 183, pp. 11-13; GEN/DNT/PV. 184, pp. 10-18; and the remarks by Wright, GEN/DNT/PV. 185, p. 3.

[17]GEN/DNT/PV. 189, pp. 5-8.

space. Since the Soviet proposal envisaged a complete prohibition on testing in these environments—which the United States phased treaty proposal of February 11 did not necessarily—Ambassador Wadsworth inquired about what type of a control system was "proposed for the installation in the high-altitude environment, what elements it would contain and at what intervals such elements of the high-altitude system would be installed." He also wanted to learn what "would be done about high-altitude or cosmic space tests which could not be identified by the initially installed system." Thus he raised a question which American policy-makers themselves had previously evaded.

Finally, Ambassador Wadsworth asked:

> As regards the underground environment, in the event that effective control of small underground explosions proved impossible and if the proposed temporary prohibition against such explosions lapsed, would the remainder of the treaty continue in effect?

Given the ideas which many in the American scientific community held about the difficulty of detecting underground nuclear explosions this was perhaps the most crucial question. The last of the non-nuclear blasts in the Cowboy series had been fired on March 4 and the evaluation of the series substantially confirmed Albert Latter's theories concerning decoupling.

Mr. Tsarapkin's responses followed the same order as Ambassador Wadsworth's questions. He repeated his previous statements that the "joint research programme" could begin immediately after the signature of the treaty. In the Soviet view the program should be drafted by the Preparatory Commission. Mr. Tsarapkin stated that the USSR felt that, although research would be a continuing aspect of the Control Organization, a suitable length for the specific program aimed at events below the threshold of magnitude 4.75 would be four or five years, and that the question of the moratorium and the research program were "closely interrelated." Mr. Tsarapkin asserted that the Soviet government did not admit the possibility that the research program might not be successful, but if it did take the most pessimistic view, it felt that the failure of the program "should not automatically release the parties to the treaty from their obligations regarding the moratorium and should not mean that the treaty would terminate or be liquidated." The governments concerned would have to discuss the situation and agree on further measures. With respect to the scope and nature of the research program, Mr. Tsarapkin asserted that experiments in the program should be conducted with "conventional chemical detonations, not nuclear weapons."

Concerning the second group of questions, the Soviet view was that the quota of on-site inspections, which would have to be determined on the basis of a political compromise, would apply both to events above and below the threshold; thus the issues of determining the magnitude of specific events would not arise. The quota would be revised in the light of the experience of the Control Organization in accordance with the periodic review article, therefore, for the first time, two years after the entry into force of the treaty, and subsequently on an annual basis.

With respect to high altitude and outer space, Mr. Tsarapkin asserted that there should be a total prohibition on testing regardless of the number or the schedule of installation of control techniques.

The answer to the last question had been given implicitly in the answers to the first group. In essence, it was that the prohibition on testing nuclear weapons should be permanent regardless of the outcome of the research program.

Simultaneously, discussion and debate began within the United States and the Western alliance about what the Western response should be. The extent to which the detailed questions raised by Ambassador Wadsworth and the responses given by Mr. Tsarapkin entered into the decision-making process is not clear. Many of the arguments were those which had been visible throughout the negotiations. Moreover, at his news conference on Friday, March 25— four days after the interchange between Wadsworth and Tsarapkin and two days after the Committee of Principals framed its recommendation—Secretary of State Herter stated that the Department had not received all of Mr. Tsarapkin's answers.[18] Of course their general nature had been reported in the press.

On Tuesday, March 22, Senator Clinton P. Anderson, then

[18]U.S. Department of State *Bulletin,* Vol. XLII, No. 1085 (April 11, 1960), p. 548.

Chairman of the Joint Committee on Atomic Energy, declared that the Soviet proposal "has the appearance of a phony."[19] It was his view that the Soviet proposal was an attempt to secure a prohibition against all testing, regardless of whether or not the agreement could be controlled. In his picturesque terms:

> Again the United States is asked to buy a "pig in the poke." We are asked to forego testing and to accept a totally inadequate inspection system. We are asked again to agree to a system based largely on trust of the Soviets rather than real controls.

John A. McCone, Chairman of the Atomic Energy Commission, was known to hold similar views.[20] To these men, the acceptance of the Soviet proposal would endanger American security because of its failure to provide adequate control.

Another force acting as an undercurrent, but in tandem with this interpretation, was the increasing pressure in the United States to resume the testing of nuclear weapons. Perhaps Freeman J. Dyson, a physicist and professor at the Institute for Advanced Study at Princeton, articulated the case most clearly. His views were advanced in an article entitled "The Future Development of Nuclear Weapons," published in the April 1960 issue of *Foreign Affairs*,[21] which was released in mid-March. In his article, Professor Dyson stressed particularly the importance and possibility of a fission-free weapon, or a neutron bomb, which would not produce fallout. He also asserted that complete control over a ban on testing nuclear weapons would be impossible without almost unlimited inspection rights.

The adverse reaction in the United States to the Soviet proposal so alarmed Prime Minister Macmillan that he hastily arranged to fly to the United States to confer with President Eisenhower about the Western response. He regarded the Soviet proposal as an extremely favorable action. Many in the United States also inclined toward this position. The day after Senator Anderson

[19]*Congressional Record,* Vol. CVI, Part 5 (1960), pp. 6219-20.
[20]*New York Times,* March 23, 1960, p. 12.
[21]Freeman J. Dyson, "The Future Development of Nuclear Weapons," *Foreign Affairs,* Vol. XXXVIII, No. 3 (April 1960), pp. 457-64.

issued his pronouncement, Hans Bethe released a statement in which he viewed the Soviet proposal favorably.[22] Senator Hubert H. Humphrey also made a lengthy speech in the Senate that day describing in detail the progress of the Geneva Conference and relating the Soviet proposal to his Pontiac speech and the United States suggestion for a phased treaty.[23] He was well informed, among other reasons because his Subcommittee on Disarmament had held a hearing on the technical problems involved in the negotiations on February 4, 1960. He pointed out that the Soviet proposal differed from his suggestion in that the number of on-site inspections was not specified and the proposed moratorium was four to five years instead of two. He also read into the record a detailed statement of the Advisory Committee on Science and Technology of the Democratic Advisory Council, which emphasized the importance of a test ban agreement. In view of all of these factors, his conclusion was that the Soviet proposal should be regarded "as a significant indication that the USSR may be willing to accept the necessary number of inspections to monitor a test-ban treaty and to work for the improvement of the control system."

Following his speech, Senators Humphrey, Anderson, and Case engaged in a low-keyed debate about the progress of the test ban talks. Perhaps the most interesting point was Senator Humphrey's insistence that from twenty to thirty on-site inspections would be necessary annually in the USSR, and Senator Anderson's reply that in informal conversations Soviet delegates had mentioned the possibility of two or three.[24] The Soviet Union still had not presented a concrete figure for the quota in the Geneva Conference, and it would not until July 26, 1960. Clearly, this issue was a factor which had to be considered in viewing the Soviet proposal.

A closed debate raged within the Administration, although the views and positions were not significantly different from those expressed in the public arena. The Committee of Principals held meetings on March 22 and 23.[25] Chairman McCone argued force-

[22]*New York Times,* March 24, 1960, p. 1.
[23]*Congressional Record,* Vol. CVI, Part 5 (1960), pp. 6356-63.
[24]*Ibid.,* p. 6362.
[25]See the account of these two meetings in Chalmers M. Roberts, "The Hopes and Fears of an Atomic Test Ban," *The Reporter,* Vol. XXII, No. 9, pp. 20-23.

fully against accepting the Soviet proposal. James H. Douglas, who had recently been promoted from the Secretaryship of the Air Force to Deputy Secretary of Defense, and who was sitting in for Secretary of Defense Thomas S. Gates, Jr., made the strongest case for a favorable response. He argued that any agreement which would "open up" the Soviet Union by stationing international inspectors within the USSR, and thus break down Soviet secrecy and insularity, would be more valuable to the United States than any gains from continued testing, and he felt that the proposal seemed to offer the possibility of such an agreement. Mr. Douglas' arguments represented a considerable shift in thinking in the Department of Defense. Although he was perhaps the most articulate exponent of the new views, they were apparently subscribed to in varying degrees by the Secretary and other senior officials. George Kistiakowsky, the President's Special Assistant for Science and Technology, supported his stand. Allen Dulles made the point that current intelligence estimates continued to indicate that the United States held a lead in nuclear weaponry, and thus that a freeze on development would be to its advantage. By the end of the second meeting a recommendation urging a conditional favorable response to the USSR was framed. Messrs. Douglas, Kistiakowsky, Dulles, and Herter supported this recommendation; Chairman McCone opposed it. The President accepted and approved the recommendation. At this point, he strongly favored attempting to achieve a nuclear test ban.[26]

Thus by March 26 when Prime Minister Macmillan arrived in the United States, his trip was rather redundant. Nonetheless, it allowed joint consultation, which had not occurred prior to this point, and a display of Western unanimity.

The Eisenhower-Macmillan Joint Declaration

On March 29, after meetings in Washington and Camp David, President Eisenhower and Prime Minister Macmillan issued a joint declaration. The most important part of this declaration, and the Western response to the Soviet proposal, was the statement that the President and the Prime Minister had agreed that as soon as a test ban treaty was signed:

[26]Robert Gilpin feels that the President's desire was the strongest factor in the decision. See *American Scientists and Nuclear Weapons Policy,* pp. 249-50.

. . . and arrangements made for a coordinated research program for the purpose of progressively improving control methods for events below a seismic magnitude of 4.75, they will be ready to institute a voluntary moratorium of agreed duration on nuclear weapons tests below that threshold, to be accomplished by unilateral declaration of each of the three powers. In order to expedite progress, the President and the Prime Minister have agreed to invite the Soviet Government to join at once with their two Governments in making arrangements for such a coordinated research program and putting it into operation.[27]

Several features of the statement are worthy of note. First, this was the first mention of a "coordinated research program." Previously the adjective "joint" had always been used. The developing differences between the Soviet Union and the Western powers concerning whether chemical or nuclear explosions would be required were responsible for this shift in terminology. American scientists of almost all persuasions were convinced that nuclear detonations were necessary for the research program, and the Administration was determined not to be put in a position whereby the Soviet Union could block this. Secondly, the statement implied that the research program should begin immediately, not after the signature of the treaty. Finally, and perhaps most importantly, the moratorium would be voluntary and accomplished by unilateral declaration. This would retain an element of freedom of action, and also meet the constitutional problem posed by President Eisenhower's departure from office in January 1961 (actually the uncertainty that this involved was soon removed by pledges from the major Presidential candidates that they would honor a moratorium commitment). Also, the duration of the moratorium was left to be determined, which implied, as various statements by officials had, that the West would not accept a period as long as from four to five years.

With the issuance of this statement the positions of the three parties to the Geneva negotiations moved significantly closer together, and the prospects for a test ban treaty appeared to rise sharply. In the following days the world press contained numerous speculations that the remaining unresolved issues could be solved

[27]*Geneva Conference*, p. 424.

at the forthcoming meeting of heads of governments, now scheduled to open May 16.

The diplomats at the conference table seem to have shared these expectations.[28] In the fifteen meetings that were held between March 29, the date on which the statement was issued and May 12, the day the Conference recessed for the summit meeting, they worked hard, as Ambassador Wadsworth put it, "to clear away as much underbrush as possible."[29] This consisted mainly of attempting to settle minor issues and clarify major ones. Significant progress was made on achieving agreement concerning the Annex on Privileges and Immunities, and the differences with respect to other aspects of the Control Organization were defined as precisely as possible. Of course, major effort was devoted to clarifying the Eisenhower-Macmillan statement and its exact relationship to the Soviet proposal of March 19. It was not until May 3 that the USSR conditionally accepted most aspects of the Western position.[30]

Meanwhile, on April 6, Ambassador Wadsworth had discussed in general terms the type of "coordinated research programme" that the United States felt should be carried out, and six days later he had proposed that scientists from the three states be brought to Geneva to advise the Conference on the technical aspects of the proposed research program.[31] This suggestion had been accepted by the Soviet Union on April 14, and on May 3 when the USSR broadly accepted the new Western position, it also agreed that the Seismic Research Program Advisory Group, as it came to be called, should hold its first session May 11. Ultimate responsibility for the research program was to rest with the Geneva Conference.

A Basic Consensus?

By May 12, when the Conference recessed, it can fairly be said that there was a mutually acceptable framework for a test ban treaty. Leaving aside issues affecting the nature of the control organization, which will be treated in a later chapter, the differences stemming from technical aspects of the matter appeared not to be insurmountable, and scientists from the three sides were already

[28]See Sir Michael Wright, *Disarm and Verify,* pp. 127, 137.
[29]GEN/DNT/PV. 198, p. 8.
[30]GEN/DNT/PV. 202, pp. 3-6.
[31]GEN/DNT/PV. 196, pp. 3-4.

at work on the research problems. Seemingly in recognition of this, on April 1 the Conference agreed that its verbatim records through February 29, 1960, and adopted portions of the draft treaty should be released on April 19 and that thereafter verbatim records would be released monthly with a one-month time lag.[32] This move also satisfied a long-standing complaint of the Joint Committee on Atomic Energy about the secrecy of the negotiations.

The Soviet Union had agreed that the moratorium could be accomplished by a series of unilateral declarations by the three governments and that as a part of the planned research there might be "a strictly limited number of joint underground nuclear explosions."[33] The Western powers had agreed that the quota of on-site inspections should apply to events both above and below the magnitude 4.75 threshold. The unresolved issues related to the size of the quota—(the Soviet Union had not yet tabled a specific proposal),—the duration of the moratorium, and what obligation the parties to the treaty would have at the end of the moratorium if the research program were not completely successful in improving the capability of the control network. The Soviet Union continued to argue that the moratorium should be from four to five years, and cited an October 29, 1959, statement of John A. McCone in which he had said that it would take from four to five years to create a reliable control system. In any case, Mr. Tsarapkin insisted that the research program and the moratorium should be coterminous. The Western representative on the other hand argued that four to five years was too long a period for the moratorium. On the other issue, the USSR also maintained its position that at the expiration of the moratorium the parties to it should not be "automatically released" from their obligations. The Western powers on the other hand felt that at the end of the moratorium each of the three powers should be "free to take any position that it deems necessary." Also, the Soviet Union continued to talk about and insist on a "joint research programme" while the Western representatives used the phrase "coordinated research programme."

However, even though the unresolved issues of a technical nature may have seemed relatively minor, some involved fairly

[32]GEN/DNT/PV. 192, p. 6.
[33]GEN/DNT/PV. 202, p. 6.

deep-rooted disagreements. The West was determined not to agree to permanent measures of arms control unless they could be policed with a high degree of assurance. Thus the length of the moratorium and what happened at its expiration were crucial issues for Western policy-makers. So too was the question of the adequacy of the research program, and consequently the desire not to allow the other side to have veto powers. The USSR had other fears. Mr. Tsarapkin expressed some of these in explaining the Soviet argument that at the expiration of the moratorium the parties to the treaty should meet to consider the situation.

> The meaning of this proposal is perfectly obvious. It is meant to preclude obstruction by any party who, in the absence of such a provision in the treaty, might under various pretexts prevent positive results from being achieved by the research and then, on the ground that the agreed time-limit for carrying out the research programme had expired, declare its freedom of action and resume testing.[34]

If the USSR assumed that within the limits of a politically acceptable control system there would always be some threshold of detectability, and that it might be extremely difficult and perhaps even impossible to compensate for such degradations in control as posed by decoupling, the Soviet fears could be well founded. In any case, the USSR had the development of the theory of decoupling as a backdrop of immediate history. The desire to exercise a high degree of control over the research work would fit with this interpretation, as would pressure for a lengthy moratorium.

Dissents From Interested Parties

These divergencies, however, remained undercurrents. The most salient signs seemed to indicate rapid and swift progress toward a test ban. As a result, those interested parties which might be affected by a test ban began to raise their voices. On April 7, President de Gaulle reiterated the position that France would only abandon its nuclear weapons development program if the three nuclear powers destroyed their nuclear weapons.[35] He repeated this

[34]GEN/DNT/PV. 192, p. 9.
[35]*New York Times,* April 8, 1960, p. 1.

several days later during a trip to the United States in an address before a Joint Session of Congress.[36] His position was underlined by the detonation of a second French nuclear device on April 1. Another "nth country" also made its position known. On April 10, Premier Chou En-lai stated that Communist China would not be bound by any accord which it did not sign.[37] At a news conference about a month later, he stated that the People's Republic of China would only take part in a disarmament conference if it were recognized by the other participating states.[38] These statements had ominous implications for the prospects of a general test ban and also for the Sino-Soviet alliance, coming as they did in the midst of the developing controversy between Communist China and the USSR in which differences concerning disarmament figured prominently.[39]

Joint Committee Hearings: The Bethe-Teller Debate

There were stirrings within the United States too. On April 11, Senator Clinton Anderson announced that two subcommittees of the Joint Committee on Atomic Energy, meeting jointly, would hold public hearings, starting April 19, on the technical aspects of the detection and inspection controls of a nuclear weapons test ban. The hearings were carried on for four days and most of the scientists who had participated in one way or another in the test ban negotiations and others as well testified.[40] Although the Chairman of the hearings, Representative Chet Holifield, strove valiantly to confine the discussion to technical matters, questions concerning the wisdom of past and possible future negotiating positions were inevitably raised. On these occasions, the positions which were by then well known were repeated. Perhaps Edward Teller and Hans Bethe portrayed best the two extremes among the scientists that testified, the former displaying great caution concerning the wisdom of a test ban and the latter controlled enthusiasm. A variety of

[36]U.S. Department of State, *Documents on Disarmament, 1960* (1961), p. 81.

[37]*New York Times,* April 11, 1960, p. 7.

[38]*Documents on Disarmament, 1960,* p. 87.

[39]See Donald S. Zagoria, *The Sino-Soviet Conflict, 1956–1961* (1962), especially pp. 290-94.

[40]For an extensive analysis of these hearings see Earl H. Voss, *Nuclear Ambush,* pp. 395-456.

estimates and judgments were involved. For Teller, the development of tactical nuclear weapons was important and promising, while Bethe viewed it as of marginal utility and as possibly being technically difficult. Teller was pessimistic about the possibility of improving the control system, while Bethe was optimistic. Teller regarded the decoupling theory as a degradation of great importance for which compensations were unlikely. Bethe, on the other hand, questioned the practicability of decoupling, particularly for large detonations in the range of tens of kilotons, and also felt that the problem could be conquered. Despite this disagreement, however, there was consensus among these two scientists and others on the capabilities of the system recommended by the Conference of Experts; they all estimated it at roughly 19 kilotons for an underground shot which had not been decoupled.

And Some New Suggestions

Other than the Bethe-Teller debate, which was framed more neatly than it had been previously, three elements stand out most in the hearings. The first of these occurred the second day when Richard Latter of the RAND Corporation testified. In the period after Technical Working Group II he analyzed the control system proposed by the Conference of Experts in more detail than anyone previously had, and in the process he experimented with some of its parameters.[41] He presented the results of this work to the Committee. No one yet knew how many control posts there would be in the Soviet Union—the issue had not been discussed in the Geneva Conference—but Dr. Latter assumed on the basis of inferences and calculations that there would be 21. If there were control posts only on the territory of the three nuclear powers—21 in the Soviet Union, 14 in the United States, and 1 in the United Kingdom—and assuming a magnitude 4.75 threshold, using earthquake tables, he estimated that this would result in about 173 unidentified events per year in the United States and 53 in the Soviet Union. If 30 percent of these were eligible for on-site inspection, there could be 52 inspections per year in the United States and 16 in the

---

[41]See his testimony: U.S. Congress, Joint Committee on Atomic Energy, Special Subcommittee on Radiation and the Subcommittee on Research and Development, *Hearings: Technical Aspects of Detection and Inspection Controls of a Nuclear Weapons Test Ban,* 86th Congress, 2d Session (1960), pp. 38-39.

Soviet Union. If control posts were established throughout the world, as recommended in the report of the Conference of Experts, he calculated that the number of unidentified earthquakes in the United States and the Soviet Union would be reduced to 143 and 28 respectively, and again assuming that 30 percent of these would be eligible for on-site inspection, the maximum number of on-site inspections would correspondingly be reduced to 43 and 8. He also calculated that by modestly increasing the number of control posts within the Soviet Union, especially in the seismic areas, the number of unidentified earthquakes could be reduced even farther. Thus, assuming control posts only in the USSR, the United States, and the United Kingdom, but increasing the number of control posts within the Soviet Union from 21 to 25 would result in there being only 20 unidentified earthquakes each year on Soviet territory. Using the 30 percent figure again, only 6 events there would be eligible for on-site inspection.

The second novel element appeared in Hans Bethe's testimony.[42] He argued that with a large number of control posts and with feasible improvements in seismological instruments, it might be possible to detect even decoupled detonations of as little yield as 20 kilotons. In his estimate, with foreseeable improvements, some 600 control posts would be required in the Soviet Union to achieve this capability. Both of these features are interesting chiefly because they indicate how the technical parameters of the control system could be changed if one were willing to alter the elements of the system. Dr. Latter's testimony illustrated the same point and was also significant because of the low number of on-site inspections involved and the differential between the number required in the United States and the Soviet Union. His figures varied greatly from those being used by the American delegates in the negotiations.

Finally, the Joint Committee hearings were interesting because they brought out in vivid detail how difficult it would actually be to conduct an on-site inspection. On the basis of this a number of Congressmen concluded that the probability of an on-site inspection's detecting evidence of a violation was very close to zero. Their conclusion had ominous implications for the possibility of Senatorial consent to ratification of a comprehensive test ban.

[42]See *ibid.*, pp. 171-86.

III

The Seismic Research Program Advisory Group

The Opening Atmosphere

The early meetings of the Seismic Research Program Advisory Group, which convened on Wednesday, May 11, 1960, seemed to sustain the general air of optimism. The excitement and tension following Premier Khrushchev's announcement on May 7 that the USSR had captured an American pilot whose U-2 aircraft had been shot down over Soviet territory six days previously seemed to have no effect on the work going on inside the *Palais des Nations*.

The technical representatives of the three states were generally younger and of lower rank than their counterparts at previous meetings. The American delegation was headed by Frank Press, a seismologist at the California Institute of Technology, and Carl Romney of the Air Force served as Associate Chairman.[43] M. A. Sadovsky, who had attended the Conference of Experts and the two technical working groups, headed the Soviet delegation,[44] and H. R. Hulme, the British delegation.[45] Although the American delegation had not had any special preparation, several members had previously participated in the negotiations at one time or another, and all were deeply involved in Project Vela, the United States research program, final approval of which had been announced on May 7. Since the purpose of SRPAG was to discuss research, this background was probably sufficient preparation. They were, however, instructed to avoid "political" issues, to refer such matters to the diplomatic conference, and to avoid anything that might give the USSR veto power over the United States research program.

The task of the Seismic Research Program Advisory Group seemed fairly clear cut, and since it involved research, this con-

[43]The other members of the American delegation were: Carlton M. Boyer, Department of Defense; Gerald W. Johnson, Department of Defense; Spurgeon M. Keeny, Jr., Office of the Special Assistant to the President for Science and Technology; Richard Latter, RAND Corporation; Robert C. Scheid, Department of Defense; and M. Carl Walske, Atomic Energy Commission.

[44]The other members of the Soviet delegation were Y. V. Riznichenko, O. A. Grinevsky, V. I. Keilis-Borok, I. P. Pasechnik, G. L. Schnierman, and A. I. Ustyumenko.

[45]The other members of the British delegation were M. Hill, H. T. Morgan, J. W. Wright, F. Panton, and R. M. Evans.

ference probably elicited more professional enthusiasm from the participating scientists than had any of the others. Also, the meeting appeared to offer the opportunity of proving the contribution of scientific research to the solution of political problems. Dr. Press's opening comments, when he spoke of the procedures and language of science as being universal and recalled the fruitful results of international scientific cooperation in the research involved in the International Geophysical Year,[46] symbolized the general tone that characterized the participation of the Western delegates in the early meetings. The Soviet scientists also seemed to be somewhat more candid in these sessions than they had been in the past and appeared to share the Western enthusiasm for the scientific character of their task. For example, in a discussion about the American plan to offer improved seismological equipment to seismological stations throughout the world, Mr. Sadovsky said: "We shall also try to use the political situation for the improvement of seismology in general."[47] The conference could conceivably allow the scientists both to further their own professional interests and to contribute to the reduction of East-West tensions.

At the first meeting, the American scientists gave a comprehensive and detailed exposition of the United States research program. The plans then in effect envisaged various theoretical and empirical studies, including the detonation of approximately 11 nuclear and chemical explosions, some of which would be designed to test Albert Latter's decoupling theory. Another aspect of the program was the scheme, mentioned above, to re-equip the seismic stations of the world. There was also a plan to establish certain model stations, some equipped according to the recommendations of the Conference of Experts. This would provide the first practical test of a so-called Geneva-type station. The next two meetings were devoted to the presentation of the much more modest British research program and to discussion of the Western plans.

At the fourth meeting, on Saturday, May 14, Y. V. Riznichenko presented a paper on the Soviet research program. Since it was not presented as the American program was in terms of cost or man-years of activity, it was rather difficult to grasp its exact magnitude. It appeared to be an extensive program, although it

46GEN/DNT/SRPAG/PV. 1, p. 3.
47GEN/DNT/SRPAG/PV. 5, pp. 62-65.

was clearly not as elaborate as that of the United States. Certain aspects of Mr. Riznichenko's presentation were moreover rather ambiguous. He stated that for the experiments two of the seismological stations in the USSR would be "equipped with the full set of equipment, bearing in mind the recommendations of the Geneva Conference of Experts in 1958 and 1959."[48] Was this or was it not a commitment to construct two Geneva-type stations? His presentation was even more ambiguous on the subject of underground nuclear explosions. At one point he stated: "The systematic recording of seismic waves produced by earthquakes and also by underground chemical and nuclear explosions carried out under different conditions and in different areas of the profile will take place during the years 1960-1963."[49] Later, he said, ". . . it seems obvious to us at the present time that a certain number of co-ordinated nuclear explosions of definite magnitude or energy will have to be carried out by us,"[50] and referred to an earlier statement on this subject by Mr. Tsarapkin. However, in response to questioning on this point, Mr. Sadovsky said that he could not give an answer until the following meeting. It was clear from Mr. Riznichenko's presentation, that the Soviet scientists planned to utilize a number of large industrial chemical explosions as sources of data, and that they would generalize from this data. The Soviet scientists also planned to make extensive use of models. Again in response to questioning, Mr. Sadovsky stated that there would be no experiments in the Soviet Union to test the theory of decoupling.[51] The reasons that he gave were avowedly political, and his statement was almost apologetic. At the following meeting on Monday, May 16, he announced that there would be no nuclear explosions in the USSR and that the references in the Soviet paper were to nuclear explosions envisaged in American program.[52]

What Conclusion?

Although the atmosphere of these early sessions was quite technical and cordial, it was not immediately clear what the out-

[48]GEN/DNT/SRPAG/PV. 4, p. 12.
[49]*Ibid.*, pp. 13-15.
[50]*Ibid.*, pp. 27-30.
[51]*Ibid.*, p. 56.
[52]GEN/DNT/SRPAG/PV. 5, p. 21.

come would be. Of course, the joint discussion and criticism of the three programs yielded certain results in itself. As a consequence of Soviet criticisms, the American scientists agreed that some aspects of the United States program should be altered; for example, they thought that the number of temporary stations should be increased and the recording times—that is, the time which a temporary station would occupy a site—lengthened.[53] In addition, there were various informal meetings where problems of methodology were discussed and some agreements reached on matters of technique. However, it was not obvious what the meeting as a collective body could or would recommend. On May 17, the British suggested various forms of cooperation, involving such matters as exchanges of data and personnel and the elaboration of uniform methodology, and these were incorporated into a draft which was submitted by the United States the following day. The principles involved and the documents elaborating these principles were discussed in SRPAG sporadically through May 24.

The Collapse of the Summit Meeting: The Changing Soviet Posture

Meanwhile, events had transpired which would seriously affect SRPAG, and indeed the entire course of the Geneva negotiations. The heads of government of France, the Soviet Union, the United States, and the United Kingdom had agreed to meet in Paris on May 16 to discuss world problems. When the four leaders gathered in Paris, Chairman Khrushchev refused to proceed farther unless President Eisenhower condemned and cancelled all U-2 flights and arranged to have those "guilty" of perpetrating such flights brought to strict account. Since President Eisenhower refused to take such action, the summit meeting collapsed. Whether the Soviet move was attributable to conflicts within the Soviet ruling group among Chairman Khrushchev and his associates, to increasing tensions in Sino-Soviet relations, or to President Eisenhower's assumption of personal responsibility for the U-2 flights and unabashed assertion at his news conference of May 11 that such activities were a "distasteful but vital necessity" when dealing with a closed society such as the USSR,[54] are matters clearly

[53]GEN/DNT/SRPAG/PV. 7, p. 36.
[54]U.S. Department of State *Bulletin,* Vol. XLII, No. 1092 (May 30, 1960), p. 851.

beyond the scope of this study.[55] For our purposes the significant issue is that from that point on the attitude of the Soviet Union toward the test ban negotiations appears to have been markedly different from what it had been previously. Annex II on Privileges and Immunities was formally adopted on October 14, 1960, but this was the only treaty language that was adopted after the collapse of the summit. Through the summer of 1960 the USSR made what could be interpreted as a few concessions on other issues, but as early as the fall of 1960, it began to retract positions which it had previously tabled.

The End of Another Try by Scientists

The sharpest indication that the Soviet posture had changed and that this would have an impact on the test ban negotiations came on Friday, May 27, eleven days after the date on which the summit conference was scheduled to begin. At the first meeting of the diplomatic conference to be convened after the recess on May 12, Mr. Tsarapkin, after a long review of the history of the negotiations, stated that, "since the Soviet Union has no doubts regarding the validity of the report of the Geneva experts of 1958, it sees no need for undertaking any research or experiments on its own territory."[56] In other words, there would be no Soviet research program. In addition, Mr. Tsarapkin demanded that Soviet scientists be allowed to participate fully in all steps of any experiments that might be carried on in the West.

This shift caused considerable embarrassment for the Soviet scientists participating in the Seismic Research Program Advisory Group. SRPAG had been meeting on a daily basis through May 25. Then several days elapsed before the final meeting on May 30. At that session, in response to questioning about the Soviet research program, Mr. Sadovsky would only say:

[55]For a good summary of the speculation which was rampant soon after the event see Richard P. Stebbins, *The United States in World Affairs, 1960* (1961), pp. 83-88.

[56]GEN/DNT/PV. 206, p. 8. Wadsworth mentions this reversal of the Soviet position in his book, *The Price of Peace,* p. 27, but he somewhat unfairly fails to put it in the context of the collapse of the summit conference.

. . . the programme of test explosions, not only nuclear but also chemical explosions, is, in our view, linked to the control system. Our view is that if we do not have definite indications that such a system will be set up in the near future, then the programme of test explosions is unnecessary and should not be carried out. We are conducting seismological research in the USSR and apparently this seismological research will continue.[57]

Obviously, in this atmosphere an agreed report was out of the question. Dr. Press, in particular, argued against separate reports on the ground that "it broadcasts to the world that the scientists have disagreed."[58] SRPAG therefore agreed on the expediency of individual private reports by each of the three technical delegations to their own diplomatic delegations.

IV

How Near an Agreement?

Remaining Differences

One can only speculate about whether or not the outcome would have been different had not the broader context of East-West relations altered so radically. It is significant though that there were important disagreements from the outset. Eastern and Western scientists had different conceptions concerning the length of the research program, an issue which had important implications for the duration of the moratorium on nuclear testing below the 4.75 seismic magnitude threshold. Also, the American scientists in particular were insistent that there had to be experiments concerning decoupling, while the Soviet scientists were adamantly opposed to this. As early as May 18, it was apparent that the Soviet scientists had serious objections to the American plans for low-yield nuclear explosions.[59] The United States program included four nuclear explosions of less than 5 kilotons, one of 500 tons and two of 100 tons, and possibly one of 2 kilotons. The first specific objection that the Soviet scientists raised to these shots was to assert they might appear "suspicious" because of the American interest in the

[57]GEN/DNT/SRPAG/PV. 13, p. 16.
[58]GEN/DNT/SRPAG/PV. 12, pp. 7-10.
[59]GEN/DNT/SRPAG/PV. 7, pp. 17-20.

development of tactical nuclear weapons.[60] The American response was that the USSR was certainly entitled to assurance that the shots would not be used for weapons development, but that the precise arrangements for this were beyond the scope of a technical group. The Soviet scientists then argued that with the current state of technology, the prospects of recording seismic signals "at distances which might be of interest for the purpose of the control system" were extremely remote.[61] The views of Western scientists were cited to support this contention. The balance of Mr. Sadovsky's statement is extremely interesting. He went on to say:

> Frankly speaking, nothing has changed so far in this respect, and we are still in a situation whereby we would be completely satisfied if we were to succeed in a relatively short time—succeed in carrying out the views which had been stated with regard to the detection and identification of five-kiloton explosions. We still believe that five-kiloton explosions can be detected and identified, but it seems to us that we should begin precisely by tackling this task. If from the outset we begin to try to tackle not only this task but alongside a second task, that of detecting and identifying much smaller explosions, I am afraid that we shall meet considerable difficulties, and we may fail in the solution of both tasks.

This was perhaps the most candid public recognition on the part of any official Soviet representative in the test ban negotiations of the technical difficulties involved in the detection and identification of underground nuclear explosions. By implication the statement recognized that the technical situation had deteriorated since the summer of 1958 and the Conference of Experts. The statement also clearly implied that there would be a threshold below which nuclear explosions could not be detected.

If the attitude of the Soviet scientists with respect to low-yield nuclear explosions is put alongside their position on decoupling, what they seemed to be saying is that they could not contemplate any experiments which might give proof that certain nuclear explosions could not be controlled without radically altering the

---

[60]GEN/DNT/PV. 10, pp. 17-20.
[61]GEN/DNT/SRPAG/PV. 10, p. 47.

framework of the control system elaborated by the Conference of Experts. The American scientists argued that all avenues of exploration had to be followed, regardless of the consequences, and were optimistic that research would yield ways of detecting both decoupled and low-yield explosions. It almost seemed as if the positions of the two sides concerning what the progress of science would yield in the technical conference were exactly the opposite of their positions in the diplomatic conference. There the Soviet side was optimistic, while the Americans were reserved.

In view of these difficulties, decisions would obviously have had to have been made at a different level for SRPAG to have succeeded. At a minimum there would have had to have been some agreement on the length of the research program and on means of assuring the opposite side that the experimental nuclear explosions were not being used for purposes of weapons development. Probably the two sides would also have had explicitly or implicitly to have reached some consensus on the threshold of detectability that the research program should attempt to achieve. American policy on this matter was no more settled than it had been in the past.

Chapter VIII

The Collapse of the Conference

I

The Diplomats Resume

Although there were sixty-eight meetings of the Geneva Conference on the Discontinuance of Nuclear Weapon Tests between May 27, when it reconvened after the collapse of the summit meeting, and December 5, 1960, when it recessed for the final time that year, and also for the final time during the Eisenhower Administration, little progress was made. The attempt to solve the differences between East and West relating to the technical aspects of a control system for a test ban had failed. Agreement had not been achieved, and the attempt to bridge the disagreement through political compromise and scientific research had collapsed.

American Policy: A Fixed Course

President Eisenhower—like many Americans—was greatly disheartened by the collapse of the summit meeting, and the obvious stalemate in the nuclear test ban talks. He virtually gave up hope of achieving a test ban treaty, and his views were shared by a number of American policy-makers. Nevertheless, Western, and more particularly American, policy seemed almost to have achieved a momentum of its own, and the policies established earlier in the negotiations were pursued with very little modification.

There were several reasons for this. The manner in which the United States, at the end of 1959, had phrased its decision to continue the moratorium meant that a positive decision would be required to resume testing, and that in the absence of such a decision, the moratorium would continue. There were a number of inhibitions against taking a positive decision to resume testing nuclear weapons. On May 28, Chairman Khrushchev warned that the USSR would resume nuclear testing if the United States did.[1] Moreover, during the late spring and early summer the Administration wanted to avoid having the matter become involved in the politics of the presidential election. That it very nearly did become involved could be seen in the debate on the Republican platform in July.[2] The Administration felt that to do anything other than maintain the status quo would affect, and perhaps in a disadvantageous way, the chances of the Republican presidential candidate.

President Eisenhower decided, however, that if Richard Nixon won the presidential election, he, Eisenhower, would announce that the United States would resume nuclear testing. His purpose in doing this would be to spare his Republican successor the burden of taking this—in his view—unpopular step. When John F. Kennedy won the election, President Eisenhower felt that the decision should be left to him, particularly since Kennedy had stated on several occasions during the election that he favored continuing and intensifying the effort to achieve a nuclear test ban.

Another factor inhibiting the possibility of changing American policy concerning the nuclear test ban negotiations was that as the year went on East-West tension rose. On June 27, the USSR walked out of the Ten-Nation Disarmament Talks. The following month the Congo crisis erupted, and despite early unanimity, by late August the USSR and the United States were at loggerheads over their own and the UN's roles in these events. To take action such as resuming nuclear tests might jeopardize a remaining point of East-West contact and also further exacerbate relations between the two powers. Furthermore, these events tended to push other matters into the background and the attention of policy-makers was focused on them rather than on the test ban negotiations.

In another way also, American policy had a momentum which carried it ahead in the previously set direction. Project Vela was now underway, and it represented a large and continuing effort. Not only were funds and people committed at this point, but also the promise that scientific research might yield means of circumventing the perceived technical difficulties remained. For all of these reasons then, American policy continued virtually without change.

[1]*New York Times,* May 29, 1960, p. 1.
[2]See *New York Times,* July 24, 1960, p. 38; July 26, 1960, p. 21; and July 27, 1960, p. 17.

1

Safeguards: Some Revolutionary Concepts

There were, however, some slight modifications in American policy. The original plan for the Vela Program had called for a series of underground nuclear explosions starting in the fall of 1960. As early as May 27, the USSR demanded precise information on the safeguards which would be established so that it could be certain that the experiments were not being used for weapons development purposes.[3] The initial American proposal merely provided for: observation of the detonations; limitations on the instrumentation which could be used at the time of the detonation; and prior placement of the devices which were to be detonated in a depository which would be guarded jointly.[4] Representatives of the other side could examine only the exterior of the devices.

The Soviet Union argued that this was insufficient and maintained that unless the Vela shots were carried out with appropriate safeguards, it would regard them as parts of a weapons development program, would consider that the moratorium had been broken, and would feel free to resume weapons testing itself.[5] As Mr. Tsarapkin explained it, appropriate safeguards would involve full Soviet participation in the detonations, the right to inspect the internal structure of the devices used and to have a veto over the type of shots to be fired. He made it clear that the Soviet Union would not allow decoupled shots.

This was where matters stood in mid-summer, 1960. Meanwhile the United States had gone ahead with its plans for chemical explosions and had invited the Soviet Union and the United Kingdom to send observers for a shot planned for July 14, with the stipulation that American scientists should receive reciprocal privileges to observe chemical explosions in those two countries. On June 27, the USSR refused to agree to this in the absence of agreement on the overall research program, including the matter of safeguards, and Mr. Tsarapkin stated that the question of reciprocity therefore did not arise.[6] The United States conducted the explosion with observers only from the United Kingdom.

On July 12, the United States introduced a new proposal on

[3]GEN/DNT/PV. 206, pp. 8-9.
[4]GEN/DNT/PV. 208, pp. 3-9.
[5]GEN/DNT/PV. 214, p. 7.
[6]GEN/DNT/PV. 220, p. 12.

safeguards. It suggested that all three powers should put a number of outmoded weapons in a pool which would be under joint surveillance and from which devices could be drawn for experimental detonations.[7] All three parties could inspect the internal structures of these devices. The United States Administration promised to seek changes in the Atomic Energy legislation so that this would be possible. The Joint Committee on Atomic Energy had been consulted before the offer was made, and had given its tentative consent. Had the offer been accepted, and appropriate legislation adopted, a most interesting situation would have resulted, for the United States would have willingly revealed to its chief adversary in the Cold War secrets regarding nuclear weapons which it would not reveal to most of its allies. That policy-makers would even consider such action is an interesting commentary on the impact of nuclear weapons on international politics.

Although Mr. Tsarapkin allowed that the new American position was a step forward, he asserted that as the USSR did not plan to conduct any nuclear explosions, it would not contribute any devices to the pool and thus would not reveal any of its nuclear weapons to the United States. Since the United States would not create a pool unilaterally, an impasse resulted, and consequently the proposed nuclear explosions in the Vela Program were postponed.

One Agreement—Continuing Disagreements

Soviet policy also was rather static during this period. Some of the same factors that were operative in the American case may have affected the USSR too. To some degree both sides were reluctant to act during the closing days of the Eisenhower Administration. In addition, during this period Sino-Soviet tensions deepened,[8] and opposition to Chairman Khrushchev's policies may well have increased within the Soviet elite. Khrushchev's views on security policy, particularly those which he expressed in his January 1960 speech concerning the composition of the Soviet armed forces, are known to have occasioned some controversy among Soviet

[7]GEN/DNT/PV. 227, pp. 3 ff.
[8]See Donald S. Zagoria, *The Sino-Soviet Conflict, 1956–1961.*

policy-makers.[9] It is also possible that the Soviet leadership had already decided to resume nuclear testing, once preparations could be completed.

One technical matter was resolved by the Geneva Conference during 1960: on July 27 the three parties agreed on a precise definition of 4.75 seismic magnitude.[10] In view of the previous disputes on this issue, and if 4.75 were to be a threshold in a treaty, this agreement was relatively important, but little other progress was made. There continued to be disagreement on the size of the quota of on-site inspections, although on July 26 the Soviet Union finally advanced a concrete figure, 3.[11] The criteria to be used for the initiation of on-site inspections and the degree of localization required were also in dispute.

In addition, it became apparent that East and West had quite different conceptions of how many control posts would be required on each other's territories. On May 12, the United States had submitted a proposal which provided that the network of control posts would be established in three overlapping phases, each lasting four years, so that within six years the entire system would be in operation.[12] The first phase provided for 21 posts in the Soviet Union, 1 in the United Kingdom, 11 in the United States, and 2 on ships and 12 on islands in the northern hemisphere.

The Soviet Union responded to this proposal on August 11. It protested that the proposal did not provide in the first phase for control posts in the southern hemisphere, where it was known that the Western powers had carried out weapon tests. The USSR also complained that the proposal provided for too many posts in the Soviet Union and too few in the United States.[13] The Soviet counter-proposal envisaged the establishment in the first phase of 15 control posts in the Soviet Union, 11 in the United States, 1 in the United Kingdom, 7 in Australia, 20 on oceanic islands belonging to the United States and the United Kingdom, 2 in North America ex-

[9]See Thomas W. Wolfe, *Soviet Strategy at the Crossroads* (1964), especially pp. 31-37.
[10]GEN/DNT/PV. 235.
[11]GEN/DNT/PV. 234, p. 15.
[12]GEN/DNT/22/Add. 1.
[13]GEN/DNT/PV. 241, pp. 12-19.

clusive of the United States, 2 in Africa, and 10 on ships.[14] In total, there would be 68 control posts, rather than 47 as in the American proposal. With a touch of irony, Mr. Tsarapkin supported the Soviet proposal by citing portions of Richard Latter's testimony before the Joint Committee on Atomic Energy in April 1960, and pointed out that Dr. Latter had assumed that there would be 14 control posts in the United States, rather than 11 as the United States proposed.[15] No progress was made toward resolving these difficulties during 1960.

In the discussion of the installation of the control posts, another related difference became apparent. In November, Mr. Tsarapkin made it known that the Soviet Union would not allow any on-site inspections until the conclusion of the first phase in the installation of control posts, a process which in its view would take four years.[16] The Western powers, on the other hand, envisaged the first phase as being divided into two two-year periods, and maintained that on-site inspections could and should begin at the end of the first period. This difference also remained unresolved.

The Acrimonious Fifteenth General Assembly

The deteriorating atmosphere of the Geneva Conference was evident in the conduct of the United States and the USSR in the fifteenth session of the General Assembly in the fall of 1960. Both gave detailed expositions and justifications of their positions.[17] The debate was acrimonious. Poland submitted a resolution which would have placed the question of the cessation of nuclear tests before a special session of the General Assembly if agreement were not reached by April 1, 1961, and which would have requested the nuclear powers to maintain the moratorium on testing until an agreement had been achieved.[18] The resolution also contained several provisions aimed at preventing the dispersion of nuclear weapons capability, some of which might have been construed as directed against NATO programs then in effect. Because of a pro-

[14]GEN/DNT/104.

[15]GEN/DNT/PV. 256, p. 10.

[16]GEN/DNT/PV. 270, pp. 11-12.

[17]UN, General Assembly, First Committee, *Official Records* (15th Session), pp. 190-92, 193-95.

[18]UN Document A/C. 1/L. 252.

cedural decision, this resolution was not put to the vote; however, three other resolutions relating more or less directly to the Geneva Conference were.

The first of these was a resolution submitted by Ireland concerning the prevention of the wider dissemination of nuclear weapons. The second was a resolution offered by Austria, India, and Sweden urging the states which were engaged in the test ban negotiations to press toward agreement and to continue their voluntary moratorium on testing. The third, sponsored by twenty-five African and Asian states and Venezuela, also made these same requests.[19]

The three resolutions were all adopted by large majorities: 68 to 9, with 26 abstentions; 72 to 0, with 5 abstentions; and 67 to 11, with 11 abstentions, respectively. The Soviet Union voted for all three resolutions, the United Kingdom abstained on the first, but voted for the second and third, and the United States abstained on all three. The position of the Western powers on the first resolution was determined by the French attitude. The French remained adamant in their determination to acquire a nuclear capability and detonated their third nuclear explosion on December 27, 1960. The United States abstained on the last two resolutions because it felt that the language of the three power draft implied that the unresolved issues in the Geneva Conference were unimportant, and because both asked for a continuation of the moratorium. As the votes indicate, the United States was as distant from the main-stream of majority sentiment in the United Nations concerning this issue as it ever had been, or would be, during the test ban negotiations.

Matters relating to these negotiations, however, were largely submerged in the broader issues that gripped the Assembly. The Soviet proposal for General and Complete Disarmament, a follow-up to Chairman Khrushchev's suggestion at the previous session of the Assembly, was debated heatedly and at length, but without resolution. Chairman Khrushchev's attack on Secretary General Hammarskjöld and demand for a reorganization of the upper levels of the Secretariat, a product of the Congo crisis, was also in the forefront, and this controversy carried over into the Geneva Conference.

[19]See General Assembly Resolutions 1576 (XV), 1577 (XV), and 1578 (XV).

II

The Kennedy Administration: A Renewed Effort

Reappraising of the American Position

On January 20, 1961, when the Kennedy Administration assumed power, American policy in the test ban negotiations seemed to have reached a dead end. The Geneva talks were clearly deadlocked, and, as evidenced by the voting on these issues in the fifteenth General Assembly, United States policy obviously commanded little worldwide support. Even the United Kingdom, America's partner in the Geneva negotiations, did not vote with the United States. These facts alone would have made a new administration reappraise past policies. Further, as a Senator and a presidential candidate, John F. Kennedy had been highly critical of the Eisenhower Administration's policies relating to disarmament and arms control.[20] During the presidential campaign, he had written a letter to Thomas E. Murray in which he had pledged that if he were elected, the United States would not be the first to begin atmospheric tests, and that if the Geneva Conference were still in progress when he assumed office, he would direct "vigorous negotiation . . . in the hope of concluding a realistic and effective agreement."[21] He had also stated that he would direct the Atomic Energy Commission to prepare for underground testing, and if agreement were not reached within a reasonable period, he would order the resumption of underground testing.

Even before his inauguration, President Kennedy appointed John J. McCloy—a prominent Republican—as his adviser on disarmament. Five days after the inauguration, the United States Disarmament Administration, a unit within the Department of State created in September 1960, and the forerunner of the United States Arms Control and Disarmament Agency, announced the appointment of a panel headed by Dr. James B. Fisk, to study and review the technical aspects of the test ban negotiations.[22] A few days

[20]See, for example, his remarks at the University of New Hampshire, *Documents on Disarmament, 1960*, pp. 58-65. See also John F. Kennedy (Allan Nevins, ed.), *The Strategy of Peace* (New York: Harper, 1960), pp. 19-30.

[21]*Documents on Disarmament, 1960*, p. 289.

[22]The other members of the panel were Dr. Hans A. Bethe; General Austin W. Betts, Division of Military Applications, Atomic Energy Commis-

later, the President named Arthur Dean—usually considered a Republican—as United States Representative to the Geneva Conference. Other personnel changes also resulted from the inauguration of the new Administration. From the point of view of the nuclear test ban negotiations, the most important of the new officials were: Dean Rusk, Secretary of State; Robert S. McNamara, Secretary of Defense; Glenn T. Seaborg, Chairman of the Atomic Energy Commission; and Jerome B. Wiesner, Special Assistant to the President for Science and Technology. Dr. Wiesner, in particular, was deeply worried about the nuclear arms race and committed to making every possible effort to obtain measures of arms control and disarmament. He had also been critical of past American policy. In an article published in the fall of 1960 he had stated that ". . . the West has always been suspicious of Soviet proposals, and furthermore has generally been ultraconservative in the inspection requirements it places upon any system."[23]

On balance, the new policy-makers probably contributed more to the reformulation of American policy than the technical review, which was after all conducted by the same scientists who had been active in the Eisenhower Administration. Moreover, at this date, early 1961, Project Vela had produced very little. Various close observers have noted how important the change in personnel at the top policy-making echelons was. Sir Michael Wright, the sometime British representative in the negotiations has asserted that President Kennedy took decisions on issues ". . . over which the previous administration had been hesitating, in some cases for

---

sion; Dr. Harold Brown, Lawrence Radiation Laboratory, Livermore, California; Spurgeon M. Keeny, Jr., Office of the Special Assistant to the President for Science and Technology; Dr. Richard Latter, the RAND Corporation; General Herbert B. Loper, Office of Secretary of Defense, Department of Defense; Dr. J. Carson Mark, Los Alamos Scientific Laboratories; Doyle Northrup, Air Force Technical Application Center, Department of Defense; Dr. Wolfgang K. H. Panofsky, High Energy Physics Laboratory, Stanford University; Dr. Frank Press, Seismological Laboratory, California Institute of Technology, Pasadena, California; General Alfred D. Starbird, Division of Military Applications, Atomic Energy Commission; and Dr. Herbert F. York, Defense Research and Engineering, Department of Defense. In addition, there were observers from interested government agencies and departments.

[23]Jerome B. Wiesner, "Comprehensive Arms-Limitation Systems," *Daedalus* (Fall 1960), pp. 915-50, at 917-18.

a year or even two years."[24] And Earl H. Voss has written that with the inauguration of the Kennedy Administration, for the first time a United States administration ". . . agreed within its own house on a complete program for ending nuclear tests."[25]

To facilitate the review of American policy, President Kennedy requested that the resumption of the Geneva negotiations be delayed.

The new American position was approved by the President and discussed with the United Kingdom toward the end of February. When the Geneva Conference resumed on March 21, Ambassador Dean presented the broad outlines of the new position,[26] and, on April 18, jointly with the United Kingdom representative, he tabled a draft treaty embodying the new proposals.[27] This was the first time that the United States had tabled a complete treaty. As in the past, prior to their formal presentation, several aspects of the new American position were discussed in the Western press.

So far as technical matters were concerned, the changes in the United States position were not major. The United States still envisaged a threshold treaty which would not cover events of less than 4.75 seismic magnitude. It was, however, willing to ban all tests at high altitudes and in outer space. The United States urged the Soviet Union to reconsider its opposition to backscatter radar, but it proposed a control system based on the principal recommendations of Technical Working Group I. The United States' views on the length of the moratorium and on events not covered by the treaty were modified somewhat. It now proposed that the research program and the moratorium should be coterminous, each lasting three years from the date of the signature of the Treaty. The United States was also willing to accept the Soviet position on safeguards on research explosions; that is, it was willing to agree that, if the United States alone conducted nuclear explosions, Soviet scientists could examine American nuclear devices without the USSR's giving American scientists reciprocal privileges. Ambassador Dean stated that the President would request that the Atomic Energy Act be amended so that this could be implemented. In terms

[24]*Disarm and Verify*, p. 127.
[25]*Nuclear Ambush*, p. 459.
[26]GEN/DNT/PV. 274, pp. 16-27.
[27]GEN/DNT/110 and corr. 1.

of implications for traditional friend-foe relationships in world politics, this change made the American proposal even more extraordinary, and underscored again the impact of nuclear weapons on the nature of politics and relations among states. The American position continued to be that a quota of 20 on-site inspections would be necessary for the Soviet Union, but it was willing for quotas of 20 to be assigned to both of the Western powers. The United States was also willing to alter the proposed distribution of control posts in Asia, so that there would be a total of 19 control posts in the Soviet Union, rather than 21.

In sum, the United States sought to meet the Soviet position by offering various compromises on points to which the USSR had objected in the past. Much of this was the result of a careful study of the record of the negotiations through 1960 by Ambassador Dean and others. With respect to the basic technical issues which had divided the Conference, however, little modification was made in the Western position. The new Administration, like its predecessor, felt bound by the "facts" as they were then understood.

Soviet Disengagement: "Troika" and France

Much to the disappointment of the new Administration, the changes in the American position were without effect in terms of advancing the negotiations. Though it did little to soften the blow, this result was predicted even before the Geneva Conference resumed.[28] The Soviet attitude toward the test ban negotiations appears to have shifted significantly by this time, and apparently Chairman Khrushchev forecast this on March 9 in a lengthy interview with the American Ambassador in the USSR, Llewelyn E. Thompson.

Mr. Tsarapkin's opening speech in the Conference on March 21 dramatically demonstrated how much the Soviet position had changed.[29] After a bitter *ex parte* account of the negotiations, he stated that on the basis of the Soviet Union's experience in "other international organizations" the USSR now felt that "the single administrator of the control system should be replaced by a collective executive organ, in which the three main groups of States would

[28]See *New York Times,* March 20, 1961, p. 1.
[29]GEN/DNT/PV. 274, pp. 3-16.

be equally represented and invested with equal rights."[30] In other words, Chairman Khrushchev's suggestion for the reorganization of the upper levels of the Secretariat of the United Nations was now applied to the proposed control system. This was the first time that this issue had permeated the Geneva Conference.

In addition, Mr. Tsarapkin raised the question of the French tests of nuclear weapons. His exact words bear analysis, for they were certainly scrutinized with care by American policy-makers.

> In conducting nuclear weapons tests, the French Government is actively spurring on the nuclear armaments race. If this development of events is not checked, the number of States possessing nuclear weapons will rapidly grow. In that case, it will be much more difficult to reach agreement on the discontinuance of nuclear tests, and all the more difficult to reach agreement on disarmament.
>
> At the same time the French nuclear explosions reveal the true meaning of the position which the Governments of the United States and the United Kingdom have taken up at our Conference, namely, by endlessly dragging out the discussions on the discontinuance of nuclear weapon tests, they, that is the United States and the United Kingdom, have provided their NATO ally—France—with time in which to conduct further nuclear weapon tests. All this looks very much like what one might term a "division of labour" among the allies. We cannot ignore in our negotiations the fact that in conducting nuclear weapon tests, France as a member of NATO can, in line with her commitments to her allies within the NATO framework, carry out for other members of this military group—in other words on behalf of the United States and the United Kingdom—definite work in connexion with the improvement of nuclear weapons and perhaps even the creation of new types of weapons. Such activity by the Western countries, while the Soviet Union is honestly fulfilling its commitment not to conduct nuclear tests, cannot be viewed in any other way except as a desire by the Western Powers to obtain for themselves one-sided advantages. All this threatens to nullify the possibility of concluding a treaty and to render it pointless.[31]

[30]*Ibid.*, p. 14.
[31]*Ibid.*, pp. 15-16.

It was difficult to know whether the USSR interjected this issue as a pretext to justify actions taken for other reasons or because of genuine concern. In one sense, the innuendo contained in the statement, that France was conducting nuclear weapons tests for the United Kingdom and the United States—which was subsequently turned into an outright allegation—was blatantly false and the Soviet Government clearly must have been aware of this. The French explosions were caused by technically simple devices, not the sophisticated mechanisms that the United Kingdom and the United States would be interested in testing, and the Soviet national monitoring system must have given Soviet leaders data that would indicate this fact.

If the statement were approached somewhat less literally, and a good case could be made for searching for allegorical meanings in Soviet statements, it perhaps had more significance. Even without elaborate inference, the meaning of the first paragraph is fairly clear and the proposition which it contains is almost axiomatic. Moreover, the development of a nuclear capability by France probably had implications for the dispersion of nuclear weapons capabilities within the Soviet bloc, and especially it may have fanned the desire of Communist China to acquire a nuclear capability. By this time, the USSR had refused to assist the Chinese in gaining an independent nuclear capability, and in mid-1960 all Soviet economic and military advisers and technicians had been withdrawn from China.[32]

With respect to the second paragraph, although it was true that the Soviet Union should have been able to tell that the devices that France had detonated were unsophisticated, and therefore of little or no interest to the United Kingdom and the United States, as the French weapons program progressed, at some future point, such discrimination might not be as easy. Moreover, the mere fact that France was developing a nuclear weapons capability had implications for the overall strength of NATO in relation to the Warsaw Pact, regardless of the initial lack of sophistication of these weapons.

[32]Alice Langley Hsieh, "The Sino-Soviet Nuclear Dialogue, 1963," *Journal of Conflict Resolution*, Vol. VIII, No. 2 (June 1964), pp. 99-115, at p. 113.

Thus it was quite plausible that the continued testing of nuclear weapons by France might be a matter of serious concern to the Soviet Union. If stopping the spread of nuclear weapons to "nth" countries was a motivating factor in Soviet policy with respect to the Geneva negotiations, the French action probably decreased the attractiveness of the negotiations, or of a test ban, for it indicated how weak an instrument these devices were and might be for controlling the spread. If the USSR were genuinely concerned about the French nuclear weapons development program, the fourth detonation in the program on April 25, 1961, probably served to heighten Soviet fears and to dramatize the fact that the United Kingdom and the United States could not or would not restrain the French.

Mr. Tsarapkin's speech signaled a sharp change in the Soviet conduct in the negotiations. From that point on the USSR was increasingly intransigent. The stalemate was obvious, but at this point the motivations for Soviet behavior were not. Were the concerns which Mr. Tsarapkin mentioned the explanation for Soviet conduct, or merely pretexts to cover courses chosen for other reasons? Did the USSR expect still further concessions, or was it seeking to provoke the West into breaking off the negotiations?[33] Within the United States, pressures to resume nuclear testing mounted.[34]

For the time being, however, the Kennedy Administration stuck to its determination to try to achieve a test ban, and refused to accept the most pessimistic interpretations of Soviet behavior. On May 29, Ambassador Dean suggested a new approach to the problem of the quota for on-site inspections.[35] He proposed that the quota should be established on the basis of a sliding scale, and that the quota for the USSR should range from 12 to 20. The lower number would prevail if there were not more than sixty located seismic events of magnitude 4.75 or above during the year. The quota would rise by one for each five located seismic events of magnitude 4.75 or above; beyond 60, however, no more than 20 on-site inspections would be authorized under any circumstances. Even with the personnel of the new Administration, achieving con-

[33]Earl H. Voss favors the latter interpretation; see *Nuclear Ambush,* p. 460.

[34]See *ibid.,* pp. 462-63.

[35]GEN/DNT/PV. 311, pp. 3-11.

sensus on this new position had been difficult, yet it and other Western concessions were ignored. '

When President Kennedy and Chairman Khrushchev met in Vienna on June 3 and 4 for a general discussion of critical world problems, the test ban negotiations seemed to be completely deadlocked. The talks between the two leaders did not change this situation, in fact, at the conclusion of the discussions the chances of a test ban treaty seemed even more remote than they had previously. Khrushchev insisted that any more than three on-site inspections per year would constitute espionage and argued that the Congo crisis had demonstrated the necessity for a "troika" arrangement in the control organization.[35a] Kennedy attempted to counter these points and stressed the dangers of nuclear proliferation. Khrushchev in return depreciated the importance of a test ban as an isolated measure of arms control. He did tell Kennedy, however, that the USSR would not resume nuclear testing until the United States did, and Gromyko said the same thing to Rusk.[35b]

During the course of the conversations, Chairman Khrushchev handed President Kennedy an *aide mémoire* which reiterated the general Soviet position as enunciated in the Geneva Conference. It went on to suggest that the difficulties facing the negotiators could be eased, and implied that the Soviet proposal for a "troika" would be dropped, if the problems of a test ban and general and complete disarmament were solved simultaneously.[36] The Soviet Union seemed to be saying that the West could only obtain the controls which it argued were necessary for a test ban treaty in the context of general and complete disarmament. Subsequent questioning in Geneva and diplomatic correspondence brought out that this was indeed the Soviet position. In Geneva, the questions led to an acrimonious exchange. Now, in contrast to the situation prior to January 1959, it was the Soviet Union rather than the West which insisted that a test ban could only be considered in combination

[35a]Detailed accounts of the Vienna meeting can be found in Arthur M. Schlesinger, Jr., *A Thousand Days: John F. Kennedy in the White House* (1965), pp. 369-72, and Theodore C. Sorenson, *Kennedy* (1965), pp. 549 and 617-18.

[35b]Arthur M. Schlesinger, Jr., *A Thousand Days,* p. 398, and Theodore C. Sorenson, *Kennedy,* pp. 617-18.

[36]*Geneva Conference,* pp. 538-42.

with other measures of disarmament. The circle was closed! As the talks dragged on in Geneva through the summer of 1961, Ambassador Dean became increasingly convinced that they were fruitless and that the USSR was preparing to resume nuclear testing. He cabled his views to the Department of State. Several policy-makers and observers shared his opinion.

To Test or Not To Test

In this atmosphere, further darkened by the developing Berlin crisis, the pressure in the United States for ending the moratorium on nuclear testing mounted, and this pressure was alluded to in the various exchanges. As early as February, the Joint Chiefs of Staff had urged the President to resume testing if agreement were not reached within sixty days of negotiations.[36a] The Joint Chiefs favored atmospheric testing. The Department of Defense, though, would have limited the resumption to underground testing. There were also pressures from Congress, especially from the Joint Committee on Atomic Energy, from the press and from public opinion. A Gallup Poll in July 1961 showed more than two-to-one public support for the United States unilaterally resuming testing.

As a response to the pressure, and also to gain advice, on June 28, President Kennedy announced the formation through the President's Science Advisory Committee of an eleven-man *ad hoc* panel, headed by Wolfgang K. H. Panofsky, to review technical questions connected with the problem of nuclear testing.[37] Their mandate was to consider whether or not the Soviet Union could be conducting clandestine nuclear tests during the moratorium, and what progress the USSR could make through such tests. The group

[36a]For accounts of these pressures see Arthur M. Schlesinger, Jr., *A Thousand Days,* pp. 454-58, and Theodore C. Sorenson, *Kennedy,* p. 618.

[37]The other members of the panel were William O. Baker, Vice President, Bell Telephone Laboratories; Hans A. Bethe, Professor of Physics, Cornell University; Norris E. Bradbury, Director, Los Alamos Scientific Laboratory; James B. Fisk, President, Bell Telephone Laboratories; John S. Foster, Director, University of California Radiation Laboratory; George B. Kistiakowsky, Professor of Chemistry, Harvard University; Frank Press, Director, Seismological Laboratory, California Institute of Technology, Pasadena, California; Louis H. Roddis, President, Pennsylvania Electric Co.; John W. Tukey, Professor of Mathematics, Princeton University; Walter H. Zinn, Vice-President, Nuclear Division, Combustion Engineering, Inc.

was also asked to consider what progress the United States could make if it resumed nuclear testing, and what would happen if both sides resumed testing. In connection with the last question the panel was specifically asked to estimate the possibility of the Soviet Union's overcoming the United States' lead in nuclear weapons.

This panel did not complete its work until early August 1961. Meanwhile, no decision was taken to resume nuclear testing, nor were large-scale preparations made for such a contingency. When the Panofsky Panel reported to the President and the National Security Council it concluded that ". . . it was feasible for the Soviet Union to have conducted secret tests, that there was no evidence that it had done so (or had not done so), and that there was no urgent technical need for immediate resumption by the United States."[37a] The Joint Chiefs of Staff filed a paper questioning the premises and the conclusions of the Panel's report. In the ensuing discussion, they and certain scientists, such as John S. Foster, the Director of the Lawrence Radiation Laboratory, argued for at least a limited resumption of nuclear testing underground. However, the President rejected their advice. During this period the Western position in the test ban negotiations seemed to enjoy considerable support among the governments of the world and in the world press, and the Administration decided that it should continue to attempt to capitalize on this. On July 15, the Western powers had requested that an item entitled "The Urgent Need for a Treaty to Ban Nuclear Weapons Tests Under Effective International Control" be inscribed on the agenda of the sixteenth session of the General Assembly.[38] For the United States to resume testing would obviously hamper Western efforts to muster support in the forthcoming Assembly. Moreover, the heads of state or government of twenty-five nonaligned states were scheduled to meet in Belgrade from September 1 through September 6. For the United States to decide to resume testing would risk condemnation by this group.

The United States not only did not decide to resume nuclear weapons testing, it did not even make preparations to do so. President Kennedy decided that in the relatively open conditions in which policy is formulated in the United States, one must decide

[37a]Arthur M. Schlesinger, Jr., *A Thousand Days*, p. 456.
[38]UN Document A/4799.

either to test or not to test. Preparations as extensive as those which would be required for a major test series could probably not be kept secret, and if they became known, he reasoned, they would surely be interpreted as indicating a decision to test, and the United States would suffer from all of the adverse consequences that it would have faced had it actually decided to resume nuclear testing. However, in mid-August, President Kennedy concluded that sometime later in the fall, the Atomic Energy Commission might announce contingency preparations for underground testing, although this would not mean that the United States had decided to resume tests.[38a]

It is true that as a part of the Vela and peaceful uses programs some preparations were made for underground nuclear testing in Nevada. This work consisted principally of readying tunnels, and in Geneva the United States sought to negotiate safeguards to assure the Soviet Union that the projected detonations would not involve weapons development.

To prove that the United States was not preparing a weapons testing program, in the summer of 1961 Ambassador Dean and Mr. John J. McCloy, Special Advisor to the President on Disarmament, offered to allow a team of Soviet or neutral experts to examine American testing sites to determine the extent of American preparations for the resumption of testing, if any, provided that the USSR would give the United States reciprocal privileges.[39] On several occasions, the proposal was rejected as "impractical." The reasons for the suggestion's impracticality soon emerged.

Actually Chairman Khrushchev hinted at these reasons in his meeting with Mr. McCloy. He told Mr. McCloy "that Soviet scientists and military leaders were urging the testing of a 100-megaton bomb that could be carried in a rocket."[40] Mr. McCloy, of course, cabled these words to the President. They were another forewarning.

The only action that was taken in response to the warnings of Mr. McCloy, Ambassador Dean, and others was to step up

[38a] Arthur M. Schlesinger, Jr., *A Thousand Days*, pp. 458-59.
[39] See GEN/DNT/PV. 341, p. 75, and John J. McCloy, "Balance Sheet on Disarmament," *Foreign Affairs*, Vol. XL, No. 3 (April 1962), pp. 339-59, at 342, note 2.
[40] Earl H. Voss, *Nuclear Ambush*, p. 467.

American surveillance of the Soviet Union, to the extent that this could be done.

In Geneva, at the negotiating table, the United States even offered new concessions. Ambassador Dean presented these to the Conference on August 28.[41] He offered to eliminate the 4.75 seismic magnitude threshold in the treaty, if the Soviet Union would agree to increasing the number of manned or unmanned control posts or of on-site inspections. Alternatively, if the threshold were kept, he proposed that six months prior to the expiration of the moratorium, a panel composed of one scientist from each of the countries on the Control Commission should be convened to propose recommendations on improved instrumentation, and on lowering the threshold. As was no doubt expected, the USSR rebuffed these suggestions, arguing that the problems could only be solved in the context of general and complete disarmament.

III

The Coup de Grâce

The USSR Breaks the Moratorium

At 12:30 p.m. on Thursday, August 30, 1961, the three-hundred-and-thirty-eighth session of the Geneva Conference adjourned. Like countless meetings before it, it had produced no resolution of the stalemate. On the other hand, the three delegates gave no indication that their governments were about to break off or in any way disrupt the negotiations. The next meeting was scheduled for Friday, September 1. Thursday evening, however, the torporific atmosphere of the negotiations was broken when Moscow radio announced that the USSR had decided to resume the testing of nuclear weapons.[42] The statement denigrated the importance of a test ban as a sole measure of arms control, and it cited the French nuclear tests and the tension surrounding the German and Berlin problems as the reasons for the Soviet resumption of nuclear testing. It disclosed that the USSR had worked out designs for creating a series of "superpowerful nuclear bombs" of from 20 to 100 megatons.

On September 1, 1961, the Soviet Union tested the first

[41]GEN/DNT/PV. 337, pp. 3-14.
[42]U.S. Arms Control and Disarmament Agency, *Documents on Disarmament, 1961* (1962), pp. 337-43.

nuclear device in what was to become its most extensive series of tests, a series which would involve the largest nuclear detonations ever conducted, and which experts estimate must have taken a minimum of six months, and more likely a year or more to prepare. It is possible that the USSR began preparing for this test series shortly after the collapse of the summit meeting in late May 1960. Clearly preparations must have been underway by the time that the Kennedy Administration completed its reappraisal of the American position and tabled the new Western proposals, that is, by March 21, 1961. This is not to say, however, that the decision to conduct the test series must have been taken by then. That decision could well have been delayed until shortly before the first detonation in the series. Meanwhile, in sharp contrast to the situation in the United States, the preparations could be conducted in secret.

Little mention was made of the tests in the Soviet press. Significantly, the USSR also tested several intercontinental ballistic missiles during September 1961, which roused the suspicion that the two developments were related, that they were designed to perfect a new series of ballistic missiles and their warheads as Chairman Khrushchev's talk with Mr. McCloy had forewarned.

The Western Riposte

The Western response was swift. Shortly after the Soviet statement, the White House issued a statement condemning the USSR's decision to break the moratorium.

Although he was bitterly disappointed, and felt personally deceived, President Kennedy chose this course, and did not follow the advice of those, including apparently Secretary of State Rusk, who argued that the United States should immediately announce its intention to resume testing.[42a] The rationale for the decision taken was that the United States should not do anything that might deflect the opprobrium of public opinion from the Soviet deed. Edward R. Murrow was the most articulate spokesman against precipitate action. Kennedy, and Vice-President Johnson too, felt that they could with-

[42a]See Arthur M. Schlesinger, Jr., *A Thousand Days,* pp. 449-50, 459, and Theodore C. Sorenson, *Kennedy,* pp. 619-20.

stand for a while the pressure of those in the Senate and elsewhere who demanded a more belligerent course.

On September 3, President Kennedy and Prime Minister Macmillan proposed that the United States, the United Kingdom, and the USSR immediately agree not to conduct nuclear tests "which take place in the atmosphere and produce radioactive fallout."[43] This agreement would require no international control measures, and the Western leaders proposed that representatives of the three states meet in Geneva not later than September 9 to sign the agreement. This proposal was almost revolutionary in terms of past Western positions. For the first time, the West announced its willingness to accept a ban on testing in some environments, without the establishment of any international control machinery. Never before had the Western powers admitted that national detection systems would be sufficient. Whenever the Western powers discussed a partial ban previously, they always maintained that at least some international control machinery would be necessary. Some in the West, Senator Gore for instance, had argued against this position from the outset. While the Kennedy-Macmillan proposal won some immediate sympathy, it also served to undermine past Western positions, and would make it difficult for the Western powers to return—as they subsequently did—to the claim that international machinery would be necessary to control atmospheric testing. The proposal also meant that the Western powers were willing to allow the USSR to realize whatever gains it might achieve from its tests without attempting to match them through a counter-series.

The Kennedy-Macmillan proposal was formulated in Secretary of State Rusk's office by a small group of British and American policy-makers and advisers. Their prime objective was to embarrass the USSR. The proposal was a serious offer, which the participants in the sessions were willing to implement. Indeed, somewhat earlier, the American ambassador in Moscow, Llewellyn Thompson, had suggested that the West should try again for a limited ban, prohibiting tests in the atmosphere and under water, and President Kennedy had relayed this suggestion to Prime Minister Macmillan in a letter in early August.[43a] On the other hand, none of those who formulated

[43]*Documents on Disarmament, 1961,* p. 351.
[43a]Arthur M. Schlesinger, Jr., *A Thousand Days,* p. 459.

the September 3 proposal seriously expected the USSR to accept it. Nor did any among them see much prospect for fruitful negotiation in the future. Although the effects of the proposal on past and possible future Western positions were discussed, because of the immediate objective and the expectations about the future, such effects were accorded little weight in the final decision.

Chairman Khrushchev scornfully rejected the Kennedy-Macmillan proposal on September 9. Following this, the Western powers asked for a recess in the Geneva Conference until the decisions of the sixteenth General Assembly were known.

On September 5, President Kennedy announced that he had "ordered the resumption of nuclear tests in the laboratory and underground, with no fallout."[44] The first American test since 1958 took place on September 15. The test series which followed was minor. The United States was not prepared to conduct major experiments! Indeed, it was not until November 2 that President Kennedy announced that atmospheric tests might be necessary and that preparations were being made. On April 24, 1962, after the Geneva Conference had ended, he announced that he had authorized atmospheric tests, and the first American atmospheric test was conducted the following day. The British did not resume nuclear tests until their underground shot on March 1, 1962.

Whether because of the quick United States decision to resume underground nuclear tests, or because of a feeling that the United States bore an equal or greater share of the blame for the fact that a test ban agreement had not been achieved (a feeling to which the Kennedy-Macmillan proposal for a nationally monitored atmospheric ban contributed in a curious way), or because of a more general reluctance to condemn one side, and especially the Soviet side in the Cold War, the neutral nations in Belgrade, while bemoaning the Soviet resumption of nuclear testing, were almost equally critical of the United States. This behavior angered President Kennedy.[44a]

The Sixteenth General Assembly

The West was somewhat more successful in mustering support in the General Assembly of the United Nations. On October 27

[44]*Documents on Disarmament, 1961*, p. 355.
[44a]Theodore C. Sorenson, *Kennedy*, p. 538.

the Assembly adopted a resolution requesting the USSR to refrain from conducting a proposed atmospheric test of a nuclear device of 50 megatons or more.[45] Only the Soviet bloc and Cuba opposed this resolution, and Mali abstained, but all other UN Member States voted for it. Despite this, on October 30, the USSR carried out its test of the "superpowerful" bomb. Subsequent evaluations estimated its yield as 58 megatons, but Hans Bethe, who headed the AEC panel which evaluated the Soviet test series pointed out that had the fusion materials been encased in uranium rather than lead, its yield would have been 100 megatons or more.[46]

The Assembly also adopted, by a vote of 71 to 11 (Soviet bloc and Cuba) with 15 abstentions, a resolution submitted by the United Kingdom and the United States entitled "The Urgent Need for a Treaty to Ban Nuclear Weapons Tests Under Effective International Control."[47] This resolution, in a sense, gave the Assembly's sanction to the Western position in the test ban negotiations. This was the first time that this had happened.

The United States and the United Kingdom voted for a resolution submitted by Ireland on the prevention of the dissemination of nuclear weapons.[48] This resolution was very similar to that which Ireland had submitted and which the Assembly had adopted the previous year, and on which the United States had abstained. The affirmative American vote at the sixteenth Assembly was another sign of the way in which the position of the Kennedy Administration on these matters differed from that of its predecessor.

Some of the Assembly's other actions in this general area were not as pleasing to the West, however. The two Western powers abstained from voting on a resolution which was submitted by several African states urging that states consider and respect the continent of Africa as a denuclearized zone,[49] since to favor such a resolution would implicitly condemn the French for their nuclear tests in the Sahara. This resolution was adopted by a vote of 55 to 0 with 44 abstentions.

[45]General Assembly Resolution 1632 (XVI).

[46]Speech delivered at Cornell University January 5, 1962. Reprinted in the *Congressional Record* (1962), pp. A1397-99. See also Ralph E. Lapp, *Kill and Overkill: The Strategy of Annihilation* (1962), pp. 36-37.

[47]General Assembly Resolution 1649 (XVI).

[48]General Assembly Resolution 1665 (XVI).

[49]General Assembly Resolution 1653 (XVI).

The United Kingdom and the United States also voted against a resolution which had originally been submitted by India, but which was ultimately sponsored by several states, urging the states concerned to resume the moratorium on nuclear testing and to maintain it until the adoption of a test ban treaty.[50] The 20 states which voted against this resolution were a curious combination of the Soviet bloc and the West; 71 states voted for the resolution, while 8 abstained.

Finally, the United States and the United Kingdom voted against a far-reaching resolution which declared *inter alia* that:

(a) The use of nuclear and thermo-nuclear weapons is contrary to the spirit, letter and aims of the United Nations and, as such, a direct violation of the Charter of the United Nations.

(d) Any State using nuclear and thermo-nuclear weapons is to be considered as violating the Charter of the United Nations, as acting contrary to the laws of humanity and as committing a crime against mankind and civilization.[51]

The resolution, which had been submitted by several neutralist states, garnered 60 favorable votes, including those of the Soviet bloc. Sixteen states voted against it, and 25 abstained. In a sense, this resolution could be interpreted as a broad attack on the basic concepts underlying Western military policy.

Whether on balance the United States could be said to have achieved important gains in terms of mustering world support for its position and against that of the Soviet Union is difficult to say. Certainly the United States fared better in the sixteenth session than it had the year before in the fifteenth, but it was far from an unblemished victory. And it is worth noting that President Kennedy rejected the advice of Assistant Secretary of State Harlan Cleveland, who argued that the United States should bring the Soviet resumption of testing before the Security Council. His reasoning was that it would look hypocritical for the United States to take such action if it had already decided to resume testing itself.[51a]

[50]General Assembly Resolution 1648 (XVI).
[51]General Assembly Resolution 1653 (XVI).
[51a]Arthur M. Schlesinger, Jr., *A Thousand Days*, p. 481.

The End of the Conference

After the passage of the Assembly resolutions on the test ban negotiations, the United States proposed that the Geneva negotiations be resumed, and the Soviet Union in due course agreed. The Conference therefore reconvened on November 28, 1961. Thirteen meetings were held between then and January 29, 1962, when the Geneva Conference finally recessed *sine die*.

The day before the Conference reconvened, the Soviet Government issued a statement, which was published in the world press and which Mr. Tsarapkin subsequently read into the record.[52] The essence of this statement was that the situation had changed radically since the test ban negotiations had begun, and that if the negotiations were to continue, they would have to do so on a new basis. Consequently, the USSR proposed the immediate conclusion of an agreement "for the discontinuance of nuclear tests in the atmosphere, under water and in outer space," to be monitored by national detection systems. The statement cited the Western proposal of September 3 as evidence that national systems were adequate. In addition, the USSR proposed that there should be a moratorium on underground tests, "pending agreement on a system of control over underground explosions as a constituent part of an international system of control over the implementation of a programme of general and complete disarmament." The Soviet Union also insisted that France should be brought into the negotiations. The USSR proposed a treaty embodying these provisions. By implication the Soviet Union no longer accepted the report of the Conference of Experts as the basis for the negotiations. In fact, in arguing that an international control system was not necessary, the USSR reverted to the position that it had held prior to 1957 London negotiations.

The Western powers implicitly rejected the new Soviet proposal immediately, and after joint British-American consultations formally rejected it on January 16, 1962. They were willing to negotiate on the basis of the proposals which they had tabled previously, including the draft treaty of April 18, 1961, and subsequent modifications, but they insisted that an international control system was necessary. With respect to the Western proposal of September 3,

[52]GEN/DNT/PV. 341, pp. 21-30.

Ambassador Dean pointed out that it was confined to the atmosphere, that it had been made in the hope of forestalling imminent Soviet tests which had been carried out, and that by its own terms it had expired on September 9, 1961.[53] At this point, among other things and perhaps above all, the Western powers wanted to retain the freedom to conduct their own nuclear tests if their evaluations of the current Soviet test series indicated that the relative military strength of the two sides had been significantly altered.

Because of this new shift in the Soviet position, the test ban talks were even more deeply deadlocked than they had been previously. Consequently, the Western powers proposed that the Conference should adjourn, and that the problem of a test ban should be referred to the Eighteen-Nation Disarmament Committee, a body which had been created by agreement between the Soviet Union and the United States during the sixteenth session of the General Assembly to consider the plans for general and complete disarmament and which was scheduled to have its first meeting on March 14, 1962. Since the Soviet Union would not agree to this, the Conference on the Discontinuance of Nuclear Weapon Tests simply adjourned on January 29, 1962. It even proved impossible to agree on a communique. When the Geneva Conference ended, the technical controversies which had divided it since January 1959 remained unsolved. The attempts both of a technical and a political nature to resolve these had been futile.

[53]GEN/DNT/PV. 342, pp. 13-14.

Chapter IX

Controversies Concerning the
Control Organization

I
An Overview

Even though they were somewhat overshadowed by the dispute about technical matters and the coverage of the treaty, controversies concerning the nature of the organization which would oversee compliance with the proposed nuclear test ban were a prominent feature of the Geneva Conference on the Discontinuance of Nuclear Weapon Tests throughout its course. These controversies too were unresolved when the Conference held its final meeting on January 29, 1962.

The controversies began in the early days of the negotiations when the parties broadly outlined their positions. The positions were developed in detail and probed, and several compromises were arranged in the succeeding two years so that by mid-1960 the gap between the positions of East and West had been narrowed considerably. In 1961, however, this agreement evaporated.

Despite the fact that there is no provision for a control organization in the partial test ban treaty which was concluded in 1963, the negotiations on these issues are of considerable interest. To some extent these negotiations explain the absence of control machinery from the Moscow Treaty. Moreover, they are one of the few detailed discussions among the Soviet Union, the United Kingdom, and the United States about an international organization which might have significant functions with respect to these powers themselves as well as to other parties. Viewed more narrowly, the Geneva negotiations represent the first concrete discussion among the three nuclear powers of an arms control or disarmament organization since the late nineteen-forties. Although it is true that related issues were raised in the talks concerning the creation of the International Atomic Energy Agency (IAEA), there was little real negotiation in this instance as the Soviet Union largely accepted the United States' draft proposal (which however had been prepared with an eye to Soviet sensibilities), and in any case, IAEA's control mechanism was not designed to apply to the nuclear powers.[1]

The positions concerning the control organization advanced by the participants in the Geneva Conference were a product of several factors. They stemmed partially from each party's understanding of the technical properties of the control mechanisms recommended by the Conference of Experts and the subsequent technical meetings. Such matters as their estimate of the reliability of the instruments, whether or not the instruments could be made tamperproof, and the clarity or ambiguity of the evidence that could be obtained of possible violations, affected their attitude toward the human elements of the control system. A related consideration involved estimates about the technical proficiency, reliability, and impartiality of personnel who might be recruited to staff the control system.

Their positions also implicitly reflected their basic assumptions about the societies which would be affected. Notions about the degree of openness of a given society and the degree of access that would be required to assure effective control and about the need for taking institutional action, for instance in the event of a violation, conditioned the concepts of a control organization which the participants advanced. Then too, their confidence in their unilateral means of obtaining information was also a factor.

In addition, each of the parties had had experience in functioning international organizations, especially the United Nations, and this affected their approach toward the constitution of a new organization. The West wanted to avoid a deadlock such as had occurred in the UN Security Council as a result of the Cold War. The Soviet Union, on the other hand, obviously had in mind the curtailment of its power in the United Nations when the center of activities shifted from the Security Council to the "veto-less" Gen-

[1]For an excellent account of the establishment of IAEA, see Bernhard G. Bechhoefer, "Negotiating the Statute of the International Atomic Energy Agency," *International Organization,* Vol. XIII, No. 1 (Winter 1959), pp. 38-59.

eral Assembly, and the Secretary General assumed important functions far beyond those originally contemplated. All parties to the Conference wanted to avoid, if at all possible, problems which they had encountered in the past.

Finally, each of the parties viewed a control organization for a nuclear test ban as a possible precedent for other organizations in the field of arms control and disarmament, and this too had an impact on their positions. In the broadest sense, the Western powers on the one hand and the Soviet Union on the other pressed for an organization that would conform as closely as possible to their ideology and image of world order.

Because so many of the questions relating to the control organization involved both scientific and political aspects, United States proposals relating to these matters had to pass through the same process of interagency agreement as did broad policy positions concerning such matters as the continuation of the moratorium and the negotiations, and the threshold problem. This meant that all of the American positions had to be approved either by the Committee of Principals or by interagency working groups at a lower level. Since it proved impossible in practice to determine precisely whether a given question was essentially political, scientific, or military, and thus to identify the agency primarily concerned, for all practical purposes each agency involved had power to block the formulation of a position on almost any issue, or to insist that its concepts should prevail. Not only was this procedure of achieving agreement within the American government a time-consuming process, it also meant that the American negotiator was quite tightly bound to rather rigid instructions.

The two Western powers tended to move in unison on issues relating to the control organization, as they did in all aspects of the negotiations. Many proposals were advanced jointly. A submission of a separate proposal by one or the other Western power usually reflected a prearranged division of responsibility for the presentation of material, rather than unilateral action, and in most cases, joint approval could be assumed.

The United Kingdom felt a greater sense of independence on these matters, however, than it did on the broader questions relating to the coverage of the treaty. It often attempted to play a leading role on these issues within Western councils, and from time to time even acted unilaterally in the Conference. British negotiators were particularly active during 1960, both before and after the collapse of the summit meeting. Occasionally, the British delegate even advanced proposals *ad referendum,* and Her Majesty's Government always ultimately accepted them and supported its delegate. In early 1960, the United Kingdom hoped to make it possible to consummate an agreement at the summit meeting. After the collapse of the summit meeting, the United Kingdom's primary objective apparently was to perpetuate the talks. The fact that the United States was in the midst of an election campaign, while the United Kingdom was not, having just completed a general election the previous year, may also explain why the latter was somewhat more active and flexible during 1960.

The Soviet Union generally left to the Western powers the task of presenting detailed proposals on the organizational aspects of the prospective treaty and expounded its position through comments and criticisms. It is true that the USSR tabled a "complete" draft treaty on the opening day of the Conference, but this was a bare skeleton.[2] Thereafter it occasionally submitted memoranda on specific points, and very infrequently, formal treaty language. However, until mid-1960, the Soviet delegate was often able to respond more quickly to new suggestions than his American counterpart.

Discussions of a control organization were interspersed throughout the 353 meetings of the Geneva Conference. Only for a few days during this period was the possibility even mooted that a test ban treaty need not provide for any control organization. As recorded in Chapter VIII, on September 3, 1961, in an effort to stave off further Soviet testing, President Kennedy and Prime Minister Macmillan proposed that a treaty banning the testing in the atmosphere of nuclear weapons which created radioactive fallout should be signed immediately and stated that such a treaty could be monitored adequately by national systems. The USSR refused this offer, and it expired on September 9, 1961. On November 28, 1961, the Soviet Union proposed a draft treaty which would rely exclusively on national detection systems, and it maintained this proposal until the end of the Conference. With the

[2]For the text, see *supra* pp. 122-23.

exception of those two periods, all three parties to the negotiations always acted on the assumption that any treaty would require the creation of some control organization. Even the phased treaty proposed by the United States on February 11, 1960, envisaged an extensive control organization and system from the outset.

While the discussions concerning a control organization went on continually throughout the Conference, there were certain periods when greater attention was devoted to these matters. The most notable of these were (1) the opening period of the Conference from October 31, 1958, through March 19, 1959; (2) the period immediately prior to the convocation of Technical Working Group II and during the early sessions of that body in late November and December 1959; (3) the period immediately prior to the summit meeting in the spring of 1960; and (4) the period from March 21 through May 31, 1961, when, following the Kennedy Administration's accession to power, the Western states advanced a series of compromise proposals. Bargaining, or the exchange of concessions, occurred only in the first three periods. These were the three periods in which the prospects for agreement appeared to be highest. Activity in the last period, that is in the spring of 1961, was confined to an exposition of positions, although it was not until this time that the West tabled an entire draft treaty.

II

The Initial Opposing Concepts of the Control Organization

The Western Blueprint

An analysis of the controversies during the Geneva Conference concerning the proposed control organization can appropriately begin by outlining the broad concepts which the two sides advanced initially. The basic Western ideas were set forth in a memorandum tabled by the British on November 13, 1958,[3] a working paper presented by the United States on November 13, 1958,[4] four draft articles tabled by the United States on December 15, 1958,[5] and a draft annex I, concerning the Detection and Identification System

[4]GEN/DNT/PV. 8, pp. 5-8.
[3]GEN/DNT/PV. 5, pp. 4-5.
[5]GEN/DNT/21.

introduced by the United States the following day.[6] Oral presentations elaborated the points made in these documents and added others.

The Western blueprint was extensive. It was an amalgam of traditional concepts of international organization prevalent in the West and the technical system proposed in the report of the Conference of Experts. It provided for a Conference, a Commission, and an Administrator. All treaty signatories would be represented in the Conference, which would hold annual meetings and could convene in special sessions. The functions of the Conference would be to approve budgets recommended by the Commission, consider and approve reports, consider amendments to the treaty, and propose matters for consideration by the Commission. The Commission would consist of the Original Parties (the three nuclear powers in the Geneva Conference) as permanent members and an unspecified number of states elected by the Conference. It would be organized, like the Security Council of the United Nations, so that it could function continuously. It would oversee the installation and operation of the Detection and Identification System, appoint and direct the activities of the Administrator of the system, authorize nuclear detonations for peaceful purposes, and prepare findings with respect to violations of the treaty. Although at an early stage the Western powers allowed that some decisions of the Commission would require the unanimous agreement of the Original Parties, these were not specified. For most decisions, only some form of majority would be required. According to the Western plans, the Administrator would be responsible for the day-to-day operation of the detection system, most aspects of which would function automatically on the basis of predetermined criteria. Thus, although the Administrator would oversee on-site inspections, decisions concerning their dispatch would depend solely on whether or not certain criteria had been met.

Following the recommendation of the Conference of Experts, the Western plan envisaged the ultimate establishment of from 160 to 170 control posts. It went no farther than the Experts had in specifying the locations of these posts, merely repeating the specifications which the Experts had outlined concerning the maxi-

[6]GEN/DNT/22.

mum permissible spacing between the posts and their distribution by continents and oceanic islands. The Western plan endorsed the Experts' recommendations concerning instrumentation. The initial Western position was that each control post should be operated by an international staff, which would consist of 32 individuals (the Experts had specified "about 30"), none of whom would be nationals of the host country. Roughly one-third of this staff would have to have relatively high-level technical qualifications, the equivalent of a British university degree, or an American master's degree. In addition to this technical staff, each post would require a communications staff of 8, who would also be recruited on an international basis, and an administrative and supporting staff of 21, who could be host country nationals. In sum, each control post would require a staff of 61, and the system of posts, depending on whether there were 160 or 170, a total of from 9,760 to 10,370, roughly one-sixth of whom would have to be highly qualified. In addition, the Western plan provided for "a sufficient number" (the Experts had recommended "about 10") of ships to maintain control over ocean areas which did not contain islands suitable for the establishment of fixed-base control posts. Presumably, these would be staffed in the same manner as the land-based control posts. Although the Western powers agreed that a time schedule would have to be elaborated for the establishment of control posts, they did not give any indication of its nature. The Western plan also included provisions for daily routine aircraft sampling flights and special aircraft sampling flights.

The Western powers envisaged that on-site inspections of events which could not be identified as natural should occur on a routine basis, and that if a state attempted to block such an investigation it would be in violation of the treaty. The Western proposals provided for the establishment of several permanent groups whose sole function would be to conduct on-site inspections. The precise number and location of these groups would be determined by the Administrator with the approval of the Commission. Nationals of the country being investigated were to be excluded from the inspection team.

The Western proposals contained provision for a headquarters, consisting of (1) a data analysis and research center, (2) a central radiochemical laboratory, and (3) a central inspection office.

Among its other responsibilities, the headquarters would conduct research relevant to the concerns of the control system. The Administrator could also, with the approval of the Commission, let contracts so that research could be done by external agencies. The Western proposals envisaged the creation of "about 10" regional offices which would provide administrative and logistical support to the elements of the control system operating in their regions.

Although the Western powers thought that a control organization for a nuclear test ban treaty should be autonomous, they felt that it should have a relationship with the United Nations similar to that of the International Atomic Energy Agency, and that it should also have some relationship with any other organizations which might be established with functions relating to arms control and disarmament.[7]

Had the Western proposals for a control organization been implemented, the staff of the organization would have been considerably larger than that of any international organization in existence. The UN Secretariat has a staff of somewhat more than 4,000; over twice that number would have been required to man the land-based control posts alone. Moreover, the control organization would have had more extensive powers with respect to the original parties than any other extant international organization. It would have been able to order an investigation on the territory of the superpowers against their wishes and to adopt a report concerning a possible violation on their part despite their opposition.

The Soviet Concept

In contrast, the concept of a control organization which the Soviet Union advanced initially was extremely limited. The draft treaty which the Soviet Union tabled on the opening day of the Geneva Conference merely stated that the parties to the agreement "shall institute machinery for control," and that this machinery "shall have at its disposal a network of control posts set up in

---

[7]For an interesting and thoughtful analysis of the problem of the relationship between the UN and a control organization for arms control measures, see Lawrence S. Finkelstein, "The United Nations and Organizations for the Control of Armaments," *International Organization*, Vol. XVI, No. 1 (Winter 1962), pp. 1-19.

accordance with the recommendations of the Geneva Conference of Experts."[8] The treaty would commit the three nuclear powers to agree to the establishment on their territories of "an agreed number of control posts." These were the only provisions for control machinery contained in the draft treaty; the Soviet view was that the details should be spelled out in a separate agreement. The similarity between this and earlier Soviet proposals concerning arms control and disarmament has already been noted. The Soviet proposal contained no provision for signature or accession by parties other than the three participating in the Conference.

Before long the Soviet Union agreed that detailed provisions concerning a control organization as well as the obligation to cease testing nuclear weapons should be contained in a single treaty, and on December 8, 1958, it tabled a draft outlining its view of the basic provisions of a control system.[9] Although this moved the USSR's position much closer to that of the Western powers, there was still a great distance between the two.

The role of states other than the three original nuclear powers was obscure in the Soviet concept. They were mentioned only implicitly in the draft in a discussion of control posts. In his oral exposition, Mr. Tsarapkin stated that after the control system had been established among the three original parties, the question of the cooperation of other states in the control system would have to be considered, and that the discussion of these matters could be entrusted to a conference of the states parties to the treaty.[10] There was no mention of a conference as a regular organ of the Control Organization in the Soviet draft.

In the Soviet concept, a Commission would be the central body in the Control Organization. Although the draft did not specify the composition of the Commission, Mr. Tsarapkin stated that the British suggestion that the Commission should consist of the three original parties as permanent members and four other states would be acceptable "provided that all major issues are settled by agreement among the three permanent members of the Commission."[11] The Commission would "direct the entire activity

[8]GEN/DNT/1.
[9]GEN/DNT/19.
[10]GEN/DNT/PV. 21, p. 37.
[11]Ibid., p. 29.

of the Control Organization." It would review evidence concerning events which could be suspected of being nuclear explosions and after reviewing additional data, including material from existing seismic stations, would inform the government concerned and request its opinion. After considering the reply of that government, the Commission would determine whether or not an on-site inspection was required. In the event of disagreement, the Commission would so inform the parties to the treaty and the Security Council of the United Nations. The Soviet draft contained no mention of an administrator or executive officer.

The Soviet draft contained provisions for land-based control posts, although no specific number was mentioned, and stated that they should be equipped in accordance with the recommendations of the Conference of Experts. In the Soviet view, the staff of each control post should consist of not more than thirty specialists and several supporting personnel. Of the thirty, four or five would be required to have a higher education and the remainder, a secondary technical education. All of these individuals would be nationals of the host country. In addition, one or two foreign control officers representing the side interested in carrying out control in the area concerned would be stationed at each control post. In the cases of control posts situated on the territories of states which were not members of either alliance system, there would be control officers from both sides. The control officers would place their seals on all instruments and would be present when data was removed and processed. They would countersign all reports to the control commission, and, when they disagreed with the chief of the control post, they would have the right to express their dissent. The control officers would have the right and the ability to check all instruments at any time, and they would enjoy diplomatic immunity. The host country would be responsible for providing appropriate means of communication for each control post so that around-the-clock transmission of information would be insured. The basic communication of each control post would be a daily coded telegraphic report. The Soviet plan called for control posts on ships, but did not specify how many. These would be staffed by personnel from the state which owned the vessel. In addition, there would be one or two control officers, including one who was a navigation specialist. The draft also contained provision for regular air sampling flights.

In contrast to the Western view, on-site inspections were to be regarded as exceptional rather than routine. This difference was symbolized by the fact that while the Western plan provided for the inspection of "unidentified events," the Soviet proposal provided for the inspection only of "suspicious events." In the Soviet scheme inspection teams would be constituted on an *ad hoc* basis. The supporting and technical personnel would be nationals of the country involved, but the inspection team would also include "a very small number of control officers, whose duties would include checking all the team's work to ensure that it was being properly carried out."[12]

The Soviet plan envisaged that the Commission would have at its disposal a technical apparatus—not a headquarters—which would consist of appropriate departments for processing and analyzing data and for providing the control organization with logistical and technical support and personnel. The Soviet draft held that the personnel of the technical apparatus should be recruited and approved by the Commission on the basis of equal representation of the two sides among the original parties. Among other things, this implied that the consent of the original parties would be required for all appointments. There was no provision for the conduct of research by the control organization. Nor was there any provision for regional offices.

The Soviet draft stated that the right of extraterritoriality should not extend to the territory and the premises of control posts and that the movements of personnel on the posts "must take place on regular terms and conditions and in accordance with the procedures existing for foreigners." Personnel for guarding the posts would be supplied by the host country. These points were not covered in the initial Western presentations.

The Deep-Seated Differences Between the Concepts

Obviously neither East nor West expected its initial position to be accepted *in toto*. They and the world had had ample evidence of their differing approaches toward international organization, and if agreement were to be reached some compromises would clearly

[12]*Ibid.*, p. 34.

be required. The foreknowledge of the disagreement and the expectation of bargaining probably led both sides to overstate their
initial positions. This is not to suggest, however, that each side
did not, rightly or wrongly, conceive its scheme of a control organization as being optimally designed to satisfy its interests, and—
according to its own interpretation—perhaps also those of the
world. It therefore is worth considering the implications of the two
positions and their rationale, both as explicitly stated and implied.

In formal constitutional terms, the Western proposals represented what can be termed the vertical or hierarchical approach to
international organization, while the Soviet proposals represented
the horizontal approach. The Western proposals implied some—
although not much—diminution of state sovereignty and transfer
of authority to an international body. The Soviet proposal, in contrast, was designed with state sovereignty as its most basic assumption. It could almost be characterized as a plan for legitimizing by
mutual agreement certain national intelligence activities. Mr. Tsarapkin repeatedly put this quite directly by saying, under our plan
you will "control" us and we will "control" you. He meant this in
the French sense of the word "control," that is in terms of gathering information. The Soviet plan went little beyond this, and
in no case could the control organization take action against the
wishes of one of the original parties.

Some analysts have distinguished between two approaches to
the control of disarmament agreements by calling one the "impartial" approach, and the other the "reciprocal" or "adversary" approach.[13] In the first as the name implies the emphasis is on gaining
control through devices and personnel disassociated from the
principal parties, while in the second the principal parties themselves exercise control. In general terms, the Western proposals
were in the spirit of the first approach, and the Soviet, the second.

The differences between the Soviet and Western proposals
represented first of all deep-seated philosophical differences. The

[13]See Fred C. Iklé and others, *Alternative Approaches to the International Organization of Disarmament* (RAND Corp., 1962, R-391-ARPA),
especially, pp. 3-4; Lawrence S. Finkelstein, "The Use of Reciprocal Inspection," pp. 82-98 in Seymour Melman (ed.) *Disarmament: Its Politics and
Economics* (1962); and Lawrence S. Finkelstein, "Arms Inspection," *International Conciliation*, No. 540 (November 1962), pp. 5-89.

West, and particularly the United States, has been committed for some time, at least on the level of declaratory policy, to the ultimate goal of an ordered and peaceful world, regulated by enforceable legal norms and powerful international institutions. In terms of this perspective, national defense forces are regarded as a temporary expedient, to be maintained and utilized only as long as this ultimate goal remains unachieved. At the time of the First World War when these concepts were originally formulated, the growth of democracy was viewed as an important means of achieving the ultimate goal as well as a basic component of it; but over the years as a result of increasing sophistication, or despair, or both, less emphasis came to be placed on this feature. Though subject to disagreement, the prevalent attitude in the West seems to be that the international goal can be achieved despite diverse domestic regimes. Being constantly exposed to and immersed in these views, and repeating them in public presentations, Western, and particularly American, policy-makers have tended to take them into account in formulating new positions. The gains of past experience are accepted and each new situation viewed as an opportunity for incremental advances. This applies *a fortiori* in situations which might involve the reduction of national armaments, given the rationale for the maintenance of national defense forces mentioned earlier. Thus the Western concept of a control organization was modeled after the United Nations and other existing international organizations such as the International Atomic Energy Agency, with the addition of certain new features.

The Soviet Union's ultimate goal, again at least on the level of declaratory policy, has been a world of Communist societies. In its view, non-Communist states and organizations dominated by these states have been hostile, or potentially hostile, to this goal. Thus, its view of international organization has been considerably different from that of the West and, given its long-run goals, it cannot have the same commitment to international organization as the West.[14] For the USSR, cooperation in international organizations has been at best a temporary expedient, not a goal in itself.

[14]For a detailed elaboration of the Soviet attitudes toward international organization, see Alexander Dallin, *The Soviet Union at the United Nations* (1962); and also, Union of Soviet Socialist Republics, Academy of Sciences, Institute of State and Law, *International Law* (1960).

According to its doctrine, the fundamental problems of society could only be solved through transformation to Communist regimes. Moreover, distrusting all non-Communists, it could not conceive an impartial or neutral international organization. In the Soviet view, therefore, international organizations including non-Communist states ought to be instruments designed to facilitate temporary cooperation between opposing sides, and consequently ought to involve only minimal indispensible limitations upon sovereignty.

Of course the two sides had also had differing experiences in existing international organizations. Particularly during the early years of the UN and its affiliated agencies, the United States and the United Kingdom were usually in a controlling position, able to command a majority for positive action and to block proposals deemed undesirable. During the same period, the Soviet Union on the other hand was a permanent minority in these institutions and frequently saw them take action against its wishes.

Initial Compromises

Despite these deep-seated differences, it was possible to effect compromises between East and West in a number of instances, and by the time of the 1959 Easter recess, several agreements had been reached which narrowed the gap somewhat. Six articles of a draft treaty had actually been adopted. One of these was purely formal, stating that the treaty and major agreements concluded by the Control Organization would be registered with the United Nations in accordance with the requirements of Article 102 of the Charter. The others, however, had greater substance. One specified that the treaty would be of indefinite duration, subject to the inherent right of the parties to withdraw if the provisions of the treaty were not being fulfilled and observed. Another provided for the periodic review of the control system.

The remaining three articles, which had been adopted by mid-March 1959, specified the obligations of the parties to the treaty and the composition of the Commission. Each signatory would undertake:

(a) to prohibit and prevent the carrying out of nuclear weapons test explosions at any place under its jurisdiction or control; and

    (b) to refrain from causing, encouraging, or in any way participating in, the carrying out of nuclear weapons test explosions anywhere.[15]

The meaning of the first of these obligations was clear; that of the second, less obvious, and the debate did not clarify it. Nor was there ever any discussion of how compliance with the second obligation would be verified. The signatories would also agree "to cooperate promptly and fully with the Control Organization . . . and to assist the Control Organization in the discharge of its responsibilities . . . ."[16]

In accepting the article on the Commission the negotiating states had implicitly agreed that other states would have a role in the Control Organization, for it provided that four other states would be members of the Commission. According to this article the four nonpermanent members of the Commission were to be chosen by a Conference in which all states would participate and which would have regular annual sessions.

The two sides also moved closer together in several other areas. The West agreed that control posts should be established first in the territories of the three nuclear powers. The Soviet Union allowed that there might have to be an administrator to oversee the operation of the control system. It also agreed that there could be from four to five "controllers" at a control post, rather than merely one or two.

Despite these compromises, there were still wide differences between the two sides. Although they agreed that the Commission should consist of seven states including the three Original Parties, they could not agree on the political distribution of the other four states. The West held that these four states should consist of one from each side and two neutrals. The Soviet Union on the other hand maintained that—considering the two-to-one preponderance of the West among permanent members—this formula would not yield a balanced Commission. It argued that the four nonpermanent members should consist of one from the Western side, two from the Soviet side, and one neutral. There continued to be differences with respect to the staffing of control posts. The West also con-

[15]GEN/DNT/14.
[16]GEN/DNT/15/Add. 1.

tinued to insist on the necessity of permanent inspection groups, while the Soviet Union denied this. To buttress his case, Mr. Tsarapkin held that this concept had been rejected at the Conference of Experts.[17] Although this was true, it was also true that the Soviet position that permanent inspection groups were unnecessary had been rejected.

Perhaps the most fundamental difference related to voting in the Control Commission. On January 30, 1959, evidently drawing upon its experience in the United Nations Security Council, the Soviet Union submitted a comprehensive list of decisions which would require four affirmative votes, including those of the three Original Parties. This was the USSR's strongest assertion that it would not agree to the proposed Control Organization's being able to take any significant action against its wishes. Or, as Mr. Tsarapkin put it, claiming the familiar defense of the veto in the Security Council, this would insure the cooperation of the Original Parties.

Prior to the March 19 recess, the Western powers agreed that unanimity among the Original Parties should be required for: amendments to the treaty, revision of the detection methods, and appointment of the Administrator. They also agreed that it might be required, if appropriate safeguards could be worked out, for the determination of sites of control posts and routes for control aircraft flights. However, they would not go beyond that. They adamantly argued that the veto could not apply to the other decisions named in the Soviet list, especially those relating to on-site inspections and violations of the Treaty. This represented the most fundamental difference between the approaches of the two sides, and it was unresolved by the time of the Easter recess in 1959. In considering these issues, it is necessary to recall that the so-called "new seismic data" was introduced by the West prior to the submission of the Soviet veto list. Perhaps the Soviet Union would have taken the same position in any case, but the new data appeared to increase vastly the number of prospective on-site inspections and thus provided a further incentive for the Soviet Union to seek iron-clad protection against imposed decisions.

[17]GEN/DNT/PV. 18, p. 16.

III
Further Compromises and Continuing Controversies, 1959–60

So far as concepts of the control organization are concerned, the period of the negotiations from the time that the Geneva Conference resumed on April 13, 1959, through the final meeting in 1960 on December 5 can be considered as a unit. Although the positions of the two sides shifted somewhat during this period, these shifts did not involve departures from the framework established in the initial phase of the Conference. Further compromises of course brought additional agreements, but some controversies remained unsolved. Since there was a basic unity to this period, the negotiations during it can be treated topically rather than chronologically. It is important to emphasize though that both sides constantly viewed the control organization as a whole and that each aspect was inextricably linked to the others. While this meant that trade offs were possible, it also meant that on important matters, piecemeal settlements were ruled out.

Areas of Agreement

During this period the three parties agreed to a preamble, eleven more articles, and two annexes for the prospective treaty.[18] The preamble and ten of the articles were adopted during the seventeen meetings held from April 13 to May 8, 1959. This achievement was in large measure the result of the momentum established in the initial phase of the negotiations. In many instances the adoption of an article merely represented ratification of a tentative understanding achieved earlier. Several of the articles adopted during this period were of a formal character, and few fundamental issues were involved.

[18]The text of the preamble, the seventeen articles, and Annex III adopted by the Conference is contained in the appendix to William J. Gehron, "Geneva Conference on the Discontinuance of Nuclear Weapon Tests: History of Political and Technical Developments of the Negotiations From October 31, 1958, to August 22, 1960," Department of State *Bulletin,* Vol. XLIII, No. 1109 (September 26, 1960), pp. 482-97, at pp. 494-97. Annex II, dealing with privileges and immunities, was adopted October 13, 1960, after this article was written. It may be found in GEN/DNT/52/Rev. 1.

(1) *"Formal" Articles*

One article concerned authentic texts. It followed the standard form in international agreements. Another article provided that the annexes should form an integral part of the treaty. Since it was envisaged that the detailed specifications for the Detection and Identification System would be contained in an annex, this met the Western insistence that these provisions should have treaty force. A third article concerned amendments to the treaty and its annexes. It provided that amendments would enter into effect when they had been adopted by a vote of two-thirds of the members of the Conference and ratified by two-thirds of the parties to the treaty, including the Original Parties. This procedure was patterned after that specified in the UN Charter, and gave the Original Parties veto power.

(2) *"Other States"*

Two of the articles touched on the question of how other states should be brought into the Control Organization. The first of these defined the parties to the treaty. The USSR, the United Kingdom, and the United States were specified as the Original Parties. It was also agreed that this article should contain a second paragraph allowing other states to become parties, but no treaty language was worked out during this period. Actually, none was even proposed until mid-1960. The Western powers nevertheless felt satisfied that they had won their point that states other than the three nuclear powers should be allowed to become members of the Control Organization.

The second article relating to this matter concerned the signature, ratification, and entry into force of the treaty. According to this article, the treaty would enter into force as soon as the instruments of ratification of the Original Parties had been deposited, thus meeting the Soviet argument that bringing other states into the Control Organization should not be allowed to delay the implementation of the treaty; other states were given a period of six months in which to sign the treaty, but no time limit was set for the deposit of instruments of ratification or acceptance.

The article on the Conference also dealt with states other than the three nuclear powers which might become parties, in that it spelled out certain powers that they would have within the

Control Organization. These were minimal. The Conference would meet annually, and could be convened in special sessions. As has already been mentioned, it would have a role in the procedure for amending the treaty. Beyond that, its powers would be to elect the nonpermanent members of the Commission, approve the budget (although the way in which this would be accomplished and the majority required were left for later specification), consider the annual report of the Commission, approve reports to the UN, and approve agreements with other international organizations. In addition, the Conference could discuss any matter within the scope of the treaty, a provision reminiscent of Article 10 of the UN Charter relating to the powers of the General Assembly. It could also make decisions on matters specifically referred to it by the Commission, propose matters for consideration by the Commission, and request reports from the Commission. All decisions, except those on budgetary matters and on amendments, would be by a simple majority of parties to the treaty present and voting, unless the Conference itself decided that a two-thirds majority would be required. It was clear from these terms of reference that the Commission and not the Conference would be the dominant body in the Control Organization, and that states other than the Original Parties would have only limited rights and responsibilities.

(3) *Obligations of the Parties Concerning the Control System*
Three of the articles which were adopted dealt with obligations of the parties to the treaty with respect to the control system. The first committed them to accept the placement on territory under their jurisdiction of the control components which would be established on the basis of the report of the Conference of Experts and installed and operated in accordance with the treaty and its annexes.

The second spelled out specific obligations of cooperation. These included: giving inspection groups "immediate and undisputed access" and refraining from any interference with them; providing "adequate and expeditious transportation" for on-site inspections; entering into arrangements for the utilization of existing aircraft flights for routine air sampling purposes; entering into arrangements for making aircraft available for special aircraft flights or permitting special flights by aircraft belonging to the control system; and, entering into arrangements for the utilization of existing weather and geophysical exploration vessels. It was agreed that another paragraph concerning the cooperation required for the high altitude detection system would be added to this article.

The third article of this group provided that representatives to the Conference and the Commission and the Administrator and other executive personnel, should enjoy such privileges and immunities as would be necessary for the exercise of their functions. The precise terms of the legal capacity of the Organization and the privileges and immunities of associated personnel were to be spelled out in an annex. This meant that these matters would have treaty force. Except for this feature, which is also found in the Rome treaties establishing the European Common Market and Euratom, the article paralleled those usually found in the charters of international organizations. Since the UN Convention on Privileges and Immunities has been ratified by the USSR and the United Kingdom, but not the United States, it is interesting that the United States readily agreed to this formulation, which was proposed by the United Kingdom. Perhaps all parties saw it as a way of circumventing the hurdle of Congressional ratification of a separate convention.

(4) *"External" Relations*

The final article on which agreement was reached in the four weeks from April 13 to May 8, 1959, concerned relationships with other international organizations. Its terms were simple. It merely stated that the Commission, with the approval of the Conference, could enter into an agreement establishing "an appropriate relationship" between the Control Organization and the United Nations, and that the same action could be taken with respect to "any international organization which may in the future be established among any of the Parties to this Treaty to supervise disarmament and arms control measures."

The implications of the article, however, are interesting. First, it signified that the Control Organization would not be a part of the United Nations. Secondly, it also implied that the functions of this complicated mechanism would be limited to the control of nuclear explosions; that further measures of arms control and disarmament would require the creation of additional international organizations. Despite popular speculation that the underlying Western ambition was to establish a control organization whose functions gradually could be expanded,[19] this possibility was never discussed in the Geneva Conference, and on several occasions it was implicitly rejected.

The only controversy surrounding the adoption of this article involved phraseology. The second paragraph of the original British proposal allowed appropriate relationships to be established with:

> . . . any international arms regulation organization which may in the future be established among any of the Parties to this Treaty to supervise arms control measures.[20]

Consistent with its general position in the disarmament debate, the USSR objected to control without disarmament and proposed that the paragraph read "international disarmament organization . . . to supervise disarmament control."[21] The final formulation mentioning both arms control and disarmament was a compromise between the Soviet and Western positions.

(5) *How Much Emotion in the Preamble?*

Related issues arose in the discussion of the preamble. Although the Western powers basically accepted a Soviet proposal, they insisted on changing the opening two paragraphs. The original draft read:

> Pursuing the aim of putting a check to the nuclear armaments race and to the further improvement and creation of new, even more destructive types of these weapons of mass destruction;
>   Endeavoring to take a practical step towards the urgent objective of prohibiting atomic weapons and eliminating them from national armaments, as indicated by the United Nations.[22]

The formulation which was adopted was:

> Pursuing the aim of reducing international competition in armaments and in the development of new weapons of war;

[19]For example, see *The Observer,* February 15, 1959, p. 14.
[20]GEN/DNT/39.
[21]GEN/DNT/PV. 76, pp. 10-11.
[22]GEN/DNT/46.

> Endeavoring to take a practical step towards the achievement of the objectives of the United Nations in the field of disarmament including the eventual elimination and prohibition of nuclear weapons under effective international control and the use of atomic energy for peaceful purposes only.

The change did little to alter the meaning of the preamble. Its principal effect was to eliminate some of the emotionalism directed against nuclear weapons, a constant component of Soviet policy until the nineteen-sixties. In addition to these paragraphs the preamble mentioned the desire of the signatories to bring about a permanent discontinuance of nuclear weapon tests; recognized that permanent, effective and continuous control was essential to achieve this objective; expressed the hope that other countries would join in the undertakings spelled out in the treaty; and asserted that a discontinuance of nuclear weapons tests would make possible "progress toward agreement on measures of disarmament." A more cautious way of expressing the last sentiment could hardly be found.

(6) *The Organization, Its Headquarters, Transitional Arrangements*

Beyond these achievements of the period from April 13 to May 8, 1959, agreement on three other matters was reached during the course of the Geneva Conference. On August 11, 1959, the three states adopted an article specifying the elements of the Control Organization. According to this article, the Control Organization would consist of: the Commission, the Detection and Identification System, the Administrator, and the Conference. The headquarters of the Organization would be in Vienna, which is also the headquarters of the International Atomic Energy Agency. The Soviet Union would not agree to this article until the Western powers had given assurances that the Administrator's powers would be limited and that he would be clearly subordinate to the Commission. As will be recalled, early Soviet formulations contained no mention of a chief executive officer.

Annex III dealing with the Preparatory Commission was adopted November 30, 1959. The provisions in this Annex are reminiscent of the Preparatory Commission which was established by the International Atomic Energy Agency Treaty. The Preparatory Commisison would come into existence on the day that the treaty was signed by the Original Parties, and would consist of one representative from each of the Original Parties. At this stage, the Preparatory Commission would plan and oversee the preliminary installation of the control system. Once the treaty came into force, the three Original Parties by unanimous agreement would co-opt four additional states from those that had signed the treaty, and the Preparatory Commission would then assume the functions of the Control Commission, until the latter could be formally constituted. It would also exercise the functions of the Administrator, until he was appointed. During this stage, the voting procedures would be those specified in the Treaty for the Commission. The Soviet Union accepted the draft for this annex, which the United States had tabled on July 27, 1959, almost in its entirety. The USSR insisted on only two changes: first, that the requirement for unanimity among the Original Parties be specified, rejecting Ambassador Wadsworth's contention that it was assumed[23]; and second, that the task of recommending the location of regional offices be omitted, since it was not agreed that there should be such offices.

(7) *Privileges and Immunities*

The final section of the proposed treaty to be adopted was Annex II, dealing with privileges and immunities, which was accepted October 17, 1960. As this section developed in detail some of the conditions under which the Control Organization would operate on the territories of each of the parties, it was among the more important to be adopted.

The Soviet Union included a proposal on this matter in the draft basic provisions which it tabled on December 8, 1958, shortly after the negotiations began.[24] This proposal merely stated that the foreign control officers should "enjoy diplomatic immunity equal to that of the staff of foreign embassies, legations and missions." In addition, as was mentioned earlier, the proposal made it clear that "the right of extraterritoriality" would not extend to the premises of control posts and that movement of foreign personnel of the posts in the territory of the state must take place in accordance with

[23]GEN/DNT/PV. 115, pp. 4, 10, 11.
[24]GEN/DNT/19.

the procedures existing for foreigners. This proposal was consistent with the modest Soviet concept of the Control Organization.

In keeping with the Western concept of an elaborate control system, Western ideas called for much more specific provisions which would ensure that the Control Organization and its personnel would receive all the privileges and immunities they might require for the performance of their novel task. This approach led to the conclusion that the privileges and immunities would have to embrace those generally granted to international organizations such as the United Nations and NATO, and also include certain special features. However, not until a year later did the United States submit a proposal reflecting this line of reasoning. The delay in tabling a Western draft for this section of the treaty was due chiefly to the necessity of working out an agreed text between the two Western partners, with the United Kingdom favoring more detail and specificity than the United States. Furthermore, Western policy-makers saw no cause for according this matter priority over other proposals on which agreement was considered more urgent. The flagging pace of the negotiations and the technical complexity of the subject may also have contributed to the delay.

The draft as finally submitted by the United States on December 7, 1959,[25] was modeled after the 1946 Convention on the Privileges and Immunities of the United Nations, the 1947 Convention on the Privileges and Immunities of the Specialized Agencies, the 1959 Agreement on the Privileges and Immunities of the International Atomic Energy Agency and, last but not least, the 1951 Agreement on the Status of the North Atlantic Treaty Organization, National Representatives and International Staff. That the Soviet Union offered no serious objection to this draft can be explained in part by the fact that it had previously agreed to substantially similar privileges and immunities in other contexts by having ratified the first and the third of these three agreements.[26]

The discussion that preceded the acceptance by the USSR of the American draft was much less extensive than the Western dele-

[25]GEN/DNT/74.

[26]The United Kingdom has ratified all four of these agreements while the United States has ratified the last only. The United States has also ratified the 1947 Headquarters Agreement with the United Nations, which contains provisions on several topics covered in the other agreements.

gations expected. The section that occasioned the most argument involved the right of the Control Organization to exchange currency, but this disagreement was not very serious. The American proposal was that the organization should be entitled to the most favorable rate of exchange. After considerable verbal sparring, Ambassador Wadsworth explained that this provision was designed to prevent countries with completely managed currencies from hampering the work of the Control Organization by establishing discriminatory rates of exchange.[27] He stated that this would be important because of the magnitude of the expenditures which would be involved. It was apparent that the provision was formulated principally because at that time the USSR maintained two rates of exchange: one of ten rubles to the dollar for tourists; and the other of four rubles to the dollar for other expenditures. The USSR strongly objected to this provision. Mr. Tsarapkin argued that the passage should follow the pattern of the UN Convention and that of the Specialized Agencies and merely give the Control Organization the right to convert currency. Although he argued generally that a country could not be forced to grant to the Control Organization an exchange rate which it had established for some special purpose, he actually seemed to be objecting more to the fact that the provision appeared on the surface to discriminate against the USSR, since in practice it was the only one of the Original Parties to which it would apply.[28] The compromise finally worked out was to delete the provision, but to agree to include in the eventual financial regulations of the Control Organization—following the example of the United Nations—the requirement that all contributions must be assessed and paid in United States dollars unless the Administrator approved another currency.

Although the Soviet Union proposed certain other amendments to the United States draft, they either concerned matters of style, or involved making explicit matters which the Western powers agreed were implicit. For example, one Soviet amendment specified that diplomatic pouch privileges should be limited to official business.

As accepted by the three powers, Annex II closely resembled, both in general structure and in substance, the four international

27GEN/DNT/PV. 222, p. 9.
28Ibid., p. 14.

agreements which set the pattern for the original American proposal. All these documents have substantially identical provisions concerning the organization's legal personality and the privileges and immunities with respect to its funds, assets, and communications. However, unlike the other agreements, the Annex contains no general provision for the settlement of disputes concerning its interpretation or application. In an early paper describing the outlines of the treaty, the United States delegation indicated that it would propose an article dealing with settlements of disputes arising out of the treaty.[29] However, such an article was the subject of disagreement within the Western councils and was never proposed.

According to the Annex, representatives of parties on the Control Commission, defined to include all members of the official staffs except those whose duties were exclusively clerical, would be given both in the country of the Organization's headquarters, and, when performing Commission duties, on the territory of another party to the treaty, the same privileges and immunities that were accorded by the respective governments to accredited diplomatic envoys. In addition, representatives of parties on any organ of the Organization together with the members of their official staffs, including clerks, would enjoy under the same circumstances (and also en route to and from meetings) enumerated privileges and immunities closely resembling those accorded to representatives of the parties in the agreements that served as models for the American proposal. Since these privileges and immunities would be accorded not for the personal benefit of the individuals but to assure their independence as officials, a party would have the duty to waive the immunity of its representatives where "in its opinion" the immunity would impede justice and could be waived without prejudice to the purposes for which it was granted. Moreover, the parties would not be required to extend privileged treatment to their own nationals or to aliens acting as their representatives.

As for the staff and experts employed by the Control Organization itself (as distinguished from the representatives of the parties and their national staffs), the top echelon, that is the Administrator and his deputies, would be given privileges and immunities "normally accorded" to diplomatic envoys. All other staff members

[29]GEN/DNT/9, par. 8.

would be accorded enumerated privileges and immunities with respect to currency facilities, personal baggage, immigration restrictions, repatriation, import duties, taxes, as well as

> Immunity from arrest or detention whenever assigned to a
> control post, an inspection group, or a routine or special
> flight; and at all times immunity from arrest, detention, or
> any legal processes with respect to words spoken or writ-
> ten and acts done by them in the performance of their
> official functions.[30]

Here, also, since the immunities would be granted in the interest
of the Organization, the Administrator would be obligated to waive
the immunity of any staff member or expert where it would impede
justice and the waiver would not prejudice the working of the
Organization.

A party's right to refuse privileges and immunities to its own
nationals, unrestricted, as was seen earlier, with respect to its representatives on the Organization's organs, would be qualified in this
section in two ways. A party would be required to grant to its
own national serving as a staff member or an expert of the Organization only one immunity and one privilege: first, the immunity for
his official acts, and second, the privilege of access to facilities with
respect to currency and exchange restrictions so far as necessary
for the effective exercise of his functions. With only one exception,
which will be noted, the international agreements upon which the
Annex is patterned contain no such restriction upon the immunities
of international staff personnel vis-à-vis their own country; by
implication, these agreements require the parties to make available
to their own nationals on the international staff the full range of
privileges and immunities. The reason for this is that the purpose

---

[30]The novel phrase "at all times" in the Annex provision quoted in the
main text was probably not intended to indicate that a staff member would
retain his immunity with respect to past official acts even after his relationship with the Organization was terminated. A more likely interpretation is
that this phrase was intended as a juxtaposition to the clause "whenever
assigned . . ." in the first part of the paragraph. However, even if this was
the purpose of the phrase the better view would be that immunity with
respect to official acts would continue after the termination of the official
position.

of international immunities is to protect the international responsibilities of international staff personnel and as one authority has written "they require protection against the State of which the official is a national as fully as, and perhaps more fully than, against any other State."[31] It is interesting to note that the limiting provision of Annex II was strikingly similar to Article 23 of the Agreement on the Status of the North Atlantic Treaty Organization, National Representatives, and International Staff,[32] and one can speculate that it was inserted in the American proposal with an eye on the United States Senate. As far as the Annex was concerned, this right of a party to refuse privileges and immunities to its own nationals was an important point as the negotiations made it clear that the control posts would be staffed in part by local nationals and that local nationals would be stationed on the territory of their own state, possibly also in other official capacities.

The exact extent to which an individual would be free from action by his government in other respects was not quite clear. There could be some question, for instance, whether the individual would remain immune from his government's action with respect to his official acts after his relationship with the Organization had come to an end, although the better view would require continuation of such immunity. Again, in the discussion of the *laissez passer* arrangements, Ambassador Wadsworth stated that they would have to include provision for enabling individuals to return either to their country of origin or to the country where the headquarters of the Organization was located.[33] Then he went on in the next sentence to state that the *laissez passer* regulations should in no way prejudice the right of a government to prescribe whatever regulations it chose with respect to its own citizens.

In considering generally the extent of the limitations imposed by the Annex upon a party's control over access to and activities on its territory, it is pertinent that the Administrator would have

[31]C. Wilfred Jenks, *International Immunities* (London: Stevens & Sons, 1961), p. 112. Jenks concludes that while the principle of enforcing stipulated privileges and immunities of international staff personnel against their own States is clear, practice has always tended to lag behind it.
[32]U.S. Department of State, *Treaties and Other International Acts Series,* No. 2992.
[33]GEN/DNT/PV. 193, p. 7.

been obliged to inform the party concerned in advance of any proposed assignment of staff members or experts to its territory, and that party would have had an "opportunity to comment" on the proposed assignment of any particular individual. This proved to be perhaps the most controversial issue of the Annex, but all three parties agreed that the opportunity to object to any individual should not be used often.[34] In this context the Annex also provided that, if in a party's view a staff member or expert posted on its territory had abused his privileges, the party would ultimately have the right to require that the Administrator arrange for an immediate replacement. A similar provision would apply *mutatis mutandis* in case of abuse of privileges by a representative of a party present in the territory of another party.

It is difficult to speculate whether the privileges and immunities defined in the Annex and fashioned after the patterns evolved for other international agencies would have met adequately the special needs and novel features of the Control Organization, particularly if applied to a large number of personnel at control posts and on inspection teams. Again, caution is in order if one desires to evaluate the significance of the Soviet acceptance of the American proposal, considering the lack of detailed Soviet comment and the limited discussion. The Soviet Union may have been content to concentrate its effort upon the important and controversial staffing provisions of the treaty on the assumption that, if these provisions were formulated to its satisfaction, it could probably agree to a standard grant of privileges and immunities in the Annex.

After the three states agreed to the Annex, they also agreed to a new and briefer article on privileges and immunities to replace that which they had already adopted in the text of the treaty. This article merely stated that the privileges and immunities which the Organization, its staff, and the representatives of parties shall enjoy,

[34]See GEN/DNT/PV. 146, p. 5; GEN/DNT/PV. 167, p. 13; and GEN/DNT/PV. 177, p. 5. There is no comparable provision for advance notification and opportunity to comment in the Conventions on the Privileges and Immunities of the UN or the Specialized Agencies or in the Agreement on the Privileges and Immunities of the International Atomic Energy Agency. But there are comparable provisions in Article XI, Section D and Article XII, Section A of the Statute of the International Atomic Energy Agency.

and the legal capacity of the Organization "shall be as set forth in Annex II of this Treaty."

These were the last agreements achieved during the Geneva Conference, and the only ones achieved after the collapse of the summit meeting.

The Remaining Disagreements

Although the parts of the treaty which were adopted represented a significant measure of agreement, several disagreements remained. They centered on four principal issues: the staffing of control posts; the composition of the Control Commission; voting in the Control Commission, especially the privileges to be given to the Original Parties; and the role and structure of executive authority.

(1) *National or International Control Post Staffs?*

As stated earlier, at the outset the Soviet Union took the position the control posts should be completely staffed by nationals of the host country except for one or two foreign controllers. The Western powers, on the other hand, had held that host country nationals should be barred from serving on the staff of control posts. Each side took the position that the view advanced by the other would not provide a sufficient guarantee of its security. The West argued that in the event of a suspected violation host country personnel would be torn between loyalty to their own state and to the Control Organization and could not be counted on to choose the latter. The Soviet Union, on the other hand, argued that under a system of international staffing, it would have no assurance that Soviet nationals would in practice be given positions which would enable them effectively to exercise control over the other side, and cited the predominantly Western character of the secretariats of the major international organizations. To buttress their position, each side developed elaborate technical arguments about the possibility of muffling and fabricating seismic signals. These then called for equally elaborate rebuttals. One slightly ironic aspect of this debate was that at the time when the Western representatives in Geneva were arguing that the only way in which the proper operation of instruments could be assured was through an international staff, the Berkner Panel suggested the introduction of large numbers of unmanned stations as one possible way around the difficulties with respect to technical issues which plagued the Conference. To put it more sharply, while Ambassador Wadsworth was arguing in Geneva that instruments could not be made tamperproof, American scientists in the United States were asserting that they could. Mr. Tsarapkin made the most of this contradiction.[35]

By the time of the recess on March 19, 1959, the Soviet Union had agreed that there might be as many as four or five foreign controllers stationed at control posts. On May 8, 1959, the Western powers met this compromise by agreeing that it might be possible for a limited number of host country nationals to serve on the staffs of control posts.[36]

Next, in mid-July, the West proposed that the staff of each control post could be divided into thirds: one third would consist of nationals of the USSR, another third nationals of the United Kingdom and the United States, and the final third nationals of other parties to the treaty.[37] This same formula had already been suggested by the West for the headquarters of the Control Organization.[38]

The Soviet Union's immediate reaction, in both instances, was to question how the final third would be apportioned. It argued that there must be some way of maintaining a balance among countries allied with the United Kingdom and the United States, countries allied with the Soviet Union, and uncommitted countries. The West, on the other hand, maintained that it would be both politically and administratively difficult to elaborate a rigid formula to define eligibility for the third third. The Western powers argued that some countries would not easily fit into the three-fold categorization proposed by the Soviet Union, that international alignments of states were subject to change, and that too rigid restrictions should not be imposed on the Administrator, whose judgment in such matters should be trusted. The Soviet rebuttal was that without a rigid formula there would be nothing to prevent the Administrator from recruiting the third third solely from Western states, thus assuring the West two-thirds of the staff at control posts.

[35]GEN/DNT/PV. 100, p. 12.
[36]Ibid., p. 7.
[37]GEN/DNT/PV. 113, p. 5.
[38]GEN/DNT/PV. 68, p. 6.

On December 14, 1959, the USSR accepted the broad principle that the staff of control posts should be divided into thirds, subject to agreement on the third third, and proposed that the third third be divided equally among Western allies, Soviet allies and uncommitted countries.[39] The Western powers were unwilling to accept this rigid formula. They did, however, propose various compromises. On May 9, 1960, they tabled detailed staffing regulations which would have required the Administrator to give preference to nationals of the host country in recruiting the third third if the control post happened to be on the territory of a state other than the Original Parties to the treaty, and to take into account the "legitimate interests" of the Original Parties.[40] On June 29, 1960, the United Kingdom went even farther and suggested that personnel appointments to the third third should "be made in such manner and proportions as to maintain an equal balance between the interests of the Soviet Union on the one hand and of the United Kingdom and the United States on the other."[41] Since these compromises were not acceptable to the Soviet Union, and the West would not go further, an impasse resulted. That was where matters stood at the end of 1960.

The differences between the two sides were not very great, but they nevertheless continued to exist. The two sides also disagreed on the nationality of the head of the staff of the control posts. The West maintained that he *could not* be a host country national while the Soviet Union maintained that he *must* be a host country national.

(2) *Power Balance in the Commission*

A second major difference concerned the composition of the Control Commission. Agreement had been reached fairly early that this body should consist of seven states, and that the three Original Parties should have permanent membership. The disagreement concerned the four other states. Even before the March 19, 1959 recess the Western powers had suggested that these four might consist of one state from the East and one from the West and two

[39]GEN/DNT/PV. 148, p. 11.
[40]GEN/DNT/89.
[41]GEN/DNT/PV. 221, p. 10.

uncommitted states, giving an overall balance of 3 (West), 2 (East), 2 (uncommitted); while the USSR had proposed one from the West, two from the East and one uncommitted state, giving an overall balance of 3 (West), 3 (East), 1 (uncommitted). Through 1960, neither side altered its position. The USSR made acceptance of its formula a part of its package proposal of December 14, 1959.[42] The West countered on August 9, 1960, by raising the status of its formula of 3-2-2 from that of a suggestion to that of a formal proposal.[43] The Soviet Union justified its position on the ground of parity between the two sides; and the West, on the ground of the necessity of reflecting actual alignments throughout the world and of avoiding too great a burden of decision on any one uncommitted state. Each side was in reality attempting to maximize its influence within the Commission.

(3) The Reach of the "Veto"

The question of voting rights in the Commission was closely linked to that of its composition, and in its package proposal of December 14, 1959, the Soviet Union actually tied the two together. As early as January 30, 1959, the Soviet Union had submitted a comprehensive list of seven categories of decisions which would require the affirmative votes of four members of the Commission, including the Original Parties, and thus be subject to a veto by the Original Parties.[44] These included:

  (a) revision of the Treaty and its annexes, and adoption of amendments thereto;
  (b) any accusation against a State of a violation of the Treaty, and other matters relating to violations of the Treaty;
  (c) appointment of the Administrator, definition or alteration of his terms of reference, recruitment of the main engineering and technical personnel of the Control Organization's headquarters, controllers and inspection groups;
  (d) adoption of a decision to despatch inspection groups for on-site investigation of an event suspected of

[42]GEN/DNT/PV. 148, pp. 10-11.
[43]GEN/DNT/PV. 240, p. 6.
[44]GEN/DNT/29.

being a nuclear explosion, and adoption of decisions on the basis of the results of such investigation;

(e) revision of existing methods and approval of new methods of observation and types of apparatus in the control system;

(f) determination of location sites of the control posts and of the routes for control aircraft flights;

(g) budgetary, financial, administrative, and economic matters connected with the Control Organization's activities, including matters relating to the recruitment and dismissal of the supporting and auxiliary personnel.

The Soviet Union was willing to have procedural decisions settled by a simple majority vote.

In the subsequent negotiations the Western powers sought to narrow the USSR's "veto list," as they called it, which had been put forward as an amendment to a paragraph of the proposed article dealing with the Commission. Two techniques were employed. One consisted of agreeing that unanimity among the Original Parties would be required with respect to a specified matter, but placing the statement of this requirement in the section of the treaty dealing with that particular matter. For example, the article which the three states adopted on amendments specified that amendments would go into effect only when ratified by two-thirds of the parties to the treaty including the three Original Parties. The other technique was to include substantive provisions which would be acceptable to the Soviet Union and render any specification of the voting requirement unnecessary. As a case in point, the Soviet Union agreed to remove the last part of section (g) relating to administrative personnel from its list when the Western powers agreed that the auxiliary and supporting personnel would be host country nationals.

By November 25, 1959, the Soviet Union had agreed or offered to delete all but one section of subparagraph (g) from the list.[45] The deletion of subparagraph (a) has already been covered. The Soviet Union agreed to delete subparagraph (b) when the Western powers agreed that the Control Organization as such

[45]See Mr. Tsararkin's summary of the negotiations on these points: GEN/DNT/PV. 13   3-7.

would not make accusations of violations. The first part of sub-paragraph (c) was deleted when the Western powers agreed that the appointment of the Administrator would require the agreement of the three Original Parties and that his terms of reference could only be changed by amending the treaty. The USSR offered to delete the remainder of subparagraph (c) relating to the Control Organization's staff if the Western powers would agree to the Soviet proposals on the distribution of the staff. It offered to delete subparagraph (d) if the Western powers would accept the proposal for an annual quota of on-site inspections. (The negotiations concerning this point have already been analyzed.) The Soviet Union agreed to delete subparagraph (e) on revisions in the system, because these would fall under the provisions relating to amendments to the treaty, since the components of the system would be specified in an annex. It agreed to delete subparagraph (f) when the Western powers agreed that the location of sites for control posts and of routes for control aircraft would be determined in agreement with the interested government. The Western powers protected their position by insisting that if the interested government rejected a proposal of the Commission it would be obliged to provide an alternative acceptable to the Commission. The Soviet Union accepted the requirement with respect to control post sites but not aircraft flights. The deletion of the final section of subparagraph (g) has already been mentioned.

Thus the principal remaining question related to those issues covered in the first section of subparagraph (g), namely "budgetary, financial, administrative and economic matters connected with the Control Organization's activities. . . ." The essential issue in controversy was whether or not the agreement of all the Original Parties would be required for the budget. The Soviet Union argued that this was necessary because of the magnitude of the expenditures which would be involved. The West on the other hand maintained that to allow this would allow one of the Original Parties effectively to block the operations of the Control Organization, and argued instead that the budget should only require a two-thirds majority in the Control Commission and a simple majority in the Conference.

On December 14, 1959, as a part of its package proposal, the Soviet Union stated that it would agree to such a provision if its proposal for the composition of the Control Commission were accepted; that is, the 3-3-1 formula.[46] As the Western powers pointed out, under such arrangements the Soviet Union would have retained the ability to block the budget and in fact to block any section of the budget since the Soviet Union insisted that the Commission should not merely vote on the total budget but also on each individual section. In the December 14 proposal the Soviet Union also insisted that the share of the contributions to be borne by each of the Original Parties would have to be specified in the treaty.

The following year brought no resolution of these differences. Although the gap between the two sides on voting procedures in the Commission was narrowed considerably in the first twenty-seven months of the Geneva Conference, it nevertheless continued to exist.

(4) *How Much Independence for the "Executive"?*

A final major controversy concerned the Administrator. As will be recalled, the original Soviet plan made no provision for a chief executive officer, and appeared to assume that the Commission would oversee the operation of the control system. However, prior to the March 19, 1959 recess, the USSR had agreed that an administrator might be required, but only after the West had affirmed that such an individual would be subordinate to the Control Commission and that his appointment would require the agreement of all the Original Parties. During the remainder of 1959 and 1960, agreement was reached on several aspects of the general functions and character of the office of the Administrator. It was agreed that he should view his task in international terms, not as a representative of any side. This was understood to mean that he would most likely be a national of an uncommitted country. It was also agreed that he would be responsible for the general management of the control system, and that in connection with this, he would prepare budget estimates, forward reports to the Commission, and encourage the staff of the system to participate in basic research.

Despite this broad area of agreement, there were various dis-

46GEN/DNT/PV. 148, p. 11.

agreements. The two sides could not agree to treaty language defining the relationship between the Administrator and the Control Commission. The original United States proposal had contained the provision that the Administrator should be "responsible to the Commission in the performance of his duties,"[47] and this was subsequently modified ". . . for the installation and operation of the control system."[48] On December 3, 1959, the Soviet Union sought to establish the dominant role of the Commission even more clearly, by suggesting that the relevant section should read:

> He shall be responsible to the Commission and is directly subordinated to it in all his acts, and shall provide to the Commission such advice, reports and assistance as the Commission may request.[49]

Although the distance between the two concepts was narrowed somewhat in the following month and a half, agreement could not be achieved. The West proposed as a compromise formulation: "He shall be responsible to the Commission and, under its supervision, shall carry out its policy directives"[50] but would go no further. The USSR, on the other hand, never accepted this formulation.

The essential issue at stake was the freedom to be given the Administrator, and the position of the two sides was in accord with that which they have taken with respect to other international organizations, particularly the United Nations. The same issue arose in the consideration of various specific powers which the West proposed to give to the Administrator, such as appointment of his staff, the authority to determine the location of control posts and bases for inspection teams, and the authority to despatch special aircraft sampling flights and on-site inspection teams. The USSR consistently sought to eliminate these provisions and hedge the Administrator's freedom. Where it did not succeed, the matters remained in dispute.

The original United States proposal had not specified any upper level staff other than the Administrator. On December 3, 1959, the Soviet Union proposed that two deputy administrators

47GEN/DNT/PV. 25, p. 12.
48GEN/DNT/PV. 106, p. 15.
49GEN/DNT/PV. 142, p. 26.
50GEN/DNT/PV. 155, p. 6.

should be appointed who "shall assist the Administrator in his day-to-day work and shall be entitled equally to participate in the preparation of questions for decision by the Administrator."[51] In his oral presentation, Mr. Tsarapkin made it clear that the two deputy administrators should represent the two sides, and asserted that their constant presence could do much to prevent friction, especially between the Control Organization and the Original Parties.[52] This appeared to the Western powers to be an attempt to intrude national elements into what they conceived of as an international staff. At first the Western powers were disinclined to compromise their concept in this way.

Movement toward agreement was only possible because of the Western powers' growing concern for another problem, on which the Soviet Union was willing to make concessions in return for counter concessions. At about the same time that the Soviet Union raised the proposal for two deputy administrators, the United States became worried about the problem of continuity in the executive authority, and proposed that the Administrator should continue to serve until his successor was appointed.[53] Obviously the United States had in mind the situation in the United Nations when the permanent members of the Security Council could not agree to a successor for Secretary General Trygve Lie, whose term of office was extended over the most strenuous Soviet opposition until agreement was reached on the new chief executive. Because of that very situation, however, and because the Western proposal would for the future "legalize" what the Western powers had done in that instance in the United Nations, the suggestion was an anathema to the Soviet Union.

On April 18, 1960, the United States tried a different approach to assure a measure of continuity in the performance of the administrative function. In January of that year the United States had agreed that there might be one Deputy Administrator, and that his appointment would require the concurrence of the Original Parties.[54] It now suggested that while the terms of both the Administrator and the Deputy Administrator would be three years, the initial term of

[51]GEN/DNT/73.
[52]GEN/DNT/PV. 142, p. 16.
[53]GEN/DNT/PV. 141, p. 18.
[54]GEN/DNT/PV. 153, pp. 3-4.

the Deputy Administrator would only be two years, so that the terms of the two officers would always overlap.[55]

On June 21, 1960, the Soviet Union proposed that there should be three deputy administrators, a first deputy who would be a national of an uncommitted country, and who could serve as Administrator in his absence, and two representing the two sides.[56] At the same time, Mr. Tsarapkin stated that the USSR would accept the Western concept of staggering the terms of the Administrator and the principal Deputy. After a series of informal meetings, Sir Michael Wright suggested *ad referendum* that there should be five deputy administrators, a first deputy from an uncommitted state, and two from each side.[57] The Soviet Union accepted this proposal on July 5, and the United States, the following day. However, agreement could not be obtained on the manner of appointment of the Deputy Administrators. The West felt that the Administrator should have some role in the selection of his principal assistants, but the Soviet Union insisted that they should all be appointed by the Control Commission.

Of course there were other differences among the three parties in the Geneva Conference, relating for example to communications and regional offices, but these four were the principal ones. Reviewing them, and considering them in conjunction with the agreements that were achieved, one can only conclude that in mid-1960, when progress in the negotiations fell sharply, issues relating to the Control Organization were not the principal obstacles to the adoption of a nuclear test ban treaty. Given the extent of the compromises which had occurred, it is hard to believe that further agreements could not have been arranged.

IV

The Renewed Western Effort

The April 18, 1961, Western Draft Treaty
In fact, the West did offer further concessions. When the Kennedy Administration assumed power in January, along with reconsidering Western positions on such fundamental issues as the coverage of

[55]GEN/DNT/PV. 195, p. 4.
[56]GEN/DNT/PV. 216, p. 6.
[57]GEN/DNT/PV. 223, pp. 3-7.

the treaty and the phasing of the installation of the control system, it also reexamined Western positions relating to the structure of the Control Organization. New positions were formulated as a consequence. The principal explanations for the changes were two. First, President Kennedy wanted to make a determined effort to achieve a treaty, and so instructed his aides. Secondly, the membership of the Committee of Principals was modified. Perhaps the most crucial change was that Glenn T. Seaborg replaced John A. McCone as Chairman of the Atomic Energy Commission. Mr. McCone was the strongest personality on the Commission and as a consequence of his departure the AEC eased its position on several aspects of the proposed treaty and Control Organization. For example, at one point the AEC had taken the position that no instrument operated by Soviet technicians could be considered reliable. After agreement had been achieved within the United States government, the new positions were presented to the British, who readily agreed.

The new Western position, several aspects of which have already been discussed, was advanced in a series of oral presentations by Ambassador Dean starting March 21, 1961, and in the draft treaty tabled April 18, 1961.[58] With one exception relating to the number of states on the Control Commission, this treaty incorporated the articles which had already been adopted in the Conference. Beyond that, it was based on previous Western positions, with certain modifications. Several of the changes were designed to eliminate outstanding controversies.

So far as staffing was concerned, the Western powers were willing to specify in the treaty that in all cases where deputies were appointed, a national of the United Kingdom or the United States should have a deputy from the USSR and vice versa. They were not, however, willing to go beyond their previous commitment with respect to the third third at control posts, and they continued to insist that the head of a control post could not be a host country national.

Perhaps the most far-reaching change in the Western position was with respect to the composition of the Control Commission. The new proposal was for a Commission consisting of eleven states: the three parties to the negotiations as permanent members; two

[58]For the draft treaty, see *Geneva Conference,* pp. 475-520.

states associated with the United Kingdom and the United States; three states associated with the USSR; and three uncommitted states; thus yielding a 4-4-3 composition with East and West represented equally. Actually Mr. Tsarapkin had casually mentioned this figure June 14, 1960, but the Western powers had not responded.[59]

As another fairly significant concession, the new Western proposal provided that decisions in the Commission concerning the scale of contributions and the total amount of each annual budget would require the unanimous agreement of the three Original Parties. By accepting substantially the Soviet position the Western powers sought to eliminate the last major point of disagreement on the scope of the "veto." Thus, contrary to the United Nations pattern where budgetary decisions are made by the veto-less General Assembly, the budgetary control in the control organization would be subject to the veto. Finally, with respect to the four deputy administrators from the two sides, the new draft treaty provided that they should be appointed by the Administrator "on the recommendation, or with the approval," of the party or parties concerned.

The new Western position also contained other innovations, the most important of which related to the accession of other states to the proposed treaty. Although the three parties had at an early stage agreed that it should be possible for other states to accede to the treaty, they had never worked out the procedures for this. On July 26, 1960, the United States had tabled two draft paragraphs on this point.[60] The paragraphs had two notable features. First, others could become parties to the treaty only if the Commission found that their adherence was "essential in order to achieve the fundamental Treaty purpose of a permanent discontinuance of nuclear weapons test explosions on a world-wide basis or that elements of control are required to be installed in territory under" their jurisdiction. Secondly, the two articles throughout used the phraseology "states or authorities." The obvious purpose of these two features was to allow the West to insist that certain states should accede to the treaty, and yet to avoid any impairment of the United States policy of nonrecognition of these or other states or their governments. The necessity of the adherence of the People's Repub-

[59]GEN/DNT/PV. 213, p. 10.
[60]GEN/DNT/102.

lic of China was one obvious case which the authors had in mind. On the other hand, these provisions would enable the West to block the accession of certain states, for example, the Democratic Republic of Germany. Mr. Wadsworth patiently explained that no one would ever know whether a party acceded to the treaty as a state or as an authority. This terminology and the entire procedure, however, were totally unacceptable to the Soviet Union.

The new Western draft attempted to meet the Soviet objection by dropping the obnoxious words "or authority." On the other hand, the West still opposed the Soviet proposal for automatic adherence of other states and would have the Commission screen membership applications. The new draft specified that in Commission decisions concerning adherence of new parties to the treaty, Original Parties "associated" with the candidate must abstain.

The question of the timing of the accession of other states was also altered in the new proposal. The six months' time limit on signing in the article on signature, ratification, acceptance, and entry into force was dropped. At the same time, a schedule in the new Annex I specified a timetable according to which elements of the Detection and Identification System would have to be installed. Among other things it specified that within five years of the entry into force of the treaty twenty-one control posts would have to be established in Asia outside of the territory of the USSR. If this commitment were not fulfilled, parties would have the right to invoke the right of withdrawal under the duration article. Thus Communist China's accession would have had to have been achieved within the five-year time period. Whether or not these arrangements would have insured this is far from clear.[61]

One final minor change was that according to the new Western draft the initial review of the effectiveness of the Detection and Identification System should occur three rather than two years after the coming into force of the treaty.

The Soviet Response

To the disappointment of the Western powers, there was little real negotiation on their new proposals. On March 21, 1961, the

---

[61]For a detailed discussion of this issue, see Ciro E. Zoppo with the collaboration of Alice L. Hsieh, *The Accession of Other Nations to the Nuclear Test Ban* (Santa Monica: The RAND Corp., 1961, RM-2730-ARPA).

day that the Conference resumed, before Ambassador Dean and Mr. Ormsby-Gore had an opportunity to speak, Mr. Tsarapkin launched an attack on the concept of a single executive head in international organizations, often illustrating his point by referring to the activities of the Secretary General of the UN in the Congo, and proposed that the Control Organization should have, rather than an Administrator, an Administrative Council, consisting of three members, representing respectively the USSR and its allies; the United Kingdom, the United States and their allies; and neutral states. According to Mr. Tsarapkin, this Administrative Council "would act as a single whole and would agree amongst themselves on all steps which they would undertake in the execution of their duties."[62] In subsequent questioning he never went beyond this brief formulation in explaining how decisions would be taken in the Administrative Council. He never gave an answer to queries about whether or not voting would take place and unanimity be required, other than to say that the members of the Administrative Council would "act in agreement."[63] Mr. Tsarapkin did state, however, that the proposal for the Administrative Council eliminated the necessity for having Deputy Administrators.

The Soviet proposal for an Administrative Council met firm opposition from Western negotiators, both because they felt that it would prevent the Control Organization from taking effective action, and because they feared the implications of any compromise on this issue, both for the UN and for other international organizations which might be established in the future.

Why the Soviet Union shifted its position is not clear. In breaking the moratorium on nuclear testing slightly over five months later, the USSR demonsrated that at that point, August 31, 1961, it was willing seriously to jeopardize the negotiations, and thus presumably had little interest in continuing them. Chairman Khrushchev had indicated as much in his meeting with President Kennedy in Vienna on June 3 and 4. Preparations for the extensive test series which the USSR initiated in the fall must have been well underway by the time that the Geneva Conference resumed on March 21. Thus Mr. Tsarapkin's move could be interpreted as designed to block the

62GEN/DNT/PV. 274, p. 14.
63GEN/DNT/PV. 298/Rev. 1, p. 32. See also GEN/DNT/325, p. 21.

negotiations. At the same time, the Soviet Union was profoundly unhappy and disturbed with Secretary General Hammarskjöld's activities in the Congo. Like the Western powers, it too was interested in implications of positions taken in the Geneva Conference for events and institutions elsewhere. Moreover, its fear of giving significant power to a single executive head of a control organization had been manifest throughout the negotiations, and the proposal for an Administrative Council was only a slight modification of its earlier stand on the question of deputy administrators.

The only one of the new Western proposals which the Soviet Union accepted was that relating to the composition of the Control Commission. On April 7, 1961, Mr. Tsarapkin agreed to the total figure of 11 and the 4-4-3 distribution.[64] On the other hand, he continued to insist that the composition of the third third of the staff of control posts had to be specified in the treaty, and that the agreement of the original parties would be necessary for individual sections of the budget as well as for the total figure. He also argued that the contributions of the USSR, the United Kingdom, and the United States would have to be equal.[65] The Western draft treaty provided for equal contributions only from the United States and the USSR. Basically, however, Mr. Tsarapkin paid little attention to the Western proposals.

Despite this rebuff, and the deep impasse on the question of the Administrator, the Western powers sought to keep the negotiations alive, and on August 30, 1961, the United States tabled further compromise proposals. The first of these would have given the Commission the right to dismiss the Administrator.[66] This would have required only the concurring votes of any seven members.

The second proposal related to the composition of on-site inspection teams. In May 1960, the Western Powers had suggested that on-site inspection teams in the USSR should be staffed by Western nationals and vice versa. They had always maintained that host country nationals could not participate, although they were willing to allow the possibility of "one or more" host country observers. Originally the Soviet Union had proposed that on-site inspection

[64]GEN/DNT/PV. 286, p. 8.
[65]*Ibid.*, p. 6.
[66]GEN/DNT/110/Add. 2.

teams should be composed of host country nationals, with one or two controllers from the other side. Subsequently it modified this stand and suggested that on-site inspection teams on the territories of the original parties should be divided equally between nationals of the USSR on the one hand, and nationals of the United Kingdom and the United States on the other. On-site inspection teams on the territories of other parties would be divided into thirds: one third from the USSR, one third from the United Kingdom and the United States, and one third from the host country. The draft treaty of April 18 had continued the previous Western position. Now, however, the United States proposed that in the case of inspections on the territories of the Original Parties, one half of the staff might consist of nationals of uncommitted states, the other half and the leader of the party being nationals of the other side.[67]

These proposals were never discussed. During the evening of the day on which they were presented, the Soviet Union announced its decision to resume testing nuclear weapons, and on November 28, 1961, it tabled a treaty which would rely solely on national detection systems.

V

Conclusions

It is obviously impossible to analyze fully the postures of East and West concerning the proposed Control Organization in isolation from their positions on other issues in the negotiations. One cannot, for example, estimate the significance of the agreements that were achieved without making some assumptions about the broad goals of the three states. Many comments and speculations can therefore best be postponed until a later stage. Some limited conclusions, however, can be drawn at this point.

The negotiations illustrated in detail the differing approaches of the United States, and to a lesser extent of the United Kingdom, on the one hand, and of the Soviet Union on the other, to the question of international organization. The Western position seemed to be dominated by a desire to establish a control organization involving if necessary thousands of personnel, the operations of which

[67]GEN/DNT/110/Add. 3.

could not be blocked by any one party and which would be capable of providing incontestable evidence if a treaty violation occurred. Western policy-makers were haunted by the fear of a situation in which violations were known to be occurring, but could not be proved conclusively. Realizing that the main if not the only sanction in case of a violation would be Western resumption of nuclear testing, they seemed to feel that they could only take such a step if they had incontrovertible evidence of a violation.

Whether or not the Control Organization proposed in the Western draft treaty of April 18, 1961, would have yielded such incontrovertible evidence may be debatable. Some have argued that the Western powers made so many concessions to the Soviet Union and in so doing mixed the "impartial" and the "reciprocal" approaches with the result that, had an Original Party been interested in violating the treaty, it would have had ample opportunity to block the effective functioning of the Control Organization.[68] Nevertheless, there can be no question about the aim of the Western powers.

The Western position implicitly contained several interesting assumptions, which deserve careful examination. First, it assumed that the evidence of a violation would most likely be ambiguous. Given the technical situation as it was understood during this period, all but underground shots of less than 50 kiloton yield or decoupled underground shots of larger yield would have been easily detected by systems independent of the Control Organization and would have been widely recognized as nuclear detonations. Moreover, single shots would have escaped detection easier than a series. Of course, certain categories of shots at high altitudes and in outer space would have been difficult to detect, but since detection in this environment relies almost entirely on mechanical means, this problem was hardly discussed in the negotiations concerning the Control Organization. The Western position therefore assumed that a violator would be interested in the kinds of technological developments that could be gained through testing in the yield ranges and in the environments where detection would be difficult. Whether or not this was a valid assumption is at least subject to question. Certainly when the Soviet

[68]See Fred C. Iklé and others, *Alternative Approaches to the International Organization of Disarmament* (1962), Appendix A, "The Western Proposal for A Nuclear Test Ban: How Would the Control Organization Function," pp. 25-37.

Union broke the moratorium it was equally if not more interested in very high-yield nuclear weapons, the detonation of which could not be concealed.

The Western position also assumed that domestic public opinion within the Western states, and the opinion of the uncommitted states, would be extremely important in determining the conduct of the Western governments. The Western position implied that Western governments would find it extremely difficult to take so serious a step as to denounce a nuclear test ban treaty on the basis of private information. Perhaps this assumption is correct, but it has never been proved. It also minimizes the ability of Western governments to influence and shape their domestic public opinion.

Finally, the Western position was based on the assumption, often explicitly stated, that it would be easier for the Soviet Union to keep clandestine activities secret than it would be for the Western powers. The most interesting aspect of this assumption is that during the period under consideration, because of important technological developments especially in the area of space reconnaissance, it was becoming less and less true.[69]

Apart from these specific policy considerations relating to possible treaty violations, the Western attitude seemed to have been influenced also by the more general philosophy that any progress toward control and reduction of armaments would require an international organization which would assure a degree of "openness" throughout the world and guarantee a measure of restraint on national action.

The Soviet position, on the other hand, was based on extreme reluctance to allow an international organization to be established which might take action over Soviet opposition. The rationale which it advanced most often for this position was that it needed to be in a position to prevent the Western powers from using the organization for espionage. The Western powers always minimized this argument, disavowing espionage aims and pointing out the limited incursions which would be involved. However, Russian regimes have traditionally maintained a tight veil of secrecy, and the Soviet gov-

[69]For an interesting discussion ot some of the techniques involved in this change see Clark C. Apt, "The Problems and Possibilities of Space Arms Control," *Journal of Arms Control,* Vol. I, No. 1 (January 1963), pp. 18-43, at 29-32.

ernment has frequently used or attempted to use secrecy to its military and political advantage.[70] The Soviet fears served to confirm, and in a sense were in accord with, the Western belief that they knew and could know less about the Soviet Union than the Soviet Union did and could know about them. Thus Soviet secrecy became a subject of and a factor in the bargaining.

In addition, Mr. Tsarapkin often asserted that the Western powers might illegitimately use the Control Organization to promote their interests, and averred that past experience in international organizations proved this possibility. Clearly this position was based on a profound distrust of the West and of any international organization in which the West played a major role, and was deeply rooted in the Soviet *Weltanschauung*. The Soviet position is perhaps only understandable in these terms. If one assumes that others are by nature hostile, one obviously cannot allow them to have important powers. Thus, even if the USSR had no intention of breaking the treaty, it might desire to be in position to block any action by the Control Organization. Soviet policy-makers probably also desired to limit their freedom of action as little as possible.

Given the different assumptions, fears, and interests of the three states, it is significant that they achieved as much agreement as they did, even though this agreement was not lasting. It is also significant that they agreed to the broad outlines of such an extensive international organization to perform so modest a function. To many of the participants from both East and West, the Control Organization envisaged in the Geneva Conference seemed to be greatly out of proportion to the limited tasks that it would have been assigned.

[70]For an insightful discussion of Soviet attitudes toward secrecy and arms control agreements, see Alexander Dallin and others, *The Soviet Union, Arms Control, and Disarmament: A Study of Soviet Attitudes* (1964), pp. 142-58.

PART III

THE PATH TO THE MOSCOW TREATY

Chapter X

The Negotiations Resume

I

The Context: Elements of Change and Continuity

Formal negotiations on a nuclear test ban treaty resumed on March 14, 1962, with the opening session of the newly constituted Eighteen-Nation Disarmament Committee, under conditions which were somewhat different from those which had prevailed during the closing days of the Conference on the Discontinuance of Nuclear Weapon Tests. Some of the changes were the result of events which occurred in the month and a half following January 29, the date of the last meeting of the Geneva Conference. Others stemmed from longer-range developments which either were beginning to come to fruition or were perceived during this period.

The Shifting Military Balance: Toward Increased U.S. Power

One of the most important longer-run developments which inevitably would have an effect on the nuclear test ban negotiations was the shifting pattern of military power. Shortly after he became President, John F. Kennedy requested a reappraisal of the entire defense strategy, capacity, commitments, and needs of the United States. On the basis of this reappraisal, and in response to a deteriorating world situation, especially in Southeast Asia, and to a developing crisis over Berlin, on three separate occasions during the spring and summer of 1961, March 28, May 25, and July 25, President Kennedy requested additional appropriations for military purposes. As a result, in August 1961 Congress finally passed a defense appropriation bill totaling $46,662,550,000, a figure which exceeded the original request prepared by the Eisenhower Administration by more than $3,750,000,000. The additional funds, plus certain savings, were allocated both to increasing the United States' strategic power and to enlarging its capacity to deal with limited and guerrilla wars. In addition, in the summer of 1961, in connection with the Berlin crisis, Congress authorized the President to mobilize 250,000 reservists, and the first troops called up under this authority reported for active duty on October 1, 1961. By the end of 1961 the effects of these measures had begun to be felt and the trend of developments was clear. The defense appropriation for fiscal year 1963 was even greater, $48,136,247,000.

In the two years from the end of 1961 to the end of 1963 the United States would double the number of nuclear warheads in its strategic alert forces, and more than double their total megatonnage. The number of American operational long-range missiles would jump from forty-five to five hundred. The United States would increase its combat-ready Army divisions by about forty-five percent, from eleven to sixteen; the number of its tactical air squadrons by thirty percent; and its airlift capacity by seventy-five percent. Ship construction and conversion to modernize the fleet would be doubled.[1]

Of course these moves to increase United States power did not pass unnoticed by the USSR. On July 9, 1961, Chairman Khrushchev announced that the Soviet Defense Ministry had been instructed temporarily to suspend the reduction of the armed forces planned for 1961, and that the Soviet Government had decided to increase defense spending in 1961 by 3,144,000,000 rubles, making the total 12,399,000,000. The arms race had been stepped up considerably, and the USSR was determined to create the impression that it would match or surpass the United States' military build-up. However, when the test ban negotiations resumed in March 1962 it was far from certain whether or not the Soviet Union could maintain the pace set by the United States. By that time it was apparent that instead of the USSR's having many more operational missiles than

---

[1]These figures are taken from a speech delivered by Secretary of Defense McNamara before the Economic Club of New York on November 18, 1963. See "Major National Security Problems Confronting the United States," the Department of State *Bulletin,* Vol. XLIX, No. 1277 (December 16, 1963), pp. 914-21. They are substantially confirmed by the analyses prepared by the Institute of Strategic Studies. See *The Communist Bloc and the Western Alliances: The Military Balance, 1961–1962*; (London: Institute of Strategic Studies, 1961); and *The Military Balance, 1963–1964* (London: Institute of Strategic Studies, 1963).

the United States, as several in the West had predicted and feared, the balance was about even. By the end of 1963 the USSR would have only about one-fifth as many long-range missiles as the United States, and only about half as many long-range bombers. The USSR would have quantitative superiority vis-à-vis the United States only in intermediate and medium-range ballistic missiles and in ground forces. Moreover, the USSR's margin of superiority would disapear if the comparison were broadened to include all NATO forces on one side and all Warsaw Pact forces on the other. The ground forces of NATO would total 3,200,000, while those of the Warsaw Pact would total only 3,000,000. NATO would have more ground forces in Central Europe than the Warsaw Pact.

The test ban negotiations would resume then in the midst of a quickening arms race from which the United States would emerge within a relatively short time with an unquestioned net military superiority, although each side would still be able to wreck horrendous damage on the other.

Exactly how this change in the distribution of military power would affect the test ban negotiations could not be foretold. Some American policy-makers predicted a favorable impact. They argued that since the USSR respected strength, the increased American military power should result in increased Soviet propensity to make concessions. They also argued that the Soviet Union would feel the costs of a spiraling arms race more than the United States, and therefore would be more desirous of ending such a race and thus more interested in a nuclear test ban. Other policy-makers, among them Jerome B. Wiesner, maintained that the American military build-up would have exactly the opposite effect, that it would make the USSR more intransigent and decrease the chances of obtaining a nuclear test ban.

The Results of the USSR's 1961 Tests: Superiority in High-Yield Weapons

A second element in the changing context was the new situation with respect to the development of nuclear weapons, resulting from the USSR's surprise abrogation in August 1961 of the nearly three-year-old moratorium on nuclear testing. The test series which the USSR began then was elaborate and extensive. Approximately fifty tests were conducted within three months. Some of these apparently related to the development of an anti-intercontinental ballistic missile. On October 30, 1961, the USSR tested a 58 megaton bomb, the largest weapon ever detonated. Furthermore, had the fusion material comprising the core of the weapon been encased in a uranium rather than a lead jacket, it is estimated that its yield would have been 100 megatons or more. Several of the other Soviet tests had yields of more than 10 megatons. As a result of these tests, the USSR became technically more advanced than the United States in the high-yield range. The Soviet Union's superior position related both to the construction of such weapons and to understanding their effects.

The largest weapon which the United States had ever tested was the 1954 15 megaton Bravo shot. General Curtis E. LeMay, as Commander in Chief of the United States Strategic Air Command, and the Air Force had recommended in that same year that the United States should develop a 50 to 100 megaton yield weapon, but this recommendation had not been accepted. The Eisenhower Administration consciously chose not to pursue this development because it felt that there was no military requirement for such high-yield weapons.

As in the past, the results of the Soviet test series were evaluated by several United States governmental groups, including a panel of scientists headed by Hans A. Bethe. In a statement published in September 1962, Professor Bethe asserted that the kinds of weapons which the USSR tested showed "that their laboratories had probably been working full speed during the whole moratorium on the assumption that tests would at some time be resumed," and that "it is very likely that they started specific preparations by March 1961 when the test ban conference reconvened in Geneva."[2] As early as January 5, 1962, Professor Bethe stated in a public lecture in Ithaca, that in his opinion a test ban as such was "no longer a desirable goal to pursue."[3] Although he was not concerned about high-yield weapons and the effects of the USSR's superiority in this area, he felt that the United States should test those designs which

[2]Hans A. Bethe, "Disarmament and Strategy," *Bulletin of the Atomic Scientists,* Vol. XVIII, No. 7 (September 1962), pp. 14-22, at 18.
[3]Representative Robert W. Kastenmeier inserted the text of his speech in the *Congressional Record,* Vol. CVIII, Appendix, pp. A1397-99, A1450-51, at A1450.

had been developed in its laboratories and which fitted its strategic needs. On the other hand, he also thought that both sides had relatively little more to learn about nuclear weapons.

In public at least, Professor Bethe did not say, as he very well could have, that what he had predicted might happen had in fact occurred. In 1958, in arguing for test ban negotiations, he had warned that the only result of continued testing of nuclear weapons would be to diminish the American superiority over the USSR in this category of military technology.

Again, the effects of this new situation on the nuclear test ban negotiations could not be foretold. Since the USSR now held a definite lead in certain areas of nuclear weapons development, one might have expected that it would try to freeze the situation to preserve this lead, following the course which Professor Bethe had urged for the United States in 1958. Conversely, one might have expected that the United States would seek to recoup its lead, to redress the balance, or to minimize the gap between its stage of development and that of the USSR.

The Debate Within the United States: To Test or Not to Test in the Atmosphere

Indeed, the most pressing issue posed by the Soviet test series for the United States was whether or not it should resume atmospheric testing. When President Kennedy ordered the resumption of nuclear tests on September 5, 1961, he confined his authorization to tests which could be conducted in the laboratory and underground. Actually, this was all that the United States was prepared to do. The grounds at Eniwetok and Bikini had been allowed to run down, and in view of their location within the Trust Territory of the Pacific Islands, there was some question about the political wisdom of using them again. Certainly there would be an outcry in the United Nations if they were used. There appears to have been little preparation in the United States' weapons laboratories during the moratorium for resumed atmospheric testing. Moreover, the skills and morale of the laboratories appear to have deteriorated to some extent during this period.[4] Even with respect to underground testing, which had

[4]See the testimony of Dr. John Foster, Jr., Director of the Lawrence Radiation Laboratory, University of California, Livermore, California, and of Dr. Norris E. Bradbury, Director, Los Alamos Scientific Laboratory:

been regarded as a more likely contingency during the moratorium, American preparations were not extensive. For example, very few holes had been prepared. As a consequence of all of these factors, the United States conducted only nine underground nuclear explosions in 1961.

Pressure for the United States to engage in an extensive test series and to test in the atmosphere began to mount immediately after the Soviet Union broke the moratorium, and it increased in intensity as the extensive nature of the Soviet test series became apparent. As early as November 2, 1961, President Kennedy announced that preparations would be made for atmospheric tests so that they could be undertaken should it be deemed necessary.[5] And in the late fall of 1961 a special task force was formed under the command of Major General Alfred D. Starbird to prepare for tests in the atmosphere and at high altitudes, and $80,000,000 was allocated for this purpose. Ultimately the task force would include 11,800 individuals. However, President Kennedy made it clear to the Pentagon that these preparations did not commit him actually to conduct a testing program.[6]

The President and Prime Minister Macmillan discussed these matters at their meeting in Bermuda in late December. British concurrence with an American decision to resume atmospheric testing would be helpful, and if the United States could use the facilities at Christmas Island, a British possession in the Pacific, as well perhaps as those at Johnston Island, an American possession, it would obviate the necessity of again testing in the United States Trust Territory. Macmillan made an eloquent plea for one more effort to break the cycle of tests and counter-tests.[6a] He had a deep horror

---

U.S. Congress, Senate, Committee on Armed Services, Preparedness Investigating Subcommittee, *Hearings: Military Aspects and Implications of Nuclear Test Ban Proposals and Related Matters*, 88th Congress, 1st Session (1964), pp. 395-96, 405. See also *New York Times*, September 26, 1963, p. 11. A popular account gives a somewhat more optimistic appraisal: George Harris, "How Livermore Survived the Test Ban," *Fortune*, Vol. LXV, No. 4 (April 1960), pp. 127, 236, 241.

[5]U.S. Arms Control and Disarmament Agency, *Documents on Disarmament, 1961* (1962), p. 567.

[6]Theodore C. Sorenson, *Kennedy*, p. 621.

[6a]See the account of the Bermuda meeting in Arthur M. Schlesinger, Jr., *A Thousand Days*, pp. 489-90.

of nuclear war and was determined to press for a test ban. He had thought that a treaty could have been achieved in 1960 and was sharply disappointed that it had not been. He had told Kennedy that the failure "was all the fault of the American 'big hole' obsession and the consequent insistence on a wantonly large number of on-site inspections."[6b] Eventually though, the Prime Minister seemed to agree that if the situation did not change he would recommend to the Cabinet that permission be given for the United States to utilize the facilities at Christmas Island. On December 22, 1961 the two leaders issued a communique which paralleled Kennedy's announcement of November 2.[6c]

President Kennedy did not announce a final decision to resume atmospheric testing until March 2, 1962. Meanwhile, a bitter debate raged within the American Administration, and the British continued to play a role in this debate, via letters to the President from Macmillan and other means. The debate concerned not only whether or not to resume atmospheric testing, but also, if such a decision were taken, the number and yield of the weapons to be tested. The division within the government paralleled many of those which had previously existed concerning issues involving the nuclear ban negotiations. Those opposed to the resumption of testing included Dr. Jerome B. Wiesner, Special Assistant to the President for Science and Technology; Adlai E. Stevenson, chief United States delegate to the United Nations; the Department of State; and the United States Information Agency. The Joint Chiefs of Staff favored the resumption of testing. As early as October, they had called for a resumption of atmospheric testing in November. The Department of Defense took a similar position. It was Secretary McNamara who had asked the President to authorize development and effect tests in the atmosphere. Still, at a lunch with Secretary Rusk and McGeorge Bundy shortly before the actual tests began, he suggested "that they were not really necessary."[6d] The Atomic Energy Commission argued for atmospheric testing, but it felt that there should be limitations on the types of tests. Several powerful members of the Joint Committee on Atomic Energy also favored the resumption of atmospheric testing. As

[6b]*Ibid.*, p. 452.

[6c]U.S. Arms Control and Disarmament Agency, *Documents on Disarmament, 1961* (1962), p. 743.

[6d]Theodore C. Sorenson, *Kennedy*, p. 622.

in the past, this intra-governmental argument both spilled over into and reflected a similar debate within the public arena. And also as in the past, the American scientific community was deeply divided.

Those favoring the resumption of atmospheric testing argued that such action was necessary because of the advances which the Soviet Union had made. Starting from this common ground the argumentation advanced by those on this side differed with the sophistication, background, and interests of the advocate. Perhaps Edward Teller developed the most elaborate rationale. He set forth his views in a book, *The Legacy of Hiroshima,* which was published on March 2, 1962.[7] Excerpts from this book were published as three serial articles in the *Saturday Evening Post,* starting February 3, 1962. Professor Teller argued that the problem of radioactive fallout "was not worth worrying about,"[8] and that because of the difficulty of policing underground tests, a nuclear test ban was a chimera. He maintained that further nuclear experiments were essential to United States's security in several ways. The most important reason, he felt, was so that the weight of nuclear warheads could be reduced in order to make the total weapons system more mobile and effective. This was necessary, in his view, to insure that the American retaliatory force could survive an enemy attack. In addition, he held out the possibility of a fission-free weapon.

Those on the other side of the argument took a much more serious view of the harm caused by the radioactive fallout resulting from nuclear weapons tests. There was little divergence between the scientific analysis of the issue by this group and that of those who minimized the problem of radioactive fallout; the difference between the two groups was in their moral evaluation of the consequences of fallout for mankind. President Kennedy himself was deeply troubled about the problem of fallout.[8a] The group opposing the resumption of atmospheric testing also raised broader moral arguments against the resumption of atmospheric tests. In general, they were more concerned about the widespread public opposition to nuclear testing both within the United States and abroad and the effects of the expression of this

[7]Edward Teller & Allen Brown, *The Legacy of Hiroshima* (1962).
[8]*Ibid.,* p. 180.
[8a]See Arthur M. Schlesinger, Jr., *A Thousand Days,* p. 455, and Theodore C. Sorenson, *Kennedy,* pp. 621-22.

opposition in such forums as the United Nations. They feared that if the United States were to resume atmospheric testing, increased tension would result and that this would diminish the prospects for achieving measures of arms control and disarmament, measures which they considered vital. So far as the military argument was concerned, they felt that the United States had sufficient nuclear weapons to devastate the Soviet Union, and that this was all that was required.

They were sceptical of the need for further testing and felt that only marginal advantages would be gained. President Kennedy shared this appraisal, and according to one of his closest advisers, "talk about a neutron bomb which destroyed only people, not buildings, struck him as foolish in the extreme."[8b]

Eventually, despite a final and moving plea by Prime Minister Macmillan, who even proposed convening a summit meeting, the advocates of the resumption of atmospheric tests carried the day. Apparently a clinching argument was one which William C. Foster, Director of the United States Arms Control and Disarmament Agency articulated privately and in public. This was that the United States could not afford to allow the Soviet Union to engage in another test series without having itself tested; that in such circumstances a second test series might give the USSR an important advantage. He felt that if these conditions were to develop it would be difficult for the United States to continue to negotiate for a test ban treaty, among other reasons because it would be unlikely that the Senate would consent to ratification.[9] The President found the argument persuasive.

At his Press Conference on February 7, 1962, President Kennedy stated that a final decision on whether or not the United States would resume atmospheric testing would be taken within a month. The following day the White House issued a statement concerning the British decision to allow the United States government to use its facilities at Christmas Island if atmospheric testing were resumed.

Finally, on Friday, March 2, 1962, in a special radio-television broadcast President Kennedy announced that he had that day authorized the Atomic Energy Commission and the Department of Defense to conduct a series of nuclear tests in the atmosphere as

[8b]Theodore C. Sorenson, *Kennedy,* p. 621.
[9]See his letter to *Washington Post,* February 10, 1962.

soon as preparations were completed, which would be sometime in April.[10] Kennedy had originally planned to give his talk on March 1, but he agreed to postpone it for twenty-four hours in response to Prime Minister Macmillan's request for further delay.[10a] By March 2 the House of Commons would be recessed for the weekend. Although the President did not announce this, the test series would also include some high altitude shots. President Kennedy said that his decision was based on the unanimous recommendation of pertinent Department and Agency heads.

This unanimity had been achieved by way of a compromise. Although the President authorized the resumption of atmospheric tests, he ordered that the series should be limited only to those tests which were absolutely necessary and could not be conducted underground, and that they should be conducted so as to restrict radioactive fallout to the minimum. Partly for these reasons, no high-yield tests were planned; the 1954 15 megaton Bravo shot would stand as the largest ever detonated by the United States. Another factor responsible for this was the continuing view of the Administration that there were no over-riding military requirements for such high-yield weapons. Moreover, because of this reason, and because they had anticipated being able to conduct only underground tests which necessarily would be relatively small, American nuclear scientists had not prepared any designs for high-yield weapons. During the actual test series, the President kept careful control to make certain that his directives were executed.

Another element of the compromise in the recommendation which President Kennedy accepted was the caveat that the decision to resume atmospheric tests would not be executed if the Soviet Union would in the meantime agree to a nuclear test ban treaty. This last feature was designed to satisfy Prime Minister Macmillan as well as elements within the American Administration. Apparently the actual proposal came first from Arthur M. Schlesinger, Jr., a former Harvard history professor serving as Special Assistant to the President.[10b] Hugh Gaitskell, the leader of the British Labour Party, also

[10]See U.S. Arms Control and Disarmament Agency, Publication 19, *Documents on Disarmament, 1962,* 2 vols. (1963), Vol. I, pp. 66-75.

[10a]Arthur M. Schlesinger, Jr., *A Thousand Days,* p. 495, and Theodore C. Sorenson, *Kennedy,* p. 623.

[10b]Arthur M. Schlesinger, Jr., *A Thousand Days,* pp. 491-92.

made a similar suggestion to Kennedy. Some within the American Administration, including Assistant Secretary of Defense John J. McNaughton, had argued that the offer be made conditional on Soviet acceptance of an atmospheric ban, policed by national detection systems, and such a proposal had even been included in an early draft of the President's 1962 State of the Union message. However, the Departments of Defense and State had objected, and when the offer not to resume atmospheric tests was finally made, they insisted that it be tied to a comprehensive ban.

The President's address was notable for its quality of reluctance and of being forced by Soviet actions into an unpalatable situation. He gave a candid appraisal of the results of the recent Soviet test series—as the United States understood them—and the course of the nuclear test ban negotiations. He found the primary reasons for the United States' decision in these events. However, he also asserted that if the United States were to refrain from atmospheric testing, the leaders of the Soviet Union would

> . . . chalk it up, not to goodwill, but to a failure of will—not to our confidence in Western superiority, but to our fear of world opinion, the very world opinion for which they showed such contempt.

He continued this line of argumentation by asserting that the Soviet Union would never agree to a "true test ban or mutual disarmament" if the West were in a position of weakness.

The Summit Correspondence: A Western Preemptive Gambit

During the same time that consensus was being achieved within the American government on resuming atmospheric testing, there was a flurry of correspondence between Western and Soviet leaders. It was inaugurated on February 7, 1962, by a letter from President Kennedy and Prime Minister Macmillan to Chairman Khrushchev in which they proposed that to facilitate progress on disarmament the three governments should be represented at the opening of the Eighteen-Nation Disarmament Committee by their Foreign Ministers, and that the Foreign Ministers should express their willingness to return to the negotiations as progress achieved by the permanent representatives warranted.[11] One of the reasons for this proposal

[11]*Documents on Disarmament, 1962, supra* note 10, Vol. I, pp. 25-26.

was to forestall a suggestion, which the two Western leaders knew Chairman Khrushchev would make, that the member states of the Eighteen-Nation Committee on Disarmament should be represented by their heads of government or chiefs of state. Macmillan originally would have been willing to accept this proposal. Indeed, he had made a similar suggestion to Kennedy in early January. Obviously, however, if such a course were to be chosen, Chairman Khrushchev would have an excellent platform from which, among other things, to denounce the Western resumption of atmospheric tests, if this decision were taken, and at that point it seemed likely that it would be. The proposal of the Western leaders reflected their continuing sensitivity to public opinion. Although their preemptive move did not prevent Chairman Khrushchev from making his proposal, it made it easier for the Western leaders to refuse his suggestion.

In all, there were three exchanges of correspondence.[12] It was not until his final letter of March 3, 1962, to President Kennedy that Chairman Khrushchev abandoned his proposal that heads of state represent their governments and accepted the Western suggestion that Foreign Ministers do this. In this letter, which was dated the same day that President Kennedy announced the United States decision to resume atmospheric testing, Chairman Khrushchev also condemned this decision, and asserted that if it were executed, the USSR would "inevitably be forced to meet this challenge too by carrying out its own series of new tests."[13] In the course of his letter he pointed out that the United States had been the first to test and to use nuclear weapons and that the West had conducted many more tests over the years than the USSR. He then asserted the right of the Soviet Union to "be the last side to complete nuclear weapons tests."

When the formal negotiations for a nuclear test ban reopened, both sides would therefore be more or less committed to another round of tests. And since each side declared that its move was a reaction to the actions of the other, it appeared as if they were engaged in an endless spiral.

At the same time that he aired his suggestion for representation by heads of states with President Kennedy and Prime Minister

[12]See *Ibid.* pp. 25-26, 32-36, 36-38, 49-57, 61-63, 64-66, and 75-81.
[13]*Ibid.,* p. 80.

Macmillan, Chairman Khrushchev also raised it in an exchange of correspondence with General de Gaulle.[14] This not only elicited the negative reaction that it had produced in the other Western capitals, but also the clear statement that France would not participate in the Eighteen-Nation Disarmament Committee because disarmament was a matter which the French felt should be handled exclusively by the nuclear or near nuclear powers.[15] France also reiterated its determination to proceed with its program to develop an independent nuclear capacity unless and until the nuclear powers agreed to ban the manufacture of nuclear weapons and to destroy those in existence.

The Detection of Underground Tests: Continuing Ambivalence

While these developments, and especially the imminent round of tests, cast a shadow over the resumption of negotiations for a test ban, there were also some apparently favorable occurrences that came to public attention during the recess in the negotiations. These related to the detection of underground nuclear explosions. On December 10, 1961, as a part of its Project Plowshare, exploring the peaceful uses of atomic energy, the United States detonated a 5 kiloton nuclear device near Carlsbad, New Mexico, in a salt cavern 1,200 feet beneath the surface of the earth. This detonation, which was named Project Gnome, was not a decoupled shot.[16] However, on the basis of the Project Cowboy experiments, it had been estimated that a tamped shot (one where the device is tightly packed in the surrounding medium) in salt, which was what the Gnome shot was, would give a seismic signal smaller by a factor of two and one-half than the seismic signal of a shot tamped in tuff, which is what all of the previous United States detonations had been. Contrary to this prediction, the Gnome shot gave a signal several times greater than Logan, the 5 kiloton tamped-in-tuff shot detonated on October 16, 1958. The Logan shot, it will be recalled, had been one of the principal sources of information for the United States'

---

[14]*Ibid.,* pp. 64-66.

[15]See de Gaulle's letter and the statement of the French Ministry of Foreign Affairs: *ibid.,* pp. 48-49, p. 81.

[16]See A. Latter, R. Latter, and W. McMillan, *The Irrelevance of the Gnome Shot to Decoupling* (The RAND Corp., 1962: Memorandum RM-3005-PR).

reevaluation of the effectiveness of the control system suggested by the Conference of Experts. By mid-December 1961, it became known that the Gnome shot had been detected at stations as far away as Sweden, Finland, and Japan.[17] In itself, this was an encouraging development, and many exaggerated its significance by assuming that the evidence disproved the decoupling theory, which in fact, it did not. The reason for this erroneous interpretation apparently was that much of the discussion concerning decoupling was framed in terms of nuclear shots conducted in large underground cavities in salt. The test did, however, indicate something about the effects of various media on the transmission of seismic signals from underground nuclear explosions; to wit, a shot tamped in salt would yield a larger signal than one of identical yield tamped in tuff.

The Gnome shot also produced some rather discouraging data, but this aspect was much less widely known and publicized. The Gnome shot made it quite apparent that because of unknown anomalies, seismic signals did not travel through the crust of the earth at uniform speeds, and, as a consequence, it was much more difficult to estimate accurately the epicenter of seismic events from distant seismic stations than had been assumed. This would greatly complicate the problem of on-site inspection of unidentified events. In fact, American scientists discovered that, applying the then current American negotiating position, the actual site of the Gnome shot would have been outside of the area which they would have picked as being legally open to on-site inspection. Moreover, on the basis of the seismic signals they estimated the depth of the shot as 80 miles rather than the actual 1,200 feet. Had they not known the actual facts, they would have concluded that the signals must have been generated by an earthquake rather than an explosion, since no one thought that explosions could be conducted that deep.[18] The reason that distant stations did not reach this conclusion was that the time, location, and yield of the shot had been announced in advance. These somewhat more technical qualifications, however, were overlooked in the public debate.

A second development which sparked public optimism concerning the problem of detecting underground explosions was that

[17]See *New York Times,* December 19, 1961, p. 1.
[18]Earl H. Voss, *Nuclear Ambush,* p. 492.

on February 2, 1962, the Atomic Energy Commission announced that the Soviet Union had apparently set off an underground nuclear explosion earlier that day.[19] So far as was publicly known in the West, this was the first time that the USSR had detonated a nuclear device underground. The announcement stated only that "the yield was well above the threshold of detectability." This vague statement allowed various interpretations. Some experts commented that this meant more than 20 kilotons, but other interpretations were possible. Only later did the United States point out that the Soviet test took place in a normally aseismic area in Central Siberia, near to a fairly well-known weapons proving ground and apparently had a yield of from 40 to 50 kilotons. Had all of these facts been publicized, no one would have doubted that it could have been detected.

The Progress of the Vela Program: Toward a Worldwide Seismological Network

Actually, at this point American scientists felt that the state of technology with respect to the detection of underground nuclear explosions had improved very little. The United States Vela Program had not yet produced significant results, although it had inaugurated a vast number of projects. During fiscal years 1960 and 1961, $51,438,000 had been appropriated for the project, and the estimated budget for fiscal year 1962 was $59,0000,000. The research inaugurated under the Vela Program was both basic and applied. As a consequence, among other results, the Vela Program would have an enormous leavening effect on the science of seismology.

Under one aspect of the program the United States Coast and Geodetic Survey undertook to construct a worldwide seismological network. It offered to supply modern calibrated and standardized instrumentation to seismological stations throughout the world, the only conditions being that copies of the records be made available to the Coast and Geodetic Survey. The program envisaged supplying instrumentation for 125 stations, most of which would be outside of the United States. Some of these stations were to be operated by governments, others by private groups, such as universities. Three million, three hundred and seventy-five thousand dollars was pro-

[19]See *New York Times,* February 3, 1962, p. 1.

vided for this purpose in fiscal years 1960 and 1961, and $1,175,000 was budgeted for fiscal year 1962. Although Vela Program officials went out of their way to assert that the purpose of this worldwide network was not to detect nuclear explosions in the Soviet Union, but rather to collect earthquake statistics, obviously within the relevant technological limitations, the stations would record all underground seismic events, including nuclear explosions. Data from the initial elements of this worldwide network would become available in quantity in the spring and summer of 1962.

Another part of the Vela Program envisaged the construction of seven seismological stations in the United States designed explicitly to detect nuclear explosions in the Soviet Union, and an analysis center, resembling in some ways the center which, according to American plans, would be established at the headquarters of the control system in Vienna. The first of the seismological stations, a prototype of the stations recommended by the Geneva Conference of Experts, was constructed at Fort Sill, Oklahoma, and became operational in October 1960. As early as July 1961 it was reported that this station appeared to be capable of detecting most seismic events of down to magnitude 4 at distances of 2,000 miles and more. At that time, American scientists thought that this meant that with this station they could locate events as small as about 1 kiloton from distances greater than 2,000 miles, but they could not begin to identify such events until they began to approach 5 kilotons.[20] Nonetheless, the capabilities of the station exceeded American expectations. The reason for this was the demonstration of the possibility of detection and identification of seismic events in what is called the "third zone"; that is, the zone at very large distances beyond "the shadow" or second zone in which detection is very difficult. Eventually the possibility would be completely substantiated. Three more seismological stations would become operational during 1962, and a fifth in April 1963. These stations would have the equipment recommended by the Conference of Experts, and would also incorporate improvements in seismological techniques developed

[20]See the testimony of Dr. Carl Romney, Assistant Director, Air Force Technical Applications Center: U.S. Congress, Joint Committee on Atomic Energy, *Hearings: Developments in the Field of Detection and Identification of Nuclear Explosions (Project Vela) and Relationship to Test Ban Negotiations,* 87th Congress, 1st Session (1962), pp. 123-24.

since that time. These improvements were also subsequently added to the Fort Sill Station.

Research with respect to decoupling proved to be the slowest in getting underway. The so-called Dribble experimental program to test the theory of decoupling was established by the Atomic Energy Commission in early 1960. The program envisaged a series of six events, involving both tamped and decoupled shots. In early 1962, because of lack of funds, the program had to be suspended. At that point only certain exploratory drilling and engineering work had been completed. When the program was resumed in September 1962, then being supported by the Department of Defense, the earliest possible date for a decoupled shot would be June 1963. Construction for the first cavity for the Dribble series, a cavity which would accommodate a 100 ton detonation, would ultimately cost $3,200,000 and would require almost a year.[21] By mid-1964 more than that had been spent and construction had not yet started for this cavity. As of September 1965 a nuclear decoupled shot had not yet been fired.

Much of the work conducted under the Vela Program operated under one basic constraint. It was generally felt that it would be impossible to achieve more access to the Soviet Union than would be allowed under the control system which had been recommended in the report of the Conference of Experts. Thus the research was always designed to find improvements which might be applied within the framework of that system, rather than those which might require a major political reorientation. At least some scientists felt that this constraint was a major handicap.[22]

Another constraint—perhaps felt more universally among the scientists participating in the program—was the prohibition prior to September 1961 on conducting any further underground nuclear explosions. This meant that all of the directly relevant work had to be done on the basis of theoretical calculations, and on the basis of the scanty empirical data gathered prior to 1959. When the

[21]See U.S. Congress, Joint Committee on Atomic Energy, *Hearings: Developments in Technical Capabilities for Detecting and Identifying Nuclear Weapons Tests*, 88th Congress, 1st Session (1963), p. 312.

[22]See the testimony of Dr. Richard Latter, *Hearings: Developments in the Field of Detection and Identification of Nuclear Explosions, supra* note 20, p. 19.

United States resumed underground testing in the fall of 1961, after the Soviet abrogation of the moratorium, this situation changed radically. The United States conducted nine underground tests in the fall of 1961. By mid-1962 this total would be increased to forty-three. Thus a relatively vast amount of new empirical data would become available simultaneously with improved instrumentation at seismological stations throughout the world. Theoretical enquiries launched under Vela were also beginning to bear fruit at about this time.

II
The Eighteen-Nation Disarmament Committee: A New Forum

The Composition of the Committee: Enter the New Eight
All of these factors came into play when the formal negotiations on a nuclear test ban resumed on March 11, 1962, with the opening session of the Eighteen-Nation Disarmament Committee (ENDC). This Committee had been created as a result of bilateral talks between the United States and the Soviet Union in the summer and fall of 1961, and its composition had been endorsed in General Assembly Resolution 1722 (XVI). In the same resolution, the Assembly requested that the Eighteen-Nation Committee should report to it, and directed the Secretary General to facilitate the Committee's work by supplying the necessary services. The Eighteen-Nation Committee therefore met, as the Conference on the Discontinuance of Nuclear Weapon Tests had previously, in the *Palais des Nations,* in Geneva. By virtue of Assembly Resolution 1722 (XVI), however, the Eighteen-Nation Committee had a somewhat more definite link with the United Nations than the previous conference, and this was underscored during the subsequent negotiations.

Reaching agreement on the composition of the Eighteen-Nation Committee had been the most difficult aspect of the bilateral negotiations. Negotiations on this point were complicated not only because of differences between the USSR and the United States, but also because of controversies among the other members of the United Nations who wished or did not wish to serve on the Committee. In the end, what was agreed to was an expansion of the old Ten-Nation Disarmament Committee, by adding eight countries belonging neither to the North Atlantic Treaty Organization nor to the Warsaw Pact. The Ten-Nation Committee had consisted of Canada, France, Italy, the United Kingdom, and the United States on one side and Bulgaria, Czechoslovakia, Poland, Rumania, and the USSR on the other. The eight states which were added to make the new Committee were: Brazil, Burma, Ethiopia, India, Mexico, Nigeria, Sweden, and the United Arab Republic.

The question of expanding the membership of the Ten-Nation Committee had actually been under consideration almost since the collapse of the negotiations on general disarmament in the summer of 1960, when the five Communist states withdrew from the Committee.[23] As early as September 1960, Chairman Khrushchev, acting as the head of the Soviet Union's delegation to the United Nations, had suggested that the Committee should be enlarged by adding: Ghana, India, Indonesia, Mexico, and the United Arab Republic.[24] The Western powers rejected this suggestion, principally because adding five nonaligned nations would give the appearance of accepting the Soviet "troika" concept. The following year, however, in bilateral discussions with the USSR in June and July, the United States proposed as alternatives adding either a chairman and two vice-chairmen or ten new members. In either case the new members would be chosen from the group of UN Member States that did not belong to NATO or the Warsaw Pact. The Soviet Union responded by repeating its suggestion of a fifteen-member committee.

These moves to expand the Ten-Nation Committee were given added impetus in September 1961 when the Conference of Heads of State and Government of Nonaligned Countries meeting in Belgrade recommended that the nonaligned states should be represented in all disarmament talks.[25] The final agreement on the composition of the new Committee was not achieved, however, until December 1961.

The figure of eighteen and the specific countries named were

[23]For an account of the collapse of the negotiations within the Ten-Nation Committee see Bernhard G. Bechhoefer, *Postwar Negotiations for Arms Control,* pp. 551-52.
[24]UN Document A/4509.
[25]See the declaration and communique, *Documents on Disarmament, 1961, supra* note 5, pp. 374-83, at 381.

both clearly compromises. Since the membership of the new Committee could not be divided into equal thirds, the West felt that it had avoided creating a precedent in favor of the "troika" principle. On the other hand, the Committee did consist of the three groups which figured in that principle. The eight new members of the Committee included three of the five originally suggested by Chairman Khrushchev: India, Mexico, and the United Arab Republic. They also included one European state, Sweden, following a United States suggestion. As the United States insisted, Latin America was given more representation than it had in the original Soviet proposal in that Brazil was added, along with Mexico, which had figured in the Soviet suggestion. Burma, Ethiopia, and Nigeria comprised the final element of the compromise. They were less anti-Western than Indonesia and Ghana, the other two states originally proposed by the USSR.

The composition of the Eighteen-Nation Disarmament Committee meant, among other things, that when the test ban negotiations were resumed within the framework of the Committee, for the first time states would be intimately involved which did not possess nuclear weapons themselves and which were not aligned with any of the nuclear powers. This experience would be quite different from the fleeting exposure of the annual General Assembly debates. Conceivably it could have an impact both on the policies of these states—for it could be a significant learning experience—and on the course of the negotiations.

The Views of the New Members

Significantly, all of the eight countries which were added to the Committee had voted for General Assembly Resolution 1648 (XVI) urging the states concerned to refrain from further nuclear weapons tests pending the conclusion of an international agreement banning such tests. All five members of the Warsaw Pact represented on the Eighteen-Nation Committee had voted against this resolution, as had France, Italy, the United Kingdom, and the United States. Canada, in contrast, had voted for the resolution, and during the sessions of the Eighteen-Nation Committee in 1962 and early 1963 it often took a position closer to that of the eight new members than to that of its NATO partners.[26] Since France boycotted the Eighteen-Nation Committee, this meant that NATO representation was effectively reduced to three. On the other hand, the five members of the Warsaw Pact acted as a solid unit.

Consisting of two states each from Latin America and Asia, three from Africa, and one from the neutral states of Europe, the eight new members of the committee roughly reflected the membership of the United Nations exclusive of those states belonging to NATO and the Warsaw Pact. Although this was never explicitly stated, it was widely assumed, both within the Eighteen-Nation Committee and in the United Nations, that the eight would represent this broad group of the UN's membership. In any case, by the nature of the situation, by their own inclination, and by the actions of East and West, the eight would introduce a new and independent element into the negotiations, and they would become, as it were, critics of the positions advanced by the two sides.[27] Beyond that, they could also obviously perform the range of functions traditionally performed by third parties in pacific settlement.

Of the eight, Sweden was the only state to have technical advisers continuously attached to its delegation. It was the most advanced state of the new members in terms of technological development and the only one which had figured in the various projections of possible nuclear powers in the foreseeable future. Whether or not Sweden should seek to acquire nuclear capability had been a matter of political discussion within the country. Throughout the negotiations on a nuclear test ban the Swedish delegation included two technical advisers. It also included military advisers. One of the technical advisers was a specialist in the mechanical effects of nuclear explosions, the other was a specialist in nuclear chemistry. Both of them were research organizers in

[26]In his account of the Eighteen-Nation Committee, the former Indian representative has noted that Canada "is jokingly referred to at Geneva as the ninth nonaligned country." (Arthur S. Lall, *Negotiating Disarmament: The Eighteen-Nation Disarmament Conference: The First Two Years, 1962–1964* (1964), p. 12.) Sir Michael Wright expressed the same view when he wrote that some of the moves which the Diefenbaker government made in the nuclear field served only to cause "embarrassment to Canadian delegates, disarray within the North Atlantic Treaty Organization in their negotiations with others, and irritation in Washington." (*Disarm and Verify,* p. 132).

[27]See the interesting self-analysis of the role of the eight by a representative of one of the states, M. Samir Ahmed, "The Role of the Neutrals in the Geneva Negotiations," *Disarmament and Arms Control,* Vol. I, No. 2 (Summer 1963), pp. 20-32.

their own fields for the Defense Research Organization in Stockholm. In addition, the Swedish delegation relied heavily on advice from the seismological station at Uppsala University. Because of its technical competence, the Swedish delegation played a special role among the eight new members of the Disarmament Committee. It should perhaps also be noted that one of the Swedish specialists on disarmament, Colonel Stig Wennerström, who worked in Stockholm, was arrested in June 1963 on a charge of spying for the Soviet Union and was subsequently convicted.

Several of the delegations of the other new members included diplomats who had had considerable experience in the United Nations, and even some who had participated in past disarmament negotiations. Ambassador Luis Padilla Nervo of Mexico was the delegate who had had the most experience of this nature. He had also been President of the General Assembly. James Barrington of Burma was another diplomat who had represented his country in the United Nations for several years, as had Arthur S. Lall of India.

The Opening of the Eighteen-Nation Committee

For the first few days of the meetings of the Eighteen-Nation Disarmament Committee, because of the acceptance of the Western proposal, most of the states were represented at the Ministerial level. In all instances but one, this meant that the delegation was temporarily headed by the foreign minister. The Indian delegation, however, was headed by V. K. Krishna Menon, Minister of Defense. This reflected the unique role Krishna Menon played for India flowing from his personal relationship with Nehru.

At the second meeting of the Committee on March 15, 1962, the Soviet Union sought to gain the initiative by tabling an entire draft treaty on General and Complete Disarmament. A month would elapse before the United States would take similar action. Tabling this draft treaty could be viewed as a tactic designed to show the reasonableness of Soviet policy; Chairman Khrushchev underscored Soviet power the following day. In a widely publicized address at a Moscow election rally on March 16, he asserted that Soviet scientists had created a new "global" intercontinental missile, which was "invulnerable to antimissile weapons."[28] He claimed that

[28]*Documents on Disarmament, 1962, supra* note 10, Vol. I, p. 152.

United States warning systems were now worthless because this missile could approach the United States from altogether different directions than those toward which these systems were aimed. The implication in his view was "that the most realistic way to prevent mass extermination of people in flames of a nuclear war is an agreement on disarmament. . . ." He laid the failure to achieve disarmament solely and squarely to the West. He repeated his threat that if the United States resumed testing nuclear weapons in the atmosphere, the Soviet Union would be forced to respond in kind.

With respect to the test ban negotiations, Chairman Khrushchev asserted, as Foreign Minister Gromyko had the day before in Geneva, that national means of detection provided an adequate basis for a treaty. He said:

> . . . what secret tests of nuclear weapons can one speak about when each one's explosions are practically under the control not only of the two countries but also of other states, including neutral ones, many of which also possess equipment for detection of nuclear explosions?[29]

In the past the USSR had only argued that tests in the atmosphere, in outer space, and underwater could be detected by national systems. Now Chairman Khrushchev extended that claim to cover underground tests as well. The inclusion of the detection capabilities of neutral states was also an interesting and perhaps significant deviation from past Soviet pronouncements on this matter.

To substantiate his point that national detection systems were adequate, Chairman Khrushchev mentioned the detection and announcement of the Soviet underground test of February 2, 1962, by the United States government. He declared that this test had been conducted to trap the United States into disproving its contention that underground tests could not be detected by national systems. Soviet negotiators would recount this incident often in the subsequent negotiations.

The American opening gambits in the Eighteen-Nation Disarmament Committee were much less dramatic. On the same day that Foreign Minister Gromyko tabled the Soviet draft treaty on General

[29]*Ibid.,* p. 155.

and Complete Disarmament, Secretary of State Dean Rusk outlined a number of proposals—which the United States would advance in the coming negotiations in concrete form—relating to general and complete disarmament and to partial measures. Somewhat later that day in a private conversation among the United States, United Kingdom, and USSR representatives, Ambassador Dean presented an *aide mémoire* to Ambassador Tsarapkin proposing modifications in the Western position with respect to a test ban. The *aide mémoire* proposed four modifications to the basic Western position as expressed in the United States-United Kingdom draft treaty of April 18, 1961, and the three amendments of May 29, 1961 and August 30, 1961.[30]

The first modification concerned provisions for safeguarding other states against a surprise abrogation. Two specific measures were envisaged: periodic declarations on the part of heads of state that there were no preparations for testing; and provision for limited and agreed rights to inspect declared test sites a certain number of times each year.

The second modification related to shortening the time spent before the inauguration of the inspection process. This involved principally the functioning of the Preparatory Commission and the scheduling of the establishment of control posts.

The third revision was more designed to appeal to the Soviet Union. The Western powers were willing to eliminate the 4.75 seismic magnitude threshold from the outset and to make the treaty comprehensive. Ambassador Dean, Jerome B. Wiesner, and others had long urged that the threshold be dropped. They felt that given the uncertainty about the determination of seismic magnitude there would be endless arguments about whether or not an underground event had generated a seismic signal that was over the threshold. Moreover, since in previous Western proposals there could be no inspections beneath the threshold, they were convinced that the USSR would have a magnificent opportunity to engage in clandestine testing. British policy-makers also shared these views.[31] Finally, Secretary Rusk and President Kennedy were persuaded and the threshold was dropped.

[30]U.S. Arms Control and Disarmament Agency, *International Negotiations on Ending Nuclear Weapon Tests, September 1961–September 1962,* pp. 200-201.

[31]Earl H. Voss, *Nuclear Ambush,* p. 471.

The final modification was also designed as a compromise to the USSR. According to it, the Western powers were willing to contemplate, within the framework of an overall quota on on-site inspections, a further limitation on the number of inspections in normally aseismic areas. Thus the greater number of inspections in the Soviet Union would be confined to an extremely limited area, mainly in East Siberia and South Central Siberia, and only a few would be allowed in the heart of the country.

In the informal meeting, the Soviet Union rejected these proposals immediately. The United States offered as an alternative suggestion the possibility of immediately signing the United States-United Kingdom draft treaty of April 18, 1961, with the three amendments. This was also unacceptable to the Soviet Union.

Deadlock in the Subcommittee

Obviously the two sides were no nearer agreement, and perhaps were even farther apart, than they had been when the Geneva Conference on the Discontinuance of Nuclear Weapon Tests ended on January 29, 1962. This became glaringly apparent in the meetings of the Subcommittee on a Treaty for the Discontinuance of Nuclear Weapon Tests. The Eighteen-Nation Committee created this Subcommittee, consisting of the Soviet Union, the United Kingdom and the United States, on March 21. The fact that the negotiations on a nuclear test ban were resumed under physical arrangements which were practically identical to those which had previously existed—the representatives of the three states met in private again in the *Palais des Nations*—should not obscure the important psychological difference. The three representatives now comprised a Subcommittee, responsible to the larger ENDC. As a consequence of this, new pressures would become operative, even though they were not immediately apparent.

In the first meeting of the Subcommittee, on March 21, the United States formally presented the new Western proposals, and the Soviet Union in turn formally rejected them. Mr. Tsarapkin bluntly asserted that no agreement would be possible "on such an utterly discredited basis."[32] He went on to assert that the USSR would only agree to a test ban which would rely solely on national

32ENDC/SC. 1/PV. 1, p. 9.

systems for control. He argued that the only reason for the Western insistence on international control was the desire to obtain opportunities to engage in espionage. The Western powers, on the other hand, maintained that they could only have confidence that a treaty banning nuclear weapon tests was being fulfilled if there were an international control mechanism. They were, however, willing to consider various possibilities: their new proposals, the draft treaty of April 18, 1961, with amendments, or any suggestion that the Soviet Union might offer as long as it met their criterion of effective control.

The Soviet position, as developed in this meeting and the next, was that it was common knowledge that all atmospheric tests could be detected by national systems. Mr. Tsarapkin cited as evidence the offer which President Kennedy and Prime Minister Macmillan made on September 3, 1961. He argued that national systems were:

> . . . equally if not more applicable in the case of nuclear explosions set off underwater or at high altitudes. And now that the techniques of detecting and identifying nuclear explosions have made considerable progress, they are also applicable to underground nuclear explosions.[33]

Nevertheless, he continued to stand by the Soviet proposal of November 28, 1961, which implied that some international control measures would ultimately be established for monitoring underground tests.

The Western position did not distinguish the problems of detecting nuclear weapons tests in the various environments, but merely asserted that the report of the Conference of Experts had demonstrated the necessity for an international control system. Thus the situation was almost the reverse of what it had previously been when the Soviet Union had argued that the negotiations had to be based on the report of the Conference of Experts and the Western powers had maintained that new information had to be introduced. Ambassador Dean stated that the proposal to eliminate the threshold in the treaty was advanced despite the fact that the United States did not think that there had been "any great advance in the ability to detect events underground below 4.75."[34] Curiously, in the plenary session

[33]ENDC/SC. 1/PV. 2, p. 10.
[34]Ibid., p. 22.

the following day Secretary of State Dean Rusk stated that the proposal to eliminate the threshold was based on "increased experience and increased scientific knowledge."[35]

The confusion which could result from these conflicting pronouncements and from the Western failure to specify the problems of detection in the various environments was exacerbated by frequent statements of Western scientists, which were widely reported in the Western press, concerning the problems of detecting nuclear weapons tests. Many of these claimed that the problems were not as difficult as the diplomats of the United States and the United Kingdom claimed. The Soviet Union used these statements to buttress its case in the Subcommittee. But other than such statements, it could offer little proof that the scientific situation had in fact changed. The position of both sides, therefore, looked somewhat murky.

In addition to stating their respective positions concerning what arrangements for the discontinuance of nuclear weapons tests would be acceptable to them, the two sides engaged in a bitter debate about the Western decision to resume atmospheric tests and the Soviet abrogation of the moratorium. Each blamed the other for increased tensions.

The Debate in the Full Committee

After two fruitless sessions, the Subcommittee reported the impasse to the full Eighteen-Nation Committee. This occasioned a full dress debate. By and large the foreign ministers of the three nuclear powers merely reiterated the positions which their representatives had voiced in the Subcommittee. There was, however, one important exception. Foreign Minister Gromyko stated that an international agreement on the discontinuance of nuclear weapons tests would only be possible if it were signed by "the Governments of all the nuclear Powers."[36] He then made it clear that this meant that France would have to sign a test ban treaty.

The only representative of the new members of the Eighteen-Nation Disarmament Committee to offer a positive suggestion at this meeting was F. C. de San Thiago Dantas of Brazil. He said:

[35]ENDC/PV. 8, p. 17.
[36]*Ibid.*, p. 25.

It is very obvious that all inspection depends, in the first place, on very accurate knowledge of the technical means available for verifying the implementation of the clauses of a treaty. An exchange of scientific information is essential, in order that States may have the same stock of knowledge and technical means for verifying the implementation of the agreements concluded. At the same time, it is clear that means of inspection must be provided, insofar as our common need requires.[37]

Although in some ways this statement could be considered an endorsement of the Western position, it also reflected the doubts among the new members about the arguments advanced by both sides caused by the conflicting claims with respect to the technical possibilities of detection. Several of them alluded to this in earlier discussions.

Prior to this debate, several of the members of the Eighteen-Nation Disarmament Committee, including many of the new members, had from time to time discussed the question of the test ban negotiations in the plenary sessions. All of the Communist countries and all eight of the new members and Canada had expressed their opposition to nuclear tests. Many of them referred to General Assembly resolution 1648 (XVI) requesting states to refrain from further testing of nuclear weapons, and several expressed the hope that the United States would not conduct the planned series of atmospheric explosions. In the view of all of the members of the Committee, the imminence of this test series made the problem of achieving an agreed treaty especially urgent. President Kennedy, after all, had pledged not to conduct the tests if an agreement could be achieved.

In addition to expressing their opposition to nuclear tests in general and to the forthcoming American series in particular, some of the eight new members introduced, always in a most tentative fashion, a number of new ideas in these early discussions. As early as the third session, F. C. de San Thiago Dantas of Brazil argued that since it was generally agreed that nuclear weapons tests underwater and in the atmosphere and in the biosphere could be detected and identified without on-site inspection or the establishment of an

[37]*Ibid.*, p. 33.

elaborate control mechanism, these tests should be suspended immediately.[38]

Two sessions later, V. K. Krishna Menon made the same point and added that tests in the atmosphere and biosphere were the main tests that people were worried about at the moment.[39] He also argued that, short of the establishment of a world state, all that could be done in the event of a violation of an arms control agreement would be to establish proof of the violation. In his view, in the case of an atmospheric test such proof could easily be obtained. Finally, the Indian Defense Minister pointed out that several stations for data collection, for instance, for measuring radiation, already existed in the world, and using these stations as an example, he suggested the possibility of establishing other "scientific detection stations" by both national and international efforts. As he put it, "The more people who watch, the less avoidance there will be."[40] In many ways his suggestion built upon a resolution which the General Assembly had adopted the previous fall, 1629 (XVI), which had urged the collaboration of national efforts and those of the World Meteorological Organization and the International Atomic Energy Agency in extending the present meteorological reporting system to include measurement of atmospheric radioactivity.

Ato Ketema Yifru, Foreign Minister of Ethiopia, introduced a final new idea at the sixth session. He asked whether or not it would be possible "to devise an international scientific system of verification where an appeal could be lodged to resolve differences in results of national detection systems?"[41]

At this point, however, these were only isolated individual suggestions. They were not advanced as proposals, and they did not appear to elicit any significant response. They did, though, constitute a nucleus around which proposals could be formulated. They also set a precedent, and a pattern was established in these early talks which was to prevail throughout 1962. It was a pattern of parallel talks. Specific negotiations would be conducted in the Subcommittee of the three nuclear powers. Meanwhile, the other members of the Eighteen-Nation Committee would scrutinize the record of these detailed talks

[38]ENDC/PV. 3, p. 9.
[39]ENDC/PV. 5, p. 39.
[40]*Ibid.*, p. 40.
[41]ENDC/PV. 6, p. 20.

and raise questions and introduce suggestions in the plenary sessions. These parallel talks would be punctuated by periodic reports from the Subcommittee to the full Committee and full dress debates. Simultaneously with these talks on the record, there would also be a series of informal discussions, both among the three nuclear powers and the entire membership of the Eighteen-Nation Committee.

The Subcommittee Resumes and American Scientists Return to Geneva

On March 28, the tripartite Subcommittee resumed its negotiations. The two sides clung adamantly to their positions. The Soviet Union continued to insist that it would only agree to a treaty based on national detection systems, while the Western powers, on the other hand, insisted that an international control system would be necessary.

Both sides elaborated the technical situation as they understood it. The Soviet Union repeated and expanded the arguments that it had developed in the first two sessions of the Subcommittee. Ambassador Tsarapkin boasted that the predictions of the Soviet scientists in 1958 had been borne out, that the situation with respect to the detection of nuclear weapons tests had improved, even more than had been expected.[42] However, he continued to differentiate slightly between the situation with respect to nuclear weapons tests in the atmosphere, in outer space, underwater, and those underground.[43] He asserted that tests in all environments could be detected by national systems, but was somewhat less positive in the latter instance. To prove his point about underground tests, he cited those which had been detected, and claimed that the detection of the Gnome shot by distant stations had disproved the decoupling theory.[44]

The two Western powers took much greater care to refute the Soviet arguments than they had during the opening sessions of the Eighteen-Nation Committee. This effort started when the interim report of the Subcommittee was presented to the full Eighteen-Nation Committee. At that time, Dr. Jerome B. Wiesner, Special Assistant to the President for Science and Technology, and other American scientists came to Geneva and made themselves available—especially

[42]ENDC/SC. 1/PV. 4, p. 8.
[43]See ENDC/SC. 1/PV. 8, pp. 22-23.
[44]ENDC/SC. 1/PV. 4, pp. 4-5.

to the eight new members of the Committee—to explain the technical situation as the United States understood it. Dr. Wiesner, in particular, was widely known among the representatives of the neutral nations and greatly respected. He and the other American scientists came to play an important teaching role in the Conference.

In the Subcommittee and in plenary sessions both Ambassador Dean and Mr. Godber developed the Western position for the record. Now they began to distinguish between the various environments and to acknowledge that most, or as they sometimes put it, "the larger," tests in the atmosphere could be detected by national systems. They maintained that although it was conceivable that tests in outer space and underwater could be detected by national systems, at present no national systems for such purposes were in existence.[45]

The Western representatives stated that they felt that the majority of underground events could be detected, but that in many cases it would be difficult to distinguish whether they were caused by earthquakes or nuclear explosions, and that in any case, the only way positively to identify an underground nuclear explosion was through obtaining radioactive debris by means of an on-site inspection. At a news conference in Washington, President Kennedy also sought to establish the difference between the detection and identification of underground events.[46] It was difficult to get many of the delegates of the eight new members of the Committee to make this distinction. Even the Swedish scientists, including those at Uppsala, were somewhat careless in this respect.

To illustrate the limitations on the distant detection of underground nuclear explosions, Ambassador Dean pointed out that of the current United States series of underground tests the Gnome shot had been the only one to be detected in Sweden. He also said that during the moratorium on nuclear testing, from the late fall of 1958 until its abrogation by the Soviet Union in 1961, United States scientists had recorded "hundreds of seismic or acoustic signals . . . and some of them may have looked as if they could have been caused by a secret underground nuclear detonation."[47] The United States did not raise questions because of its fear of upsetting the negotiations.

[45]ENDC/PV. 19, p. 38, and ENDC/SC. 1/PV. 8, p. 6.
[46]See *Documents on Disarmament, 1962, supra* note 10, Vol. I, pp. 215-17.
[47]ENDC/SC. 1/PV. 4, p. 23.

Concerning the Gnome shot, Ambassador Dean agreed that it had confounded the predictions of American scientists with respect to the effects of various media on the transmission of seismic signals.[48] However, he pointed out that since it was tamped the Gnome shot was irrelevant to the question of decoupling.

It was not long before the presence in Geneva of the American scientists began to have an impact. As early as April 2, the Swedish delegate, R. Edberg, stated that to the best of his knowledge there was "no real or marked discrepancy between the view of American scientists and our own as to the detectability and possibility of identifying seismic events."[49] The Western representatives sought to press this advantage by suggesting that there should be a meeting of scientists from East and West to go over the technical situation. The Soviet rebuttal was to cast aspersions on the motives of the scientists that the Western governments had sent to Geneva in the past.[50]

Simultaneously with their efforts concerning the technical situation, the Western representatives sought to prove that the Soviet fears with respect to espionage were groundless. They pointed out the elaborate safeguards that they were willing to have the host country establish and the minute portion of the Soviet Union which would be subjected to on-site inspection in any year.

The Eight-Nation Memorandum: A Synthesis with Deliberate Ambiguity

Despite the fact that the West might have had the better of the oral presentations during this period, it was the side that was about to open a series of atmospheric tests, and thus was in many ways the more vulnerable to criticism. Even as early as the interim report of the Subcommittee, though, it was apparent to many that the Soviet Union was at least equally, if not more, determined than the West to hold another round of atmospheric tests.[51] In the plenary sessions, several of the delegates of the eight new members stated their belief that both East and West were determined to carry out new series of atmospheric tests. Since the American tests were imminent (and perhaps for other reasons as well), however, they con-

[48]ENDC/SC. 1/PV. 6, p. 18.
[49]ENDC/PV. 13, p. 47.
[50]See ENDC/SC. 1/PV. 4, p. 32.
[51]*New York Times*, March 25, 1962, p. 1.

centrated their pressure on the United States. On April 12, Ambassador Lall of India, on the instruction of his government, appealed to the governments of the nuclear powers "not to resume nuclear tests during the pendency of this Conference. . . ."[52] It should be noted parenthetically that on this occasion and on each subsequent occasion when he asked the nuclear powers to forego testing, he stressed the "nth country" problem as a primary reason, arguing that if the nuclear powers continued to test, other powers would do so also. Obviously India was perturbed by a particular "nth country" problem, the People's Republic of China. In October of 1962 heavy fighting would break out on the Sino-Soviet border. The Soviet response to Ambassador Lall's appeal was to reiterate its stand that it would pledge not to conduct tests during the meetings of the Eighteen-Nation Committee if the Western powers did also.[53] The Western powers retorted that they could not again agree to an unpoliced moratorium; they would only agree to forego their planned tests if a treaty with effective control were signed in the interim.[54]

An exchange of statements and correspondence between Prime Minister Macmillan and President Kennedy on the one hand and Chairman Khrushchev on the other produced virtually the same result.[55] It also gave Chairman Khrushchev an opportunity to restate his threat that the Soviet Union would resume testing if the United States inaugurated its planned atmospheric series.

As the days went by, the eight new members of the Committee became increasingly concerned about the imminence of resumed atmospheric testing. Several of them thought that they should break off the Conference if the United States executed its plans, and some members of the United Nations Secretariat who were providing the supporting services for the Conference also took this position.

Meanwhile, in the discussions in the plenary sessions, individual representatives of the eight had added their suggestions to those which some of them had already made. James Barrington, of Burma, suggested the creation of an international scientific commission, though not as elaborate as the organization envisaged in the Western plans,

[52]ENDC/PV. 19, p. 7.
[53]*Ibid.,* p. 21.
[54]*Ibid.,* pp. 21-23.
[55]*Documents on Disarmament, 1962, supra* note 10, Vol. I, pp. 292-94, 318-28.

which could settle disputes which might arise from conflicting interpretations of data derived from national detection systems.[56] He thought that such a commission would probably have to have the right to conduct an agreed number of on-site inspections. Other delegates further developed this and the previous suggestions.

Eventually, the delegations of the eight nations decided that they should combine their efforts in a concerted attempt to break the deadlock in the negotiations. Actually, the origins of this move can be traced to the reactions of some of the eight delegates to the initial report of the Subcommittee, which made the impasse plainly apparent. Sweden and India played a leading role in formulating the concerted action for the eight. India mainly contributed ideas of a constitutional and legal character. The Swedish delegation brought to the task considerable technical knowledge, as well as definite ideas about the political and legal arrangements that could be implemented in an arms control agreement. Swedish scientists were convinced that the chances of an on-site inspection's actually obtaining radioactive debris were not very great and this diminished the importance of such inspections in their view. (As time went on, American scientists would increasingly share this pessimism with respect to the results of on-site inspections.) Moreover, the Indian and the Swedish delegations concluded that in the event of a violation of a nuclear test ban agreement, the only recourse and sanction would be for the other side to resume testing. Finally, the Swedish delegation felt that control mechanisms should be constructed as far as possible as appendages to other more normal activities of scientific installations.[57] The Swedish delegation thought that General Assembly Resolution 1629 (XVI) which dealt with increasing the capacity of the existing world meteorological network to measure radioactivity was an example of the kind of thing that should be done. In developing this notion, the Swedish delegation was in close touch with the head of the International Union of Geodesy and Geophysics. This group was actively promoting the creation of an international center for seismology, and international cooperation in this field was

[56]ENDC/PV. 13, p. 7.

[57]Many of these thoughts are summarized in a speech given by R. Edberg on April 2, 1962: ENDC/PV. 13, pp. 47-49.

an item on the agenda of the United Nations Economic and Social Council in 1962.

After considerable deliberation, the representatives of the eight new members of the Committee ultimately formulated a memorandum, a process which took several weeks. Many of the speeches of the representatives of the eight, mentioned above, in which suggestions were tentatively broached, reflected this process. The actual drafting of the memorandum was done by the representatives of Ethiopia, India, and Sweden, and the Indian delegate, Arthur S. Lall, was particularly influential in preparing the final version of the proposal.[58] In the American view Ambassador Lall's influence was not helpful; it resulted in a "less intelligent document." Ambassador Lall himself, who was particularly close to Krishna Menon and resigned his post after Mr. Menon resigned as Defense Minister, felt that his contribution was to make the proposal more equidistant between the positions of East and West.

The Eight-Nation Memorandum was presented to the plenary meeting on April 16, ten days before the United States atmospheric tests were scheduled to begin. It was, however, shown to the Soviet and American representatives prior to its formal presentation, and had been shown to the Canadian delegation even earlier. The memorandum was an amalgam of the views of the eight, especially those of India and Sweden. In this memorandum, the eight urged the nuclear powers to persist in their efforts to achieve a test ban treaty.[59] After noting that despite the differences that existed among the nuclear powers concerning a test ban treaty there were "also certain areas of agreement," the memorandum proclaimed their belief that "possibilities exist of establishing by agreement a system for continuous observation and effective control on a purely scientific and nonpolitical basis."

> Such a system might be based and built upon already existing national networks of observation posts and institutions, or if more appropriate, on certain of the existing posts designated by agreement for the purpose together, if necessary, with new posts established by agreement. The existing networks already include in their scientific en-

[58]Arthur S. Lall, *Negotiating Disarmament,* pp. 20-21.
[59]ENDC/28. The following quotations are taken from that document.

deavors the detection and identification of man-made explosions. Improvements could no doubt be achieved by furnishing posts with more advanced instrumentation.

In addition, the memorandum suggested that "the feasibility of constituting an International Commission, consisting of a limited number of highly qualified scientists, possibly from non-aligned countries together with the appropriate staff might be considered." It then went on to outline the functions of such a commission.

> This Commission should be entrusted with the tasks of processing all data received from the agreed system of observation posts and of reporting on any nuclear explosion or suspicious event on the basis of thorough and objective examination of all the available data. All parties to the treaty should accept the obligation to furnish the Commission with the facts necessary to establish the nature of any suspicious and significant event. Pursuant to this obligation the parties to the treaty could invite the Commission to visit their territories and/or the site of the event the nature of which was in doubt.
>
> 5. Should the Commission find that it was unable to reach a conclusion on the nature of a significant event it would so inform the party on whose territory that event had occurred, and simultaneously inform it of the points on which urgent clarification seemed necessary. The party and the Commission should consult as to what further measures of clarification, including verification *in loco,* would facilitate the assessment. The party concerned would, in accordance with its obligation referred to in paragraph 4 above, give speedy and full cooperation to facilitate the assessment.

After the International Commission had made a full examination of the facts, according to the Eight-Nation Memorandum, it would inform all of the parties of the treaty of the circumstances of the case and of its assessment. The parties to the treaty would be free to determine their reaction after receiving this report. The eight nations offered their suggestions, in their words, "so as to save humanity from the evil of further nuclear tests."

As would soon become apparent, the two paragraphs quoted above could be subject to varying interpretations. An earlier draft had more clearly stated an obligation to accept on-site inspections, but this had been obfuscated at the insistence of Ambassador Lall.

The Response to the Eight-Nation Memorandum

The nuclear powers responded to the Eight-Nation Memorandum in rather different ways. The day after it was presented, both the American and the British representatives raised a series of detailed questions, seeking clarification so that they could better inform their governments.[60] Essentially these questions were designed to probe the scientific, technical, and political implications of the general propositions in the memorandum. One of the most important was whether on-site inspections would be obligatory or voluntary. The delegates of the eight nations did not give an immediate answer, but the Burmese delegate did suggest that the question should be submitted in writing.[61] Two days later, speaking for the eight, P. Sahlou stated that the memorandum would have to stand by itself; they would not interpret it.[62] He said that the memorandum had been put forward in the hope of facilitating a new approach and that only the nuclear powers themselves could negotiate a treaty. Mr. Sahlou added, though, that the eight nations would be willing to cooperate with the nuclear powers in any or all aspects of the new negotiations and that they were prepared to offer whatever scientific collaboration they could. In addition some of the eight did discuss their views in private.

There were several reasons for the eight taking the position that they did. In the first place, Ambassador Lall was adamant that they should. Secondly, the memorandum represented several compromises among the eight. To eliminate the ambiguities and to elaborate the general provisions would have risked destroying these compromises. It probably would have been impossible to draft a joint explanation, and individual explanations would have been divergent. Thirdly, had the eight been more explicit in their memorandum, they would have been drawn into the heart of the controversy between the two nuclear sides. The eight were firmly convinced that a test ban treaty could only be achieved by agreement among the nuclear powers, and that they would not facilitate such an agreement by seeming to favor one or the other side. Finally, several of the delegates of the eight states felt that if they were to be more explicit than they had been in the

[60]See ENDC/PV. 22, pp. 20-26.
[61]*Ibid.*, p. 26.
[62]ENDC/PV. 24, pp. 5-7.

memorandum, they would risk going far beyond their technical depth.

Immediately after Mr. Sahlou spoke, Ambassador Zorin read a prepared statement which praised the memorandum and stated that the Soviet Government accepted it as a basis for the continuing negotiations.[63] Ambassador Dean was more cautious.[64] Although he declared that his delegation was prepared and willing "to give the most serious consideration" to the Eight-Nation Memorandum, he said that he was concerned that there was an element of voluntariness with respect to on-site inspections. He stated that the United States could not sign a treaty in which there was any ambiguity about the commitment of each party to agree to effective international control and to objective, scientific on-site inspection's taking place under certain specified conditions. He went on to say that the United States never expected that an inspection team could force its way onto the territory of a state where an unidentified event had occurred to conduct an inspection, but that the United States wanted it to be clear which side was guilty of breaking international law. If a state legitimately could refuse an on-site inspection, then the onus of breaking a treaty would fall, not on the state which might have violated the treaty, but on the other side.

Continued Deadlock: An Exercise in Exegesis

From that point until the Eighteen-Nation Committee recessed on June 14, 1962, the Eight-Nation Memorandum in fact became the basis for the negotiations. All of the discussions in the tripartite Subcommittee were based on it, and it served as the focal point in those plenary meetings when the nuclear test ban issue was discussed. Despite this new element, however, the negotiations continued to flounder.

Since the eight new members of the Committee refused to interpret their memorandum, each side was free to place whatever construction it chose on the document. Both tended to interpret it in terms of their past proposals.[65] As early as April 24, 1962, the Western powers were arguing that the Eight-Nation Memorandum

[63]*Ibid.*, pp. 7-11.
[64]*Ibid.*, pp. 15-21.
[65]See, for example, the speeches of Dean and Tsarapkin: ENDC/SC. 1/PV. 10, pp. 12-19, and ENDC/SC. 1/PV. 12, pp. 3-6.

provided for obligatory on-site inspection. The Soviet Union, of course, staunchly denied this. Of all the points of difference, this was the most crucial. As the days wore on, the speeches of the two sides became increasingly complicated by divergent exegeses of the memorandum.

From the outset, the United States had suggested that it might be helpful to have one or more of the eight nations sponsoring the memorandum participate in the work of the Subcommittee.[66] But the USSR rebuffed this suggestion, arguing that the matter should either be discussed among the states principally concerned, that is the nuclear powers, or in the full Committee. Since this was the original pattern, no change in organizational structure was made. When the test ban was discussed in the meetings of the plenary Committee, the eight nations continually refused to be drawn into an interpretation of their memorandum to resolve the conflicting interpretations that had developed.[67] Thus the schism grew in the fashion of medieval theological controversies.

III

The Sign and Poignance of Failure

The United States Resumes Atmospheric Testing

Meanwhile, on April 26, 1962, the United States resumed atmospheric testing. Two days previously, Ambassador Lall, on behalf of the government of India, had made a last minute appeal to the nuclear powers "not to undertake any testing of nuclear weapons" during the period that the Eight-Nation Memorandum was being considered.[68] That same day, President Kennedy authorized the Atomic Energy Commission and the Department of Defense to proceed with the planned tests.[69]

On the day of the United States' resumption of atmospheric testing, only the delegates of Italy, the United Kingdom, and the United States supported the American action in the Eighteen-Nation Disarmament Committee. All of the other delegates expressed regret, and varying degrees of sorrow, dismay, and recrimination. The fact that

[66]ENDC/PV. 24, p. 15.
[67]ENDC/PV. 34, p. 5.
[68]ENDC/PV. 26, p. 14.
[69]*New York Times,* April 25, 1962, p. 1.

as recently as April 24 the Soviet Union had proclaimed its intention to reply in kind,[70] increased the distress of many of the delegates, but also made some of them slightly less harsh in their criticisms of the West.

Within the United States, even after the decision to resume atmospheric testing was a foregone conclusion, the debate about this policy continued. Now it was phrased exclusively in terms of the extent to which the test series should be limited.[71] The Department of Defense wanted the series to be enlarged to include proof testing of existing weapons systems in the American stockpile to test their actual effectiveness as systems and to measure the extent of deterioration.[72] This was opposed by the Atomic Energy Commission and the President's science advisers who wanted to minimize the number of tests. Although the President ultimately allowed some proof tests, he insisted that the overall number of tests and their yield should be kept to an absolute minimum. As a consequence, the total series had a yield of approximately twenty megatons. The Soviet series in the fall of 1961 had had a yield of almost ten times as much. When the Soviet, American and British, and French test programs were totaled, more nuclear weapons had been tested in 1962 than in any other year, and the megatonnage of the tests conducted from September 1961 until December 1962 surpassed that of all previous years.

Efforts to Break the Stalemate

Several members of the Eighteen-Nation Committee vainly sought to break the stalemate. Some of these efforts again sought to use science and scientists as a means of achieving agreement. At a very early stage, Italy suggested convening a meeting of scientists from the three nuclear powers and the eight new members of the Committee to go over the implications of the Eight-Nation Memorandum.[73] Somewhat later, in the Subcommittee, the United Kingdom suggested the convocation of a meeting of technical experts to

[70]See the speech of Foreign Minister Gromyko to the Supreme Soviet, *Documents on Disarmament, 1962, supra* note 10, Vol. I, pp. 423-46.

[71]See *New York Times,* April 17, 1962, pp. 1, 2, and May 1, 1962, pp. 1, 20.

[72]Earl H. Voss has stated that the repeated false starts in the 1962 program appeared to confirm the need for proof testing (*Nuclear Ambush,* p. 474).

[73]ENDC/PV. 27, p. 37.

assess national systems of detection so that their adequacy could be evaluated and the extent to which they needed to be supplemented could be estimated.[74] As the prompt and cursory rebuff which the Soviet Union gave these proposals indicated, they were partially designed to embarrass the USSR. At the same time, they also seem to have stemmed from a genuine belief that there must be a "scientific" and objective solution to these problems. This is attested to by the fact that one of the eight new members of the Committee, Sweden, suggested that a scientific inventory of the existing facilities and a blueprint of how they might be brought into more effective cooperation would be useful as a starting point for more fruitful negotiations.[75]

As another way of attempting to induce agreement, Ambassador Padilla Nervo of Mexico suggested the establishment of a cut-off date for the discontinuance of nuclear weapons tests.[76] As he explained it, this would be a way of ending the seemingly endless spiral of tests and answering tests and it would also be a means of putting some pressure on the negotiators. After making these comments, he went on to single out atmospheric tests as being "the greatest stimulus to the arms race" and also the most harmful to public health. They also could "be recorded and identified without any doubt." Therefore, in his view, these tests especially should obviously be discontinued. Sweden backed the Mexican suggestion in a later public meeting, and several other of the eight new members also did so in private.

In the Subcommittee, the United Kingdom sought to indicate flexibility—a tactic which occasionally caused some concern within the United States delegation and in broader American circles—and to emphasize areas of agreement. Some among the eight new members of the Committee also stressed the extent of agreement. By June the delegates of Sweden and India proclaimed that the gap between the sides had been narrowed somewhat.[77]

Despondency Among the Eight

Ambassador Padilla Nervo, on the other hand, felt that the nuclear powers were no nearer to agreement than they had been in

[74]ENDC/SC. 1/PV. 14, p. 6.
[75]ENDC/PV. 52, p. 29.
[76]ENDC/PV. 34, pp. 13-19.
[77]See ENDC/PV. 52, pp. 27-29; and ENDC/PV. 53, pp. 15-18.

March when the Eighteen-Nation Disarmament Committee opened.[78] He spoke bitterly of the continued nuclear testing, especially the plans to conduct shots in outer space, an environment which he felt was *res communis*. In his view this demonstrated how the nuclear powers ignored the wishes and interests of other states. The Brazilian delegate echoed his sentiments:

> There is an understanding between the two great powers that they will use their power, their strength, their determination, and their will to carry out these tests, taking advantage of their technical abilities in order to use universal property, the property of all the peoples of the world— space, the seas and all the possibilities of nature—and that in the exercise of this will and taking advantage of this property, they will commit acts which are obviously in their own interest, but are against the interests of all the other Powers.[79]

He, and others from the delegations of the eight new members of the Committee, protested but with a sense of futility. He feared the historical situation would not be favorable for a resumption of real negotiations on a nuclear test ban until the end of the following year, after both sides had conducted tests, and the results had been collected, examined, and studied.

Perhaps history would prove the correctness of his views. Meanwhile, transferring the test ban negotiations to a new forum and interjecting the views of the non-nuclear powers appeared to have had no effect toward advancing an agreement.

[78]ENDC/PV. 53, pp. 23-26.
[79]*Ibid.*, p. 28.

Chapter XI

Another New Western Position

I
A Reformulation in Washington

Even though it was not immediately visible in Geneva, the West was again in the process of reformulating its position. This began formally in late April when an *ad hoc* committee was formed within the United States Administration. The Committee was sponsored by the Arms Control and Disarmament Agency (ACDA), which had been established in September 1961. The Committee was chaired either by ACDA's Deputy Director, Adrian S. Fisher, or by Franklin Long, the Assistant Director, who was in charge of the Bureau of Science and Technology. The other agencies represented were the Department of Defense, including the Joint Chiefs of Staff, the Atomic Energy Commission, the Department of State, the Executive Office of the President, and the Central Intelligence Agency. This group met periodically during the succeeding two months; its last regular meeting was held on July 3, 1962. By that time a tentative version of a new United States position had been evolved.

Contributing Factors

Several factors contributed to the reformulation of the American position. Perhaps what did most to trigger the reexamination was the reaction in the Eighteen-Nation Committee, among world leaders, and within the United States to the resumption of atmospheric testing. The widespread opposition to atmospheric testing made American leaders hesitant to order its resumption and also compelled them to search for ways of avoiding such action in the future.

A related point was the fact that during the spring of 1962, as a consequence of the Soviet and American test series, the level of radioactivity resulting from fallout increased significantly.[1] Later that year it would reach its highest levels. Some scientists felt that the concentration of certain elements, especially Iodine 131, reached dangerous heights, and suggested that, if atmospheric testing continued at existing rates, some protective measures might have to be taken to guard against contaminated foodstuffs, particularly milk for children.

Simultaneously with these developments, American strategic doctrine was changing. The United States was, to some extent, becoming disenchanted with nuclear weapons. This was partly a product of their very abundance. Since 1958 the United States' stockpile of nuclear weapons had increased tremendously, so that by 1962 nuclear weapons were readily available not only for American strategic forces, but also down to the company level in ground formations. This proliferation of nuclear weapons caused serious problems of command and control and led to deep concern about the triggering of accidental war. In addition, the Kennedy Administration was much less sanguine than its predecessor had been about the possibilities of fighting limited nuclear war and of using nuclear weapons in tactical situations. Moreover, it became increasingly clear to the Administration that a neutron bomb was still technologically a long way off and that arguments for it were dubious; that a pure radiation weapon would have very little value in tactical situations involving close engagements. And as the situation in Southeast Asia demonstrated, limited and guerrilla actions seemed to be those which the United States would be most likely to face, and for which it was least adequately prepared. The changing pattern of strategic thought was reflected in President Kennedy's ordering the Department of Defense in the spring of 1962 to cut back its orders for nuclear warheads by several thousand.[2]

Secretary of Defense Robert S. McNamara sought to develop some aspects of this new strategic doctrine in his commencement address at The University of Michigan on June 16, 1962.[3] Review-

[1]U.S. Congress, Joint Committee on Atomic Energy, Subcommittee on Research, Development, and Radiation, *Hearings: Radiation Standards, Including Fallout,* 87th Congress, 2d Session (1962).

[2]*New York Times,* May 4, 1962, p. 1.

[3]"Defense Arrangements of the North Atlantic Community," U.S. Department of State *Bulletin,* Vol. XLVII, No. 1202 (July 9, 1962), pp. 64-69.

ing the defense arrangements of the North Atlantic Treaty Organization, he stressed the necessity of building up NATO's conventional forces so that the Alliance would be capable of action other than simply a nuclear response in the event of a limited attack. He pointed out that the United States had taken steps to build up its conventional forces and that it expected its NATO allies to follow a similar course.

In the event of a general nuclear war, Mr. McNamara said that the Administration had concluded that basic military strategy:

> . . . should be approached in much the same way that more conventional military operations have been regarded in the past. That is to say, principal military objectives, in the event of a nuclear war stemming from a major attack on the alliance, should be the destruction of the enemy's military forces, not of his civilian population.[4]

The implications of this statement for nuclear weapons policy were far-reaching. It meant that the Administration rejected the notion of a "finite deterrent." According to this doctrine, a state could deter possible opponents by merely having sufficient nuclear capacity to inflict serious harm on them. Presumably, with such a doctrine centers of population would be the major targets. By choosing other targets, the Administration hoped to give an opponent a strong incentive to refrain from attacking American cities. Under the evolving Administration doctrine, the number of nuclear weapons which the United States would require would be related to the numbers of enemy military installations rather than to the more constant number of population centers. Another implication of such a strategic doctrine was that extremely high-yield weapons would have relatively little attraction since they could be used most effectively against population centers. Moreover, such weapons went against the whole trend of the new doctrine, which was that only the minimum force necessary to achieve the stated military objectives should be used.

While the new doctrine therefore required more nuclear weapons than would be needed under the "finite deterrent" concept, since it was essentially responsive in character, and since the Administration recognized that there was no feasible way that the United States

[4]*Ibid.*, p. 67.

could prevent an opponent from causing serious harm to American society, the Administration did not see an unlimited, or infinite need for more and more nuclear weapons. The number required could be gauged by the situation at hand. Because of the build-up of American strategic power then in progress, the Kennedy Administration was beginning to feel that American nuclear strength was adequate.

Therefore, as a consequence both of changes in its strategic doctrine and the shifting military balance, the United States was already becoming much less interested in the possible gains that it could achieve from further nuclear testing.

A final element entering into the reformulation of the American position was the changing appreciation of the difficulty of the problem of detecting underground nuclear explosions. This was partly attributable to the fact that the research of the Vela project was beginning to produce results. It was also attributable to a fortuitous circumstance, which will be dealt with first since it served as a focal point.

On May 1, 1962, France carried out an underground nuclear explosion with an estimated yield of about 30 to 50 kilotons in a desolate region of Algeria in the Sahara near the Hoggar Mountains. Although it was not announced immediately, this shot was detected in the United States and also by a number of seismological stations throughout the world which had been equipped by the Coast and Geodetic Survey.[5] It was the first relatively low-yield shot conducted at a long distance from the United States and detected in the United States, and consequently drew attention to the possibilities of long-range detection, underscoring again the possibility of detection in the so-called "third zone."

The Vela Program was also beginning to produce significant results at about this time. Although, as is often the case, the increased knowledge pointed in several directions, the overall effect was to make the problem of the detection of underground nuclear explosions seem easier.

First, it was discovered that the number of shallow earthquakes in the Soviet Union was substantially less than American scientists had previously thought. The previous estimate had been that there would be about 100 shallow earthquakes above seismic magnitude

[5]See *New York Times*, July 24, 1962, p. 1.

4.75, or the presumed equivalent of a 19 kiloton nuclear explosion in tuff, and about 600 above seismic magnitude 4.00, or the equivalent of a 2 kiloton nuclear explosion in tuff. Now it was estimated that there would be only 40 shallow earthquakes above seismic magnitude 4.75 and 170 above seismic magnitude 4.00.[6] Previously the United States had based its calculations of the number of earthquakes in the Soviet Union on extrapolations from records collected in 1932 and 1936. With more recent and a greater total supply of data, the earlier estimates proved to be much too large.

Secondly, it was discovered that the sensitivity of seismographs could be increased by a factor of five or ten by placing them in deep holes rather than at the surface.[7] In addition, on the basis of experimentation with surface arrays of seismic instruments, it was discovered that improvements greater than previously considered possible could be obtained through the use of special filtering techniques. Also, some useful experimentation was being done with ocean-bottom seismometers, which offered promise of increased capabilities. All of these developments indicated that the capability for the detection of underground seismic events was better than had previously been estimated.

On the other hand, certain data indicated unforeseen difficulties. The problem of travel time anomalies first discovered as a result of the Gnome experiments has already been mentioned. It was also discovered, on the basis of the Gnome and subsequent experiments, that there were pronounced differences in the strength of seismic signals when measured in different directions from an underground explosion. Having conducted underground nuclear explosions in a variety of mediums, American scientists had now learned that the size of the seismic signal depended greatly upon the medium and that a shot conducted in alluvium would generate a signal about 7 times

[6]See the testimony of William C. Foster, Director of the United States Arms Control and Disarmament Agency, U.S. Congress, Senate, Committee on Foreign Relations, Subcommittee on Disarmament, *Hearings: Renewed Geneva Disarmament Negotiations*, 87th Congress, 2d Session (1963), p. 12. Mr. Foster testified on July 25, 1962; however, the hearings were not published until the following year.

[7]See "Department of Defense Statement on Project Vela, July 7, 1962," in U.S. Arms Control and Disarmament Agency (Publication 9), *International Negotiations on Ending Nuclear Weapon Tests, September 1961—September 1962*, pp. 246-48.

smaller than it would have had it been conducted in tuff, or 14 times smaller than if it had been conducted in granite.[8] It was also discovered, however, that underground shots in alluvium were likely to produce a cavity on the surface of the ground which could be seen.

In the spring of 1962, for the first time, the United States was beginning to have adequate technical information on which to base its negotiating position. On balance this information indicated that the task of detecting underground nuclear explosions would be somewhat easier than most American scientists had thought in 1958, and certainly easier than they had thought from early 1959 through mid-1962. Simultaneously with this development, the Administration had become less interested in the further development of nuclear weapons and more concerned about the general reaction against continued nuclear testing, particularly in the atmosphere. It was the confluence of these factors that produced the new Western proposals.

The Range of Choices

In formulating these proposals, the *ad hoc* group explored in depth four possible courses.[9] The first course which they considered was that of continuing to advance the Anglo-American draft treaty of April 18, 1961, and refusing to make any changes in that proposal. The Administration concluded that this course was unsatisfactory first because standing firm would do little to increase the prospects of obtaining a treaty since the Soviet Union obviously would not accept the 1961 draft. Standing firm would also make the United States seem unresponsive to the Eight-Nation Memorandum. Finally, it would make the United States seem to ignore the progress of science.

The second course considered was that of presenting a simplified treaty banning nuclear weapon tests in the atmosphere, and also in outer space and underwater. Such a treaty would not necessitate control posts or on-site inspections on Soviet territory. As has been mentioned earlier, Ambassador Thompson, John McNaughton, and others within the Administration had argued for this course for some time, and Arthur Dean had become converted to their view, after initially opposing it. Of course others, for example Senator Gore, had

---

[8]*Hearings: Renewed Geneva Negotiations, supra* note 6, p. 11.
[9]See the testimony of William C. Foster before the Subcommittee on Disarmament: *Hearings: Renewed Geneva Negotiations, supra* note 6, pp. 2-38.

proposed that the United States take such action as early as 1958. William C. Foster, Director of the Arms Control and Disarmament Agency, explained the situation with respect to detection under such a treaty to the Senate Subcommittee on Disarmament in this manner:

> Except for small atmospheric tests, tests in the atmosphere can be detected from outside the territory of the Soviet Union. Underwater tests are also reasonably easy to detect. Tests in outer space are difficult to detect at some altitudes, but an inspection system on Soviet territory increases the capability of detection in outer space only modestly over that of a U.S. unilateral system.[10]

Such a treaty would stop those tests which produced radioactive fallout and caused the greatest public concern, and in the view of ACDA, this would be an important achievement. It would also do something to prevent the proliferation of nuclear weapons among the non-nuclear powers and to slow down the nuclear arms race. It would be a simple treaty and would not require the establishment of an elaborate and expensive international control system. It would also permit the United States to continue testing and thereby to make advances in its weapons program. Furthermore, since the weapons laboratories would be kept active, the United States "would be in a better position to resume full-scale testing should the Soviets breach or abrogate the treaty and begin testing themselves."[11]

On the other hand, the Arms Control Agency also felt that a partial ban would have serious disadvantages. As it would not stop all nuclear weapons tests, it would not be as effective a restraint on the proliferation of nuclear weapons capabilities as a comprehensive ban. A second disadvantage in ACDA's view was that it "would make very little, if any, advance in the principle of inspection and control."[12] Also, ACDA felt that to propose a partial treaty might result in a failure to take full advantage of the technological improvements that had been made. The Agency also feared that the USSR would attack the proposal as a device to insure that the United States could continue testing, and that the Soviet Union would insist that such a treaty be accompanied by an unpoliced moratorium on

[10]*Ibid.*, p. 5.
[11]*Ibid.*, p. 6.
[12]*Ibid.*

underground testing. Finally, the Agency thought that the eight new members of the Eighteen-Nation Committee would feel that the United States had ignored their efforts to find a compromise basis for a comprehensive test ban.

The third course considered was for the United States to propose a modified comprehensive treaty responding "as closely as technical knowledge will permit to the eight-nation proposal of April 16."[13] Such a proposal would continue to insist on the necessity of some on-site inspections on the territory of the USSR, but it would rely on "internationally coordinated and standardized national control posts." The Arms Control and Disarmament Agency estimated that a system based on national seismic stations would be able to detect seismic events equivalent to nuclear explosions of down to 1 kiloton in granite, 2 kilotons in tuff, and 14 kilotons in alluvium. Such a system would obviously cost much less than it would to establish an international system *de novo*. It could also begin operations immediately. In the view of the Arms Control and Disarmament Agency, an important reason for making such a proposal would be that it "would continue to place pressure on the Soviet Union to agree to open up its territory to some inspection and control."[14] The Arms Control Agency admitted that a country that was willing to run the risk of detection might be able to violate the treaty clandestinely and to do some weapons development by testing underground devices with yields in the low kiloton range.

A fourth course considered was simply for the United States to present to the Eighteen-Nation Committee a technical evaluation of the capability of the system provided for in the eight-nation proposal, and not to present any new draft treaty. The rationale for doing this would be that it was a way of being responsive to the Eight-Nation Memorandum. The United States could explain its unwillingness to offer a new draft treaty on the ground that the Soviet Union had rejected out of hand suggestions reported in the press that the United States might modify its position.

These four possibilities were discussed in the *ad hoc* committee and preliminary draft treaties were prepared to implement the second and third possible courses of action. After the final meeting of this

13*Ibid.*, p. 10.
14*Ibid.*

group on July 3, the two drafts were sent to the relevant agencies for formal comment. On July 20, the Committee of Deputies (composed of deputies to the members of the Committee of Principals) met to discuss the formal comments. Following this meeting two new drafts were prepared, and these were submitted to the Committee of Principals on July 26. This Committee met that day with the President, and it also met with the President again the following day, on July 30, and on August 1. The Chairman of the Joint Chiefs of Staff accompanied the Department of Defense Representative at each of the four sessions. Ambassador Dean was recalled from Geneva to participate in these meetings of the Committee of Principals; and two members of the General Advisory Committee of the Arms Control and Disarmament Agency, Mr. John J. McCloy and Mr. Robert Lovett, also took part. After these meetings some consultations continued on a lower level and additional drafts were circulated for comment. There were also meetings with key members of Congress, including members of the Joint Committee on Atomic Energy. The result of this intragovernmental consultation was that on August 27, 1962, the United States submitted two new draft treaties to the ENDC.

II

A Preview in Geneva

While these deliberations were in progress in Washington, the Eighteen-Nation Disarmament Committee had reconvened in Geneva. As a consequence of this simultaneity, the negotiations in Geneva had some impact on the reformulation that was going on in Washington, and the new Western position was revealed in a piecemeal and somewhat confusing fashion.

Initial Confusion

Some of the confusion surrounding the introduction of the new Western position probably could have been averted. Returning from Washington to Geneva on July 14, 1962, two days before the Conference resumed, Ambassador Dean stated, at a press conference held at the airport, that because of new scientific discoveries the United States might be able to modify its position with respect to a nuclear test ban.[15] He said that it might be possible for the United States to accept a system of nationally manned, internationally supervised control posts, and that control posts in the Soviet Union might not be necessary. However, he declared that on-site inspections would still be needed. Two days previously, also at a news conference, Secretary of State Rusk had said that he did not think that the new scientific information would make it possible to do without control posts in large countries such as the Soviet Union.[16] Immediately after word of Ambassador Dean's remarks reached Washington, the Department of State felt compelled to issue a statement asserting that the results of the Vela Program did "not demonstrate the possibility of doing away with control posts and on-site inspections to determine the precise nature of suspicious events."[17] Although the Department of State statement was issued as a denial of Ambassador Dean's comments, and was treated as such by the press,[18] it of course was not, since no one had talked about the possibility of doing away with control posts altogether or with on-site inspections. It was not until August 1 that President Kennedy announced—again at a press conference—that the United States could accept internationally supervised, nationally manned control stations.[19] His remarks were prefaced by a negative response to a question concerning whether or not the United States position had changed.

Both the delegates in Geneva, who carefully analyzed pronouncements from officials of the nuclear powers, and readers of the world press were befuddled by this succession of statements. The problem was partly attributable to the personality traits of the individuals involved. In a more general sense it was attributable to the pressure placed on busy officials by an inquiring and insistent press corps. This pressure forced policy-makers to speak for the public record when their own minds may have been made up, but official United States policy had not yet been determined. Dean may also have

[15]See the transcript of the Press Conference: *Hearing: Renewed Geneva Negotiations, supra* note 6, pp. 22-23.

[16]*International Negotiations on Ending Nuclear Weapon Tests, September 1961—September 1962, supra* note 7, pp. 249-50.

[17]*Hearing: Renewed Geneva Disarmament Negotiations, supra* note 6, p. 25.

[18]See *New York Times,* July 16, 1962, p. 1; and July 17, 1962, p. 1.

[19]*Documents on Disarmament, 1962,* Vol. II, pp. 709-13.

attempted to use his press conferences to force a decision within the Administration. The press corps further exacerbated the problem by reading their own meaning into the statements and exaggerating their differences.

Another aspect of the problem was the fact that the Administration had to explain the change in its policy to several different audiences. When dealing with the world at large and particularly with the representatives of the eight new members of the Disarmament Committee, the Administration wished to emphasize its flexibility, the extent to which its policy had changed, and the ways in which it had been responsive to new suggestions. At home, when facing critics of its policies and those who feared that the Administration might make concessions which could endanger United States' security, the Administration sought to emphasize continuity and to underplay the changes. Thus different things were said to different groups. Since the statements to each group were almost immediately available to the other, however, the differences in emphasis were apparent to all and both confusion and cynicism were the result.

Another complication arose from the fact that the new scientific information appeared to support the opponents of the American position rather than that position. A final difficulty was that the Administration, following the rules of careful bargaining, did not wish fully to reveal the extent of the concessions which it might offer until it had time to judge its opponent's intentions.

Vela Data and Changes in Western Position Introduced

At the first meeting of the resumed session on July 16, Ambassador Dean introduced the Department of Defense announcement outlining the results of the Vela Program, and said that the United States would develop these findings in detail in the near future. Interestingly, he said that the United States did "not envisage the establishment of a technical working group in the pattern of those previously established, nor any formal report of recommendations and conclusions on the scientific aspects of the question."[20] As he put it, the Committee's negotiating time and efforts should be devoted toward agreement on a nuclear test ban, not scientific conclusions.

This position was in sharp contrast to that which the Western

[20]ENDC/PV. 57, p. 13.

powers had taken during the winter of 1958–59 when the question of new data had first arisen. There were several explanations for this change in attitude, which went farther in the case of the United States than that of the United Kingdom. The United Kingdom, as a matter of principle, continued to look with favor upon meetings of technical experts, and its delegates to the Geneva talks continued to suggest from time to time that experts from all sides should meet together. The United States, on the other hand, had become rather disenchanted with the idea of separate meetings of scientists. The experience of Technical Working Group II had left a profound impact in Washington, and American policy-makers now seriously doubted that scientists could function apolitically in a highly political situation. They were also aware of the costs of forcing scientists to become public participants in political conflicts. The Administration decided that what was essential was first to have a clear understanding of the technical situation within the American government itself, and then to convince others of the correctness of the United States' position. The Administration felt that the best way to achieve the latter goal was again to bring distinguished American scientists to Geneva to explain the technical situation as it was now understood in the light of the results of the Vela Program to all interested listeners at informal sessions. And this is what was done. Finally, it should be recalled that an important reason for the United States' preference for technical meetings during the Eisenhower Administration was that this was a neutral device to which both those who favored and opposed a test ban treaty could agree. The Kennedy Administration was not plagued with this division of opinion; it was much more unanimously in favor of a test ban treaty.

In this particular instance, both the United States and the United Kingdom recognized that the Soviet Union would not be likely to agree to the establishment of another technical working group. The experience of the Seismic Research Program Advisory Group wherein Soviet diplomats had had to retract positions taken by Soviet scientists had proved especially embarrassing for the USSR. Moreover, Western policy-makers reasoned that if the Soviet Union felt that its scientists could effectively support its negotiating position, it would have brought them to Geneva to attempt to convince the eight new members of the Committee, as the United States had done. The two Western powers also realized that the representatives of the eight nations generally felt that the problem of obtaining a nuclear test ban was preeminently political and were somewhat impatient with the Western emphasis on the technical aspects of the question.

The Soviet Union and other Communist states on the Eighteen-Nation Committee greeted the introduction of the results of the Vela Program with derision. A number of delegates representing the eight new members of the Committee also expressed scepticism.[21] Gradually, however, in the six weeks between the resumption of the Conference and August 27, the day that the United States introduced the two new draft treaties, it was able to win the confidence of this latter group. The presentations by the American and British scientists, including Dr. Wiesner, who returned to Geneva, were quite effective. The Western case was also helped by the fact that on July 21, 1962, the Soviet Union announced that it would resume nuclear tests. The first blast in the new series was detonated on August 5. With an estimated yield of 30 megatons, it was the second largest nuclear explosion, the Soviet Union having detonated the largest the previous fall. Although the Soviet action was not criticized in the Eighteen-Nation Disarmament Committee nearly as much as the American decision to resume atmospheric testing earlier in 1962 had been, it made it impossible for pressure to be directed solely against the United States.

On August 5, immediately after his return from a hasty trip to Washington to participate in the meetings of the Committee of Principals, Ambassador Dean began to outline in more specific terms what changes might be forthcoming in the Western position. He did this in an informal meeting with Ambassador Zorin that day, in a meeting of the tripartite subcommittee four days later, and before the plenary sessions of the ENDC several days after that.[22] Ambassador Dean stated that the United States felt that the new scientific developments did not eliminate the necessity of on-site inspections. On the other hand, they would make it possible for the United States to consider a reduction in the number of on-site inspections and also to consider a network of detection stations that would be considerably smaller than that which had previously been envisaged and which

[21]See for example Ambassador Lall's comments: ENDC/58, pp. 29-30.
[22]See ENDC/SC. 1/PV. 23, pp. 3-30, and ENDC/PV. 69, pp. 6-21.

would be nationally manned, though internationally supervised, rather than internationally operated. If such changes were made, the area open to an on-site inspection might have to be increased. Negotiation on these issues, he explained, would be contingent on the USSR's acceptance of the principle of obligatory on-site inspection.

The Soviet Union's reaction, expressed each time Ambassador Dean outlined the new Western position, was that it represented no change. The chief factor cited to support this charge was the fact that the West still continued to insist on obligatory on-site inspection. Soviet representatives dismissed the offer to reduce the number of on-site inspections and to have a smaller number of control stations which would be manned by national rather than international personnel as mere details. They also asserted that by continuing to demand obligatory on-site inspections the Western powers were ignoring the Eight-Nation Memorandum.

Suggestions of the Eight Nations

Representatives of the eight new members of the Committee were more impressed with Ambassador Dean's presentations, and by this time the work of the American scientists in Geneva had had an important effect. However, it was also apparent to the delegations of the eight nations that the nuclear powers continued to be at loggerheads. They therefore continued their efforts to break the impasse. For some, this meant hortatory appeals to both East and West. Others attempted to achieve the desired results by going over the remarks of the representatives of the nuclear powers and giving glosses on them, which in their view proved that the two sides were moving closer together.

In the realm of practical suggestions, on July 25, the Brazilian delegate noted that the divergencies between the two nuclear sides concerned underground tests, and that the control required for atmospheric and outer space tests did not appear to present as many difficulties.[23] He therefore suggested that the Committee might concentrate its efforts on stopping tests in the latter two environments, which he said "are the most dangerous, actually and potentially, and the ones which have a most disturbing effect on mind, body and nerves." This notion of a partial ban had been mentioned previously,

[23]ENDC/PV. 61, p. 36.

and after its reintroduction by Brazil, several other delegations from the eight nations supported it. By early August all of the eight had, with varying degrees of enthusiasm, given their support to the idea of a partial ban, and on August 15, Italy did this also.[24] Some felt that a partial ban should cover atmospheric tests. Others added those in outer space and underwater as well. In most cases, approval of a partial ban was coupled with approval of the Mexican suggestion for a cut-off date on nuclear testing. Gradually there came to be a consensus among the eight that this date should be January 1, 1963.

Another practical attempt to break the stalemate was made by Sweden on August 1, 1962. Mrs. Myrdal presented a fairly detailed analysis of the existing facilities for meteorological and seismological observation, which could be used for the detection of nuclear detonations, and the present extent of international collaboration among them. She suggested that the nuclear powers carry this inventory further, and that they make plans for the immediate creation of the international commission which would be responsible for processing the data from the observation stations, and that they also make plans for sharing the financial burdens associated with exchanging the data.[25]

Even her rather superficial inventory was impressive. The Swedish delegation had discovered from public sources that there were 7,800 land stations making meteorological observations and 12 anchored weather ships. In addition some 3,000 ships had agreed to make observations while crossing the oceans. At that time the United States also had at least two satellites in orbit making meteorological observations. Under arrangements for the transmission of data then in effect, data gathered at one of the stations would be available throughout the world in about one hour. Not all of the stations were equipped to monitor nuclear tests, but such equipment could be provided at a modest cost. The General Assembly of the United Nations had asked the World Meteorological Organization, the International Atomic Energy Agency, and the United Nations Scientific Committee on the Effects of Atomic Radiation to study the feasibility of such a move.[26]

[24]ENDC/PV. 70, p. 20.
[25]ENDC/PV. 64, pp. 5-18.
[26]General Assembly Resolution 1629 (XVI).

So far as seismology was concerned, the Swedish delegation had discovered that there were approximately 800 stations in operation and that about half of them had participated actively in the International Geophysical Year in 1957. Mrs. Myrdal mentioned the collaboration of many of the stations with the United States Coast and Geodetic Survey and stated that 65 nations throughout the world had reported the French underground nuclear test of May 1 to the Coast and Geodetic Survey within six weeks of its occurrence. She singled out twenty-four countries or territories, stations in which had reported most rapidly. These were Bolivia, Canada, the Congo, Czechoslovakia, Ethiopia, Finland, France, the Federal Republic of Germany, Eastern Germany, Greece, Greenland, Iran, Israel, Italy, Morocco, Norway, Peru, Puerto Rico, Spain, Sweden, Southern Rhodesia, Turkey, the United States, and Yugoslavia. The combination of countries, representing East and West as well as North and South was indeed impressive. Mrs. Myrdal's broad point was that a substantial measure of international collaboration already existed in these matters.

In the course of her presentation, Mrs. Myrdal gave what to her was the most imperative reason for preferring to utilize existing observation stations rather than creating a new international network. She felt that only in this way could one be certain "that scientists, attracted as they are by the full freedom of research, being subservient to nothing but truth will feel a lasting propensity for playing an additional role in this international scheme for promoting peacemaking."[27] Under such circumstances scientists would be free to continue their normal work. On the other hand, Mrs. Myrdal doubted that scientists would have much enthusiasm for participating in a system which had as its exclusive task policing a nuclear test ban. She also emphasized how much less expensive it would be to rely on existing stations.

As the month of August passed by and September 18, the date of the opening of the seventeenth session of the General Assembly, drew near, the pleas of eight new members of the Disarmament Committee became increasingly urgent. They strongly desired to be able to present some tangible evidence of progress to the General Assembly, which the previous fall had sanctioned their participation.

[27]*Ibid.*, p. 15.

They seemed to be encouraged by the knowledge that a new Western position would be forthcoming, but at the same time it was fairly obvious from the Western outline of the changes and the USSR's advance reaction to them that the deadlock would remain.

III

The Two Draft Treaties of August 27, 1962

Partly because of the anticipated Soviet rejection, and partly because so much of its contents had been foretold, the new draft comprehensive treaty which the United Kingdom and the United States tabled on August 27, 1962, did not receive much acclaim in Geneva. However, the United Kingdom and the United States also tabled, at the same time, a draft partial treaty outlawing nuclear weapons tests in the atmosphere, outer space, and underwater. This treaty did not require the creation of any international control features. Prior to late August, the Western powers had given no indication that they would make such a move, although the United States had not reacted adversely when Italy endorsed the Brazilian suggestion for a partial ban.[28] Actually, the Italian delegate had seen Ambassador Dean's instructions.

As mentioned previously, the idea of proposing a partial ban had been under consideration in Washington for some time. The draft treaty for a partial ban had been approved in the meetings of the Committee of Principals during the last days of July and August 1. It was approved then, though only as a fall-back position. The decision to introduce it on the same day as the new comprehensive treaty was tabled was based on the negative Soviet reaction to the outline of what the new Western position would be and on the positive endorsement of the idea of a partial ban by the eight new members of the Disarmament Committee. Because it was unexpected (except for the indiscretion of the Italian delegate), and because it fitted in with the developing current of thought in the ENDC, the draft partial treaty received more attention in the Committee than the draft comprehensive treaty. Before considering this reaction, however, the main features of the two new draft treaties should be analyzed.

[28]See *New York Times,* August 19, 1962, p. 1; August 22, 1962, p. 3; and August 26, 1962, p. 1.

The Draft Comprehensive Test Ban Treaty: Obligations and Organs

Although the new draft comprehensive treaty was considerably shorter than that which the United Kingdom and the United States had tabled more than a year before on April 18, 1961, it was still a complicated document.[29] Essentially, the new draft treaty was a simplified version of the earlier one, modified in the light of the Eight-Nation Memorandum and the new appraisal of the technical situation.

The first article stated the obligations of signatories. It was taken directly from the first article of the 1961 draft. According to it, signatory states would undertake:

(a) to prohibit and prevent the carrying out of nuclear weapon test explosions at any place under its jurisdiction or control; and

(b) to refrain from causing, encouraging, or in any way participating in, the carrying out of nuclear weapon test explosions anywhere.

As in the previous proposal, all of the surveillance machinery provided for in the treaty was designed to check compliance with the first obligation; there was no machinery to oversee the second.

The surveillance machinery consisted of these elements: an International Scientific Commission, an International Staff, and a Verification System.

The International Scientific Commission was the principal organ. This body would consist of fifteen members. The USSR, the United Kingdom, and the United States would be permanent members. The other twelve members would be elected for three-year terms by a majority vote in a conference of all of the signatories. Of the twelve, three would have to be elected from among states, parties to the treaty, nominated by the Soviet Union, two from states nominated jointly by the United States and the United Kingdom, and the remaining seven, from states nominated jointly by the three nuclear powers. The division of the Commission among East, West, and nonaligned states therefore presumably would be four-four-seven. The 1961 draft treaty had provided for an eleven-member commis-

[29]For the text see *International Negotiations on Ending Nuclear Weapon Tests, September 1961—September 1962, supra* note 7, pp. 286-97. The draft was circulated as document ENDC/58.

sion, with a presumed distribution of 4-4-3. The eight new members of the Disarmament Committee had raised the possibility that all members of the Commission might come from nonaligned states. Although the Western powers were willing to increase the representation of this group, they strongly felt that the nuclear powers must have permanent representation on an organ dealing with such a vital matter as compliance with a test ban. The eight new members had also suggested that the Commission should be composed of scientists. The Western powers virtually disregarded this suggestion, except for the inclusion of the word "scientific" in the title of the organization. Their draft provided for membership by states, not individuals, and there were no restrictions in the draft on the right of states to select their own representatives. By taking this position, the Western powers clearly indicated their feeling that the issues which would come before the International Scientific Commission would be political and diplomatic, not technical.

According to the new draft comprehensive treaty, the Commission would be organized so that it could meet on twenty-four hours' notice. Each state would have one vote, and all except a few specified decisions would be by majority vote. Those specified decisions which would require the concurring votes of the permanent members were essentially the same as in the 1961 draft treaty and will be treated topically in the appropriate section of the following description.

The Commission would be the keystone of the organization. It would approve the total amount of the annual budget, and it would also appoint the Executive Officer, who would recruit, organize, and oversee the functioning of the International Staff. As in the earlier draft treaty, both of these decisions would require the concurring votes of the permanent members.

The Commission would supervise all elements of the Verification System. In fulfilling this function it would "establish and monitor adherence to standards for the operation, calibration, and coordination of all elements of the [Verification] System." Since the performance of this function was not one of the stated exceptions to the normal voting procedure, standards would be established by a simple majority vote. These would then be imposed on the various elements of the Verification System, including the nationally owned and nationally manned stations. In this sense the rights of the nuclear powers were less than they had been in the previous draft, for there the nature of the international Verification System was specified in the draft treaty and by reference to the reports of the Conference of Experts and the various technical working groups, and changes in these specifications would have required the concurring votes of the nuclear powers. The new draft treaty stated that:

> The Commission shall arrange for observers to be permanently stationed at, and to make periodic visits to, elements of the System in order to ensure that established procedures for the rapid, coordinated and reliable collection of data are being followed.

In many ways this resembled the old Soviet proposal for controllers, except that the nationality of the permanent observers was not specified.

The Commission could consult with parties to the treaty concerning the nature of unidentified events reported to it by the Staff and it could issue reports to all parties to the treaty concerning the nature and origins of such events.

The Commission would also be charged with the responsibility of establishing such laboratories as might be necessary and of facilitating the participation of the International Staff in research. Until the first elections to the Commission, the three nuclear powers, acting by unanimous agreement, would exercise the functions of the Commission.

The new draft, as the previous one, provided for a conference of all of the parties; however, its status and functions were considerably reduced. It would meet only triennially, rather than annually, and on the call of the Commission. Its sole functions would be to elect members of the Commission, "discuss matters pertaining to the treaty," and "examine the facts and assess the significance of the situation" in a special session in the event of a party's desiring to withdraw from the treaty.

Similarly, the Executive Officer was a somewhat shrunken version of the Chief Executive Officer or Administrator of the 1961 draft treaty. In the earlier version he was listed as one of the principal elements of the control system, but in the new version he was not given this status. The Executive Officer's functions were reduced because international elements of the Verification System were substantially diluted as compared with the earlier Detection and Identification System. Other than differences necessitated by this, the provisions of the two treaties were virtually identical. The new draft treaty also contained a provision, similar to the amendment which Ambassador Dean had tabled on August 30, 1961, for the removal of the Executive Officer. Such a decision would require the affirmative votes of eleven members of the Commission; in other words, all of the members of one side and all of the nonaligned members. (The amendment which Ambassador Dean tabled on August 30 would have required seven affirmative votes, which, with the composition of the Commission then envisaged, would have had the same political effect.) Under the new draft the Executive Officer would serve for a term of four years, one year longer than provided in the 1961 draft.

The functions of the International Staff would be to man such elements of the system as might be established by the Commission and to analyze the data collected by the Verification System. The Executive Officer and the International Staff would be international civil servants and the new draft treaty contained the usual provision found in the constitutions of international organizations attempting to insure their independence from national governments and policies. Unlike the 1961 version, the new draft treaty contained no provisions specifying the nationality distribution of the International Staff.

The Verification System

The biggest difference between the old and new draft concerned the Verification System. In the earlier treaty the Detection and Identification System was patterned on the rather elaborate recommendations of the Conference of Experts and the various technical working groups, and all elements would be established and operated on an international basis. In the new draft the Verification System would consist of three elements:

1) Stations constructed at sites listed in an annex to the treaty. Although the Commission would finance the construction of these stations and would train the personnel to operate them, they would be maintained and manned by nationals of the state or the territory on which they were located. These stations would have observers from the International Commission.

2) Existing stations provided, maintained and manned by signatories to the treaty.

3) "Stations to be constructed, maintained and manned by the Commission in agreement with individual Parties if the Commission deems such stations desirable." Ambassador Dean explained that this last category would apply principally to states which felt that they could not afford to maintain and operate stations themselves or which felt that they did not have sufficient trained manpower for this purpose.

Stations in the first category would have to be in operation within twelve months from the entry into force of the treaty and those in the second category, within six months.

Although these provisions showed considerable movement in the direction of the suggestions embodied in the Eight-Nation Memorandum, the Western powers obviously were much less confident of the facilities of existing stations than the eight were. The Western powers wanted new stations so that they would be spaced appropriate distances apart, so that they would be located on sites with relatively low background noise, and so that they would have the most modern equipment. The requirement for an observer from the Commission was designed as a means of checking on the operation of the stations and the prompt and complete transmission of data to the international headquarters. No figures were listed for the numbers of such new stations, although the Western representatives indicated that they would be willing to accept fewer than the 19 previously envisaged for the USSR. In one oral presentation, Mr. Godber mentioned the figure of "only a handful."[30]

The new treaty gave the Commission broad freedom to include in the Verification System any detection instruments that it desired in outer space, on and beneath the surface of the earth, and underwater. These could either be provided, maintained, and manned by the Commission or by signatories to the treaty, the choice being left to the Commission. The treaty did not include any provision for routine or special air sampling flights.

On-Site Inspections

The criteria stated in the new draft for determining eligibility for on-site inspection were the same as those which had been contained in the 1961 draft, except that the 4.75 seismic magnitude threshold

[30]ENDC/PV. 75, p. 23.

was eliminated. As a special safeguard, the new draft stated that data from stations on the territory of the state in which the unidentified event occurred could not be used to render an event ineligible for inspection, but could be used to establish its eligibility. The Executive Officer would certify the unidentified events which according to the standards specified in the treaty would be eligible for on-site inspection. As in the case of the earlier draft, quotas for on-site inspections on the territory of the USSR, the United Kingdom, and the United States would be fixed in the treaty, and they would be identical. Incorporating the proposal which the Western powers made at the opening of the Eighteen-Nation Disarmament Committee, only a limited percentage of this quota—the specific figure was left open to negotiation—could be applied to the aseismic areas of the nuclear powers, thus there would be very few inspections in European Russia. Also as in the earlier version, the United States or the United Kingdom would have the right to select which of the unidentified events in the Soviet Union should be inspected and the Soviet Union would have the right to select which of the unidentified events in the United Kingdom and the United States should be inspected.

Although the quota number for the nuclear powers was left blank, subject to negotiations, both the American and British delegates said that it would be less than the 12 to 20 previously requested, and in one speech Mr. Godber said it would be "a double handful at most."[31] If there were no unidentified events, there would be no on-site inspections. Ambassador Dean stated that the United States now estimated that there would be from 50 to 75 unidentified events each year in the Soviet Union, most of which would be concentrated in a small area of the USSR, the area of Kamchatka Peninsula.[32]

Previously the United States had thought that there would be roughly two and a half times as many unidentified seismic events in the Soviet Union. However, until the opening of the Eighteen-Nation Disarmament Committee in March 1962, the United States' position had been that only those events which generated a seismic signal of 4.75 or more would have been eligible for on-site inspection. No one

[31]ENDC/SC. 1/PV. 24, p. 16.
[32]ENDC/PV. 71, p. 18.

knew exactly how many unidentified events there would have been in the USSR above this threshold; the usual estimate was from 60 to 100. On the basis of the Vela Program American scientists discovered that the figure probably would be from 10 to 15.[33] It is to this figure that the pre-March 1962 quota proposal of 12 to 20 on-site inspections would have been applied.

Ambassador Dean admitted that the number of unidentified seismic events in the United States would be somewhat larger than in the Soviet Union;[34] however, the provision contained in both the new and old Western draft treaties was that the quota for the United States and the Soviet Union should be equal. Of course, the United Kingdom would also be subject to an equal number of on-site inspections, and this quota could be used in any territory under that country's jurisdiction or control.

The new draft treaty provided that the maximum number of inspections annually on the territory of states other than the USSR, the United Kingdom, and the United States would be three "or such higher number as the Commission, after consultation with the Party, may determine by a two-thirds majority of those present and voting." In the 1961 draft the Commission's prerogatives were the same; however, the standard quota figure was two unless the signatory had more than 1,000,000 square kilometers of territory under its jurisdiction, in which case there would be one inspection for each 500,000 square kilometers or fraction thereof. The Western Powers decided that two was too small a number to constitute a practical safeguard. In cases involving inspections on the territories of states other than the USSR, the United Kingdom, and the United States, the Commission would decide whether or not to exercise the option of an on-site inspection. In the 1961 draft, the Commission could only take such a decision if it were requested by a party to the treaty.

The new draft treaty differed from the previous Western proposal in that the Executive Officer was given complete freedom in staffing on-site inspection teams, except that nationals of the state which was being inspected could not be included. Thus the previous

[33]See U.S. Congress, Senate, Committee on Foreign Relations, *Hearing: Test Ban Negotiations and Disarmament,* 88th Congress, 1st Session (1963), p. 15.
[34]ENDC/PV. 71, p. 18.

requirement that in the case of on-site inspections involving the nuclear powers or permanent members of the Commission the team should be comprised of nationals of the other nuclear side was dropped. Such individuals could or could not be included as the Executive Officer chose.

The area to be subject to on-site inspection was left blank in the new draft treaty, reflecting the Western desire to have a larger area eligible than had been provided for in the 1961 draft. The area normally eligible for on-site inspection under that treaty would have been 200 square kilometers. In certain instances, however, it would have been 500 square kilometers.

Other Modifications

The August 27, 1962, draft treaty allowed nuclear detonations for peaceful purposes only if the permanent members of the Commission unanimously agreed, or if they were carried out in accordance with provisions to be specified in an annex. This annex was not tabled. As will be recalled, the 1961 draft treaty contained an elaborate series of safeguards for peaceful detonations.

Unlike its predecessor, the new Western draft treaty provided that the Commission could make appropriate arrangements for the Commission, the International Staff, and the Verification System "to become part of, or to enter into an appropriate relationship with, an international disarmament organization, or any international organization which may in the future be established among any of the Parties to this Treaty to supervise disarmament or related measures."

The earlier version of the article on finance had stated that the financial contributions of the Soviet Union and the United States should be equal. In the new draft the contributions for the three permanent members would be fixed in percentages, as they would for all signatories, but the specific figures were left for negotiation.

The amendment procedure differed somewhat in the new draft treaty in that the consent of the three permanent members of the Commission was necessary to approve an amendment as well as for its entry into force.

The new draft stated that all parties to the treaty would have the right to inspect the data gathered by the Verification System and reports prepared on these data by the International Staff. The absence of such a provision in the 1961 draft had been felt to be a weakness by some Western analysts on the ground that vital information might be withheld.[35]

The new draft treaty also contained a provision in which a date could be inserted specifying when the treaty would come into effect. The Western powers asserted that this provision was included in response to the Mexican suggestion for a cut-off date on which nuclear testing would cease.

The Withdrawal Article

The withdrawal article—which must be compared with the duration article of the 1961 draft—was a final and important modification. The duration article had stated that the treaty would remain in force indefinitely subject to the inherent right of parties to withdraw if the provisions of the treaty, including those relating to the installation of the Detection and Identification System, were not being fulfilled. This provision would have meant that the failure of certain states such as France and Communist China to cooperate with the control system would have constituted grounds for withdrawal. The new draft treaty contained a complicated withdrawal provision. The first step was the determination by a signatory that (1) another signatory had violated its obligations under the treaty; (2) another signatory was not fulfilling its obligations under the treaty including those relating to on-site inspection and that such nonfulfillment might jeopardize the national security of the determining party; (3) nuclear explosions had been conducted by a state not a signatory to the treaty under circumstances which might jeopardize the national security of the determining party; or (4) nuclear explosions had been conducted under circumstances in which it was not possible to determine the responsible state and that such explosions would either constitute a violation of the treaty if conducted by a signatory or if conducted by a state not a party to the treaty might jeopardize the national security of the determining party. After a state had made such a determination, it could request a conference of all of the parties to the treaty. The conference would take into account the evidence and "examine the facts and assess the significance of the situation." After the conclusion of the conference

[35]See Fred C. Iklé and others, *Alternative Approaches to the International Organization of Disarmament,* pp. 36-37.

or after sixty days from the date of the request for the conference, whichever was earlier, the state concerned could give notice of withdrawal from the treaty, if it decided this course was necessary for its national security. The withdrawal would take effect on a date specified in the notice, which in any event could not be sooner than sixty days from the receipt of the notice by the Depositary Government.

Under the procedure outlined in the treaty, to withdraw legally would probably take from ninety to a maximum of one hundred and twenty days. Western policy-makers assumed that it would take approximately this long to ready the most likely sanction that a state might choose to invoke, a retaliatory testing program.

The withdrawal procedure represented an effort to devise a response to a violation within the limitations of the present world order, including three types of sanctions: (1) world publicity of the violation through the conference debate, hopefully with an authoritative political determination of the facts and consequent public opinion pressures upon the violator; (2) termination of the agreement by the opposite nuclear power which would regain freedom of action; and (3) prompt retaliatory testing by such power which could not be delayed by procedural maneuvers at the conference beyond the minimum time which would be required for the preparation for testing.

The Americans who prepared the draft sought to make the withdrawal procedure as "sticky" as possible, and yet to retain a high incentive for a signatory state to withdraw legally. They wanted the Soviet Union to have practice in and to develop the habit of complying with international accords.

It is very possible, however, that the procedure would have seriously complicated American and Western policy in the contingency which most concerned American policy-makers; that is, the situation which would result if the Soviet Union were to engage in a clandestine testing program but the West could produce at best ambiguous evidence of a treaty violation. In such an instance, having to prove a violation before an audience of all of the signatory states, many of whom might be more interested in preserving the framework of the treaty than in Western security, might have been both embarrassing and cumbersome.

While the new Western draft comprehensive treaty may not

have been much of a concession to the Eight-Nation Memorandum, it did reflect a much greater willingness to have nonaligned states participate in the control system and greater confidence in their impartiality. This can be seen in the increased number of seats on the Commission allotted to this group; in the acceptance of national staffing of control posts; and in the dropping of the requirement that the nuclear powers participate in on-site inspections. In this sense, the Western powers moved away from the reciprocal inspection features that had been built into the April 18, 1961, draft as a result of the negotiating process and back toward their original concept of an impartial system.

Some of the changes in the new draft treaty were obviously designed to eliminate perceived faults in the previous treaty and to make the proposed control system more effective from the Western point of view. Thus it is difficult to describe the entire draft as a concession to the Soviet point of view, although it certainly contained important compromises in this direction.

The Capability of the New System

Shortly after the new Western comprehensive treaty was tabled, Paul H. Nitze, who at that time was Assistant Secretary of Defense for International Security Affairs, attempted to evaluate for the Preparedness Investigating Subcommittee of the Senate Committee on Armed Services the capability of the system which the Western powers had just proposed. He estimated that the system would be capable of detecting underground nuclear explosions down to from 10 to 20 kilotons if the shots were in alluvium.[36] The system's capability with respect to underground explosions in tuff and granite would be respectively seven and fourteen times greater. There are only two small areas in the Soviet Union where deep deposits of dry alluvium are known to exist. Both are near the Aral Sea, one close to the border of Iran and the other about 500 miles inland. Mr. Nitze said that such a detection system would permit "clandestine shots up to 2 or 3 kilotons with some confidence that they will not be detected by seismic means."[37] This of course assumed that such

[36]U.S. Congress, Senate, Committee on Armed Services, Preparedness Investigating Subcommittee, *Hearings: Arms Control and Disarmament,* 87th Congress, 2d Session (1962), p. 13.
[37]*Ibid.*

shots were conducted in alluvium. If the shots were decoupled by being detonated in a large cavity, Mr. Nitze estimated that this "would allow yields well in excess of 10 kilotons to take place below the detection threshold."[38] Earlier he had stated that "most of the important scientific principles can be effectively studied below 3 kilotons including what, if anything, might be done about all fusion weapons; and development of improved weapons of greater efficiency and lowered cost are attainable under this 3-kiloton threshold."[39]

By comparison, in the light of the new scientific information, he appraised the capability of the system proposed in the 1961 draft treaty as 7 kilotons in alluvium. Again this system's capability with respect to underground explosions in tuff and granite would have been respectively seven and fourteen times greater.

On balance, the new draft comprehensive treaty was probably influenced more by the new scientific information than it was by the Eight-Nation Memorandum. The new draft treaty reflected increased confidence in the ability to detect underground explosions at long distances rather than a new appraisal of the utility of using existing national seismic stations. Since the capability of the new system was roughly what the capability of the old system had been estimated to be prior to the reappraisal of the technical situation resulting from the Vela Project, it meant that the Western powers were willing to accept virtually the same risks that they thought they were taking in March 1962 when they announced their willingness to drop the threshold from the 1961 draft treaty. Had the West stuck to its earlier negotiating position it would have faced even less risk than it had thought in 1958 that it would face with the system recommended by the Conference of Experts. The system proposed in the 1961 draft treaty would have been able to detect underground explosions down to 1 kiloton in tuff. The Experts, on the other hand, had felt that the system which they proposed (the same system) would have been relatively ineffective in the range from 1 to 5 kilotons in tuff.

The Draft Partial Test Ban Treaty

The draft partial treaty which the Western powers also tabled on August 27, 1962, was much simpler than the alternative com-

[38]*Ibid.*
[39]*Ibid.*

prehensive proposal.[40] It was brief, consisting merely of a preamble and six articles. It did not involve the creation of an international organization or control system.

The preamble was like that of the draft comprehensive treaty, except that it expressed confidence that a partial test ban would facilitate progress toward a comprehensive agreement. The obligations of the treaty were also identical with those of the other draft treaty except that they were confined to tests:

(a) in the atmosphere, above the atmosphere, or in territorial or high seas; or

(b) in any other environment if such explosion causes radioactive debris to be present outside the territorial limits of the State under whose jurisdiction or control such explosion is conducted.

In accepting these obligations states would agree not to conduct tests in the prohibited environments at any place under their jurisdiction or control and also "to refrain from causing, encouraging, or in any way participating in, the carrying out of any nuclear weapon test explosion anywhere" in the prohibited environments. Subsection (b) was phrased as it was for several reasons. One was that, in the absence of any provision for aircraft sampling flights over the territories of signatory states, nuclear weapons tests could only reliably be detected and identified if radioactive debris escaped beyond the territorial limits of the state where the tests were conducted. Secondly, this subsection was designed to prevent a state from throwing a shovelful of dirt over a nuclear device and saying that it was underground. Finally, it took account of the fact that many nuclear devices which were completely sealed underground caused some venting when they were detonated; for example, this had occurred with the Gnome shot.

The article on peaceful explosions was like that in the comprehensive draft except that the obligation was limited to the prohibited environments. The withdrawal articles in the two treaties were iden-

---

[40]For the text of the treaty see *International Negotiations on Ending Nuclear Weapon Tests, September 1961—September 1962, supra* note 7, pp. 297-300. The draft was circulated as document ENDC/59.

tical, as were the articles on signature, ratification and entry into force, and authentic texts. The basic process for amending the two treaties was the same: an amendment would require the approval and ratification of two-thirds of the signatories including the USSR, the United Kingdom, and the United States. However, since there was no provision in the draft partial treaty for regular meetings of a conference of all of the parties, if a state desired to propose an amendment it would circulate it to all of the signatories; and then, if one-third or more of the parties so requested, a conference would be convened.

In presenting the draft treaty for a partial ban, Ambassador Dean asserted that such a treaty could and should be accepted immediately.[41] He argued such a treaty would exercise something of a brake on the arms race, would to some extent inhibit non-nuclear powers from attempting to develop independent nuclear capacities, and would stop the radioactive pollution of the atmosphere, outer space, and the oceans. He emphasized, however, that the United States could not agree that a partial ban should be accompanied by a moratorium on underground testing, and his British colleague underscored this position.[42] In the latter's words, "Once bitten, twice shy." With a moratorium, of course, the draft treaty for a partial test ban would be almost equivalent to the USSR's proposal of November 28, 1961.

In discussing the draft treaty for a partial test ban, before both domestic and international audiences, Administration officials emphasized that the West had twice before suggested such a move; in President Eisenhower's letter to Chairman Khrushchev of April 13, 1959, and in the joint offer which President Kennedy and Prime Minister Macmillan made on September 3, 1961. There were, however, some important differences between these proposals and the draft treaty. The partial ban suggested by President Eisenhower would have applied only to tests in the atmosphere up to 50 kilometers. This ban would have been the first step in the phased achievement of a comprehensive treaty, and there would have been some international control features. The offer made by President Kennedy and Prime Minister Macmillan would not have involved

---

[41]See his remarks: ENDC/PV. 75, pp. 10-18.
[42]See *ibid.*, p. 26.

any international control features. Like President Eisenhower's suggestion, however, it was confined to tests in the atmosphere.

Interestingly, neither new draft treaty contained provisions attempting to prevent the signatories from preparing to engage in nuclear weapon tests, a provision which President Kennedy had demanded immediately after the Soviet Union broke the moratorium in the fall of 1961. Indeed, Ambassador Dean proclaimed that the United States intended to keep itself in a state of readiness.[43] The Administration had decided that being ready to respond quickly with a retaliatory series of tests would be a better deterrent to a violation than any formal treaty provisions.

The Capability Under the Partial Treaty

In the same hearing before the Preparedness Investigating Subcommittee in which Paul Nitze appraised the capability of the new draft comprehensive treaty, he and other officials also appraised the capability of the partial treaty. Since the draft treaty would rely exclusively on national detection systems, this was essentially an appraisal of the United States' unilateral detection system. Mr. Nitze stated that the United States had "a very limited and unevaluated capability of detecting nuclear explosions in outer space," but that it had a program to further develop this capacity.[44] This program was the Vela Hotel Program. The first detection satellites developed under this program would not be launched until the fall of 1963. Meanwhile, Mr. Nitze admitted that the United States had no way of knowing whether or not the USSR was testing in deep outer space. Dr. Franklin Long, Assistant Director of the Arms Control and Disarmament Agency in charge of the Bureau of Science and Technology, stated that the United States had a reasonable ability to detect underwater tests by its seismic system, but that on the basis of an evaluation of the likelihood of underwater tests by the USSR and of the cost of a hydrophone system, which would be the best for detecting and locating underwater tests, the United States had decided not to install such a system.[45] Thus for the present, the United States' ability to detect and identify underwater tests was also

[43]*Ibid.*, p. 16.
[44]*Hearings: Arms Control and Disarmament, supra* note 36, p. 27.
[45]*Ibid.*, p. 61, also, pp. 62-63.

limited. So far as tests in inland waters were concerned, there would be no means for the United States to establish positive identification through the collection of radioactive debris short of an on-site inspection. Since there was no provision for on-site inspections in the partial ban there was no way of enforcing this particular prohibition. However, it was decided that since the United States itself would not wish to test nuclear weapons in any of its inland waters such as Lake Michigan this environment might just as well be included in the proposal in the hope that the USSR would abide by the treaty and feel constrained. No one questioned the capability of the United States' system to detect atmospheric tests; however, it was clear that small atmospheric tests in the USSR—those with yields less than 1 kiloton—could not be detected without monitoring stations in that country.

IV

The Response to the Western Draft Treaties

Soviet Rejection

In Geneva, the Soviet Union immediately gave a firm negative reaction to both of the new Western draft proposals.[46] The USSR rejected the comprehensive treaty, alleging that it was merely a restatement of the previous Western position and that it contained no qualitative changes. As could be expected, the feature to which the Soviet Union objected most was that concerning obligatory on-site inspection. Soviet delegates repeated their contention that national instruments were adequate for the detection of underground nuclear explosions, and that the only reason for the Western powers' insistence on obligatory on-site inspection was their desire to obtain military and especially targeting information concerning the USSR. Although the Western delegates did not change the USSR's position, they at least scored a debating point in the Eighteen-Nation Committee when they pointed out that under the new proposals inspection teams could consist exclusively of nationals of nonaligned states.

The Western powers balked, however, when Ambassador Barrington of Burma carried this line of reasoning a step further and suggested that the Commission should be entrusted with the decision

---

[46]For samples of the Soviet reaction, see ENDC/PV. 76, pp. 14-23, and ENDC/SC. 1/PV. 24, pp. 18-25.

as to which unidentified events on the territories of the nuclear powers should be investigated.[47] This increase in the Commission's authority at the expense of the nuclear powers would strengthen the "impartial" features of the system at the expense of its reciprocal aspects. But the Western powers insisted that for maximum deterrent effects, this choice would have to be left to the opposite nuclear side. Obviously they were counting on using their unilateral intelligence as a fundamental aid in the selection of the events for inspection within their quota.

The USSR rejected the partial treaty because it was not comprehensive, or, as Soviet delegates put it, because it "legalized" underground nuclear tests. The USSR's representatives denied that a partial ban would do much to stop the proliferation of independent nuclear capabilities or that it would put a brake on weapons development. With repect to the Western argument that a partial ban would end the peril of radioactive fallout, Soviet delegates took the line that nuclear war was a far more dangerous and serious threat than fallout and that a partial ban would be likely to increase the threat of nuclear war because it would lead to an intensification of the arms race. Mr. Kuznetsov alleged that in proposing a partial ban the United Kingdom and the United States were

> . . . striving to retain for themselves a loophole for the purpose of continuing the nuclear weapon race and at the same time they want to pinion the arms of the Soviet Union in regard to ensuring its own defensive capacity, although they attempt to hide this fact, and, of course, deny it. In such circumstances the Soviet Union would be compelled to conduct nuclear tests likewise in order to improve its weapons and create new types.[48]

He seemed to be saying that, if the Western powers were to continue testing underground, the Soviet Union would continue atmospheric tests.

The Reaction of the Eight Nations

The reaction of the eight new members of the Disarmament

[47]ENDC/PV. 78, p. 9.
[48]ENDC/SC. 1/PV. 24, p. 22.

Committee was no doubt colored by the Soviet Union's quick and blunt rejection. In view of this, and committed as they were to maintaining a neutral position between the two nuclear sides, they could not have been overly enthusiastic even if they had wanted to be. All of those that spoke, like the Western powers, asserted that their real goal was a comprehensive test ban, but having said this, they expressed varying degrees of enthusiasm for a partial ban as an initial step.

The representatives of the eight new members continued to try to find ways of bringing the two nuclear sides together. For the most part, their efforts consisted of attempts to link a moratorium on underground testing with the Western proposal for a partial ban so as to bring the proposal closer to the Soviet position. In deference to the Western position, however, they avoided the word moratorium, using such euphemisms as "a voluntary restraint." They also groped for safeguards which might accompany a moratorium, such as declarations by heads of states, the immediate establishment of an international scientific commission, and fixing time limits for the duration of the moratorium. The Western powers, though, were adamant. Some of the representatives of the eight new members themselves were troubled by the idea of a moratorium. Ambassador Barrington of Burma spoke of it as a "double-edged weapon."[49] After acknowledging that a moratorium might facilitate—and even be a necessary component of—an agreement, he expressed the concern that a moratorium which did not last would lead to the failure of the treaty and expressed doubt that in the present tensions a moratorium would last.

January 1, 1963, continued to receive prominent mention as the target date for a cut-off for nuclear weapon tests. Soviet delegates mentioned this date, saying that it deserved consideration; then, on August 29, at his news conference, President Kennedy said that the United States would regard this "as a reasonable target date."[50] He added, however, that the negotiations would have to proceed quickly so that the Senate would have time to ratify a treaty containing such a date.

[49]ENDC/PV. 78, p. 7.
[50]*International Negotiations on Ending Nuclear Weapon Tests, September 1961—September 1962, supra* note 7, p. 312.

On September 7, 1962, when the Eighteen-Nation Disarmament Committee recessed for the seventeenth session of the General Assembly, it was debatable whether after seven months of discussions in a new forum and all of the efforts of the eight new members the positions of the two nuclear powers were in reality any closer together. In one of the final sessions of the Committee, Mexican Ambassador Padilla Nervo expressed some of the frustrations of the new members when he said that although on the surface the explanation for the lack of progress seemed to be the difference between the two sides concerning on-site inspection, this was not the basic explanation. He continued by saying that:

> The cause is complex and many-sided. It seems to consist of considerations of internal politics and international prestige which for the moment the Powers cannot or do not know how to overcome. It also consists of suspicion and the tempting dream of obtaining, by further nuclear tests, some military advantage or an important lead from possible discoveries in that field.[51]

Accepting this analysis, the representatives of several of the eight new members of the Committee were frustrated because they felt that at the Conference table in Geneva they could only deal with the apparent and surface sources of disagreement. Thus many of them were not unhappy to move to New York, where in the widely publicized meetings of the General Assembly they might have a better instrument for bringing pressure to bear on the nuclear powers.

Meanwhile, in response to an American proposal, the tripartite Subcommittee would continue to meet in Geneva. No one, though, predicted success. A test ban agreement seemed as distant as it had before the tabling of the new Western proposals.

[51]ENDC/PV. 80, p. 33.

Chapter XII

False Hopes

I

A Debate, an Inventory, a Showdown, a Schism

The next period in the nuclear test ban negotiations brought certain significant changes. Although it started inauspiciously, suddenly both sides—but particularly the Soviet Union—demonstrated greater flexibility, and some observers felt that an agreement might be in sight. Hopes soared, but by the end of the period this optimism had been dashed.

The Seventeenth General Assembly

While the Subcommittee of the Eighteen-Nation Disarmament Committee continued to meet in Geneva—an American suggestion which the USSR reluctantly accepted—the spotlight of attention turned to New York and the United Nations General Assembly, where all three groups within the ENDC hoped to gain support for their positions. The Soviet Union, though, may well have had certain special expectations. Soviet leaders may have expected that the series of nuclear tests which the USSR was then conducting could be completed in sufficient time to enable them to make some dramatic move, such as announcing another unilateral suspension. Making such a move during the Assembly session would put great pressure on the Western states to take similar action. The USSR's assertions that the date set for the reopening of the full Eighteen-Nation Committee, November 12, could easily be adjusted and set back so that there need be no deadline on the Assembly's deliberations and its insistence that the subcommittee's sessions in Geneva should not in any way inhibit the Assembly,[1] support the suspicion that Soviet leaders may have considered such a move.

The item, "The urgent need for suspension of nuclear and thermonuclear tests," had been placed on the Assembly's agenda at

[1]ENDC/SC. 1/PV. 26, p. 24.

417

the request of India. When the Assembly opened, the First Committee decided to make it the first order of business. The debate in the Committee lasted from October 10 through November 5, and the two resolutions recommended by the Committee were adopted on November 6. For the most part the debate consisted of an expanded version of that which had occurred previously in the ENDC. The addition of ninety-three more states to the debate brought little that was qualitatively new.

The introduction of so many states which had not had previous detailed contact with the negotiations, however, complicated the Western position. In the Eighteen-Nation Committee the United States and the United Kingdom had attempted to build an elaborate technical case to substantiate their position, and had devoted considerable effort to explaining their views to the eight new members of the Committee.

To undertake a comparable effort in the Assembly would have been impossible. Immediately after the debate opened in the First Committee, the United States submitted two memoranda: the first outlining the technical aspects of the detection and identification of underground nuclear explosions and the second explaining the findings of the Vela Program as they related to a nuclear test ban.[2] Obviously, though, these memoranda were not as effective as the briefings with top Western scientists held in Geneva. Nevertheless the Soviet Union, for the first time in 1962, felt constrained to issue a technical reply, though it did not do so until November 11 after the Assembly debate on a nuclear test ban had been concluded, and did so then only in the form of an article by three Russian scientists in *Izvestia*.[3] Subsequently the Soviet article was circulated as a document of the Eighteen-Nation Disarmament Committee.[4]

During the course of the debate, speakers from several Latin American states (Argentina, Brazil, Colombia, and Peru), states belonging to the Western alliance system (Australia, Canada, China, Denmark, Greece, Iran, Italy, Japan, New Zealand, Norway, and

2UN Document A/C. 1/873.
3For the text of the article, see *Documents on Disarmament, 1962,* Vol. II, pp. 1042-46. The article was signed by Mikhail A. Sadovsky, V. Keilis-Borok, and N. Kondorskaya. The first two individuals had participated in some of the meetings of scientists connected with the Conference on the Discontinuance of Nuclear Weapon Tests.
4ENDC/67.

the Philippines), as well as from the Federation of Malaya, Spain, Ireland, and Somalia, supported the idea of a partial test ban treaty as a first step toward a comprehensive ban. On the other hand, spokesmen from Communist states (Albania, Bulgaria, Cuba, Czechoslovakia, Poland, Romania, Yugoslavia, and the USSR), certain African and Asian states (Afghanistan, Algeria, Burma, Ceylon, Ethiopia, Ghana, India, Indonesia, Iraq, Mali, Nepal, Niger, Saudi Arabia, and Syria) and Austria emphasized the importance of having a test ban treaty apply to all environments.

Two draft resolutions were introduced, both on October 19. The first was proposed by thirty African, Asian, and Latin American states, including the eight new members of the Disarmament Committee.[5] Seven other states from the same geographic regions later became additional cosponsors. The other resolution was proposed by the United Kingdom and the United States.[6]

The thirty-seven power resolution condemned all nuclear tests, asked that all such tests should cease immediately and in any event not later than January 1, 1963, endorsed the Eight-Nation Memorandum "as a basis for negotiations," called upon the parties concerned "to negotiate in a spirit of mutual understanding and concession in order to reach agreement urgently," and asked the ENDC to pursue the matter and to report to the General Assembly on or before December 10, 1962. With the exception of certain preambular paragraphs, the Soviet Union supported this proposal.

The Western resolution urged the Eighteen-Nation Disarmament Committee to work toward the conclusion of a comprehensive treaty "with effective and prompt international verification," but asserted that if this proved impossible, the ENDC should

> . . . seek the conclusion of an interim treaty prohibiting nuclear weapon tests in those environments where radioactive fall-out is a matter of international concern and where nuclear weapon tests can be detected and identified without international controls, namely, the atmosphere, the oceans, and space.

It also urged the negotiating powers to agree on a date on which a treaty prohibiting nuclear weapon tests should enter into force, noted

5UN Document A/C. 1/L. 310.
6UN Document A/C. 1/L. 311.

the reports of the Committee, and requested the Secretary General to bring the records of the Assembly debate to the attention of the Committee. Essentially, it was an endorsement of the Western position.

Canada submitted a number of amendments to the thirty-seven power proposal.[7] The most important of these involved the addition of a paragraph recommending that if agreement were not reached on a comprehensive ban by January 1, 1963, the parties concerned should enter into an immediate agreement prohibiting nuclear tests in the atmosphere, underwater, and in outer space. Subsequently, Canada modified this, incorporating a Ghanian subamendment, so that the paragraph recommended that a partial ban be accompanied by an interim arrangement, limited in time, suspending underground tests, on the basis of the Eight-Nation Memorandum.[8] The United States and the United Kingdom proposed to add to this:

> Such limited interim agreement shall include adequate assurances for effective detection and identification of seismic events by an international scientific commission.[9]

At the suggestion of Ambassador Arthur Lall of India, who again as on many previous occasions manifested concern for the position of the USSR, the two Western powers agreed to delete the word "limited." As revised, the United Kingdom and United States subamendment was adopted by a vote of 65 to 11, with 28 abstentions. The Soviet bloc states and Cuba voted against the proposal. All of the eight new members of the Eighteen-Nation Committee except the United Arab Republic, which abstained, voted affirmatively. The alignment on the vote on the paragraph as a whole was similar, although there were minor differences. The vote was 62 to 11, with 31 abstentions.

The First Committee then turned to the thirty-seven power resolution itself.[10] The condemnation of all nuclear tests in the first operative paragraph was adopted by 81 votes to 0, with 25 abstentions. The major states of both East and West abstained. The second

[7]UN Document A/C. 1/L. 313.

[8]For the Ghanian subamendment, see UN Document A/C. 1/L. 314.

[9]UN Document A/C. 1/L. 316.

[10]For the record of the voting see UN, General Assembly, First Committee, *Official Records*, 17th Session, pp. 110-13.

operative paragraph establishing the cut-off date of January 1, 1963, was adopted, 88 to 10, with 8 abstentions. Only Australia, Belgium, Greece, Italy, Portugal, South Africa, Spain, Turkey, United Kingdom, and the United States voted against the paragraph. China, France, Luxembourg, the Netherlands, New Zealand, Norway, the Philippines, and Thailand abstained. The states voting for the paragraph even included three members of NATO, Canada, Denmark, and Iceland. The disarray within the ranks of the Western alliance demonstrated, among other things, the strength of support for an immediate, unconditional cessation of nuclear testing.

The thirty-seven power resolution as a whole was adopted in the First Committee by a vote of 81 to 0, with 25 abstentions, and in the plenary session, 75 to 0, with 21 abstentions.[11] The major states of both East and West abstained, though as can be seen from the votes on the parts of the resolution, for different reasons: those from the East because of the condemnation of all nuclear tests and those from the West for the same reason and also because of the cut-off date.

Just before the vote on their resolution, the United States and the United Kingdom dropped the paragraph endorsing a partial ban. With this change, the resolution was adopted in the First Committee by a vote of 50 to 12, with 42 abstentions, and later in the plenary session, 51 to 10, with 40 abstentions.[12] In the Committee vote, Mali and Cuba joined the Soviet bloc in opposing the resolution. In the plenary session, Mali did not participate and Cuba was absent. The eight new members of the Disarmament Committee split evenly: Brazil, India, Mexico, and Sweden voted for the resolution; and Burma, Ethiopia, Nigeria, and the United Arab Republic abstained.

The results of the General Assembly's consideration of the nuclear test ban issue were therefore somewhat contradictory. Because of the adoption of their resolution, the Western powers could claim something of a victory, although in their efforts to muster a majority they had had to abandon the idea of obtaining an endorsement for their partial ban proposal. Even after this concession was made, less than half of the UN's membership had actually voted for their resolution. The Soviet Union was pleased with the establishment

[11]General Assembly Resolution 1762 A (XVII).
[12]General Assembly Resolution 1762 B (XVII).

of the cut-off date and the endorsement of the Eight-Nation Memorandum in the thirty-seven power resolution which had been adopted by substantial majority of all members. However, the USSR strongly opposed the Canadian amendment referring to verification arrangements. The meaning of this amendment as it was finally adopted was not very clear. The Western powers would have to exercise their interpretative skills to see it as supporting their position. Those who fared best in the Assembly were the eight new members of the Disarmament Committee, to the extent that their Memorandum was endorsed without qualification. Perhaps this could be explained by the very ambiguity of the Memorandum! In any case, the two Assembly resolutions constituted a charge of sorts for the ENDC, which now had to report back to the Assembly by December 10, 1962.

The other actions of the General Assembly at its seventeenth session with respect to disarmament and arms control were also rather ambiguous. It decided not to take any decision on the suggestion of certain Latin American states that Latin America should be established as a denuclearized zone. It also did not take a decision on the Soviet-sponsored item relating to propaganda favoring preventive nuclear war, accepting instead the Soviet recommendation that the matter be referred to the Eighteen-Nation Disarmament Committee. The resolution which the Assembly adopted on General and Complete Disarmament was procedural and hortatory. It was adopted unanimously, except for the vote of France, which abstained. In another resolution, the Assembly postponed the question of convening a conference to sign a convention prohibiting the use of nuclear and thermonuclear weapons by asking the Secretary General to carry on further consultations with the governments of Member States. At that point, 59 states had replied to the Secretary General's inquiries. Thirty-three, including the USSR had favored the convocation of such a conference, and 26, including the United States and the United Kingdom, had expressed negative views or doubts.

Continued Testing

Although the General Assembly debate and the resolutions which were adopted may have had some influence on the nuclear test ban negotiations, events which occurred outside the meeting halls in Geneva and New York had a much more significant impact.

Both sides continued their test programs. The Kennedy Administration authorized an extension of the United States atmospheric and high altitude testing program, so that the series, originally scheduled to end in July, was continued into the fall. The extension was made partly to allow shots which had originally been scheduled, but for various reasons had not been conducted. It was also made to allow American scientists to follow up leads gained during the spring and summer. Finally, on November 4, President Kennedy announced that the atmospheric and high altitude series had been concluded. Underground shots, however, would continue in Nevada. By the end of the year, including both series, the United States would have conducted over ninety tests.

The Soviet series, which started in early August, was in full operation during the Assembly debate. Both within and outside of the United Nations, Soviet officials continued to assert the right of the USSR to test last. On November 7, Chairman Khrushchev predicted that the current Soviet test series would end on November 20. By the end of the year, the Soviet Union would have conducted some 40 explosions. In all there would have been more nuclear detonations in 1962 than in any other year.

What was perhaps more significant than the conclusion—or prospective conclusion—of the two test series was the fact that both sides appeared to be losing interest in testing nuclear weapons in the atmosphere, at high altitudes, and in outer space. Even when the decision to start the 1962 series of tests was taken that spring, there was some discussion in the United States that that series would be the last in these environments. In their 1962 test series, both sides appeared to be approaching the theoretical limits of development which had been postulated by nuclear scientists. This meant that there was less and less to learn through further testing, and also that each gain became more and more difficult. The two sides, though, appear to have emphasized and to have learned different things. The Soviet Union had detonated more high-yield weapons and appeared to know more in this area, while the United States had detonated a larger number of lower yield weapons and seemed to have the lead here.

Military Crises

Another event, or series of events, external to the negotiations which would have an important impact on them was the Cuban crisis, which came to a climax in late October 1962. In this crisis, the United States and the USSR faced the grim possibility of nuclear war more directly than ever before. Apparently this had a profound impact on the leadership of both states, and led them to seek a détente. Most analysts think that this crisis was an important—if not the most important—factor explaining the subsequent change in Soviet policy which ultimately led to the signature of the Moscow Treaty.[13] In withdrawing its nuclear tipped missiles from Cuba, the USSR accepted a resounding defeat and also abandoned the hopes that it seemed to have harbored of overcoming or at least counterbalancing American strategic superiority through this move.[14] Moreover, in the process the USSR accepted the idea of international verification, though not on Soviet soil. Finally, Soviet actions in this instance added fuel to the already smouldering Sino-Soviet dispute.

Almost simultaneously with the Cuban crisis, heavy fighting broke out on the Chinese-Indian border. As a result, India was forced to explore the possibility of obtaining defense assistance from the West, and its entire relationship with the major Western powers became more cordial. One repercussion of this development was the dismissal of Krishna Menon as the Indian Minister of Defense and this in turn led to the replacement in Geneva of Arthur Lall, who left the diplomatic service. The Sino-Indian dispute created a dilemma for the Soviet Union. Allied with China, but also interested in retaining good relations with India, the USSR was forced to choose between the two. By seeking to avoid this choice, it weakened its ties with both parties.

While these important events were taking place and the Assembly debate was in progress representatives of the three nuclear powers continued to meet in the tripartite Subcommittee in Geneva. Yet their instructions obviously were unchanged, for their efforts in eighteen sessions were repetitive and sterile. Outside events were hardly mentioned.

---

[13]See, for example, Marshall D. Shulman's testimony: U.S. Congress, Senate, Committee on Foreign Relations, *Hearings: Nuclear Test Ban Treaty,* 88th Congress, 1st Session (1963), pp. 792-813.

[14]For an excellent analysis in these terms see Arnold L. Horelick, "The Cuban Missile Crisis: An Analysis of Soviet Calculations and Behavior," *World Politics,* Vol. XVI, No. 3 (April 1964), pp. 363-89.

II

Will the Deadlock Dissolve or Endure?

Signs of Change

The pace of the negotiations, however, would soon quicken. In one of the final exchanges of correspondence between Chairman Khrushchev and President Kennedy relating to the Cuban crisis, both leaders expressed the hope that the nuclear test ban issue could be solved.[15] In early November there were hints in New York, Moscow, and Geneva that the USSR might change its position.[16] Specifically, it was indicated that the USSR might propose the adoption of a suggestion which had been raised by three American and three Soviet scientists at the Tenth Pugwash Conference on Science and World Affairs, which had been held in London in early September. In a signed published statement, the six scientists suggested that the use of sealed, automatic recording stations, later dubbed "black boxes," might provide a way out of the test ban impasse.[17] The scientists concluded their statement by saying that a system designed along the lines they suggested would produce enough objective data so that an International Control Commission would "need to request very few on-site inspections." They thereby implicitly acknowledged that some on-site inspections would be necessary. In private conversations during the Pugwash meetings some American scientists suggested that they thought that the West would be satisfied with very few on-site inspections.

At the same time that there were indications that the Soviet position might change, the West began to make new efforts. For the first time since the revelation of the new data it disclosed the number of on-site inspections and control stations in the USSR that it would be willing to accept. In a private meeting in New York on November 7, the day after the General Assembly adopted the two

[15]See Chairman Khrushchev's letter of October 27 and President Kennedy's letter of October 28, *Documents on Disarmament, 1962,* Vol. II, pp. 991-94, 1000-1001.

[16]See *New York Times,* November 2, 1962; November 11, 1962; and ENDC/SC. 1/PV. 43, pp. 17-31.

[17]For the text of their statement, see *Documents on Disarmament, 1962,* Vol. II, pp. 863-65. The statement was signed by D. R. Inglis, R. S. Leghorn, and A. Rich of the United States and L. A. Artsimovitch, Y. V. Riznichenko, and I. Y. Tamm of the Soviet Union.

resolutions concerning a nuclear test ban, Ambassador Dean revealed to Ambassador Kuznetsov that the United States might be willing to accept as few as from 8 to 10 on-site inspections annually in the Soviet Union, and from 8 to 10 nationally manned control posts on Soviet territory. In an earlier meeting, on October 30, Ambassador Dean had said that he thought that a mutually satisfactory arrangement covering all tests could be arranged, and that the United States had in mind a small number of on-site inspections.

At about the same time, in late October 1962, Jerome B. Wiesner, Special Assistant to the President for Science and Technology, had occasion to meet privately with Soviet scientist Fedorov in Washington, D.C., a friend from his Pugwash days. Trying to get the USSR to modify its position so that negotiations would again be possible, Wiesner told Fedorov that if the Soviet Union would come back to its earlier position and accept a small number of inspections, he felt confident that the United States would be able to reduce the number which it would ask for. Till that point the minimum American demand had been for 12. Wiesner continued saying that once the principle of on-site inspection had been established he would hope that the two sides could arrive at some satisfactory number. Dr. Wiesner did not intend to mislead Fedorov, nor to create the impression that the United States could accept as few as 3 or 4 on-site inspections, but merely sought to take action that would get the negotiations started again.

Apparently, however, Chairman Khrushchev interpreted the reports of the Dean and Wiesner conversations as indicating that the United States would be willing to agree to a comprehensive test ban treaty if the USSR would merely accept 3 on-site inspections annually. According to his own account (as relayed by Norman Cousins), Khrushchev presented this information to the Council of Ministers and got the Council to agree to reinstate the Soviet offer of 3 on-site inspections annually.[18]

The Eighteen-Nation Disarmament Committee Reconvenes

When the Eighteen-Nation Disarmament Committee reconvened on November 26, 1962, it was faced with two imminent deadlines.

---

[18]Norman Cousins, "Notes on a 1963 Visit with Khrushchev," *Saturday Review*, Vol. XLVII, No. 45 (November 7, 1964), pp. 16-21, 58-60.

First, it had to report its progress on the test ban issue to the General Assembly by December 10. Secondly, there was the cut-off date of January 1, 1963, established by Assembly Resolution 1762 A (XVII). According to the schedule originally established the Committee would have had more time, but to accommodate Soviet desires the opening date of the Committee had been moved back two weeks from November 12, the date set at the time of the recess and written into the General Assembly resolution. As it was, the Soviet Union had just completed its series of aboveground tests when the Committee reconvened, although it, like the United States, was still conducting tests underground.

Since it was obvious that the nuclear powers would not be able to reach agreement on a comprehensive test ban treaty within the specified time, and since at the conference table the USSR continued to reject the alternative of a partial ban, the eight new members of the Committee concentrated their efforts on the solution suggested in paragraph 6 of General Assembly Resolution 1762 A (XVII), a partial ban accompanied by an interim arrangement suspending underground explosions. Canada, continuing to follow a course somewhat independent of its NATO allies, also participated in these efforts.

A number of concrete suggestions emerged. Sweden again raised its suggestion that the international scientific commission proposed in the Eight-Nation Memorandum should be constituted immediately.[19] In the Swedish view this body could act as an interim commission and it could (1) provide the conference with scientific information and undertake certain scientific investigations, (2) assist in elaborating the detection and data exchange system, and (3) perform the functions which the Eight-Nation Memorandum envisaged for the permanent commission. The Swedish delegate even suggested that it might be helpful if it were possible for this interim commission to undertake an on-site inspection. Brazil, Burma, Canada, Ethiopia, Mexico, and the United Arab Republic supported this suggestion. Canada maintained that an interim arrangement would have to be of limited duration, perhaps a year or six months.[20] Various delegations also echoed this sentiment. Others, however, such as Ethiopia, argued that an interim arrangement should not be bound by a time limit

[19]ENDC/PV. 84, pp. 11-23.
[20]ENDC/PV. 85, p. 17.

and that to impose a time limit would violate the sense of the Assembly resolution. This was also the USSR's position.

Ambassador Lall of India suggested that it might be possible for the states concerned to agree to an annual quota of invitations for on-site inspections.[21] In the course of his remarks about on-site inspection, he also said that the Eight-Nation Memorandum put "an obligation upon all countries to supply all that is required in order to establish the nature of an event."[22] He went on to say that "under the normal rules governing equity and responsibility a country which was in breach in this respect would in fact have broken the agreement, which would no longer subsist." Although these remarks seemed to favor the Western position, they had been submitted to Ambassador Zorin seventy-two hours before they were delivered, and he apparently raised no objection to them. Furthermore, in response to later questioning, Ambassador Lall admitted that his formula did not involve an obligation.

On the same day that Ambassador Lall spoke, Ambassador Padilla Nervo made a similar point. He maintained that "refusal by one of the parties to invite scientific groups would have the same consequences as the violation of a provision for compulsory inspection."[23] The consequence, he felt, in both cases would be to release the injured party from its political and legal obligations—to terminate the treaty.

The "Black Boxes"

The first sign of loosening in the Soviet position came on December 3, 1962. The USSR proposed, although somewhat obliquely, that control over underground nuclear explosions could be established through the use of automatic seismic recording stations in the territory of the nuclear powers and in adjacent countries.[24] In subsequent discussions it emerged that the USSR felt that the use of "black boxes" would obviate the need for internationally supervised, nationally manned control stations and also for on-site inspections. The Western powers were willing to consider the use of "black boxes"—indeed, the United States had made such a suggestion to the Soviet

21ENDC/PV. 85, p. 24.
22*Ibid.*, p. 25.
23*Ibid.*, p. 37.
24ENDC/PV. 86, p. 33.

Union in private meetings in New York before the Eighteen-Nation Committee resumed—but felt that at most they would merely reduce the number of manned stations and on-site inspections required. Moreover, the Western powers wanted to explore the technical details of the "black boxes." The United Kingdom proposed that a group of experts should be convened for this purpose.[25] Later the United States joined the British in urging a technical meeting. Western experts were confident that scientific evidence could not be marshalled to support the Soviet stance. This probably explains why the United States was again willing to support a proposal for technical talks. The USSR, in contrast to the Western powers, insisted that the concept had to be accepted in principle first, then the relevant technical details could be elaborated jointly. Thus the deadlock remained on December 7, 1962, when the Eighteen-Nation Committee filed its required report with the General Assembly.[26]

In the almost two weeks before the Committee recessed on December 20, there were three more meetings of the tripartite sub-committee on nuclear testing and six-plenary sessions. On December 10 the USSR expanded its "black box" proposal by listing three sites where such installations could be located: near Yakutsk for the Far Eastern zone, near Kokchetav for the Central Asian zone, and near Badaibo for the Altai zone.[27] The United States felt that a larger number of "black boxes" would be required and thought that only one of the three suggested sites would be acceptable. Nevertheless it welcomed this Soviet move as providing at least some details.[28] In the same statement, the USSR also announced that it would be willing to have foreign personnel from the international center participate in the delivery and replacement of the "black boxes," it being understood that the USSR could establish appropriate precautionary measures and that Soviet personnel and aircraft would be involved. This was a significant step, for it was the first time since November 28, 1961, that the USSR had been willing to commit itself to allowing some foreigners to enter Soviet territory in connection with a nuclear test ban. For this reason, even though it was not directly related, it had some bearing on the controversial question of on-site inspections.

[25]ENDC/PV. 87, p. 13.
[26]ENDC/ 68.
[27]ENDC/PV. 90, p. 15.
[28]ENDC/SC. 1/PV. 49, pp. 7-9.

It certainly did not solve this conflict, however; and, when the ENDC recessed, the deadlock on nuclear testing persisted. Moreover, on December 13, 1962, the USSR resumed atmospheric testing, and there was some speculation in the West that it might have engaged in atmospheric testing before that date.

The Khrushchev-Kennedy Correspondence: Back to On-Site Inspections

The next moves of the negotiations occurred outside the Eighteen-Nation Committee. This was partly because of the recess. More importantly, however, at this point the two parties principally involved, the Soviet Union and the United States, appear to have desired privacy.

On December 19, 1962, as a part of the private correspondence between the two heads of government inaugurated during the Cuban crisis, Chairman Khrushchev sent President Kennedy a letter which dealt exclusively with the nuclear test ban issue. [29] The most notable feature of the letter was the statement that the USSR would be prepared to agree that two to three on-site inspections should be carried out each year "when it was considered necessary," in seismic areas on the territory of the nuclear powers. The effect of this was almost to bring the Soviet position back to what it had been prior to November 28, 1961. At that time, however, the USSR had not limited the inspections to seismic areas. The offer was cleverly phrased so as not to denigrate the Soviet claim that on-site inspections were unnecessary. Khrushchev stated that he understood from the President and his representatives that the United States Senate would not ratify a nuclear test ban which did not provide for a minimum number of on-site inspections and that this was preventing an agreement. The offer was made, Khrushchev stated, to overcome this obstacle. The Chairman also stated that precautions, such as the use of Soviet aircraft flown by Soviet crews to transport inspection teams on Soviet territory, the screening of windows on the aircraft, and a prohibition on members of inspection teams carrying cameras, would have to be taken to preclude the misuse of inspections for intelligence purposes.

Khrushchev finally repeated the Soviet offer with respect to the three automatic recording stations, and stated that if the sites which

[29]*Documents on Disarmament, 1962*, Vol. II, pp. 1239-42.

had been proposed were not acceptable, the Soviet Union would be willing to discuss the matter and "to seek a mutually acceptable solution."

Western policy-makers were puzzled by two of what they considered to be outright misstatements of fact. First, Khrushchev's letter asserted that at the recent Pugwash meeting, English scientists had proposed the use of automatic seismic recording devices. It was the Western understanding that the idea had been introduced by Soviet scientists, and the public recommendation had been signed by three American and three Soviet scientists. Secondly, the letter declared that in his meeting with Deputy Foreign Minister Kuznetsov on October 30, Ambassador Dean had stated "that in the opinion of the United States Government 2–4 on-site inspections a year in the territory of the Soviet Union would be sufficient." That meeting was conducted in English. During it, Kuznetsov read a draft of the letter which Chairman Khrushchev would send to President Kennedy. Ambassador Dean claims that he told Kuznetsov, both at that meeting and at the one on November 7, that 2 or 3 on-site inspections would not be sufficient. He mentioned a figure from 8 to 10 as being the one which the West would accept. At this point, no mention was made of the Wiesner-Fedorov conversation. For the moment Western policy-makers attributed these two—from their point of view—errors to hasty composition, of which there was other evidence in the letter.

Despite this puzzlement Western policy-makers thought that the letter advanced the negotiations considerably. President Kennedy himself was "exhilarated" on receiving it.[29a] Now at least both sides agreed on the principle of on-site inspections.

President Kennedy replied on December 28, 1962.[30] The President welcomed the change in the Soviet position. He repeated that the United States would be willing to allow "reasonable" security provisions relating to on-site inspection, so long as the inspectors could assure themselves that they were taken to the intended area and had the necessary freedom within the designated inspection area. He also said that an effective test ban treaty was of such importance to him that he "would not permit such international arrangements to become mixed up with our or any other national desire to seek other

[29a]Arthur M. Schlesinger, Jr., *A Thousand Days,* p. 896.
[30]*Documents on Disarmament, 1962*, Vol. II, pp. 1277-79.

types of information about the Soviet Union." Thus he gave his personal pledge not to use on-site inspections for intelligence purposes.

Elsewhere in his letter, the President corrected what he considered the factual errors in Chairman Khrushchev's message. He gave the American version of the Dean-Kuznetsov conversations and stated that the only figures that Ambassador Dean had mentioned were from 8 to 10. He also stated his understanding that the proposal for the use of automatic recording stations had been introduced by Soviet scientists, not British. In passing, he noted that none of the three American scientists who had signed the recommendation were seismologists and that they had been acting as private citizens, not as governmental officials. He also refuted the suggestion that Congress was the sole reason for the American insistence on on-site inspections, asserting that this issue went to the "heart of a reliable agreement."

The President argued that on-site inspections should be allowed in aseismic as well as in seismic areas. He maintained that the automatic recording stations should be established in the areas of greatest seismicity, and thus that there "would be a need for a number of stations in the vicinity of the Kamchatka area and a number in the Tashkent area."

At last the differences between the two sides appeared to be susceptible to negotiation. With this in mind, President Kennedy suggested that a Soviet representative meet with William C. Foster, Director of the Arms Control and Disarmament Agency, to attempt to resolve the differences.

The Washington and New York Talks

Chairman Khrushchev agreed to this course in a letter dated January 7, 1963, and talks between Mr. Foster and Soviet representatives began in Washington one week later. After several days the talks were moved to New York, and British representatives were added. On January 26, President Kennedy ordered the Atomic Energy Commission to postpone the underground nuclear tests which were scheduled to occur in Nevada. (The United States had continued its underground testing program despite the exhortation contained in General Assembly Resolution 1762 A (XVII). However, no tests had as yet been conducted since January 1.) Many thought that a nuclear test ban treaty was finally in sight, but as so often in the past, these hopes were dashed. Questions relating to on-site inspections continued to be at the center of the most important disagreements.[31]

In his letter of January 7 Chairman Khrushchev had agreed that inspections should occur in aseismic as well as seismic areas. The Western powers now wanted to probe the technical details relating to on-site inspections. The United States made proposals concerning the criteria to be used in locating suspicious seismic events; the method of choice for exercise of the quota; the size and shape of the area to be inspected; the personnel and techniques to be utilized in the inspections; and the safeguards to be established surrounding inspections. The Western powers indicated that they would be willing to allow procedures whereby sensitive defense installations could be excluded from on-site inspections, provided that there would also be a remedy for abuse of this privilege. While the Western powers stuck to their position that they would require a quota of from 8 to 10 on-site inspections annually on the territory of the Soviet Union, they indicated that they might be willing to reduce this figure somewhat if they were satisfied that the arrangements would ensure the effectiveness of on-site inspections. The Soviet Union argued that the Western powers were attempting to put off the conclusion of a treaty by the discussion of technical detail, and that these technical matters could be discussed after the quota figure of from 2 to 3 on-site inspections on the territory of the nuclear powers had been accepted. Thus there was once more a deadlock.

Again according to his own account, Chairman Khrushchev felt betrayed by the Western powers, since he had thought that they would accept his offer of 3 on-site inspections annually. Because of domestic opposition to his policy of détente with the West, and because of the opposition of Communist China, he has claimed that he felt that he could not ask that the USSR make still one more concession to the West, since he had asserted that the first would be sufficient.[32] Both the domestic and international forces opposing his policies would

[31]Although there are no public records of the talks, the major participants all gave detailed accounts before the ENDC. See the remarks by Foster (ENDC/PV. 96, pp. 9-14; ENDC/PV. 104, pp. 15-21); Stelle (ENDC/PV. 116, pp. 10-16); Godber (ENDC/PV. 96, pp. 30-33); and Kuznetsov (ENDC/PV. 96, pp. 20-23).

[32]See Norman Cousins, "Notes on a 1963 Visit With Khrushchev," *supra* note 18, pp. 21, 58.

argue, he has said that he felt, that if another concession were made, the West would merely raise its demands again.

In the private talks the Western powers agreed with the Soviet Union that the control system should consist of nationally owned and operated control stations which would submit data regularly and in a uniform manner to an international data-collection center. The Soviet Union and the United States exchanged preliminary lists of seismographic stations from which a control network might be formed (the United States submitted a list of 76 stations and the USSR, 73 stations), and the United States gave the Soviet Union a general description of the instrumentation at each of the United States' stations. The Western powers also agreed that the nationally owned and operated stations would be supplemented by automatic recording stations. The United States suggested ten sites in the United States where automatic recorders might be installed and furnished information on the average seismic noise levels at each site. The Soviet Union accepted one of these, declined the other nine, and requested two additional sites. The United States did not object to these two sites, and furnished seismic noise-level data on them. The United States specified ten general areas within the Soviet Union where it felt automatic recorders might be located, and requested that the Soviet Union designate specific sites within those areas. The Soviet Union countered that there need only be three automatic recording stations on its territory. Ultimately, agreement was reached on three sites in both the USSR and the United States, and on January 31 the Soviet Union provided background noise information on these sites, but there continued to be a debate about whether or not more sites were necessary. The United States eventually stated that its requirements might be met by as few as seven stations, but the Soviet Union refused to agree to more than three. The United States made a number of specific proposals relating to the installation, operation, and removal of the "black boxes," to which the Soviet Union made no response. Implicit in the discussion of "black boxes" and nationally owned and operated stations was the fact that the West no longer insisted on internationally supervised stations.

On the surface, and to much of the press, the disagreement seemed to be quantitative, about the numbers of stations and on-site inspections. In reality, it may well have been considerably broader since the Soviet Union refused to discuss the modalities of conducting on-site inspections. This made many participants in the formulation of American policy pessimistic that negotiations on numbers would prove useful. On January 31, 1963, the Soviet Union requested that the private talks be ended, and that the negotiations be taken up again when the Eighteen-Nation Disarmament Committee resumed. This was widely interpreted as an attempt to use that body as an instrument to bring pressure on the West to agree to Soviet terms.

III
Plans, Fears, Explanations, and Frustrations

Plans for a NATO Multilateral Nuclear Force

Meanwhile, other events had occurred which would have an impact on the test ban negotiations. Prime Minister Macmillan and President Kennedy met at Nassau in the Bahamas from December 18 to 21, 1962. Their discussions centered on matters relating to national security. The principal topic with which they had to deal was the American decision to abandon the development of the Skybolt medium-range air to surface missile, on which the United Kingdom had counted to maintain and extend the useful life of its bomber force. In searching for an alternative, the United States offered to provide the United Kingdom with a certain number of Polaris missiles, without nuclear warheads, which could be installed on British submarines. A condition of this offer was that the British agree to employ the missiles not as an independent deterrent, but as part of a NATO nuclear force.[33] The United States agreed to make available equal forces for inclusion in such a multilateral force. The President and the Prime Minister took the occasion, therefore, to attempt to solve the strategic crisis in NATO, as well as to solve the immediate British problem. The creation of new instrumentality, a NATO multilateral nuclear force (MLF) was implicit in their resolution of the Skybolt controversy. By this move, which would mean giving a larger voice in nuclear strategy to their allies—although exactly how much larger was not clear—the two leaders hoped to head off the development of further independent nuclear forces and to increase confidence in and the viability of NATO. As an immediate start on the creation of a multilateral nuclear force, the Prime Minister suggested, and

[33]See the communique, *Documents on Disarmament, 1962,* Vol. II, pp. 1274-76.

the President agreed, that some elements of the United States Strategic Forces and the United Kingdom Bomber Command could be assigned to NATO and targeted in accordance with NATO plans.

Whether or not the creation of a NATO multilateral nuclear force would actually achieve the results for which the two leaders hoped was moot. The detailed plans for implementation, of course, would have to be worked out. However, it was clear that the United States had no intention of assigning more than a fraction of its Strategic Forces to NATO, thus it still would have the ability to inaugurate a nuclear war without the consent of its allies. On the other hand, it was fairly clear that the United States would insist that it would have to agree to any decision to employ the MLF. Therefore the defense of Europe through nuclear weapons would continue to be dependent upon an American decision. France indicated clearly that a multilateral nuclear force would not solve the problems relating to NATO which concerned it. France turned down a United States offer similar to that which was made to the British to supply Polaris missiles and refused to participate in the discussions of plans for a multilateral nuclear force. Some other Western European members of NATO, especially Western Germany, were more receptive to the plan, which would give them greater access to nuclear weapons and a larger voice in NATO nuclear strategy than they had had previously. For this very reason the MLF had implications for the "nth country" problem, one of the issues at stake in the test ban negotiations.

Rising Republican Opposition

A second development during this period was the growth of serious opposition within the ranks of Republican Congressmen to American policy in the nuclear test ban negotiations. The two draft treaties which the United States tabled on August 27, 1962, had been cleared with the relevant congressional committees. At that time some members of Congress had not paid much attention to the shifts in United States policy because they were convinced that the Soviet Union would reject the new American proposals.[34] When the negotiations began to look more serious as a result of the Khrushchev-Kennedy correspondence, some of these Congressmen began to have second thoughts. One, Representative Craig Hosmer, a Republican

[34]See *New York Times*, August 3, 1962, p. 3.

from California, the ranking minority member of the Joint Committee on Atomic Energy, and the individual who as an Army officer had led the first United States occupation forces into Hiroshima in 1945, concluded that the Kennedy Administration might well agree to arrangements which, in his view, would prejudice American security. He expressed his concerns in a speech in the House of Representatives on January 24, 1963.[35] What he appeared to fear most was that the United States would agree to the Soviet offer of three on-site inspections annually. He was also concerned that the United States would accept three "black boxes" in lieu of a much larger number of international control posts. He further worried that the Soviet Union had made significant gains through its atmospheric tests in December and that the United States was acting before these gains could be properly analyzed and their impact on the United States assessed. He recommended that President Kennedy restate the American 1958 terms and that these be made nonnegotiable. By this he seemed to mean an international control system involving 20 on-site inspections and 19 internationally manned control posts on Soviet territory.

After his speech the Republican leadership took the unusual step of establishing a Republican Conference Committee on Nuclear Testing, with Representative Hosmer as its head. Initially this Committee planned to arrange for the personal appearance by experts before a meeting of the Republican Conference on January 29. However, when President Kennedy announced the suspension of nuclear testing on January 26, Hosmer thought that an agreement was near, and changed his plans. He then decided to issue a series of papers prepared by experts. The first of these, written by Edward Teller, was issued on January 31, 1963. In it, Teller argued that acceptance of the current Soviet proposals would constitute acceptance of an unpoliced moratorium. Other scientists who prepared subsequent papers reiterated this position, and also argued that further tests were needed to explore and develop nuclear weapons and to create a pure fusion weapon. The Kennedy Administration attempted to answer these criticisms with a paper prepared for the Republican Conference Committee by William C. Foster, Director of the Arms Control and Disarmament Agency, and also a lifelong Republican and former official in the Department of Defense. He argued that the United

[35]*Congressional Record,* Vol. CIX, Part 1, pp. 950-51.

States was ahead of the Soviet Union in many areas of nuclear weapons development and that a test ban would slow down or "freeze" Soviet efforts to catch up. He also maintained that as a first step toward other measures of arms control, a test ban would offer important advantages. Although he conceded that there would be risks in a test ban, he maintained that on balance the advantages would outweigh the disadvantages.

With these developments, the domestic battle was joined. The Republican Conference Committee on Nuclear Testing would continue its attack throughout the spring of 1963.

The Eighteen-Nation Disarmament Committee Resumes

The Eighteen-Nation Disarmament Committee reconvened on February 12, 1963, almost a month later than had been planned. Both East and West sought to gain the support of the eight new members of the Committee for their position. The Western representatives gave a detailed explanation of their position, and attempted to indicate its reasonableness and flexibility, however, the British delegates put considerably greater stress on the latter point than the Americans. Soviet representatives, on the other hand, argued that the USSR had made major concessions to the West and that it was the West which was blocking agreement. They also strongly criticized the current American underground tests, the first of which was conducted on February 8, 1963—President Kennedy rescinded the suspension after the New York talks collapsed—underscoring that these tests violated General Assembly Resolution 1762 A (XVII). In contrast, the Soviet Union, so far as could be determined, had not conducted any nuclear tests since the conclusion of its Arctic series in December 1962.

As in the January private talks, the principal differences between East and West involved on-site inspections. Soviet delegates argued that they had made a major concession in accepting obligatory on-site inspections. They maintained that this was a political concession, since the USSR did not feel that such inspections were necessary. They also developed the argument, touched upon in Chairman Khrushchev's letter of December 19, that the USSR had been led to believe that if it accepted 2 or 3 on-site inspections, the West would agree to a treaty banning all nuclear tests. In seeking to substantiate this case, Soviet delegates reiterated their version of the Dean-Kuznetsov conversations, and maintained that in the private conversations in January Mr. Foster had been very cautious in denying this, saying merely that Mr. Dean was not authorized to offer any figure other than 8–10.[36] They also quoted a number of statements made in the Eighteen-Nation Committee and the seventeenth General Assembly by British and American representatives to the effect that all that was needed to achieve a comprehensive treaty was for the Soviet Union to accept the principle of obligatory on-site inspection, and to revert to the position which it had held prior to November 28, 1961. At that time the Soviet Union was willing to accept 2 to 3 on-site inspections. Soviet delegates also stated that in the second half of October, 1962, Jerome B. Wiesner, during two informal meetings in Washington and New York with Soviet academician Fedorov, had requested that the Soviet Union should agree to on-site inspections, and that a small quota of 2 to 3 inspections annually would open the way to an agreement.[37] The USSR held that by now insisting on more than three on-site inspections the West was acting in bad faith.

Western delegates denied most of the Soviet charges. As President Kennedy had in his letter of December 28, they refuted in unambiguous terms the Soviet version of the Dean-Kuznetsov talks. They argued that Soviet delegates were distorting the statements made in the Eighteen-Nation Committee and in the General Assembly. They also said that "no official representative of the United States" had ever said that 2 or 3 on-site inspections would be acceptable to the United States, and pointed out the number of occasions, including President Kennedy's letter of December 28, on which a higher figure had been named. However, they never denied the Soviet account of the Wiesner-Fedorov conversation. Moreover, some American officials have conceded that the USSR may have "honestly misunderstood" some of the private meetings that preceded the December correspondence between the two heads of government.[38]

The American failure and inability to deny the Soviet accounts of the Wiesner-Fedorov conversations damaged its case before the eight new members of the Committee. Dr. Wiesner, beyond being an important administration official, had after all borne the burden of

[36]ENDC/PV. 113, p. 35.
[37]See ENDC/PV. 101, p. 48; and ENDC/PV. 113, p. 16.
[38]*New York Times*, April 23, 1963, p. 8.

explaining to them the technical situation as the United States understood it.

In his initial presentations to the Eighteen-Nation Committee, Mr. Foster continued to maintain that the minimal number of on-site inspections annually on the territory of the USSR which the United States could accept would be from 8 to 10. In one session, he argued that in order adequately to deter a would-be violator, a country would have to save at least one or two of its quota of inspections until the end of the year.[39] If the annual quota were only three, this would mean that a country would only be able to call for one on-site inspection during most of the year. Senator Hubert H. Humphrey, who was a member of the American delegation during the first days of the resumed session, emphasized in private conversations with other delegations that the United States Senate would not ratify a test-ban treaty which provided for only three on-site inspections in the USSR annually.[40] According to the testimony of some of the representatives of the eight new members of the ENDC, he did state, however, that the Senate might accept a figure lower than 8–10. American negotiators continued to maintain that before the United States would agree to any quota figure, the Soviet Union would have to specify its view concerning several aspects of the overall verification system.

During the week of February 18, Mr. Foster met privately with Deputy Foreign Minister Kuznetsov. In this meeting he explained a new American position on several features of the inspection system, and then stated that in the context of the verification system which he had described, the United States could accept an annual quota of seven on-site inspections for each side.[41] The Western press had widely forecast that the United States would reduce its demands, and some within the Kennedy Administration were arguing that the United States could go still further. Secretary McNamara was reportedly willing to settle for 6.[41a] Jerome B. Wiesner maintained that 5 inspections per year would provide adequate security against clandestine testing.[42] Five is the number which the representatives of the

[39]ENDC/PV. 99, p. 21.

[40]Washington Post, February 21, 1963, February 22, 1963.

[41]ENDC/PV. 102, pp. 23-24.

[41a]Arthur M. Schlesinger, Jr., A Thousand Days, p. 897.

[42]Jerome B. Wiesner, Where Science and Politics Meet (1965), p. 167. Interestingly and perhaps significantly Wiesner states that the United States formally reduced its demand to 6 or 7 (ibid.).

eight new nations in the ENDC expected the United States to ask for. The other changes in the Western position which Mr. Foster described related to the conduct of on-site inspections. Western delegates presented them in more detail to the ENDC at various times during the next month, and then summarized them in a memorandum submitted on April 1, 1963.[43] As of mid-March, the United States actually had a new draft treaty prepared. However, it did not table anything more than the memorandum.

These changes shifted the most important elements of the on-site inspection process in the case of the nuclear powers to representatives of the other side. Thus they moved away from the impartial concepts that had been written into the August 27, 1962, draft comprehensive treaty and in the direction of reciprocal or adversary inspection. The other nuclear side would not only have the right to select which events it chose to inspect (as in the 1962 draft treaty) but in addition it would supply the leader of the inspection team and over half of the team's technical personnel. Only the remainder of the personnel would be selected from the international staff. Beyond this, the Western position specified various time limits. The most important of these were that the other nuclear side would have up to sixty days after a seismic event to request an on-site inspection, and, unless drilling were required or mutual agreement for an extension obtained, an on-site inspection team would have only six weeks in which to complete an inspection. The inspection area would consist of an ellipse with a semi-major axis of no more than 15 kilometers, with a maximum area of 500 square kilometers. The country on whose territory the inspection was to take place would be responsible for transporting the team to the inspection area. It could use its own aircraft and pilots, and could select the flight routes. It could have its own personnel including observers accompany the team. The number of such personnel could equal the team. The Western powers also spelled out their concept of the use of the "black boxes."

Despite repeated requests in private and plenary sessions, Soviet delegates refused to comment on these matters. They argued that the Western powers were seeking to block an agreement by having the negotiations become involved in a morass of technical details. They

43See ENDC/PV. 108, pp. 5-10; ENDC/PV. 110, pp. 19-26; ENDC/-PV. 113, pp. 5-9; and ENDC/78.

continually asserted that if the West would agree to the number of "black boxes" and on-site inspections proposed by the Soviet Union, there would be no difficulty reaching agreement on the details. Since the Western powers would not do this, the deadlock continued.

The eight new members of the Committee were perplexed and irritated by the situation. Because of the Washington and New York talks, they had returned to Geneva in an optimistic mood. When their expectations were not fulfilled, they became irked, yet they did not know what to do. Some of them made rather halting attempts at suggesting compromise solutions, and they were even encouraged to do this by the United Kingdom, but these attempts were virtually ignored by the United States and the USSR. The two states even discouraged the eight new members of the Committee from submitting compromise proposals which they had formulated but not tabled. While the eight agreed not to act—apparently because of pressure applied by both Soviet and American diplomats in their national capitals[44]—some of them warned that if agreement were not forthcoming soon, they might submit their proposals even if these proposals met the displeasure of both powers.[45] The United Kingdom suggested that the tripartite Subcommittee of the three nuclear powers should be revived, and the United States and other countries supported this proposal, but the Soviet Union refused, insisting that the discussion should be conducted in the plenary sessions.

IV
For the Moment: Pianissimo

In mid-March the United States and the Soviet Union, as Co-chairmen of the Eighteen-Nation Disarmament Committee, suggested that the Committee should also discuss the other items on its agenda, and thereafter normally only one of the three weekly meetings of the Committee was devoted to discussion of the nuclear test ban.

The Soviet Union appeared to be quite interested in the discussion of other matters. When the Eighteen-Nation Committee had resumed in February, it had tabled two new proposals. The first was

[44]Arthur S. Lall, *Negotiating Disarmament*, p. 25. Eventually, in a public address in Copenhagen, on May 9, 1963, Mrs. Alva Myrdal exposed most of the details of the proposals (*ibid.*, pp. 27-28).
[45]ENDC/PV. 123, pp. 48-49.

for a declaration on renunciation of use of foreign territories for stationing strategic means of delivery of nuclear weapons, and the second was for a nonaggression pact between the parties of the Warsaw and North Atlantic Treaties.[46] In the debates Soviet delegates linked both of these proposals with the Western efforts now in progress to develop a NATO Multilateral Nuclear Force. They asserted that such a force would be dangerous, among other reasons, because it would give Western Germany access to nuclear weapons. These delegates argued that the MLF, in widening access to nuclear weapons, would contradict one of the aims of a nuclear test ban. Western delegates, on the other hand, explained that the purpose of the MLF was to prevent the development of independent nuclear capabilities and that it was consonant with long-standing Western policies opposing the proliferation of nuclear weapons capability. The French nuclear test in the Sahara on March 18, 1963, furnished Soviet delegates ammunition for their attack on Western policy. Obviously, all of these issues were linked with the test ban negotiations in Soviet strategy.

What this new development in the test ban negotiations meant was the subject of speculation. Did it mean that these other issues would have to be solved before or simultaneously with the achievement of a test ban treaty? Various answers were given. Regardless of their answer to this question, many, both within and outside of the Committee, regarded the lower priority now accorded the test ban issue as a sign that the high hopes raised by the correspondence between the heads of government in December 1962 and the private talks the following month would not be fulfilled.

[46]ENDC/75, and ENDC/77.

Chapter XIII

The Moscow Treaty

I

Prelude

The Administration Moves to Rebut Domestic Criticisms

While the negotiations in Geneva continued at a low key and reduced tempo, the domestic opposition to the Administration's efforts to achieve a nuclear test ban, which had begun to make itself felt in late January 1963, continued its attacks and appeared to gain strength. However, the Kennedy Administration also moved to rebut the criticisms and demonstrated that it would fight for its policies.

On February 21, 1963, Senator Thomas J. Dodd, a Democrat from Connecticut, gave a long, critical analysis of the American position in the negotiations in a major address on the Senate floor.[1] He argued that the United States had made a number of unwarranted concessions, and that it should return to its "original Geneva formula." On February 28, Senators Richard B. Russell, Stuart Symington, and Henry Jackson, all Democrats especially influential in defense policy matters, sent a letter to President Kennedy advising him that they could not approve the 1962 draft comprehensive treaty in its present form.[2] In early March, the Joint Committee on Atomic Energy conducted six days of hearings on the technical aspects of verification of a nuclear test ban. In these hearings, Dr. Carl Romney admitted that the seismic system currently being proposed by the United States would generally be unable to detect fully coupled underground nuclear explosions of below 1 kiloton if they were conducted in granite, below 2 to 6 kilotons if they were conducted in tuff, and below 20 kilotons if they were conducted in alluvium.[3] He added that some tests below

[1]*Congressional Record*, Vol. CIX, Part 2, pp. 2798-2809.
[2]See *Washington Post*, March 5, 1963.
[3]*Hearings: Developments in Technical Capabilities for Detecting and Identifying Nuclear Weapons Tests*, 88th Congress, 1st Session (1963), p. 104.

that level might be detected and that the United States would of course have its unilateral intelligence capabilities. On the other hand, decoupling would raise the threshold even higher. The current estimate was that decoupling would muffle a seismic signal by a factor of 200 or more.[4]

The most optimistic statement which the American scientists who had been working on the problem of on-site inspection under the Vela Program would make was that the system envisaged in the Western 1962 draft comprehensive treaty would give some probability, which they could not evaluate, of identifying an underground nuclear explosion.[5] They also admitted that with careful planning an underground detonation could be executed so that proof of its occurrence would probably be lacking. Thus far there had been no field exercise involving on-site inspection techniques, because the scientists involved did not think that their techniques were "sufficiently advanced," and because the Arms Control and Disarmament Agency was not convinced that given the conditions in the United States—limited areas in which to test and limited abilities to maintain secrecy—such exercises would be useful.[6]

Representative Craig Hosmer played an active role in the hearings, which provided ample material for the use of his Republican Conference Committee on Nuclear Testing. This group continued its assault on the Administration position.

As the attacks against the Administration's efforts mounted, those who favored these efforts rallied to their support, and members of the Administration launched a major effort to justify their course. In early March, Adrian Fisher, Deputy Director of the Arms Control and Disarmament Agency, took the unusual action of writing a letter to the Editor of the *Washington Post,* in reply to a letter which that paper had printed from Senator Dodd.[7] Senator Humphrey made a major speech in the Senate on March 7.[8] Four days later, the Senate Committee on Foreign Relations held a hearing which provided a

[4]*Ibid.*, pp. 71, 297.

[5]See the statement of Theodore A. George, General Engineer, Advanced Research Projects Agency, *ibid.*, p. 257.

[6]*Ibid.*, pp. 251, 475.

[7]*Washington Post*, March 1, 1963 (Dodd); and, March 4, 1963, (Fisher).

[8]*Congressional Record*, Vol. CIX, Part 3, pp. 3711-24.

platform from which Secretary of State Rusk could defend the Administration's efforts. Senator Pastore arranged it so that Messrs. Foster and Long of the Arms Control and Disarmament Agency were the concluding witnesses before the Joint Committee on Atomic Energy. President Kennedy utilized his news conferences personally to defend the Administration's position.

These individuals all argued that the ability to detect underground explosions had substantially increased. They also pointed out that the thresholds of detectability were not absolute, that some events under the commonly assumed thresholds would be detected. They maintained that the possibility that an on-site inspection would discover incriminating evidence of a nuclear explosion would be a powerful deterrent to a would-be violator, and they pointed out that unilateral intelligence capabilities could be used in selecting events to be inspected. Presumably such intelligence capabilities would include agents, observation satellites, and other devices. In their view, this would substantially increase the probability of an on-site inspection's being successful. They also argued that the new United States' position emphasizing reciprocal inspection would enhance the effectiveness of inspections. Finally, they argued that the risks of a continued unfettered arms race would outweigh the acknowledged risks of a comprehensive test ban. President Kennedy, in his public remarks, seemed to be particularly impressed with the dangers which he felt would result from the proliferation of nuclear capabilities.[9]

Steps to Break the Deadlock

Although there seemed to be major obstacles to a test ban treaty both in Geneva and Washington, more promising signs soon appeared. On April 5, 1963, in the Eighteen-Nation Disarmament Committee, toward the end of a somewhat polemical speech, Mr. Tsarapkin announced that the Soviet Union was ready to consider the United States proposal, tabled the previous December, to establish a direct line of communication between the governments of the USSR and the United States.[10] The difficulty of insuring reliable communications between the two states had become painfully evident during the Cuban crisis, and the United States had come to emphasize this proposal as an important means of preventing war arising through accident or

[9]See his news conference remarks of March 21, 1963.
[10]ENDC/PV. 118, p. 52.

miscalculation. After this announcement, talks began on the technical modalities of establishing a "hot line," as it was called. A memorandum of understanding on this subject was finally signed on June 20, 1963.[11] Also in April, negotiations were begun between the Soviet Union and the United States to renew their agreement on cooperation in nuclear research. A new agreement was signed the following month.

In late April, in an interview with an Italian newspaper editor, Chairman Khrushchev raised the possibility that if the Western powers did not soon agree to accept the Soviet offer of from two to three on-site inspections annually, the offer might be withdrawn.[12] At about the same time the American and British Ambassadors in Moscow jointly approached first Foreign Minister Gromyko and then, on April 24, Chairman Khrushchev on the test ban issue.[13] The move was taken at British urging and without great American enthusiasm. The two ambassadors delivered a letter to Chairman Khrushchev from President Kennedy and Prime Minister Macmillan. This "letter concluded by saying that the writers would be ready in due course to send to Moscow very senior representatives empowered to speak for them directly with Khrushchev."[13a] Despite Chairman Khrushchev's unpromising initial reply, this touched off another round of correspondence between the heads of government in May and June.

There were also developments within the United States. On May 8, the Atomic Energy Commission and the Department of Defense announced that they would detonate three low-yield nuclear explosions in Nevada later that month. Five days later the two agencies announced the cancellation of these shots.[14]

On May 27, Senator Dodd submitted a resolution stating that it was the sense of the Senate "that the United States should again offer the Soviet Union an immediate agreement banning all tests that contaminate the atmosphere or the oceans, bearing in mind that such tests can already be monitored by the United States without on-site inspection on Soviet territory."[15] The resolution suggested that if the Soviet Union should reject this offer, the United States should reiterate

[11]ENDC/97.

[12]The transcript was published in *New York Times*, April 22, 1963, p. 1.

[13]*New York Times*, April 23, 1963, p. 1; April 25, 1963, p. 1.

[13a]Arthur M. Schlesinger, Jr., *A Thousand Days*, p. 898.

[14]*New York Times*, May 14, 1963, p. 1.

[15]*Congressional Record*, Vol. CIX, Part 7, p. 9483.

it, and seek the widest possible international support for it. If the Soviet Union should continue to refuse such an agreement, the resolution proposed that the United States should commit itself "before the world to conduct no nuclear tests in the atmosphere or under water so long as the Soviet Union abstains from them." As far as was known in the West, the USSR had not conducted any nuclear tests since its December 1962 series. The resolution added that the United States should maintain its readiness so that it would not be unprepared if the Soviet Union suddenly resumed nuclear testing in the atmosphere or underwater. Senator Humphrey joined Senator Dodd as the principal cosponsor of the resolution. Thirty-two other senators from both parties also became cosponsors,[16] making a total of thirty-four. Although Senator Dodd informed the Administration of his proposal in advance, he did not act at its behest. Indeed, President Kennedy had some concern that it might undercut American efforts to achieve a comprehensive test ban.[16a] During the course of his speech introducing the resolution, Senator Dodd stated that although he felt that a comprehensive test ban would be preferable to a partial ban, he had serious reservations about the current American proposal for a comprehensive treaty, which he knew several Senators shared.

Ten days earlier, Senator William Proxmire had asserted in a major address that it was unlikely that the Senate would ratify the comprehensive treaty currently being proposed by the Administration,[17] and after a private survey conducted by members of his staff during the month of May, Senator Joseph S. Clark concluded that, at that time, at most, fifty-seven Senators would support the current American proposal.[18] This was ten less than the required two-thirds

[16]They were Senators: Bartlett, Brewster, Burdick, Case, Church, Clark, Dominick, Douglas, Engle, Gruening, Hart, Hartke, Inouye, Javits, Keating, Kefauver, Lausche, McCarthy, McGee, McGovern, Metcalf, Morse, Moss, Muskie, Neuberger, Pell, Prouty, Randolph, Ribicoff, Scott, Sparkman, and Yarborough.

[16a]Arthur M. Schlesinger, *A Thousand Days*, p. 899.

[17]*Congressional Record*, Vol. CIX, Part 7, p. 8894. Jerome B. Wiesner has gone even farther. In his book, he wrote that "Many times during the bitter Senate hearings on the partial test ban treaty we [The Kennedy Administration] had reason to wonder whether a comprehensive treaty would indeed have been acceptable given any number of inspections." (*Where Science and Politics Meet*, p. 167.)

[18]Senator Joseph S. Clark, "Would the Senate Ratify a Nuclear Test Ban Treaty?," *War/Peace Report*, Vol. III, No. 6 (June 1963), p. 6.

majority. On the other hand, it was obvious that the resolution submitted by Senator Dodd commanded much wider support.

The extent to which the Senate resolution affected the Soviet position cannot be known. It must have been obvious, though, if that many Senators had grave reservations about the American proposal involving 7 on-site inspections annually, to obtain Senatorial consent to a treaty involving only 3 on-site inspections annually would have been virtually impossible.

On June 10, Harold Wilson, leader of the British Labour Party, stated, at a news conference in Moscow where he was visiting, that he had gained the impression in a three-hour interview with Chairman Khrushchev that the prospects for an immediate agreement on a comprehensive test ban were not very hopeful.[19] Mr. Khrushchev apparently implied that the Soviet Union had withdrawn its offer of two or three on-site inspections annually. Mr. Wilson also said, though, that he thought that prospects for a partial ban were fairly good.

That same day President Kennedy delivered the commencement address at The American University. He titled his remarks "Toward a Strategy of Peace."[20] Earlier in the spring, the President had decided that he would make a speech about "peace."[21] Norman Cousins contributed to the timing of the speech by suggesting in a letter to Kennedy on April 30 that such a step at this time might affect the course of Soviet policy and would certainly help the American image in the world. The letter was written just after Cousins' return from a trip to the Soviet Union, during which, among other things, he told Khrushchev—at Kennedy's request—that the President really did want a test ban treaty.

In his address, President Kennedy called for a reexamination of American attitudes toward peace itself, toward the Soviet Union, and toward the Cold War, and called for a new context for world discussions and increased understanding with the USSR. He announced—as Harold Wilson did also—that he, Prime Minister Macmillan, and Chairman Khrushchev had agreed that high level discussions would begin shortly in Moscow on a nuclear test ban treaty. Unlike Mr. Wilson, however, he stated that the negotiations would be "looking for

[19]*New York Times*, June 11, 1963, p. 1.
[20]U.S. Department of State *Bulletin*, Vol. XLIX, No. 1253 (July 1, 1963), pp. 2-6.
[21]Theodore C. Sorenson, *Kennedy*, p. 730.

ward toward early agreement on a comprehensive test ban treaty."[21a] The President apparently was determined to pursue the objective of a comprehensive ban despite the feeling in the Senate and the apparent retraction by the Kremlin.[22] As evidence of American good faith, President Kennedy declared that "the United States does not propose to conduct nuclear tests in the atmosphere so long as other states do not do so." His hand was strengthened in this regard by the resolution which Senator Dodd had introduced. Moreover, as far as is known, neither side had tested in the atmosphere since the end of December 1962. Some within the Administration had proposed that the United States also suspend underground testing for a limited period, but the President rejected this suggestion.[22a]

Apparently, the agreement to hold the meeting resulted from the exchange of correspondence between the heads of government initiated in April, and more specifically from Chairman Khrushchev's response on June 8 to a joint proposal of Prime Minister Macmillan and President Kennedy, delivered on May 31, 1963.

Prior to this there had been important developments on the Soviet scene. The quarrel between the Soviet and Chinese Communist parties had deepened, and a conference between the two groups on their ideological differences had been scheduled to meet on July 7. A plenum of the Central Committee of the Communist Party of the Soviet Union had also been scheduled to open on June 18. Thus it seemed that events on various fronts were moving toward a climax.

II
Drafting the Treaty

American Preparations

Even before President Kennedy's American University speech, the Administration had begun preparing for the forthcoming Moscow negotiations. The first steps consisted of the relevant agencies of the Administration reviewing current Western positions. Most of the American preparation concerned a comprehensive treaty. Almost simultaneously, the Preparedness Investigating Subcommittee of the

---

[21a]"Toward A Strategy of Peace," *supra* note 20, p. 6.
[22]See *New York Times*, June 3, 1963, p. 1.
[22a]Theodore C. Sorenson, *Kennedy*, p. 730.

Senate Committee on Armed Services began a series of executive session hearings.

In the process of the review of American policy, the Joint Chiefs of Staff concluded that the current Western proposal for a comprehensive nuclear test ban was "not consistent with the national security," because it was "not adequate to prevent the Soviet Union from making important advances in nuclear weaponry that could alter the present military relationship in favor of the Soviets."[23] There were several reasons for their decision. First, they concluded that the present proposal would prohibit all tests, including those "which have essentially no probability of detection."[24] They felt that this would prevent the United States from testing while providing "the opportunity for the Soviets to test clandestinely." The Joint Chiefs felt that any test ban treaty should "permit testing below appropriately specified and realistic detection thresholds." The Joint Chiefs also concluded that 7 on-site inspections "would not provide a reasonable deterrent considering the number of suspicious events likely to occur in the Soviet Union annually." They regarded the criteria for initiating an on-site inspection as too restrictive, and the area within which the inspection would be confined as being too small. They objected to the fact that the host country would provide the logistic support. They disliked the fact that the International Commission would have the sole right to order inspections on the territory of the nonnuclear powers. Finally, they felt the withdrawal provisions were too time consuming, and that at most 60 days should be required to complete a legal withdrawal. What the position of the Joint Chiefs was when the 1962 draft treaty was formulated has never been satisfactorily explained.

After the individual agency reviews, the American position was discussed in the Committee of Principals. Interestingly, on May 22, 1963, the Chairman of the Joint Chiefs of Staff was made an official member of the Committee of Principals; prior to that time he had routinely attended the Committee, but as an advisor. The change was made to mollify Congressional criticism. On June 14 the Committee of Principals met, and decided that in the forthcoming Moscow nego-

---

[23]U.S. Senate, Committee on Armed Services, *Hearings: Military Aspects and Implications of Nuclear Test Ban Proposals and Related Matters,* 88th Congress, 1st Session (1964), 2 vols., Vol. I, p. 305.
[24]*Ibid.*, p. 303.

tiations the United States should continue to give priority to efforts to achieve a comprehensive treaty, essentially on the basis of the draft which had been prepared in March. The Joint Chiefs of Staff dissented. The Secretary of Defense, however, concurred in this recommendation, which the President accepted. It was in accord with his own thinking on the matter.

Two days earlier it was announced that W. Averell Harriman, onetime Ambassador to Moscow and then the Under Secretary of State for Political Affairs, would head the American delegation to Moscow.[25] Lord Hailsham, who was Minister of Science, was chosen to head the United Kingdom delegation.[26] He was known to take a passionate interest in achieving a nuclear test ban treaty. On June 18, the United Kingdom pledged that it would not be the first nation to resume atmospheric testing.

President Kennedy visited Prime Minister Macmillan during his Western European trip on June 29 and 30. The two leaders coordinated Western strategy for the forthcoming talks, and Kennedy arranged to have the American delegation take the lead in the negotiations. He had much more confidence in Harriman than in Hailsham.

Before the American delegation departed for Moscow, according to Theodore C. Sorenson, President Kennedy

> . . . made clear his belief (1) that this was the last clear chance to stop the diffusion of nuclear tests and poisons and to start building mutual confidence with the Russians; (2) that the delegation should keep in daily contact with him; and (3) that extreme precautions should be taken to prevent their prospects of success from being ruined by any premature leak of their position.[26a]

[25]The other members of the American negotiating team were: Adrian W. Fisher, Deputy Director of the Arms Control and Disarmament Agency; Carl Kaysen, Deputy Special Assistant to the President for National Security Affairs; William R. Tyler, Assistant Secretary of State for European Affairs; John T. McNaughton, General Counsel, Department of Defense; Frank E. Cash, Department of State; Alexander Akalovsky, Franklin A. Long, and Nedville E. Nordness, Arms Control and Disarmament Agency; and Frank Press, a seismologist at California Institute of Technology.

[26]The other members of the British delegation were Duncan Wilson, Under Secretary of the Foreign Office, and Sir Sully Zuckerman and Sir William Penney, scientific advisors.

[26a]Theodore C. Sorenson, *Kennedy,* p. 734.

Again according to the same source, "he made arrangements for only six top officials outside the White House (Rusk, Ball, McNamara, McCone, Thompson, and Foster) to read the cables from Moscow on a hand-delivered, 'for-your-eyes-only' basis." When the actual negotiations were in progress, he would meet each evening with these six officials to discuss the progress of the talks, and he insisted that all communications to the delegation in Moscow be cleared through him.

Soviet Preliminary Moves

As these developments were in process, the USSR gave various indications of the position which it would take. On June 14, in an interview with a Pravda correspondent, Chairman Khrushchev stated that the USSR would not permit any on-site inspections as part of a nuclear test ban treaty.[27] He also said, though, that President Kennedy's American University speech had made "a favorable impression." Immediately after it was broadcast, Khrushchev had told Harold Wilson that it was "the greatest speech by any American President since Roosevelt."[27a] Moreover, Soviet jamming of the BBC and the Voice of America, which had begun to slacken off in May, was stopped completely shortly after the President's speech. When the speech itself was rebroadcast, the USSR did not jam a single passage.

On July 2, in East Berlin, Chairman Khrushchev gave what could be considered a formal reply to the President's speech. Much of his address was devoted to an analysis of the past negotiations. He argued that underground nuclear tests could be monitored by national detection systems combined with automatic seismic stations, and that on-site inspections were not necessary. He reiterated the Soviet charge that the Western powers sought on-site inspection for intelligence purposes, and then went on to say:

> . . . it is time for the imperialist gentlemen to know that the Soviet Government will never abandon the security interests of its country and of all the Socialist countries and will not open its doors to NATO intelligence agents. This is no subject for bargaining.[28]

[27]*New York Times*, June 15, 1963, p. 1.
[27a]Arthur M. Schlesinger, *A Thousand Days*, p. 904.
[28]U.S. Congress, Senate, Committee on Foreign Relations, *Hearings: Nuclear Test Ban Treaty*, 88th Congress, 1st Session (1963), p. 1000.

After asserting that a treaty banning nuclear tests in all environments was impossible because of the Western position, he declared that the Soviet Government would be willing to conclude a treaty banning nuclear tests in the atmosphere, in outer space, and under water. He said that the USSR had "made this proposal before, but the Western Powers had frustrated an agreement by advancing supplementary conditions which envisaged large-scale inspection of our territory." The record of the negotiations contains no evidence to substantiate this claim of a prior Soviet offer. Until June 1963 the USSR had always refused to consider a partial ban without an unpoliced moratorium on underground testing. Now for the first time, the USSR did not insist that a moratorium on underground tests accompany a partial ban. At the conclusion of his speech, Khrushchev attempted to link the conclusion of a partial nuclear test ban with the signature of a nonaggression pact between the NATO countries and the Warsaw Pact states; however, it was not clear whether or not he intended the latter to be a condition of the former.

On July 3, seemingly in response to Chairman Khrushchev's speech, Prime Minister Macmillan declared in the House of Commons that although the West ought to seek a comprehensive test ban, an agreement banning tests in the sea, the atmosphere, and space "would still be an advance." That same day the Administration officials in Washington also revealed that the United States would be willing to accept a partial test ban.

The Moscow Negotiations

Negotiations between the three nuclear powers opened in Moscow on July 15, 1963. The day before, in the midst of the Sino-Soviet ideological talks, the Soviet Communist Party chose to make public a full statement of its grievances against the Chinese Communist Party. The Moscow test ban talks thus would be held in the context of seriously deteriorating Sino-Soviet relationships.

Chairman Khrushchev opened the first meeting of the treaty negotiations, and during the course of this meeting he tabled a draft treaty banning nuclear tests in the atmosphere, in outer space, and under water. Except for the fact that it provided for a partial ban, it bore a strong resemblance to the treaty which the USSR had tabled on October 31, 1958, the opening day of the Conference for the Discontinuance of Nuclear Weapon Tests and to the USSR's draft treaty of November 28, 1961. It was simple and brief. It merely stated that the three governments agreed to ban nuclear tests in the three environments. There was no withdrawal clause or provision for peaceful detonations. Significantly, however, there was provision for the accession of other states.

In response the Western powers tabled their draft partial test ban treaty of August 27, 1962. The Western delegates also attempted to engage the Soviet Union in negotiations on a comprehensive ban but without avail. They even were unsuccessful in their attempts to arrange meetings between Professor Press, the seismologist member of the American delegation, and Soviet seismologists, all of whom were said either to be out of town or otherwise engaged. After a few days, the Western delegates abandoned their efforts to achieve a comprehensive treaty, and by mutual agreement discussion was based on the Western draft partial test ban treaty of August 27, 1962. Even after accepting this draft as a basis for discussions, however, Soviet delegates continued to argue for the title from their draft, "Treaty Banning Nuclear Weapon Tests." They finally agreed, but with great reluctance, to the more accurate but more cumbersome Western title —"Treaty Banning Nuclear Weapon Tests in the Atmosphere, in Outer Space, and Under Water."

There was some talk of the "nth country" problem, both with respect to France and Communist China, and for a while the USSR maintained that France would have to be brought into the treaty. However, it soon dropped this condition. On the other hand, the USSR, despite Western queries, refused to be drawn into a discussion of the problem of the adherence of Communist China.

The USSR pushed, although not too hard, for the signature of a nonaggression pact between the governments of the North Atlantic Treaty and the Warsaw Pact. The Western delegations made it clear that they were not authorized to negotiate such a treaty. Eventually the matter was disposed of by a sentence in the final communique stating that the three delegations had discussed the matter and had agreed "fully to inform their respective allies in the two organizations concerning these talks and to consult with them about continuing discussions on this question with the purpose of achieving agreement satisfactory to all participants."[29] This met the contention of the

---

[29]U.S. Department of State *Bulletin*, Vol. XLIX, No. 1259 (August 12, 1963), p. 239.

Western powers that they could not negotiate on such an issue without involving all of the NATO allies.

On July 25, 1963, Soviet Foreign Minister Gromyko, Lord Hailsham, and Mr. Harriman initialed a treaty, which was formally signed, again in Moscow, on August 5 by Mr. Gromyko, Foreign Secretary Lord Home, and Secretary of State Dean Rusk. Prime Minister Macmillan had wanted to convene a summit meeting to sign the treaty.[29a] President Kennedy had thought this unwise, but he had told Harriman that he would go to a summit meeting if necessary. Happily from his point of view, it was not. The President regretted that because it would be politically inexpedient he could not include Adlai Stevenson in the delegation which accompanied Secretary of State Rusk when he signed the treaty. Stevenson, of course, regarded the treaty as a vindication of his proposal made in the midst of the 1956 Presidential election campaign.

The Moscow Treaty

The Moscow Treaty closely resembled the Western August 27, 1962, draft proposal. There were two principal differences. The first was that the 1962 draft contained a provision allowing nuclear detonations for peaceful purposes if the original parties agreed, or if the detonations were carried out in accordance with the provisions outlined in an annex. The Moscow Treaty did not include such a provision. The Soviet Union took the attitude that it was already allowing the West to conduct nuclear explosions underground and that it did not want to extend this right to explosions in other environments. The Western delegates argued for retention of the provision. They had an annex partially worked out, although there were some uncertainties concerning the degree of disclosure which the United States would insist upon and accept. The USSR was adamant, however, and President Kennedy eventually ruled that the American delegates should agree to the Soviet position, even though he knew that the Atomic Energy Commission would oppose this and that the absence of such a provision would create certain difficulties for the Plowshare peaceful uses program. The necessary change in the text was effected by including the phrase "or any other nuclear explosion," in the first paragraph of the first article immediately after the state-

29aTheodore C. Sorenson, *Kennedy,* p. 735.

ment that the parties were not to carry out any nuclear weapon test explosion, and again prior to the listing of the environments in which nuclear explosions are prohibited. This same phrase was also included in the second paragraph of this article, which imposed the obligation to "refrain from causing, encouraging or participating in" nuclear weapon tests in the prohibited environments. In other words, the broadened provisions prohibited the signatories to the treaty both from conducting peaceful nuclear explosions in the prohibited environments themselves and also from assisting others to conduct such explosions. As a consequence of agreeing to drop the provision allowing nuclear detonations for peaceful purposes, the Western Powers insisted on reducing the number of ratifications required for amending the treaty from that of two-thirds of the parties, including the original parties, to that of a majority, including the original parties. They hoped that this would make it easier in the future to obtain an amendment allowing such explosions.

The second principal difference concerned the withdrawal clause. As will be recalled, the 1962 draft treaty embodied a complicated procedure for withdrawal, which would have taken up to 120 days and would have involved the convocation of a conference of all signatory states. In addition, the permissible grounds for withdrawal were specified in a fairly detailed fashion. The Moscow Treaty simply stated:

> This Treaty shall be of unlimited duration. Each Party shall in exercising its national sovereignty have the right to withdraw from the Treaty if it decides that extraordinary events, related to the subject matter of this Treaty, have jeopardized the supreme interests of its country. It shall give notice of such withdrawal to all other Parties to the Treaty three months in advance.

At first, Foreign Minister Gromyko argued that there was no need for a withdrawal clause; that the right to withdraw was an inherent right of sovereignty. The Western negotiators insisted that the treaty had to have a withdrawal clause because they felt that the absence of such a clause would be a more severe restraint on the Western powers than on the Soviet Union. In all, two days were spent on this issue. One of the complicating problems was that the Western delegates wanted to specify the grounds for withdrawal in as much detail as possible. These would have included testing by "nth countries."

Soviet delegates, in contrast, apparently wanted to avoid pointing too directly at Communist China, which obviously was not going to sign the treaty. The compromise, ultimately suggested by the United States and accepted by the other parties, was to insert the qualifying phrase "related to the subject matter of this Treaty," after the words "extraordinary events." Thus a conference as a possible forum for discussion of violations of the treaty and an instrument for mobilizing political pressure, as well as the enumeration of specific grounds for withdrawal were dropped from the treaty. Both features had been designed by American policy-makers to make withdrawal as difficult as possible. In the opinion of the Joint Chiefs, it will be recalled, they would have made it too difficult.

A third change involved listing all three of the Original Parties as depository governments, instead of naming just one government as is the normal practice. The reason for this was to ease the embarrassing problems which might arise from the attempted accession of governments which an Original Party did not recognize, such as East Germany and Nationalist China. Because of this change, there is no single agreed list of the parties to the treaty, since each depository government keeps its own list. The only circumstances in which this conceivably could cause a problem would be in determining whether or not a majority of parties had ratified an amendment.

A final change consisted of the addition of a hortatory paragraph in the preamble which proclaimed the objective of an agreement on general and complete disarmament under strict international control.

During the negotiations the delegates had ample time to go over the Treaty word by word and to achieve a consensus on the meaning to be attached to each. Among other things, they agreed that the Treaty in no way inhibited the use of nuclear weapons in time of war. Chairman Khrushchev publicly confirmed this understanding in replying to written questions from Soviet correspondents the day after the Treaty was initialed.

III
The Epilogue to the Negotiations

Ratification of the Treaty

President Kennedy submitted the Treaty to the Senate for its advice and consent to ratification on August 8, 1963. Hearings in the

Committee on Foreign Relations began on August 12 and lasted through August 27. The Committee had, however, been shown the Treaty as early as July 23, before it was initialed, and a bipartisan group of Senators had been included in the delegation for the official treaty-signing ceremony. The hearings before the Preparedness Investigating Subcommittee, which had started in May, also continued through this period. Administration witnesses before both committees appeared to be quite candid in their appraisal of the Treaty. All of the civilian officials, though with varying degrees of enthusiasm, argued that on balance the admitted risks of the Treaty—which they assessed in much the same terms as Paul Nitze had the previous September— were outweighed by its advantages. The Joint Chiefs of Staff individually and collectively recommended ratification, though somewhat ambiguously. They concluded that while there were military disadvantages to the Treaty, they were "not so serious as to render it unacceptable."[30] Because of its "broader advantages," they felt that the Treaty was "compatible with the security interests of the United States," and consequently supported its ratification. The Joint Chiefs insisted that if the Treaty were ratified, certain safeguards would have to be implemented to protect the security interests of the United States.

It transpired that General Curtis LeMay, Chief of Staff of the Air Force, probably would have been against the Treaty if it had not already been signed.[31] Appearing before the Preparedness Investigating Subcommittee, General Thomas S. Power, Commander in Chief of the United States Strategic Air Command, stated that he did not feel that the Treaty was "in the best interest of the United States."[32] In somewhat oversimplified form, his position was that the United States could only maintain its security through the further development of nuclear weapons.

Edward Teller also opposed the Treaty before both committees.[33] His arguments essentially were that the United States needed to know

---

[30]*Hearings: Nuclear Test Ban Treaty, supra* note 28, p. 275.

[31]*Ibid.,* p. 372.

[32]*Hearings: Military Aspects and Implications of Nuclear Test Ban Proposals and Related Matters, supra* note 23, p. 790.

[33]*Hearings: Nuclear Test Ban Treaty, supra* note 28, pp. 417-506, and *Hearings: Military Aspects and Implications of Nuclear Test Ban Proposals and Related Matters, supra* note 23, pp. 542-84.

more about the effects of nuclear weapons and this information could be gained only through atmospheric testing. He also wanted more proof tests and more work on the development of a defense against intercontinental ballistic missiles. Dr. John Foster, Director of the Lawrence Radiation Laboratory at Livermore, California, did not go quite as far as Dr. Teller, but he concluded that "from purely technical-military considerations," the Treaty appeared to him to be "disadvantageous."[34]

Interestingly, one of the principal witnesses from the Administration was Dr. Harold Brown, Director of Defense Research and Engineering, Department of Defense. He had been on the staff of the Lawrence Radiation Laboratory from 1952 through 1961, ultimately serving as Director from 1960 through June of 1961. He was also one of the two American scientists who did the basic work in Geneva on the system recommended by the Conference of Experts. In supporting the Treaty, he was in effect arguing against his former colleagues. One might speculate that one of the reasons for this was that as the Defense Department's Director of Defense Research and Engineering, the position which he then occupied, Dr. Brown had to face daily choices of trying to assess value in making decisions on expenditures for military purposes. In such a role, taking the position that cost did not matter when national defense was at stake, as many Livermore scientists were prone to, was simply not feasible. Dr. Norris E. Bradbury, Director of the Los Alamos Scientific Laboratory, the other center for nuclear weapons development in the United States, speaking for himself and for the majority of his staff, also supported the Treaty.[35] He acknowledged that it had risks, but felt that they could be minimized through a vigorous program of underground testing. Throughout the negotiations the scientists at Los Alamos had generally been more sympathetic toward efforts to achieve a nuclear test ban than their counterparts at Livermore.

Among those who had been associated with the test ban negotiating over the years, Harold E. Stassen and Arthur H. Dean, John J. McCloy, Hans Bethe, and Dr. Herbert York, the first director of the Lawrence Radiation Laboratory and Director of Defense Research and Engineering in the Eisenhower Administration, Professors

---

[34]*Hearings: Nuclear Test Ban Treaty, supra* note 28, p. 616.
[35]*Ibid.*, p. 583.

I. I. Rabi, Linus C. Pauling, and Edward M. Purcel supported the Treaty. Dr. Willard F. Libby and Dr. George B. Kistiakowsky did also, though somewhat less enthusiastically.

Admiral Lewis L. Strauss, although he did not oppose the Treaty, gave essentially negative testimony. Former members of the Joint Chiefs of Staff, Admirals Burke and Radford and General Twining, went somewhat further and expressed grave misgivings about the treaty.

Former President Eisenhower ultimately gave the Treaty a qualified endorsement.[36] He said that his recommendation that the Treaty should be ratified was conditional upon the safeguards recommended by the Joint Chiefs of Staff being implemented. He also suggested that a reservation might be added to the Treaty specifying "that in the event of any armed aggression endangering a vital interest of the United States this Nation would be the sole judge of the kind and type of weaponry and equipment it would employ, as well as the timing of their use." Later, he said that he did not have in mind a formal reservation.

In the course of their testimony Administration officials, who included Secretary of State Rusk, Secretary of Defense McNamara, and Chairman of the Atomic Energy Commission Seaborg, emphasized that the Treaty did not affect the use of nuclear weapons during war. They also emphasized that the Administration intended to do all that it could to maintain American readiness, including increasing the underground testing program. As if to underscore this point, on the day that the hearings of the Senate Committee on Foreign Relations opened, the Atomic Energy Commission detonated a nuclear device with intermediate yield underground in Nevada. Administration officials also declared that in their view the Treaty would not interfere with the development of a NATO Multilateral Force. Finally, Secretary of State Rusk asserted that, in the event of a Soviet abrogation of the Treaty, the United States would not feel itself bound by the Treaty and would feel free to resume testing whether or not it had complied with the withdrawal provision.[37]

On September 3, 1963, the Committee on Foreign Relations filed its report on the Moscow Treaty. By a vote of 16 to 1, the

[36]*Ibid.*, pp. 846-48.
[37]*Ibid.*, p. 37.

Committee recommended that the Senate give its advice and consent to ratification. The lone dissenter was Senator Russell B. Long, of Louisiana.

Six days later, the Preparedness Investigating Subcommittee filed its report. Although this committee did not make a recommendation, it concluded that the Treaty would "result in serious, and perhaps formidable, military and technical disadvantages."[38] It also concluded that it was not convinced that comparable military disadvantages would accrue to the USSR. Senator Symington signed the report, although in a separate statement he said that he would vote for the Treaty, because of its other advantages. Senator Saltonstall filed a dissenting statement in which he said that he felt that the conclusions drawn were "overly adverse."[39] The other five members of the Subcommittee presumably approved the report without reservation.

Floor debate in the Senate opened on September 9, 1963. On September 11, President Kennedy sent a letter to Senators Mansfield and Dirksen, the majority and minority leaders respectively, giving them several "unqualified and unequivocal assurances."[40] These were (1) that the underground testing program would be "vigorously and diligently carried forward"; (2) that the United States would maintain its readiness to test in the prohibited environments, and that it would "resume atmospheric testing 'forthwith' if the Soviet Union violated the treaty"; (3) that the United States facilities to detect nuclear weapons tests "will be expanded and improved as required"; (4) that the Treaty in no way limited the "authority of the Commander-in-Chief to use nuclear weapons for the defense of the United States or its allies"; (5) that if the Island of Cuba should be used to circumvent or nullify the Treaty, the United States would take all necessary action in response; (6) that the Treaty in no way changed the status of East Germany; (7) that the government would "maintain strong weapons laboratories in a vigorous program of weapons development," and that it would "maintain strategic forces fully ensuring that this Nation will continue to be in a position to destroy any aggressor, even after absorbing a first strike by a surprise attack"; and (8) the

[38]U.S. Congress, Senate, Committee on Armed Services, Preparedness Investigating Subcommittee, *Interim Report on the Military Implications of the Proposed Limited Nuclear Test Ban* (1963), p. 11.

[39]*Ibid.*, p. 14.

[40]*Congressional Record,* Vol. CIX, Part 12, pp. 16790-91.

United States would continue to pursue the development of nuclear explosives for peaceful purposes underground, and when developments made possible constructive uses for peaceful shots in the atmosphere, the United States would seek international agreements to permit this. The President also gave assurances that any amendments to the Treaty would be submitted to the Senate for its approval.

Again, as if to underline the President's assurances, on September 13, the Atomic Energy Commission detonated two underground explosions in Nevada. One of these was reported to have a yield equivalent to 1 megaton.

President Kennedy intervened in the Senatorial debate in other ways too.[40a] He was concerned that a sufficient number of Southern Democrats might join with Republicans and prevent the necessary two-thirds majority. He wanted a large majority, and he wanted to ward off possible formal reservations. He spoke individually with key Senators. He encouraged the creation of a private "Citizens Committee for a Nuclear Test Ban," a group of leaders from both parties organized to gain support for the Treaty. He "advised them which Senators should hear from their constituents, . . . counseled them on their approach to the unconvinced, and suggested particular business and other leaders for them to contact."[40b] Kennedy felt so strongly that he remarked to his associates on one occasion "that he would gladly forfeit his re-election, if necessary, for the sake of the Test Ban Treaty."[40c]

On September 24, the Senate, by a vote of 80 to 19 gave its advice and consent to ratification of the Moscow Treaty. According to Theodore C. Sorenson, President Kennedy called the vote " 'a welcome culmination.' No other single accomplishment in the White House ever gave him greater satisfaction."[40d] The 19 who voted against the treaty included 11 Democrats and 8 Republicans.[41] The list included Senator Goldwater, who would become the Re-

[40a]See Theodore C. Sorenson, *Kennedy,* pp. 737-40.
[40b]*Ibid.,* p. 739.
[40c]*Ibid.,* p. 745.
[40d]*Ibid.,* p. 740.
[41]They were Senators: Bennett (Utah), H. F. Byrd (Va.), R. C. Byrd (W. Va.), Curtis (Neb.), Eastland (Miss.), Goldwater (Ariz.), Jordan (Idaho), Lausche (Ohio), Long (La.), McClellan (Ark.), Mechem (N.M.), Robertson (Va.), Russell (Ga.), Simpson (Wyo.), Smith (Me.), Stennis (Miss.), Talmadge (Ga.), Thurmond (S.C.), and Tower (Tex.).

publican presidential nominee in 1964. Four of the 19 were members of the 7-man Preparedness Investigating Subcommittee, and 2 more were members of the parent Committee on Armed Services. The 19 included 1 member of the Joint Committee on Atomic Energy and 2 members of the Committee on Foreign Relations. Senator Lausche, in keeping with his maverick style, voted against the Treaty, even though as a member of the Committee on Foreign Relations he had voted for the report recommending that the Senate give its advice and consent to ratification. Of the 19, all but 4 (Senators Byrd [W.Va.], Curtis [Neb.], Lausche [Ohio], and Smith [Me.]) were from the conservative strongholds of their parties in Southern or Western states. Some of the Senators who voted for the Treaty—most notably Senator Jackson, another member of the Preparedness Investigating Subcommittee—indicated that they did so reluctantly and with some misgivings.

President Kennedy signed the Moscow Treaty on October 7, completing the United States ratification. The Presidium of the Supreme Soviet unanimously voted to ratify the Treaty for the USSR on September 25, the day after the Senate completed its action. The Treaty formally entered into effect at 1:00 p.m. on October 11, 1963. That same day, it was announced in Oslo that the Nobel Peace Prize for 1962 had been awarded to Linus C. Pauling. Among American scientists, he had clearly been the most outspoken critic of nuclear testing.

"Nth" and Potential "Nth Countries"

While the nuclear powers were completing their ratification, more than 100 other countries signed the Moscow Treaty. By the end of the year this total, so far as those states which signed or acceded to the Treaty in Washington, D.C., were concerned, rose to 116. There were, however, certain notable exceptions. The day after the Treaty was initialed in Moscow, a leading Chinese Communist official flatly asserted that China would have nuclear weapons in the not-too-distant future, and he condemned the efforts of a small number of nuclear powers to restrict nuclear capabilities.[42] As the days wore on, Chinese denunciation of the Moscow Treaty increased. Of course it did not sign, and on October 16, 1964, Communist China detonated

[42]New York Times, July 27, 1964, p. 1.

its first nuclear explosion, in the atmosphere. Both Albania, China's ally in the ideological struggle within the Soviet camp, and Cuba also refused to sign the Treaty.

President Kennedy and Prime Minister Macmillan made a personal appeal to President de Gaulle for France's adherence. They even offered some assistance with the development of the French nuclear weapons program as an inducement. President Kennedy was prepared to declare that France had achieved a nuclear capability within the meaning of the 1958 amendment of the Atomic Energy Act, thereby rendering it eligible for the same assistance that the United Kingdom received from the United States.[42a] However, at a news conference on July 29, President de Gaulle definitely ruled out the possibility that France would sign, restating the position that France had maintained during the negotiations.

The Eighteenth General Assembly

When the eighteenth session of the General Assembly opened in September 1963, the Moscow Treaty was widely welcomed. However, there was also a fairly general feeling that it should be extended to cover all environments, which, according to the preamble to the Treaty, was the objective of the three nuclear powers too. The eight new members of the Eighteen-Nation Disarmament Committee wanted the Assembly to adopt a resolution which would pledge the Committee to continue to seek an accord banning all nuclear tests with adequate provision for inspection. Both the USSR and the United States balked at such specific instructions and would agree to no more than a paragraph instructing the Committee to continue its efforts "to achieve the objectives set forth in the preamble of the partial test ban treaty."[43] Both the USSR and the United States apparently wanted to avoid reopening the controversial question of monitoring a ban on underground tests, and the USSR gave no indication that it was willing to renew its offer of a limited number of on-site inspections on Soviet territory annually.[44] Only Albania opposed the resolution, which the Assembly adopted in November, and which was tailored to the nuclear powers' specifications.

[42a]Arthur M. Schlesinger, Jr., *A Thousand Days*, p. 914, and Theodore C. Sorenson, *Kennedy*, p. 573.
[43]General Assembly Resolution 1910 (XVIII).
[44]See *New York Times*, October 24, 1962, p. 1; October 29, 1962, p. 1.

Since then there have been no serious negotiations on a ban on underground tests. It may well be accurate to say, as Jerome B. Wiesner has said, that political and military conservatism on the part of both sides prevented the achievement of a comprehensive test ban.[45] Important groups within the Soviet Union appear to have been most reluctant to agree to a treaty which would involve lifting the USSR's veil of secrecy beyond the most miniscule amount. Important groups within the United States, on the other hand, were unwilling to agree to a treaty which might involve significant risks of the Soviet Union's being able to engage in clandestine testing. Some of these same individuals were also strongly desirous, for a variety of reasons, of being able to continue testing nuclear weapons. The leaders in both camps, Chairman Khrushchev and President Kennedy, both appear to have been willing to go farther than several other policy-makers within their respective countries. But achieving an international agreement in an age of mass and bureaucratic government requires a broader coalescence of forces than agreement merely between two heads of state. There was this broader coalescence for a partial test ban treaty, but not for a comprehensive one.

[45]Jerome B. Wiesner, *Where Science and Politics Meet*, pp. 167-68.

PART IV

SOME CONCLUDING OBSERVATIONS

Chapter XIV

The Test Ban Negotiations and Treaty in Retrospect

I

Introduction

Did the signature of the Moscow Treaty Banning Nuclear Weapon Tests in the Atmosphere, in Outer Space and Under Water mark a turning point in the nuclear era? Obviously it is too early to answer this question. Only in the future will it be possible accurately to assess the significance of the Moscow Treaty. Unfortunately though, except for the purposes of historical analysis, it is impossible to wait to make judgments. To act rationally in formulating policy the outcome of each step must be scrutinized with care and analyzed before a choice is made among the possible courses for the next move. An assessment must be made, however tentative it may be and subject to reevaluation. Similarly, although a single case study is hardly an adequate basis for formulating answers to the questions raised in the introductory chapter concerning the processes by which United States security policy was formulated and executed, the nature of these policies, and the characteristics and modalities of the contemporary international system, these too demand immediate answers.

Fortunately, the nuclear test ban negotiations probably provide as good a basis for generalizations as any single set of diplomatic talks that have occurred since the end of the Second World War. The nuclear test ban talks involved, in one way or another, most of the actors in the contemporary international system, and the most important states—the super-powers—were deeply engaged. There were significant differences among the political systems of the three states principally involved. The negotiations covered a long time period. During this period, the distribution of military power in the international system shifted. Again as a result of their length, the

469

negotations spanned two administrations within the United States. Among other things, the change in administrations brought changes in personnel, in administrative organization and procedures, and in presidential-legislative relationships. The nuclear test ban negotiations were conducted in a variety of forums, ranging from bilateral talks, through a tripartite conference and a larger committee, to the general international organization with the broadest membership, the United Nations. In several respects, therefore, the negotiations offer the opportunity of comparative analysis. And as an unique series of events, because of their importance, the negotiations had sufficient salience to permit at least some conclusions to be drawn.

II

The Formulation and Execution of American Security Policy

With respect to the formulation and execution of American security policy, analysis of the test ban negotiations yields not so much new insights as confirmation and refinement of the consensus-building model. The circle of participants in the consensus-building process widened or narrowed depending upon issues and circumstances. In most instances during the course of the negotiations decisions concerning what American policy should be, or how it should be executed, could be made by the executive branch acting alone. Since the end product of the negotiations was envisaged as being an international treaty, however, the Senate always had a potential role; and, because certain inspection procedures could have required modifications in American legislation concerning atomic energy, the House of Representatives also had such a role.

Except for a few brief periods, such as when the USSR abrogated the moratorium on nuclear testing or immediately before and after the signature of the Moscow Treaty, the test ban negotiations elicited little public interest. Certain segments of the public, however, followed the negotiations very carefully and were deeply and often emotionally interested. These groups included large numbers of scientists. Those scientists who worked on weapons development obviously had a direct professional interest. Other scientists were involved through their feeling of personal or collective responsibility for the consequences of the development of nuclear weapons. Among the lay public, attentiveness was largely confined to those especially concerned about peace on the one hand and the United States military posture on the other. Members of SANE and the Women's Strike for Peace provide examples of the former; members of veterans' organizations the latter. Given the nature of the issues and the limited extent of Congressional involvement, the interested members of the public had few means at their disposal, other than publicity, to give effect to their views.

Consensus-Building in the Eisenhower Administration

In these circumstances the process of consensus-building was more often than not confined to the executive branch. This did not necessarily make the process smoother or easier. The Eisenhower Administration was deeply divided on several questions relating to the nuclear test ban negotiations, including even the wisdom of attempting to negotiate on this issue. President Eisenhower himself saw little advantage from the viewpoint of American security policy in a test ban as such, and—responding to the advice of the Atomic Energy Commission—he was not convinced of the great danger of the radioactive fallout that would result from continued testing. Fundamentally, he was doubtful that when the chips were down the Soviet Union would agree to a treaty acceptable to the United States, or that a treaty, even if agreed upon, would be followed by a substantial slowdown in the arms race. Although it entails great oversimplification and some distortion of their detailed positions, the various interested agencies in the Eisenhower Administration can be ranked along a continuum.[1] The Atomic Energy Commission, which had the greatest doubts about the wisdom of a nuclear test ban, would be at one extreme. The Department of Defense would be next to the AEC. It tended to be somewhat more favorably inclined toward a test ban than the Commission. Next, in a center, although slightly positive position, would be the Central Intelligence Agency. The Department of State would come next, and then the President's Science Advisory Committee, at the opposite extreme from the AEC. Both on balance were favorably inclined toward a nuclear test ban.

As a consequence of these divisions, when policy was made by

---

[1]Compare this ranking with that given by Sir Michael Wright, *Disarm and Verify*, p. 120.

committee, as it usually was, the result tended to be a compromise which straddled the issues and occassionally contained contradictory elements. The position which the United States adopted at the outset of the political negotiations in the fall of 1958 is an example. The United States was willing to agree to a nuclear test ban, but it insisted that after a specified period, the continuance in force of the ban would be dependent upon satisfactory progress being made in other areas of arms control and disarmament. This "link" with other measures of arms control and disarmament was eventually dropped, but it was dropped only at the time when the "new seismic data" had raised serious obstacles to achieving a nuclear test ban. Thus one set of obstacles replaced another. The American insistence on technical conferences in 1959 can be seen as a neutral policy, acceptable both to those who were enamored with the prospects of obtaining a nuclear test ban and to those who seriously doubted the wisdom of such a measure. When the United States did hint at the possibility of a partial ban in 1959 as a first step toward a comprehensive ban, it failed to specify in detail what control measures it would demand, but in any case made it clear that they would be fairly extensive. Yet a year earlier Senator Gore had stated that an atmospheric ban could be policed by control instruments under the unilateral control of the United States, and this is what the United States eventually proposed in 1961, and in 1962, and it is what was finally accepted in 1963.

In addition, under the Eisenhower Administration largely because of the deep divisions of opinion, decisions were taken at an extremely slow pace. Countless examples can be recalled. To cite only one, although Technical Working Group I accepted virtually all of the American proposals, a month and a half elapsed before the American Ambassador could even accept "the report as a correct technical assessment . . . in the light of presently available scientific knowledge."[2] It was not until after the Kennedy Administration had assumed power that the United States would finally submit treaty language based on the report.

Under the Eisenhower Administration, consensus-building also tended to exercise a gyroscopic effect on policy. In the period from 1958 through 1960, once negotiations were underway, it proved

[2]GEN/DNT/PV. 127, p. 4.

almost impossible for the United States to break them off, or to radically alter their course.

This is not to imply that all of the agencies which participated in these decisions did not have vital interest in them and an important contribution to make, nor that American policy necessarily would have been better had it been formulated exclusively by one agency. At least one major decision during this period was not made within an elaborate committee structure. This was the proposal for a conference of experts. In this instance President Eisenhower acted solely on the advice of Secretary of State Dulles. This meant that the participants in the decision were confined to the White House Staff and the Secretary of State with a few of his advisors. This decision has been and can be criticized. In proposing a conference of experts, the United States committed itself to a course of action with potentially far-reaching consequences without having fully explored the consequences and without having formulated appropriate and adequate contingency policies. Of course, proposing a conference of experts solved certain immediate tactical problems, and provided a needed response to a Soviet initiative. Two questions, however, can be raised. The first is whether or not the short-range gains outweighed the longer-range difficulties. The second is whether or not the short-range gains could not have been obtained without also incurring the longer-range difficulties.

The Advent of the Kennedy Administration

From 1961 on decisions within the executive branch concerning a nuclear test ban flowed more rapidly and smoothly.[3] This was partly because different personnel headed the relevent agencies, and the new men held more homogeneous views concerning the wisdom of a nuclear test ban. However, the change in administrations did not bring a complete change in personnel. Allen W. Dulles continued to serve as Director of the Central Intelligence Agency until September 27, 1961, when he was replaced by John A. McCone. Mr. McCone had also been a member of the Committee of Principals during the Eisenhower Administration, in which he had served as Chairman of the Atomic Energy Commission. Moreover, the extent to which

[3]See Sir Michael Wright, *Disarm and Verify*, pp. 121, 127.

prinicipal officers are bound to the collective viewpoints of their agencies should not be underestimated.

A second factor explaining the smoother flow of decisions after the advent of the Kennedy Administration was that the institutional balance was altered. In September 1961, the United States Arms Control and Disarmament Agency was established. The Director of ACDA immediately became a member of the Committee of Principals, and even before ACDA was established, President Kennedy's adviser on disarmament, John J. McCloy, met with the Committee. Thus, starting in 1961 the balance on the Committee of Principals was altered by the addition of an individual more or less institutionally committed to advocate measures of arms control and disarmament. The creation of ACDA also meant that many more resources within government were devoted to analyzing issues of arms control. Positions could be explored more thoroughly before being advocated and the analyses would be done from the point of view of trying to achieve agreements. Furthermore, there were many more people available for consensus-building efforts. Unlike the State Department in the past, ACDA had its own scientific advisers.

On balance, however, the fact that the quest for a test ban was approached with a new intensity and drive in the Kennedy Administration seems to have been more important than the institutional changes. The advent of a new Administration brought the appointment of a new principal negotiator in Geneva, Arthur Dean. Although his predecessor held a strong personal conviction of the desirability of a test ban and was an experienced and skillful negotiator, it is demonstrable that Ambassador Dean made a greater effort to understand the technical issues involved in the negotiations, devoted more energy toward trying to stimulate new policies, and at least partially as a consequence was more actively involved in the formulation of American policy. More importantly, President Kennedy himself seems to have devoted more attention and energy to this issue than President Eisenhower. President Kennedy appears to have been more interested in achieving a nuclear test ban that President Eisenhower was. He certainly was more willing to take risks, in terms of both domestic and international politics, to gain such an agreement than President Eisenhower. This was in large measure a reflection of President Kennedy's general policy of seeking to engage the Soviet Union in a continuing realistic dialogue designed primarily to clarify positions and remove misunderstandings and also to explore avenues toward possible agreements. The test ban negotiations offered an obvious opportunity in this respect. President Kennedy also made a greater effort to understand the technical intricacies involved in the test ban negotiations. Jerome B. Wiesner, the President's science adviser, has written that President Kennedy "made himself an expert on these subjects."[4] It was only by becoming an expert that he could successfully cope with the expert advice which he received. President Kennedy gave his Administration a greater sense of direction on this issue, and his Administration responded with a more forthcoming process of decision-making.

It was only after President Kennedy assumed office that the United States tabled an entire draft treaty for a nuclear test ban. Such a draft had been in existence for some time, but it had been impossible to obtain agreement among the relevant interested agencies to table it, and President Eisenhower had not insisted that agreement be achieved. It was only during the Kennedy Administration that the United States submitted alternative draft treaties. All of these steps were at least partly attributable to the President's leadership. Without this leadership, a test ban might never had been achieved. In a decision-making structure as decentralized as that of the American government, Presidential leadership is necessary for action to be taken.

The Contribution of Congress

Much has been written about the decline of the legislative branch of government in the modern era. On the surface the test ban negotiations might be viewed as another case supporting this general thesis. Yet full examination reveals that Congress played an important role in the shaping of United States policy.

In the first place, the record indicates that Congress had ample opportunity to obtain information relevant to the test ban negotiations. Congressional hearings produced a wealth of technical and political data. It is true that different Congressional committees tended to develop different kinds of data. The Joint Committee on Atomic Energy tended to rely mainly for its information on the Atomic Energy Commission and sources provided or sponsored by that agency. The Senate Committee on Foreign Relations and its

---

[4]Jerome B. Wiesner, *Where Science and Politics Meet*, p. 11.

Subcommittee on Disarmament, on the other hand, tended to rely mainly on the Department of State and later on the Arms Control and Disarmament Agency. Partly as a consequence, the policy positions of the two committees tended to reflect the differences between the executive agencies. However, any individual Congressman, if he had the inclination and the time, could read the records of both committees. Moreover, some Congressmen, notably Senator Albert Gore and Bourke B. Hickenlooper, served on both committees, thus providing a bridge and an element of continuity. These two men also served as Congressional advisers to the American delegation in Geneva and were able to gain additional data through this means. In sum, so far as obtaining data, Congress was not at a serious disadvantage in relation to the executive branch. It could not engage in research itself, it is true, but almost all of the governmental experts and all of the private experts within the United States were available to it. Careful staff work on the part of the staffs of the committees made it possible to utilize the expertise rationally and wisely. The only group of experts within the administrative branch not available to Congressional committees were those within the Executive Office of the White House, namely the Special Assistant to the President for Science and Technology and his immediate staff. In this instance, the inability to question these individuals does not appear to have been a serious obstacle to obtaining relevant information. In broad terms, Congress appears to have been as well informed as the executive branch was on this issue.

In the formal or procedural sense, the initiative in formulating policy, of course, always rested with the executive. However, Congress and Congressmen were able to influence in important ways the manner and purposes for which the executive branch utilized its powers. At the very outset, the hearings of Senator Humphrey's Subcommittee on Disarmament clearly contributed to the pressure on the executive to separate the test ban issue from other measures of disarmament and to enter negotiations on this issue alone. On the other hand, during the course of the next several years the frequent hearings of the Joint Committee on Atomic Energy kept before the public the difficulty of controlling underground nuclear explosions and no doubt this inhibited the executive's freedom. Whether or not the executive branch would have followed a more flexible policy had it not been for this is naturally an unanswerable question. At least prior to 1961 it probably would not have; however, even if the executive had wanted to make concessions, it would have found it difficult to do so in view of the activities of the Committee. Indeed there can be serious doubt that the Senate would have ratified the comprehensive treaty which the United States proposed in 1962 and 1963 had the USSR accepted it.

In October 1959, Senator Humphrey suggested in a public speech, that the United States should propose that a partial ban should be accompanied by a moratorium of limited duration on testing in those environments where control techniques were not at the moment adequate, the hope being that by the end of the moratorium adequate control measures would have been discovered so that the ban could be extended to cover all environments. The following spring the United States made such a proposal.

Toward the end of the negotiations, the resolution sponsored by Senator Dodd and others and adopted by the Senate clearly strengthened President Kennedy's hand. Although the content of the President's American University speech might have been the same even without this resolution, clearly it was easier for him to announce that the United States would forego further testing of nuclear weapons in the atmosphere after the Senate had recommended that this country should take such action.

The test ban negotiations also indicate the limits of Congressional influence on the formulation of policy by the executive. As early as November 1958, Senator Albert Gore proposed that the United States should abandon the attempt to negotiate a comprehensive ban on nuclear weapons tests and concentrate its efforts on attempting to achieve a partial ban. Several other Congressmen repeated this suggestion in the following years. Despite this, it was not until August 1962 that the United States seriously proposed a partial treaty; and as late as the Moscow talks in July 1963, American negotiators were still instructed to give priority to a comprehensive ban. But even here, Congressmen can be said to have shaped the environment in which a partial ban became the most feasible outcome.

Science and Security Policy

Implicit in the foregoing discussion of the formulation of United States policy is the assumption that judgments on scientific issues played a crucial role. It is self-evident that any rational decision on the wisdom of attempting to negotiate a nuclear test ban would postulate in the first place some judgment about the danger to human life resulting from the fallout and other by-products of past and continued testing of nuclear weapons both with respect to immediate and long-range genetic effects, if any. Again, one would have to form some estimate of the gains that could be achieved in weapons technology through further testing, and of the gains that could be made without testing. Finally, one would have to assess the technological feasibility of establishing control measures to insure the observance of a test ban. Each of these is almost a purely scientific question.

In addition, there are several questions which, although not as purely scientific, involve, in varying degrees, important scientific elements. One would want to have an estimate of the types and qualities of nuclear weapons presently held by other states and a sense of how these compared with one's own nuclear arsenal. One would also want to have some sense of the possibilities of the dispersion of nuclear weapons capabilities among the presently non-nuclear countries and of the consequences of this. It would finally be necessary to make judgments about the role of nuclear weapons in military strategy in the light of all the available knowledge of their effects.

Finally, there are essentially nonscientific questions containing nevertheless a limited scientific component. Thus a decision-maker would want to make some estimate about the likelihood of the opponent state violating the treaty. In part this would involve the scientific issue of the risk of detection through available technical devices that a potential violator would have to face. But it would also involve a perhaps more important judgment concerning the general attitude and willingness of the potential violator to run such a risk. Again a decision-maker would also have to have some notions about the dangers arising from the nuclear arms race, such as the possibility of war by accident, which would have to reflect, among other things, an evaluation of the technical safeguards. Finally, he would have to make an estimate of what kind of treaty the Senate, the American people, and other states would be likely to accept. While this would call for an exercise of political judgment, the scientific component is readily identifiable.

To take a position on a nuclear test ban, any policy-maker would have to deal in some fashion with all of these questions. He could of course choose to ignore one or more of them, but even that would be dealing with them. Moreover, a policy-maker's task is complicated by the fact that many of these questions involve issues concerning which there is great scientific uncertainty. It is highly unlikely that any given forecast of future scientific developments would prove to be completely accurate. Nor are the first answers formulated in any scientific inquiry always the best, and many technical questions were raised in the test ban negotiations for the first time. Again, the scientific element is often so closely intertwined with nonscientific factors that it would require great restraint and discipline to limit a judgment to the scientific element. Concerning all such questions a scientist can give a wide range of answers without violating his scientific integrity. The answer that a scientist gives will depend partly upon his personal preferences and predilections, including his concept of international relations and his political orientation, and on his experience and maturity. It will also depend on the way in which the question is phrased and asked and the form and type of answer permitted.

Scientists as Policy Advisers

In a theoretical model of rational decision-making, it might be desirable for the decision-maker to permit each of his advisers to speak only on matters affecting his special area of expertise. In such a scheme scientists would confine their observations to scientific questions, economists to economic questions, lawyers to legal questions, military experts to military questions, and political experts to political questions.

There is a great deal to be said for keeping this model as an ideal goal that participants in the American system ought to strive to approximate. Much has been written demonstrating what poor advisers specialists are when they stray beyond their areas of special competence, and Albert Wohlstetter has persuasively demonstrated the weaknesses of some scientists when they have ventured into the realm of military strategy.[5] Clearly certain scientists such as Linus Pauling and Edward Teller blatantly violated the precepts of this

[5]See "Strategy and the Natural Scientists," pp. 174-239 in Robert Gilpin and Christopher Wright (eds.), *Scientists and National Policy-Making* (1964).

ideal model in their public comments on the nuclear test ban issue. To say that the risk from radioactive fallout caused by continued testing in the atmosphere was intolerable or could be ignored, or to maintain that the control system devised by the Geneva Conference of Experts was adequate or inadequate, implicitly involved judgments on a number of issues, some of which were not at all scientific in character. On the other hand, other scientists, Wolfgang K. H. Panofsky, for example, phrased their pronouncements very carefully, distinguishing as well as they could between the scientific and nonscientific elements which were involved.

It is difficult to estimate with any degree of accuracy the effect in this instance of the tendency of scientists like Linus Pauling and Edward Teller to stray beyond the areas of their expertise. Probably public and perhaps even official understanding would have been easier had these individuals distinguished more clearly between their role as scientists and their role as citizens. Unquestionably, the policy-maker had to scrutinize their scientific advice and judgments with greater care, and their standing in this respect was impaired. However, to ask them to refrain from speaking freely on any issue risks robbing the American system of one of its most dynamic elements. These men played important roles in the test ban negotiations because they had deep convictions extending far beyond their scientific expertise. There is little question that they contributed to the motive force without which policy might have atrophied on dead center. Moreover, the admixture of nonscientific elements in the pronouncements of individuals such as Teller and Pauling was often so obvious that its discovery was not a task of inordinate intellectual difficulty. Admittedly, there has been a tendency in American society to transfer authority earned in one field to other fields; but if this is a problem, a better corrective might be to strive to develop greater official understanding and more sophisticated public attitudes, than to harness the scientists.

In the nuclear test ban negotiations the subtle mixing of scientific and nonscientific elements in judgments offered by scientists was much more bothersome than the blatant mixing mentioned above. As has been shown, when a scientist was asked to give advice on certain seemingly scientific questions, his personal, nonscientific views almost inevitably intruded. In these instances, it could be extremely difficult for the nonscientist decision-maker to detect the nonscientific elements implicitly interwoven into the answer. How could the decision-maker know whether his scientist adviser had been, within the range of scientific uncertainty, excessively optimistic or excessively pessimistic? The problem was complicated by the fact that, despite their uncertainty, the scientists could answer questions in quantitative terms, which could give a misleading impression of precision.

In retrospect, it would seem that the scientists advising the President and the Secretary of State prior to and during the time of the Conference of Experts may well have allowed their hopes for a more orderly international political system to interfere with their giving as properly qualified technical answers concerning control possibilities as they should have on the basis of the scientific evidence then available to them.

At the same time, the scientists did not have an unlimited opportunity to present their views. Issues concerning a nuclear test ban were only a few of countless numbers facing top decision-makers. The amount of attention that the decision-makers could devote to any individual issue was inevitably limited. Furthermore, even concerning a nuclear test ban, there were several technical issues which had to be considered. In this case, a second factor explaining why the principal decision-makers perhaps did not understand the technical complexities relating to the control of nuclear explosions as fully as they might have during most of 1958 is simply that they did not spend enough time on these issues. Within the limited amount of time that they could spend considering what position the United States should adopt with respect to a nuclear test ban, most of their attention—perhaps rightly—was devoted to considering issues other than control. They were particularly concerned about comparing American and Soviet nuclear strength and about the possibilities for future developments in the realm of weapons technology. The point is not to question the allocation of their attention, for these may well have been the most important questions, but merely to point out that little time was left for considering the technical aspects of control.

The Need for "Scientific Literacy" Among Nonscientists

A final, more subtle, factor also seems to have been involved in the communications difficulties which were apparent in American policy-making during the earliest stages of the negotiations. To understand fully what a scientist means when he says, *"On the basis of one experiment,* we think that . . . ," one must have some notions about the way in which science progresses from initial tentative estimates to more fully documented and more definitive judgments. Similarly, if one is to understand all of the ramifications of the scientists' report that the seismic magnitude of the Rainier explosion appears to be 4.1 on the Richter scale rather than 4.25 as had previously been thought, one must know something about how many more earthquakes there are at the smaller seismic magnitude. It would also be helpful to know something about the way in which these figures are calculated, and that measurements in this area of the Richter scale are usually given with the understanding that the margin of error may be plus or minus .4.

Understandably, the individuals who were the principal decision-makers in the United States during the earliest stages of the negotiations seem to have known little about modern science. They had received their education prior to the First World War, and thus prior to the great expansion in scientific activity which has occurred after that time. During most of their earlier careers both President Eisenhower and Secretary of State Dulles had not been deeply involved in science. Their background for fully comprehending scientific advice was not especially strong. Of course, one could use intelligent questioning to make up for an inadequate background. Often, however, the ability to ask intelligent questions is dependent upon having at least a minimal background. Moreover, questioning takes time, which was in extremely short supply in this instance, and probably will be in similar cases.

Thus it is clear that the first prerequisite to adequately coping with the problems posed by the growth of the role of science in security policy is the development of more "scientific literacy" among policy-makers, both politicians and diplomats. Only then will the nonscientists be able to make the best use of their scientist colleagues. In this connection, it should be noted that at least some of the scientists found the higher level policy-makers more willing to be concerned with and to make an effort to understand the technical details which were involved in the nuclear test ban negotiations than the professional diplomats, members of the Foreign Service. These scientists felt that many of the latter group tended to take the attitude that what was important was the technique of negotiation, that a personal knowledge of the substance was secondary and might in fact be disturbing toward reaching an agreement. Obviously, the need for "scientific literacy" is as great among the diplomats as it is among the politicians. Just as the process of formulating policy cannot be divided into rigid compartments horizontally, and experts confined to their area of expertise, it also cannot be divided vertically. Improper understanding of technical issues at a lower level may be equally as damaging as improper understanding at a higher level; among other possibilities it could prevent important questions from ever reaching the higher level.

Scientific Advice at the Highest Levels of American Government

The experience in the nuclear test ban negotiations suggests that for communications between scientists and nonscientist decision-makers at the highest levels of American government to be as effective as possible, policy-makers must receive advice from several scientists rather than one. This appears to be the most effective means of guarding against the tendency for advice on scientific matters to be colored by personal predispositions. The President's Science Advisory Committee, with about twenty members and additional scientists who serve as regular consultants, can adequately meet the need for divergent viewpoints. If the Committee is to meet this need, however, it must develop adequate techniques for transmitting divergent views. The President and other top decision-makers must also be willing to receive conflicting advice and to assume the responsibility for deciding which advice they should accept as bases for policy. Ideally the top policy-makers should have the opportunity to witness in some manner a confrontation between scientists who hold divergent views. If a scientist is to remain true to the training and to the canons of his work, he must acknowledge certain facts. The test ban negotiations supply evidence that scientists will behave in this manner. Thus Hans Bethe readily acknowledged the correctness of Albert Latter's decoupling theory even though it presented a new obstacle on the road to a test ban agreement which Bethe strongly favored in principle. One of the virtues of the Congressional hearings was that they provided forums for confrontation among scientists holding divergent viewpoints. Such confrontations, by clearly developing the points concerning which the scientists agree and disagree, can significantly clarify the issues and thereby ease the policy-makers' problem of choosing among divergent advice.

There is also another reason why policy-makers at the highest level should receive advice from several scientific sources if they are to act as rationally as possible. Most problems with which policy-makers must deal have several facets. Their scientific segments alone often involve not one but several academic disciplines. In the light of the difficulties concerning the detection of underground nuclear explosions which plagued American policy during the test ban negotiations, it may have been significant that there was no seismologist on the President's Science Advisory Committee until 1962. The Committee headed by Hans Bethe which conducted an overall appraisal of the situation with respect to the nuclear test ban in early 1958, and on which initial American policies were based, did not include a seismologist either. The President's Science Advisory Committee has generally been dominated by scientists who specialized in aspects of nuclear energy, particularly physicists. It can be argued that PSAC might have been a more effective source of advice if its membership had included a wider spectrum of disciplines. The counter-argument that scientists in all disciplines are employed by the government and therefore available to PSAC does not completely meet the problem, because having the proper mixture of disciplines is as important in the final stages involving evaluation of data and drafting of recommendations as it is in early stages involving data collection.

Scientific Expertise Within the Bureaucracy

Providing advice for policy-makers at the highest level is only one aspect of the problem of integrating scientists into the procedures for formulating American security policy. Obviously, decisions which are taken at a lower level also involve scientific questions. In addition, frequently scientific and technical research must be conducted in order to develop necessary data. An overwhelming number of the scientists who have been involved in the formulation of American security policy thus far have been employed by the Atomic Energy Commission and the Department of Defense. There can be no doubt that these two agencies have had the greatest need for scientists. However, the experience during the test ban negotiations illustrates that other agencies, such as the Department of State, also deal with questions which have scientific elements, and it can be argued that

American policy would have been better had scientific expertise been interspersed more widely throughout all of the agencies working in the area of security policy. It is not sufficient merely to have access to scientists in another agency. For one thing, having to go to another agency immediately raises all of the physical and psychological problems involved in inter-agency coordination. For another, as was apparent during the test ban negotiations, there are what can be called "agency viewpoints" on policy questions, and the views of most individuals are affected more or less strongly by the milieu in which they work. Moreover, an individual's tasks and responsibilities are bound to be defined in terms of the priorities of the agency for which he works.

It is easy to argue that governmental agencies which have only peripheral responsibilities in scientific fields ought to have more scientists on their payroll. Unfortunately, implementing this recommendation is extremely difficult. A scientist long in the employ of an agency such as the Department of State will soon lose his expertise. On the other hand, short term service involves considerable waste in terms of time lost in gaining familiarity with problems and procedures of the agency and in preparing to leave government service. Furthermore, employment in a nonscientific government agency has few attractions for a promising young scientist, deeply interested in and committed to his discipline. Joining the Department of State, for example, means substantial risk of losing contact with his discipline.

With respect to getting research done and investigating technical problems, the typical pattern, much in evidence during the test ban negotiations, has been either to assign the tasks to scientists employed by the government or to let contracts to institutions outside the federal government, and then to have the results reviewed by panels of governmental and nongovernmental scientists convened on an *ad hoc* basis. This system has much to recommend it. It involves independent checks and is in accord with the pluralistic pattern and structure of American life. However, it is cumbersome and time-consuming. For this reason, it is not responsive to the needs of modern diplomacy. In addition, it has meant that within the government the only agencies dealing with security policy equipped to conduct scientific research themselves have been those which have had as their primary responsibility maintaining the nation's military strength or developing uses of nuclear energy. Since the Vela Program has always been administered by the Department of Defense, even after the establishment of the Arms Control and Disarmament Agency, it seems that these are also the only agencies deemed capable of administering large-scale scientific research programs, regardless of their purpose. Inevitably, the approach of these agencies to security problems has been colored by their primary responsibilities.

A possible and perhaps the best way of overcoming the difficulties involved in getting high quality scientists to serve in nonscientific government agencies at the lower and middle ranks, and also easing those connected with the conduct of research, might be to establish a national scientific institute or to expand some existing facility, such as the Bureau of Standards. Such an institute would have to allow scientists great freedom to pursue their own interests, but it might also be capable of responding to some of the government's needs. If a promising young scientist could look forward to a career in such an institute, the prospect of a brief assignment with a nonscientific government agency might not seem so unpalatable. Presumably the scientific staff of the institute would be chosen so that their interests would have some relevance to governmental needs. Given this concurrence of interests, the institute might be able to conduct certain research itself and to monitor projects entrusted to institutions outside the government which would be of immediate use to the government.

Scientists in Negotiations and as Negotiators

During the nuclear test ban negotiations, scientists were not only involved in the formulation of American policy, they also served at various times and in various capacities as negotiators. There were four conferences conducted primarily by scientists: the Conference of Experts, Technical Working Groups I and II, and the Seismic Research Program Advisory Group. During the Geneva Conference on the Discontinuance of Nuclear Weapon Tests, at least one scientist was always assigned to the American negotiating team. Later, during the meetings of the Eighteen-Nation Committee on Disarmament, several senior American scientists went to Geneva and presented briefings to members of other delegations. Finally, scientists accompanied diplomats to Moscow when the partial test ban treaty was drafted and initialed.

Evaluating the wisdom of the decisions to assign scientists to these roles and appraising their performance depends upon assumptions about the purposes of the tasks which they were given. In negotiating, any specific move may be made for a variety of reasons, some of which may have little intrinsic relationship to that particular move. Given the decentralized system of formulating security policy within the United States, the probability is high that any move will reflect a variety of motives, and it is by no means inconceivable that these motives might conflict. Thus, any move may at the same time successfully fulfill certain motives and fail to fulfill others. Moreover, a move which satisfied certain short-range motivations of policy-makers may prove to be disfunctional in terms of their longer-range goals or other criteria.

No one can question the use of scientists as advisers to diplomatic negotiators during the test ban negotiations. This was obviously necessary, and as far as can be determined from the public record, the scientists assigned to these missions performed their tasks creditably. The use of scientists as negotiators, however, was more controversial. Robert Gilpin, for one, has been quite critical of the performance of the American scientists as negotiators. His analysis of the 1958 Conference of Experts led him to conclude that the American scientists "lacking sufficient political guidance, fell into a number of regrettable errors."[6] It might be fairer, though, to include in an evaluation an assessment of the tasks assigned to the scientists and of the motives for these assignments.

One of the motives behind the original American proposal to hold a meeting of experts was a desire to neutralize the public pressures against testing so that the United States could conduct its planned series of nuclear weapons tests in the summer of 1958. A second motive was a desire to test Soviet intentions; it was thought that this would offer a means of establishing whether or not the Soviet Union would really accept control. The third motive was to provide a tactical response in a diplomatic situation where some Western move was considered advisable. In terms of the first and third motives, the Conference of Experts was undoubtedly a suc-

[6]*American Scientists and Nuclear Weapons Policy*, p. 219.

cess, and it probably was also successful in terms of the second. If other criteria are used, however, the Conference of Experts appears in a less favorable light.

After the new seismic data was discovered and the theory of decoupling developed, some writers criticized the American scientists at the Conference of Experts because they had agreed to a report which then appeared to be excessively optimistic about the possibility of detecting and identifying underground nuclear explosions.[7] Now that there have been further experiments, this criticism no longer appears valid. So far as the technical work of the American scientists at the Conference of Experts including their part in the drafting of the report, it was probably as good as could be done, given the existing state of knowledge.

Other criticisms, though, can be made of the Conference of Experts. By their report the Experts virtually committed the United States to engage in negotiations, and—what was perhaps even more crucial—to negotiate on the basis of the particular control system which they recommended. As a strategy for getting the United States to take positive action, this course may have been wise. Without some such development, because of the difficulty of formulating an agreed policy within the American government, the United States might never have engaged in the negotiations.

On the other hand, practical as this course may have been, it fell far short of criteria for rational decision-making. Entering negotiations in this manner meant that the threshold of detectability which would be acceptable to the United States was determined in Geneva by a group of scientists temporarily serving as negotiators, with very skimpy instructions, not through a deliberate decision at the highest levels of government. It also meant that until the accession of the Kennedy Administration, the government was not united in support of the negotiations. Thus the United States often seemed to be pulling back; reluctant to accept what its scientists had proposed.

The wisdom of committing the United States to a particular control system at an early stage in the negotiations can also be

[7]See, for example, Freeman Dyson, "The Future Development of Nuclear Weapons," *Foreign Affairs*, Vol. XXXVIII, No. 3 (April 1960), pp. 457-64.

questioned. Doing so severely limited American flexibility. Any control system is composed of variable elements, some predominantly technical, others predominantly nontechnical. All of these elements are interrelated, and changes in one area can be compensated for by adjustments in another. For example, one can compensate for a smaller number of on-site inspections by having a greater number of control posts. Similarly, one might also compensate for less efficient or trustworthy operating personnel by having a greater number of control posts. The ability to make such trade-offs, however, was greatly reduced as long as the Report of the Conference of Experts remained the immutable basis for the nuclear test ban negotiations, and the Soviet Union certainly viewed the report in this light for several years.

The American motivation for insisting on convoking Technical Working Groups I and II was always rather ambiguous. Calling for additional technical conferences was a course which was acceptable within the American government, both to those who wanted to abandon and to those who wanted to continue the negotiations. Since it could be viewed as a means of testing Soviet intentions, it was also agreeable to those who wanted a nuclear test ban treaty, but only under "acceptable" conditions.

From the point of view of the utilization of scientists as negotiators, Technical Working Group I appears to have been by far the more sensible of the two. In TWG I the scientists were given a narrowly defined task—to elaborate a control system for high altitudes and outer space—on which there was substantial agreement among the negotiating partners. The American scientists obviously had profited from their earlier experience at the Conference of Experts: they insisted on much more careful phraseology and on recommending alternative systems rather than a single one.

In Technical Working Group II, the scientists were in effect asked to solve the deep controversies which plagued the negotiations, an obviously impossible task. Moreover, they were asked to do this at a time when the United States was in the process of empirically testing the theory of decoupling, the development of which had done the most to dampen American enthusiasm for a test ban. In addition to failing to accomplish their mission, the scientists participating in Technical Working Group II jeopardized the intricate and delicate network of their personal relationships extending across national frontiers, which they had so carefully nurtured. One cannot but question whether this was a sensible assignment.

The Seismic Research Program Advisory Group was another matter. It is hard to conceive of any way of planning a joint or coordinated research program other than to have scientists themselves meet and produce agreed elements of a program.

After this meeting, American policy placed less emphasis on formal meetings of scientists, and probably wisely. If the purpose of bringing scientists into the negotiations was either to convince the opposite side or neutrals of the legitimacy of the Western position, there was no inherent reason why this could not be done as well, if not better, through informal sessions rather than through formally constituted meetings of scientists. The use of scientists after 1960 for elucidating and buttressing Western positions seems to have accomplished these goals, to the extent that they could be accomplished, and yet avoided the difficulties of the formal meetings of scientists.

In this connection, the Kennedy Administration had a distinct advantage over its predecessor—and this must be kept in mind in any evaluation or comparison of the conduct and contributions of the two administrations. It was under the Eisenhower Administration that the decision-makers were faced for the first time with the novel and complex scientific issues involved in the test ban and with the difficult task of finding the proper men and devising organizational patterns and procedures through which scientific advice could be integrated in the governmental process. By the time the Kennedy Administration took office a number of career diplomats and other governmental officials had acquired basic background in these problems and some lessons could be drawn from earlier experience. This was necessarily reflected in both the policy formation and in the later shapes of the negotiations.

III

The Substance of American Security Policy

Vacillation and Ambiguity

Much of what has already been said concerning formulation and execution of American security policy obviously has implications for the substance of that policy. Because the Eisenhower Administration was deeply divided concerning the wisdom of a nuclear test ban, and because President Eisenhower did not take decisive steps to end this division, until 1961 American policy toward the nuclear test ban negotiations was characterized by ambiguity and vacillation. The United States often appeared not to know whether or not it wanted a test ban or what the minimum conditions were that it would accept. It is difficult, if not impossible, to say whether this situation was due primarily to President Eisenhower's basic belief that the Soviet Union was not prepared to accept any agreement except on terms disadvantageous to the United States or to his reluctance to resolve differences within the Administration. In fact, he remained skeptical of the wisdom of the Moscow Treaty even after it was negotiated.

Inadequate Technical Preparation

A second major problem was that throughout the negotiations the level of the United States technical preparation left much to be desired. During the Conference of Experts, the United States based its calculations for elaborating control measures over underground nuclear explosions on one experiment. Subsequent experience proved that this base was too narrow. Several times American scientists discussed and agreed to control devices which did not exist and the real operational capacities of which therefore could not fully be known. An operating prototype of the control station recommended by the Conference of Experts in 1958 did not exist until October 1960. The satellites recommended by Technical Working Group I for the detection of nuclear explosions in outer space were not put into orbit until the fall of 1963, three years before an entire system would be operational. Twice during the negotiations the United States attempted to settle technical issues despite the foreknowledge that relevant experiments would be conducted during the technical discussions or after their conclusion. This occurred, as will be recalled, in the case of the Conference of Experts. It also occurred with respect to Technical Working Group II. The first major experiment in Operation Cowboy, a series of chemical explosions designed to test Albert Latter's decoupling theory, was conducted on December 17, 1959, the day before the Working Group recessed. The tests in this series would continue until mid-March 1960.

This is not to suggest that the level of American technical preparation was inferior to that of the Soviet Union, for the record certainly does not indicate this. On the contrary, the United States scientists provided by far the largest proportion of the technical data. Given the asymmetrical interest in control, which regardless of whether or not it is desirable will probably continue as long as Western societies maintain a higher degree of openness than Communist regimes, the situation requires that the West be better prepared technically than the East. Nor is it to attempt to set absolute and ideal standards by which to judge the American performance. It is merely to state that the United States' level of technical preparation was not adequate to the seriousness of the task. This criticism of course applies with even greater force to the Soviet Union. Admittedly, it is impossible always to foresee or control the pace of negotiations, but in 1958 a test ban was an issue of long-standing, and the United States was unprepared despite its salience.

In part, technical preparation is a function of administrative and financial support. The United States' position in 1958, among other things, reflected the relatively low priority accorded to arms control and disarmament matters within the government then. Presumably the situation has at least been improved with the establishment of the Arms Control and Disarmament Agency. Clearly more human and physical resources within the government are now devoted to tasks in this area. Whether or not sufficient resources are allocated to these matters, though, is an unanswered question. And one curious effect of the establishment of ACDA has been that because there has now been amassed a wealth of technical detail it has become progressively more difficult for creative outsiders to get a foothold in this field, and therefore the number of technical people not in government employ who are willing to concern themselves actively with trying to find radical solutions has been reduced.

Technical preparation is also a function of the linkage between political intelligence and technical research. Forthcoming technical issues have to be defined far enough in advance so that scientists have ample time to probe their complexities. Again, establishment of the Arms Control and Disarmament Agency should help to create and maintain this linkage. Moreover, the office of the Special Assistant to the President for Science and Technology and the President's Science Advisory Committee—both created as responses to the Sputnik crisis of the fall of 1957—are now much more firmly established as parts of the governmental structure than they were in 1958. Representatives of the scientific community now have an unquestioned place in the nation's highest policy councils. Perhaps as much has been done as is possible in terms of institutional arrangements. The questions which remain—and which by their nature are presently unanswerable —center on whether sufficient thought is given to future problems. As far as the role of ACDA is concerned, there is also a question whether—in the absence of arms control agreements that would give it operating responsibilities—the Agency will be able to retain high quality personnel and assert its place in the mainstream of policy-making in Washington.

The Linkage Between Controlling the Arms Race and Altering the State System

A third substantive problem was the linking of the nuclear test ban issue with American schemes for and concepts of world order. The United States originally proposed and argued that a grandiose organization would be required to monitor a nuclear test ban. This body would have dwarfed all existing international organizations. Interestingly, few of the American participants in the negotiations felt that such a huge organization could long stand with such a limited function; they felt that it would either have to assume additional functions in the field of arms control or collapse. Of course one reason for the extent of the American proposals in this realm was that those within the United States government who questioned the wisdom of a nuclear test ban treaty found this a convenient way of working against a test ban without engaging in a frontal attack. However, more fundamental factors were also responsible. American concepts of world order ultimately looked forward to the hierarchical organization of the world. In considering the organizational requirements of a nuclear test ban the United States drew from past experience with such organizations as the United Nations and also tried to insure that whatever new organizational developments were implemented in connection with the nuclear test ban would fit in with the general long-range goal. Little thought was given to the relationship between the limited arms control functions to be performed and the organizational requirements. As a result, in many ways the United States was as unprepared for serious arms control negotiations when it came to determining the appropriate organizational arrangements as it was lacking in the essential technical data.

Inferring from the American proposals, it appears that little thought had been given in the earlier years of the negotiations to the problem of how to reduce the possibility of nuclear holocaust without at the same time reforming the world political system. Reciprocal or adversary control (more accurately in this instance unilateral control), the technique eventually embodied in the Moscow Treaty, was one obvious response to this problem, but the United States did not even suggest this possibility until 1962. It is apparent from the record that the Soviet Union was equally if not more deficient in thinking about these problems. Throughout the negotiations there was no evidence that within the Soviet government the organizational aspects of disarmament were being considered separate from other policy questions.

The Consequences of the American Position

An assessment of the consequences of the policies pursued by the United States may be made on several levels. It seems clear that these policies caused certain difficulties for the United States in the realm of propaganda, and on these grounds it can be argued that the United States would have been in a better position had it maintained its original position of clearly insisting on linking a nuclear test ban with other measures of arms control and disarmament rather than taking the positions that it did. At least then the United States could not have been accused of negotiating in a disingenuous fashion.

A more fundamental consequence was that Soviet intentions were never fully explored. It may well be that the Soviet Union would not have agreed to any formally binding commitment prior to 1963, nor at any time to a treaty that would have involved on-site inspection. The point is that since American policies were not flexible and generous enough to allow ultimate testing of Soviet motivation these assertions cannot be made with certainty and without fear of contradiction. As the record stands, it is always possible to argue that if only American policies had been framed in terms a bit more acceptable to the Soviet Union, a more far-reaching agreement would have been possible earlier.[8]

[8]Both American and British negotiators have implicitly stated this. See James J. Wadsworth, *The Price of Peace*, p. 73, and Sir Michael Wright, *Disarm and Verify*, p. 109.

On the level of negotiating tactics, the decision to proclaim a one-year moratorium on the testing of nuclear weapons at the outset of the diplomatic negotiations has been seriously questioned. Many have argued that this deprived the United States of one of its most important means of bringing pressure on the Soviet Union to reach an agreement. It is clear that regardless of the course of the negotiations it became very difficult, if not impossible, for the United States to end the moratorium. On the other hand, whether or not the Soviet Union would have consented to engage in negotiations had the United States insisted on continuing its testing is problematical. Furthermore, had it chosen to pursue this course, the United States government would have had to have been willing to face serious pressures from both internal and external sources, the latter especially in the United Nations.

IV
The International System

Open and Closed Societies
The way in which the two sides handled the important issue of the moratorium on testing brings out as clearly as any example drawn from the nuclear test ban negotiations the tactical advantages that a closed society enjoys over an open society in international negotiations. The former can shift course quickly and radically, and can plan its moves in secrecy, thus maintaining the advantage of surprise. Open societies, in contrast, except during crises, tend to move more slowly and to give ample forewarning of their moves. Thus the Soviet Union could break the moratorium suddenly, while the West could not.

A somewhat different disadvantage but stemming from the same cause was that the open and pluralistic societies of the West gave off ambiguous signals. Some in the West spoke in more severe terms than the official policy, others in more lenient terms. Those who took lines which diverged from official policy sometimes even included individuals with policy-making responsibilities. The Kremlin could read these divergent signs as indicating on the one hand that the official policy might be only a cover for a harsher line, or, on the other, as indicating that further concessions would be forthcoming, and that to gain these one need only wait. Of course, the openness of Western society could also be an advantage to the extent that it allowed the West to introduce "feelers" into the negotiations. To make use of this advantage requires skill and care, and also greater control over circumstances than sometimes exists in reality.

Policy-makers in a closed society are less subject to external and internal pressures than their counterparts in an open society. The test ban negotiations indicate that the Western states tended to take such matters as UN resolutions and pronouncements of neutrals more seriously than did the Soviet Union. However, they also show that both sides were affected by such matters to some extent, and that both would ignore them if they felt that their vital interests were at stake. Thus both sides tried to have their position endorsed by the UN, and both also did things that UN resolutions exhorted them not to.

A related difference is that the USSR could appeal to segments of the Western public, over the heads of the Western governments, while the Western states could not as easily engage in similar operations with respect to the Soviet people.

The differences in the nature of Soviet and Western societies, however, affected the negotiations in more fundamental ways than simply with respect to the tactics and relative freedom of action on the part of the negotiators of the two sides. At least partly because of its closed society, the USSR's attitude toward the establishment of control measures was significantly different from that of the United States and the United Kingdom. To the end of the negotiations, the Soviet Union firmly resisted any outside intrusions that it could not control. For a while the Soviet Union appears to have been willing to accept the intrusions connected with the establishment of a limited number of fixed control posts manned by at least some non-Soviet personnel. This position was in a sense an unprecedented step but it was retracted in November 1961 and never reinstated. The Soviet position toward on-site inspection was always so hedged, that—partly for reasons suggested earlier in connection with the United States policies—it is impossible to say that the USSR was ever entirely willing to accept such intrusions. The rationale for the Soviet Union's penchant for secrecy has been amply analyzed elsewhere;[9] it is only necessary here to note how deeply it affected the

[9]See especially Alexander Dallin and others, *The Soviet Union, Arms Control and Disarmament*, pp. 142-58.

USSR's policy in this instance. No doubt the Soviet Union's secrecy contributes something to its military security, though it is also clear that this secrecy is an important part of the regime in its own right, and as such has a vital effect on arms control negotiations. These remarks are of course not intended to suggest an absence of secrecy and concern with secrecy in the West, but rather to indicate an important difference.

A related point is that the USSR never consented to the establishment of a control organization in connection with a nuclear test ban which could take significant action against its wishes. No doubt the positions of East and West are colored by the experience of the two sides in and with existing and past international arrangements and institutions such as the United Nations, an experience which thus far has been much more favorable to the West in East-West confrontations. But the more important explanation of the differences in the attitudes toward control and inspection probably lies in the differences between the two societies.

The Effects of Technology

The record of the test ban negotiations is interesting in this respect for it showed how these fundamental differences between the two societies—and particularly the closed character of the Soviet society—were being altered among other factors by the growth of modern technology. In 1963 the United States felt that it could do as good a job of detecting underground nuclear explosions within the Soviet Union with stations outside of the territory of the USSR as it had felt in 1958 that it could do with a significant number of stations within the USSR. The development of observation satellites also sharply inhibited the ability of any society to act in secret. Thus the Soviet system has become more open, not necessarily by its own conscious design, but simply because technology has made it easier for others to observe Soviet territory, regardless of Soviet wishes. In the long run, this factor should reduce at least to some extent the difficulty of negotiating arms control agreements, particularly if it is reinforced by the conscious efforts toward greater openness such as increased exchange of persons and scientific cooperation between East and West. As a result, the USSR should become less reluctant to accept intrusions, and the West less insistent on their necessity.

The Role of Nonnuclear States

The proposition that other powers can affect the policies of the superpowers is implicit in what has already been said. The United Nations was one forum available to virtually all states during the test ban negotiations, and many of them sought to and did exercise influence through it. The Eighteen-Nation Disarmament Committee was a more effective instrument for those states which were members; there can be no doubt that both the USSR and the United States were more sensitive to pressures brought to bear and suggestions raised in this organ than in the more diffuse General Assembly. It is also demonstrable, as many British leaders have claimed, that the United Kingdom had influence far greater than that of other states of equivalent size, mainly, in this case, because of its possession of nuclear weapons.[10] It is further clear, though, that ultimately the superpowers, the USSR and the United States, or more accurately political configurations within them, determined whether or not there should be a nuclear test ban treaty. Other states and international organizations could influence the superpowers, and their internal political configurations, but they could not determine the course of events.

Power and Agreements

The record of the test ban negotiations also has relevance for long-debated questions about the relationship between the distribution of power and the achievement of agreements. When the Moscow Treaty was signed, the relative position of the Soviet Union and the United States with respect to the development of nuclear weapons was very different from what it had been when the negotiations began in 1958. In 1958 the United States apparently held the technological lead with respect to all areas and levels of nuclear weapons development. By 1963 the Soviet Union had detonated larger weapons than the United States, and the test ban treaty would make it difficult if not impossible for the United States to develop weapons of such magnitude. In more general terms, the USSR appeared to have become technologically more advanced than the United States in the development of high-yield weapons; that is, weapons with a yield of 5 or 10 megatons or larger. The situation with respect to weapons

[10]See Sir Michael Wright, *Disarm and Verify*, p. 141.

with intermediate yield was indeterminate. The United States definitely held the lead in low-yield weapons; that is, weapons with a yield of less than one megaton. However, since continued underground testing was permitted under the treaty, and since weapons with such yields can be tested underground, presumably the Soviet Union could attempt to equal or surpass the United States level of achievement. This consideration might have made the treaty more attractive for the Soviet Union in 1963. It should be noted though that since the signature of the treaty the frequency of underground tests conducted by the United States has exceeded that of tests conducted by the Soviet Union by almost a factor of ten. Whether this is due to a lack of preparation on the part of the USSR, to a low opinion of the value of such tests, or to their high cost and complexity, it is impossible to know.

What was perhaps equally as significant as the exact state of the technological race was that both sides appeared to have neared the theoretical limits of nuclear weapons development in their last series of tests, and also to have discovered most or all that was "interesting" to them in terms of their concepts of military strategy. The Soviet Union, having apparently decided under Khrushchev to put great emphasis on deterrence, had developed the counter-city weapons that it needed for this strategy. The United States under President Kennedy, on the other hand, moved to deemphasize the role of nuclear weapons in its strategy, and in particular became less interested in the development of tactical nuclear weapons.

The changes in positions of the two sides with respect to the development of nuclear weapons should be viewed against the changes concerning total military strength. In 1963 the United States' margin of superiority was significantly greater than it had been five years earlier.

In sum, with respect to military power, in 1963 there were reasons for both sides to have greater confidence in their own abilities to achieve the missions that they might assign to their military establishments than they had in 1958. This bears on the question of whether in an arms race an increase in one side's security necessarily decreases that of the other side, and also on the degree of confidence necessary to achieve arms control agreements. P. M. S. Blackett's argument, though, that the Western superiority in missile strength made the USSR unwilling to accept an international control system for a test ban on the ground that such a system would detract from Soviet security by possibly revealing the location of Soviet missile sites, should be noted.[11] He feels that the USSR counted on the secrecy of these sites to offset the Western numerical superiority. Many strategists disagree with his argument, and in any case observation satellites have to some extent made it obsolete.

The Decline of Bipolarity

At the same time that both the United States and the Soviet Union became more confident concerning their own military capabilities vis-à-vis one another, they each became more worried about other problems on the world scene. In the first place, both appear to have become more concerned about the consequences of the dispersion of nuclear weapons capabilities, and this has marked the emergence of a common interest of the two nuclear superpowers in the status quo. More specifically, for their own reasons both the Soviet Union and the United States became interested in inhibiting increases in Communist China's military power. Again, the Soviet Union had always been concerned about the spread of nuclear weapons capabilities in the West, and especially to Western Germany. Although the United States was never as concerned about the spread of nuclear weapons capabilities within the West as it was within other areas, it foresaw a connection between the spread within the West and elsewhere and increasingly came to oppose the spread within the West also. One purpose behind the American proposal for a multilateral nuclear force under NATO was to foreclose pressures for new national nuclear forces in the West and particularly in Germany although the Soviet Union has refused to view the proposal in this light.

To say that both the Soviet Union and the United States became increasingly interested in a nuclear test ban because they became increasingly interested in inhibiting the nuclear capabilities of other states, implies that this arms control agreement was partially a consequence of decreasing bipolarity. Paradoxically, signing the agreement hastened the dilution of bipolarity, for it meant that each coalition leader had to oppose the wishes of a major ally: the Soviet

[11]P. M. S. Blackett, *Studies of War: Nuclear and Conventional* (Edinburgh: Oliver and Boyd, 1962), p. 160.

Union, those of Communist China and the United States, those of France.

The Problem of Controlling Modern Technology

The experience with the nuclear test ban negotiations confirms the immense difficulty inherent in the task of controlling modern technology in an environment of the multi-state system. The negotiations brought out how hard it was to arrange matters so that the interests of just two sides (and three states) coincided enough to allow for an agreement. The refusal of Communist China and France to adhere to the Moscow Treaty, although anticipated, reduced the value of the treaty for the two sides and showed that bargains made essentially bilaterally cannot easily be extended to other parties.

The makeup and interests of states are not identical and agreements affect them differently. Constructing an agreement that has an equal range of benefits and disadvantages for many disparate partners is a task of great intellectual difficulty, and one which is made even more laborious if it must be worked out through the mechanisms of multi-governmental bargaining and complex intragovernmental processes such as those existing in the United States.

The fact that modern technology is subject to swift changes— as was amply evidenced during the nuclear test ban negotiations— makes this task even more complicated. The insistence by the West in 1959 that "new data" be brought into the negotiations after the scientists had agreed on the relevant technological basis in 1958— and the refusal by the Soviet Union to agree to this proved a major stumbling block in the negotiations.

If it is difficult to strike a bargain among several disparate parties for a static situation, it is even more difficult to strike one that will accommodate technological change and yet any agreement without such accommodation would be of limited value. Sovereign states are most unlikely to accept agreements which have a built-in potentiality for unpredictable alterations. Thus the Soviet Union would be very unlikely to accept a treaty that would at the outset provide for 20 on-site inspections on its territory annually but might under certain circumstances require several hundred.

The conceivable solutions for this problem are limited. The participating states could give broad powers to a panel of scientists to modify the control system in accordance with new technology, but during the test ban negotiations neither side seemed very eager or willing to accept such a solution. If the panel of scientists were given such powers the states would be exposed to the danger that the distribution of benefits and disadvantages built into the treaty could be radically altered by a group beyond their control. Moreover, the test ban negotiations show how many different interpretations of some data are scientifically plausible. Thus the margin of discretion would be quite wide and the scientists could not be expected to achieve universally accepted decisions. Another possibility would be to require a periodic review of the control provisions, but what this actually would amount to is a provision for periodic renegotiation, if significant technological changes occurred which vitally affected the subject matter of the treaty. That this renegotiation would be conducted within the framework of the treaty might provide some guidelines and an additional incentive for agreement, but little beyond that. Of course, if an adversary or reciprocal control system were used, as it was in the Moscow Treaty, accommodating technological change could be accomplished on the basis of unilateral decisions by interested parties. Of the various ways of treating the problem, this is clearly the easiest to negotiate and the least cumbersome, but whether or not it can be applied to other than essentially bilateral relationships is open to serious question.

Although it does not show in the terms of the Moscow Treaty, the nuclear test ban negotiations made it apparent that some control measures can be developed as a by-product of peaceful activities. The use of weather stations to collect information on radioactive fallout and of seismological stations to collect information on underground nuclear detonations are examples. Interestingly, as the level of technology has risen, effective exploitation of such developments has often required increased international collaboration. The territories of states are often just too small to exploit new technological developments. The position of the United States in the test ban negotiations concerning the use of already existing stations shows the doubts that many states would have about the reliability of information from such national sources, but perhaps this problem could partially be overcome by having redundant systems for gathering information. Moreover, it is possible that there may be more sources that a state could trust in a multipolar world than in a bipolar world, and for this reason the movement of the world from bipolarity may make it increasingly possible to rely on information gained from such sources. One can envisage a relatively high degree of control over technology resulting from overlaying the world with multiple networks based on international arrangements for scientific collaboration, established principally to facilitate other purposes such as weather prediction and high-speed, long-distance communication.

As the nuclear test ban negotiations so clearly demonstrate though, the questions of whether or not such control will be established, and the extent of this control, are preeminently political and diplomatic, not technical. Science and scientific research can contribute to the solution of arms control and disarmament problems; it cannot solve them.

It is obviously impossible to give a definitive answer at this stage to the crucial question of whether or not the signature of the Moscow Treaty marked a turning point in the nuclear era. What can be said, though, is that the Treaty represented an attempt to create a turning point; that the attempt has been made is important and it has had an impact on international atmosphere. Furthermore, what has been learned in the process of making the attempt may have been as important as the actual Treaty, for mankind now knows a good bit more about how to proceed in efforts to create a more peaceful world. Finally, the record of the test ban negotiations also shows that the growth of technology may contain within itself important potentialities for control.

Appendix

Treaty Banning Nuclear Weapon Tests in the Atmosphere, in Outer Space, and Under Water

The Governments of the United States of America, the United Kingdom of Great Britain and Northern Ireland, and the Union of Soviet Socialist Republics, hereinafter referred to as the "Original Parties,"

Proclaiming as their principal aim the speediest possible achievement of an agreement on general and complete disarmament under strict international control in accordance with the objectives of the United Nations which would put an end to the armaments race and eliminate the incentive to the production and testing of all kinds of weapons, including nuclear weapons,

Seeking to achieve the discontinuance of all test explosions of nuclear weapons for all time, determined to continue negotiations to this end, and desiring to put an end to the contamination of man's environment by radioactive substances,

Have agreed as follows:

Article I

1. Each of the Parties to this Treaty undertakes to prohibit, to prevent, and not to carry out any nuclear weapon test explosion, or any other nuclear explosion, at any place under its jurisdiction or control:

(a) in the atmosphere; beyond its limits, including outer space; or underwater, including territorial waters or high seas; or

(b) in any other environment if such explosion causes radioactive debris to be present outside the territorial limits of the State under whose jurisdiction or control such explosion is conducted. It is understood in this connection that the provisions of this subparagraph are without prejudice to the conclusion of a treaty resulting in the permanent banning of all nuclear test explosions, including all such explosions underground, the conclusion of which, as the Parties have stated in the Preamble to this Treaty, they seek to achieve.

2. Each of the Parties to this Treaty undertakes furthermore to refrain from causing, encouraging, or in any way participating in, the

504

carrying out of any nuclear weapon test explosion, or any other nuclear explosion, anywhere which would take place in any of the environments described, or have the effect referred to, in paragraph 1 of this Article.

Article II

1. Any Party may propose amendments to this Treaty. The text of any proposed amendment shall be submitted to the Depositary Governments which shall circulate it to all Parties to this Treaty. Thereafter, if requested to do so by one-third or more of the Parties, the Depositary Governments shall convene a conference, to which they shall invite all the Parties, to consider such amendment.

2. Any amendment to this Treaty must be approved by a majority of the votes of all the Parties to this Treaty, including the votes of all of the Original Parties. The amendment shall enter into force for all Parties upon the deposit of instruments of ratification by a majority of all the Parties, including the instruments of ratification of all of the Original Parties.

Article III

1. This Treaty shall be open to all States for signature. Any State which does not sign this Treaty before its entry into force in accordance with paragraph 3 of this Article may accede to it at any time.

2. This Treaty shall be subject to ratification by signatory States. Instruments of ratification and instruments of accession shall be deposited with the Governments of the Original Parties—the United States of America, the United Kingdom of Great Britain and Northern Ireland, and the Union of Soviet Socialist Republics—which are hereby designated the Depositary Governments.

3. This Treaty shall enter into force after its ratification by all the Original Parties and the deposit of their instruments of ratification.

4. For States whose instruments of ratification or accession are deposited subsequent to the entry into force of this Treaty, it shall enter into force on the date of the deposit of their instruments of ratification or accession.

5. The Depositary Governments shall promptly inform all signatory and acceding States of the date of each signature, the date of deposit of each instrument of ratification of and accession to this Treaty, the date of its entry into force, and the date of receipt of any requests for conferences or other notices.

6. This Treaty shall be registered by the Depositary Governments pursuant to Article 102 of the Charter of the United Nations.

Article IV

This Treaty shall be of unlimited duration.

Each Party shall in exercising its national sovereignty have the right to withdraw from the Treaty if it decides that extraordinary events, related to the subject matter of this Treaty, have jeopardized the supreme interests of its country. It shall give notice of such withdrawal to all other Parties to the Treaty three months in advance.

Article V

This Treaty, of which the English and Russian texts are equally authentic, shall be deposited in the archives of the Depositary Governments. Duly certified copies of this Treaty shall be transmitted by the Depositary Governments to the Governments of the signatory and acceding States.

In witness whereof the undersigned, duly authorized, have signed this Treaty.

Done in triplicate at the city of Moscow, the fifth day of August, one thousand nine hundred and sixty-three.

Bibliography

Frequently used abbreviations or short titles are given in brackets following the entry.

I. Documents

Conference of Experts to Study the Methods of Detecting Violations of a Possible Agreement on the Suspension of Nuclear Tests. *Documents.* [EXP]

———. *Verbatim Records.* [EXP/PV.]

Conference on the Discontinuance of Nuclear Weapon Tests. *Documents.* (Mimeographed; "Private.") Geneva, 1958-62. [GEN/DNT]

———. *Verbatim Records.* (Mimeographed; "Private.") Geneva, 1958-62. [GEN/DNT/PV.]

Eighteen-Nation Committee on Disarmament. *Documents.* (Mimeographed; "Private.") 1962-63. [ENDC]

———. *Verbatim Records.* 1962-63. [ENDC/PV.]

United Nations. Disarmament Commission. Subcommittee 1. Relevant *Documents* and *Summary Records.* 1957. [DC/SC.1] and [DC/SC.1/SR]

———. General Assembly. Relevant *Documents* and *Summary Records.* 1957-63. [A and A/SR]

———. Security Council. Relevant *Documents* and *Summary Records.* 1957-63. [SC and SC/SR]

U.S. Arms Control and Disarmament Agency (Publication 5). *Documents on Disarmament, 1961.* Washington, D.C.: Government Printing Office [GPO], 1962.

———. (Publication 19). *Documents on Disarmament, 1962,* 2 vols. GPO, 1963.

———. (Publication 24). *Documents on Disarmament, 1963.* GPO, 1964.

———. (Publication 9). *International Negotiations on Ending Nuclear Weapon Tests, September 1961—September 1962.* GPO, 1962.

U.S. Congress. *Congressional Record.* Vols. 104-6, 108, 109.

U.S. Congress. Joint Committee on Atomic Energy. *Amendment to the Atomic Energy Act of 1954,* Senate Report No. 1654, 85th Congress, 2d Session. GPO, 1958.

———. *Hearings: Developments in the Field of Detection and Identification of Nuclear Explosions (Project Vela) and Relationship to Test Ban Negotiations,* 87th Congress, 1st Session. GPO, 1962.

———. *Summary-Analysis of Hearings: Developments in the Field of Detection and Identification of Nuclear Explosions (Project Vela) and Relationship to Test Ban Negotiations,* 87th Congress, 2d Session. (Comm. Print) GPO, 1962.

———. *Hearings: Developments in Technical Capabilities for Detecting and Identifying Nuclear Weapons Tests,* 88th Congress, 1st Session. GPO, 1963.

————. Special Subcommittee on Radiation. *Hearings: The Nature of Radioactive Fallout and Its Effect on Man,* 3 parts, 85th Congress, 1st Session. GPO, 1958.

————. Special Subcommittee on Radiation and the Subcommittee on Research, Development, and Radiation. *Hearings: Radiation Standards, Including Fallout,* parts 1 and 2 and Appendix, 87th Congress, 1st Session. GPO, 1962.

————. *Hearings: Technical Aspects of Detection and Inspection Controls of a Nuclear Weapons Test Ban,* 2 parts, 86th Congress, 2d Session. GPO, 1960.

U.S. Congress. House of Representatives. Appropriations Committee. *Hearings: Atomic Energy Commission Appropriations for 1960,* 86th Congress, 1st Session. GPO, 1959.

U.S. Congress. Senate. Committee on Armed Services. Preparedness Investigating Subcommittee. *Hearings: Arms Control and Disarmament.* 87th Congress, 2d Session. GPO, 1962.

————. *Interim Report on the Military Implications of the Proposed Limited Nuclear Test Ban,* 88th Congress, 1st Session. GPO, 1963.

————. *Hearings: Military Aspects and Implications of Nuclear Test Ban Proposals and Related Matters,* 2 vols., 88th Congress, 1st Session. GPO, 1964.

U.S. Congress. Senate. Committee on Foreign Relations. *Hearing: Test Ban Negotiations and Disarmament,* 88th Congress, 1st Session. GPO, 1963.

————. *Hearings: Nuclear Test Ban Treaty,* 88th Congress, 1st Session. GPO, 1963.

————. Subcommittee on Disarmament. *Final Report: Control and Reduction of Armaments,* Senate Report No. 2501, 85th Congress, 2d Session. GPO, 1958.

————. *Hearings: Control and Reduction of Armaments,* 85th Congress, 2d Session. GPO, 1958.

————. *Hearings: Disarmament and Foreign Policy,* 86th Congress, 1st Session. GPO, 1959.

————. *Hearing: Geneva Test Ban Negotiations,* 86th Congress, 1st Session. GPO, 1959.

————. *Hearings: Renewed Geneva Disarmament Negotiations,* 87th Congress, 2d Session. GPO, 1963.

————. *Hearing: Technical Problems and the Geneva Test Ban Negotiations,* 86th Congress, 2d Session. GPO, 1960.

————. *Staff Study No. 10: Control and Reduction of Armaments: Detection of and Inspection for Underground Explosions: Replies from Seismologists to Subcommittee Questionnaire.* 85th Congress, 2d Session. (Comm. Print.) GPO, 1958.

U.S. Department of Defense. Press Release, January 16, 1959.

U.S. Department of Defense (Samuel Glasstone, ed.). *The Effects of Nuclear Weapons.* Washington, D.C.: U.S. Atomic Energy Commission, revised ed. 1962.

U.S. Department of State (Publication 7172). *Documents on Disarmament, 1960.* GPO, 1961.

————. *Treaties and Other International Acts,* Nos. 3521, 4078, 4267, 4268, 4271, 4276, 4277, 4278, 4292, 4764, 4876. GPO, 1959.

————. (Publication 7008). Historical Office. Bureau of Public Affairs. *Documents on Disarmament, 1945-1959,* 2 vols. GPO, 1960.

U.S. Disarmament Administration. Department of State (Publication 7258, Disarmament Series 4). *Geneva Conference on the Discontinuance of Nuclear Weapon Tests, History and Analysis of Negotiations.* GPO, 1961. [*Geneva Conference*]

II. Unpublished Manuscript

Zoppo, Ciro E. *The Test Ban: A Study in Arms Control Negotiations,* Ph.D. Dissertation, Columbia University, 1963.

III. Books

Bechhoefer, Bernhard. *Postwar Negotiations for Arms Control.* Washington, D.C.: The Brookings Institution, 1961.

Blackett, P.M.S. *Studies of War: Nuclear and Conventional.* Edinburgh: Oliver and Boyd, 1962.

Brennan, Donald G. (ed.). *Arms Control, Disarmament and National Security.* New York: George Braziller, 1961.

Dallin, Alexander. *The Soviet Union at the United Nations.* New York: Frederick A. Praeger, 1962.

————, and others. *The Soviet Union, Arms Control and Disarmament.* New York: School of International Affairs, Columbia University, 1964.

Dupré, J. Stefan, and Lakoff, Sanford A. *Science and the Nation: Policy and Politics.* Englewood Cliffs: Prentice-Hall, 1962.

Eisenhower, Dwight D. *Waging Peace, 1956-1961; The White House Years.* Garden City: Doubleday, 1965.

Gardner, Richard N. *In Pursuit of World Order: U.S. Foreign Policy and International Organizations.* New York: Frederick A. Praeger, 1964.

Gilpin, Robert. *American Scientists and Nuclear Weapons Policy.* Princeton: Princeton University Press, 1962.

————, and Wright, Christopher (eds.). *Scientists and National Policy-Making.* New York: Columbia University Press, 1964.

Henkin, Louis (ed.). *Arms Control: Issues for the Public.* Englewood Cliffs: Prentice-Hall, 1961.

Herz, John H. *International Politics in the Atomic Age.* New York: Columbia University Press, 1959.

Holborn, Hajo. *The Political Collapse of Europe.* New York: Alfred A. Knopf, 1951, with contributions by David C. Elliot, Louis Henkin, Hans A. Linde, Robert B. von Mehren, and Ciro E. Zoppo.

Hsieh, Alice Langley. *Communist China's Strategy in the Nuclear Era.* Englewood Cliffs: Prentice-Hall, 1962.

Iklé, Fred Charles, and others. *Alternative Approaches to the International Organization of Disarmament.* Santa Monica: The RAND Corporation, R-391-ARPA, 1962.

————. *How Nations Negotiate.* New York: Harper and Row, 1964.

Institute of Strategic Studies. *The Communist Bloc and the Western Alliances: The Military Balance, 1961-1962.* London: Institute of Strategic Studies, 1961.

————. *The Communist Bloc and the Western Alliances: The Military Balance, 1963-1964.* London: Institute of Strategic Studies, 1963.

Jenks, C. Wilfred. *International Immunities.* London: Stevens & Sons, 1961.

Kramish, Arnold. *The Peaceful Atom in Foreign Policy.* New York: Harper and Row, 1963.

Lall, Arthur S. [Anand]. *Negotiating Disarmament: The Eighteen-Nation Disarmament Conference, The First Two Years, 1962-64.* Ithaca: Center for International Studies, Cornell University, 1964.

Lapp, Ralph E. *Kill and Overkill: The Strategy of Annihilation.* New York: Basic Books, 1962.

Melman, Seymour (ed.). *Disarmament: Its Politics and Economics.* Boston: The American Academy of Arts and Sciences, 1962.

———— (ed.). *Inspection for Disarmament.* New York: Columbia University Press, 1958.

Murray, Thomas E. *Nuclear Policy for War and Peace.* New York: The World Publishing Company, 1960.

Nogee, Joseph L. *Soviet Policy Towards International Control of Atomic Energy.* Notre Dame: University of Notre Dame Press, 1961.

Schelling, Thomas C. *The Strategy of Conflict.* Cambridge: Harvard University Press, 1960.

Schlesinger, Arthur M., Jr., *A Thousand Days: John F. Kennedy in the White House.* Boston: Houghton Mifflin Co., 1965.

Sorenson, Theodore C. *Kennedy.* New York: Harper and Row, 1965.

Speier, Hans. *German Rearmament and Atomic War: The Views of German Military and Political Leaders.* Evanston: Row, Peterson, 1957.

Stebbins, Richard P. *The United States in World Affairs, 1957.* New York: Harper and Brothers, 1957.

————. *The United States in World Affairs, 1958.* New York: Harper and Brothers, 1959.

————. *The United States in World Affairs, 1960.* New York: Harper and Brothers, 1961.

————. *The United States in World Affairs, 1961*. New York: Harper and Row, 1962.

————. *The United States in World Affairs, 1962*. New York: Harper and Row, 1963.

————. *The United States in World Affairs, 1963*. New York: Harper and Row, 1964.

Strauss, Lewis L. *Men and Decisions*. Garden City: Doubleday and Company, 1962.

Stromberg, Roland N. *Collective Security and American Foreign Policy: From the League of Nations to NATO*. New York: Frederick A. Praeger, 1963.

Teller, Edward, and Albert Latter. *Our Nuclear Future: Facts, Dangers and Opportunities*. New York: Criterion Books, 1958.

————, with Allen Brown. *The Legacy of Hiroshima*. Garden City: Doubleday, 1962.

Union of Soviet Socialist Republics, Academy of Sciences, Institute of State and Law. *International Law*. Moscow: Foreign Languages Publishing House, 1960.

Voss, Earl H. *Nuclear Ambush: The Test Ban Trap*. Chicago: Henry Regnery, 1963.

Wadsworth, James J. *The Price of Peace*. New York: Frederick A. Praeger, 1962.

Wiesner, Jerome B. *Where Science and Politics Meet*. New York: McGraw-Hill, 1965.

Wolfe, Thomas W. *Soviet Strategy at the Crossroads*. Cambridge: Harvard University Press, 1964.

Wright, Sir Michael. *Disarm and Verify: An Explanation of the Central Difficulties and of National Policies*. New York: Frederick A. Praeger, 1964.

Zagoria, Donald S. *The Sino-Soviet Conflict, 1956-1961*. Princeton: Princeton University Press, 1962.

IV. Newspapers and Periodicals

Bulletin of the Atomic Scientists
The Current Digest of Soviet Press
The Houston *Post*
The New York *Times*
The Observer
United States Department of State *Bulletin*
The Washington *Post*

V. Articles and Pamphlets

Ahmed, M. Samir. "The Role of the Neutrals in the Geneva Negotiations," *Disarmament and Arms Control*, Vol. I, No. 2 (Summer 1963), pp. 20-32.

Apt, Clark C. "The Problems and Possibilities of Space Arms Control," *Journal of Arms Control,* Vol. I, No. 1 (January 1963), pp. 18-43.

Bechhoefer, Bernhard G. "Negotiating the Statute of the International Atomic Energy Agency," *International Organization,* Vol. XIII, No. 1 (Winter 1959), pp. 38-59.

Bethe, Hans A. "Disarmament and Strategy," *Bulletin of the Atomic Scientists,* Vol. XVIII, No. 7 (September 1962), pp. 14-22.

———. "The Case for Ending Nuclear Tests," *Headline Series,* No. 145 (January-February 1961), p. 17.

———. "The Hydrogen Bomb," *Bulletin of the Atomic Scientists,* Vol. VI, No. 4 (April 1950), pp. 99-104, 125.

Bloomfield, Lincoln P. "The Politics of Administering Disarmament," *Disarmament and Arms Control,* Vol. I, No. 2 (Autumn 1963), pp. 118-32.

Clark, Senator Joseph S. "Would the Senate Ratify A Nuclear Test Ban Treaty?" *War/Peace Report,* Vol. III, No. 6 (June 1963), p. 6.

Cousins, Norman. "Notes on a 1963 Visit with Khrushchev," *Saturday Review,* Vol. XLVII, No. 45 (November 7, 1964), pp. 16-21, 58-60.

Davis, Saville R. "Recent Policy Making in the United States Government," in Donald G. Brennan (ed.), *Arms Control, Disarmament, and National Security.* New York: G. Braziller, 1961.

Dulles, John Foster. "Policy for Security and Peace," *Foreign Affairs,* Vol. XXXII, No. 3 (April 1954), pp. 353-64.

———. "Challenge and Response in United States Policy," *Foreign Affairs,* Vol. XXXVI, No. 1 (October 1957), pp. 25-43.

Dyson, Freeman J. "The Future Development of Nuclear Weapons," *Foreign Affairs,* Vol. XXXIX, No. 3 (April 1960), pp. 457-64.

Finkelstein, Lawrence S. "Arms Inspection," *International Conciliation,* No. 540 (November 1962), pp. 5-89.

———. "The United Nations and Organizations for the Control of Armaments," *International Organization,* Vol. XVI, No. 1 (Winter 1962), pp. 1-19.

———. "The Uses of Reciprocal Inspection," in Seymour Melman (ed.). *Disarmament: Its Politics and Economics.* Boston: American Academy of Arts and Sciences, 1962.

Gehron, William J. "Geneva Conference on the Discontinuance of Nuclear Weapon Tests: History of Political and Technical Developments of the Negotiations From October 31, 1958 to August 22, 1960," Department of State *Bulletin,* Vol. XLIII, No. 1109 (September 26, 1960), pp. 482-97.

Harris, George. "How Livermore Survived the Test Ban," *Fortune,* Vol. LXV, No. 4 (April 1960), pp. 127, 236, 241.

Hilsman, Roger. "Congressional-Executive Relations and the Foreign Policy Consensus," *The American Political Science Review,* Vol. LII, No. 3 (September 1958), pp. 725-44.

———. "The Foreign Policy Consensus: An Interim Research Report,"

The Journal of Conflict Resolution, Vol. III, No. 4 (December 1959), pp. 361-82.

Horelick, Arnold L. "The Cuban Missile Crises: An Analysis of Soviet Calculations and Behavior," *World Politics,* Vol. XVI, No. 3 (April 1964), pp. 363-89.

Hsieh, Alice Langley. "The Sino-Soviet Nuclear Dialogue: 1963," *Journal of Conflict Resolution,* Vol. VIII, No. 2 (June 1964), pp. 99-115.

Jacobson, Harold K. "Our 'Colonial' Problem in the Pacific," *Foreign Affairs,* Vol. XXXIX, No. 1 (October 1960), pp. 56-66.

———. "The Test-Ban Negotiations: Implications for the Future," *The Annals* of the American Academy of Political and Social Science, Vol. 351 (January 1964), pp. 92-101.

Johnson, G. W., and others. "The Underground Nuclear Detonation of September 19, 1957—Rainier, Operation Plumbbob" (February 4, 1958).

Khrushchev, Nikita S. "On Peaceful Coexistence," *Foreign Affairs,* Vol. XXXVIII, No. 1 (October 1959), pp. 1-18.

Kissinger, Henry A. "Nuclear Testing and the Problem of Peace," *Foreign Affairs,* Vol. XXXVII, No. 1 (October 1958), pp. 1-18.

Latter, A., Latter, R., and McMillan, W. *The Irrelevance of the Gnome Shot to Decoupling.* Santa Monica: The RAND Corporation, RM-3005-PR, 1962.

Latter, A. L., LeLevier, R. E., Martinelli, E. A., and McMillan, W. G. *A Method of Concealing Underground Nuclear Explosions.* Santa Monica: The RAND Corporation, RM-2347-AFT, 1959.

Margolis, Emanuel. "The Hydrogen Bomb Experiments and International Law," *The Yale Law Journal,* Vol. LXIV, No. 5 (April 1955), pp. 629-47.

McCloy, John J. "Balance Sheet on Disarmament," *Foreign Affairs,* Vol. XL, No. 3 (April 1962), pp. 339-59.

McDougal, Myers S. and Schlei, Norbert A. "The Hydrogen Bomb Tests in Perspective: Lawful Measures for Security," *The Yale Law Journal,* Vol. LXIV, No. 5 (April 1955), pp. 648-710.

McNamara, Robert S. "Defense Arrangements for the North Atlantic Community," The Department of State *Bulletin,* Vol. XLVII, No. 1202 (July 1962), pp. 64-69.

———. "Major National Security Problems Confronting the United States," The Department of State *Bulletin,* Vol. XLIX, No. 1277 (December 16, 1963), pp. 914-21.

Morton, Louis. "The Decision to Use the Atomic Bomb," United States of America, Department of the Army, Office of the Chief of Military History, *Command Decisions,* Washington, D.C.: GPO, 1960, pp. 493-518.

Murphy, Charles J. V. "Nuclear Inspection: A Near Miss," *Fortune,* Vol. LIX, No. 3 (March 1959), pp. 122-25, 155-62.

Roberts, Chalmers M. "The Hopes and Fears of an Atomic Test Ban," *The Reporter,* Vol. XXII, No. 9, pp. 20-23.

Schilling, Warner R. "The H-Bomb Decision: How to Decide Without Actually Choosing," *Political Science Quarterly,* Vol. LXXVI, No. 1 (March 1961), pp. 24-46.

Speier, Hans. "Soviet Atomic Blackmail and the North Atlantic Alliance," *World Politics,* Vol. IX, No. 3 (April 1957), pp. 307-28.

Taubenfeld, Howard J. "A Treaty for Antarctica," *International Conciliation,* Vol. 531 (January 1961), pp. 245-322.

Teller, Edward. "Alternatives for Security," *Foreign Affairs,* Vol. XXXVII, No. 2 (January 1958), p. 204.

USSR Academy of Sciences, Institute of State and Law. *International Law.* (English translation) Moscow: Foreign Languages Publishing House, 1960? .

Wiesner, Jerome B. "Comprehensive Arms-Limitations Systems," *Daedalus* (Fall 1960), pp. 915-50.

Zoppo, Ciro E. *The Issue of Nuclear Test Cessation at the London Disarmament Conference of 1957: A Study in East-West Negotiation.* Santa Monica: The RAND Corporation, RM-2821-ARPA, 1961.

————. *Technical and Political Aspects of Arms Control Negotiation: The 1958 Experts Conference.* Santa Monica: The RAND Corporation, RM-3286-ARPA, 1962.

————, with the collaboration of Alice L. Hsieh. *The Accession of Other Nations to the Nuclear Test Ban.* Santa Monica: The RAND Corporation, RM-2730-ARPA, 1961.

Index

Accidental war, 382
Adenauer, Konrad, 31
Administrative Council, proposed by USSR, 330
Administrator (Control of Organization), 302; manner of appointment, 322, 326; privileges and immunities of, 313-14; replacement by "troika," 272-73, 276; two to five deputy administrators, 324-27
Afghanistan, 419
African states, 22, 268, 284, 419
Afro-Asian Solidarity Conference, 34
Agreement for Cooperation, US-UK, 1958, amended in 1959, 37
Ahmed, M. Samir, 359n
Air Force Technical Applications Center, 178
Akalovsky, Alexander, 452n
Alamogordo, New Mexico, 3
Albania, 419, 465
Algeria, French underground nuclear explosion in, 384
Allen, George V., 86
Alpert, J. L., 186n
American Embassy in Moscow, 98
American Friends Service Committee, 25
American Unitarian Association, 25
Anderson, Clinton P., 35, 243-45, 251
Antarctica Treaty, 211

Antimissile weapons, 146, 360
ANZUS, 103
Apt, Clark C., 334n
Argentina, 418
Argus experiments, 192
Arms control, link to world order, 7-9, 493
Arms Control and Disarmament Agency, 388, 445, 476
Arms limitation, in agreed area of Europe, 167
Arms race, 340-41
Artificial earth and solar satellites, 190-92
Artsimovitch, L. A., 425n
Asian states, 268, 419
Atmospheric tests, opposition to resumption of, 381-82; plans for announced by Kennedy (Nov. 2, 1961), 344; Soviet plans for new series, 370
Atomic Energy Act of 1954, amended (July 2, 1958), 36, 175; amendment considered, 30-31, 265, 271
Atomic Energy Commission, US (AEC), 29, 35, 43-45, 70, 88n, 91-92, 172, 178-79, 377-78, 381; approval of atmospheric tests with limitations, 345-48; Chairman of, 85-86; limitation on test ban recommended, 157-58; position on proposed treaty and Control Organization, 327; scientific panel, 45

515